Cinematic Cuts

SUNY series, Insinuations: Philosophy, Psychoanalysis, Literature

Charles Shepherdson, editor

Cinematic Cuts

THEORIZING FILM ENDINGS

EDITED BY

SHEILA KUNKLE

Cover art entitled Double Shadow XXVII, collage, 2014.
Photographed by John Stezaker.
Reproduced with permission from the Approach Gallery.

Published by State University of New York Press, Albany

© 2016 State University of New York

For information, contact State University of New York Press, Albany, NY
www.sunypress.edu

Production, Diane Ganeles
Marketing, Anne M. Valentine

Library of Congress Cataloging-in-Publication Data

Cinematic cuts : theorizing film endings / edited by Sheila Kunkle.
        pages cm — (SUNY series, Insinuations: Philosophy, Psychoanalysis, Literature)
    Includes bibliographical references and index.
    ISBN 978-1-4384-6137-3 (hardcover : alk. paper)—978-1-4384-6136-6 (pbk : alk. paper)
    ISBN 978-1-4384-6138-0 (e-book)
    1. Motion pictures—Philosophy.   2. Motion pictures—Editing.   3. Motion
pictures—Psychological aspects.   I. Kunkle, Sheila, editor.

PN1995.C533 2016
791.4301—dc23   2015036552

10 9 8 7 6 5 4 3 2 1

Contents

Preface

The essays in this collection all address the importance of the cinematic cut, both in terms of a film's ending and the formal elements deployed within a film. They engage various philosophical and psychoanalytical authors and ideas, preeminently: Jacques Lacan's cut of the Master Signifier, which allows retroactive meaning to emerge; Slavoj Žižek and Todd McGowan's treatment of the Real (the objects *a* or gaze and voice) in film, which conveys the subject's ontological ambiguity and gives expression to an excess enjoyment beyond signification; Gilles Deleuze's concept of the irrational cut, which reconfigures montage in modern cinema, setting it free from the commensurability of time and its measurement in movement that marked the classical era; and Hegel's dialectic, which suggests ways to imagine a film ending's counternarrative, thereby exposing the hidden dimension of its underlying fantasy, among many other thinkers and theoretical traditions.

The essays presented here, however, go beyond the analyses of cuts found in a film's narrative structure and ending to theorize the marking of endings in our time. They consider how a film ending is linked to our anxieties and fears about the end of the world and our existence, for instance: how new technologies signal the end of traditional orientations to temporality and closure with the use of computer-generated imagery, the glitch, and other digital interventions in filmmaking; how a film that ends with a traumatic and inexplicably violent act also reveals the impotence, and thus an ending, of patriarchy and its authority; how the end of the American Dream can be detected in the cuts of failure of masculinity depicted in American films of the 1970s; and ultimately, how the era of cinema itself might "end." Will film be able to reinvent itself (as did the medium of television and its seriality) in our late-stage capitalist age when the repetitions of the drive offer the prevailing mode of enjoyment? Our authors address these and related themes that bear not only on film theory but also on theories of the subject and political change.

In one sense, this collection continues the exploration of a long-standing question that traces back to the beginning of both filmmaking (the continuity editing of D. W. Griffith) and film theory (the play of composition and continuity of images by the early Soviet montage theorists): how do cinematic cuts (the gaps configured through both the formal elements of editing and technique and in countless variations of endings) engage a spectator in the film narrative; how are we to experience continuity through cuts and ruptures of discontinuity? The influence of the early montage theorists can be traced outward and is found in German Expressionism, the French *nouvelle vague*, in the work of American filmmakers such as Alfred Hitchcock and directors of film noir, and in contemporary films that experiment with duration, sequencing, composition, and novel endings. The question of continuity as it informs theory can be traced from the early Soviet montage school to realist theories, such as André Bazin's and Apparatus theory's critique of continuity editing as a form of ideological manipulation. And it becomes a primary influence in the theory of Gilles Deleuze, who detects a paradigm shift in film after World War II, when the continuity of the movement-image in the classical era was displaced by the irrational cut and discontinuity in the time-image of modern cinema. Finally, in psychoanalytical film theory after Lacan, we see how the cut of the Master Signifier and materializations of the objects *a* (gaze and voice) allow both the formulation of a retroactive meaning and the experience of enjoyment of non-sense through film cuts and endings.

Our authors in this collection not only add depth and another dimension to former theories of continuity in film, they further reverse the original question. That is, instead of asking how the cinematic cut provides a certain continuity for the spectator in the filmic experience, they seek to detect how the subject is already constituted as split; how reality itself is structured by way of gaps, ellipses, repetitions, and retrospection; and how both meaning and enjoyment are only accessed through the play of discontinuity and rupture. In this regard film cuts and endings often work to short-circuit the dimensions of being and meaning, knowledge and *jouissance*, contingency and necessity, and immanence and transcendence. The underlying political import of this approach to film theory is the proposition that cinematic cuts can work to free spectators from the Symbolic and Imaginary identifications that determine them, and it is this freedom that opens the space for any radical political change that might follow.

Acknowledgments

First and foremost, I wish to thank the contributors for their brilliant and innovative essays. Special thanks to Hilary Neroni, a great friend and outstanding film scholar, who along with Hugh S. Manon and Brian Wall, provided the motivation to begin this project during a lively discussion around a pub table in Boston in 2012. Thanks also to jan jagodzinski for his supportive camaraderie and inspiring creativity over the years and to A. Kiarina Kordela for her incomparable intellect and contribution to this project. I am profoundly grateful to Todd McGowan, my longtime friend and intellectual collaborator, whose brilliant and prolific work in the areas of philosophy, politics, and film studies continues to inform and inspire my own thoughts. His generosity is boundless and his astute critical commentary unparalleled. Thanks also to Elizabeth, David, and J. Kunkle for their ongoing support, to Jane Krueger for her congenial and expert help throughout this project, and to my valued colleague and accomplished screenwriter and filmmaker, James Byrne. Thank you to The Approach in London for allowing me to use the image of John Stezaker's "Double Shadow XXVII" (Collage 2014) provided by FXP Photography on the cover. Finally, I wish to thank Metropolitan State University, which awarded me a sabbatical in the fall of 2014 to finalize work on this project.

Introduction

On the Subject of Endings

Sheila Kunkle

The main thing is that the ending does not mark the end.

—Siegfried Kracauer, *Theory of Film:*
The Redemption of Physical Reality

A film never really ends, according to realist film theorist Siegfried Kracauer, because it partakes in "the flow of life."[1] As the camera works to record and reveal limitless reality, the spectator can at once experience life in all its uncertainties and simultaneously imagine a way to go on. Even the happy ending, according to Kracauer, is not a final resolution but rather marks our desire for indestructibility, our search to find something of necessity in the human condition. In the recurring final shots of Charlie Chaplin's silent films, for example, as the little Tramp waddles away time after time, he personifies "a desire to exalt the power of resistance of the seeming weak who time and again cheat destiny."[2] The fantasy of indestructibility is indeed the standard of the epic Hollywood ending, from *Gone with the Wind* (Victor Fleming, 1939) where Scarlett O'Hara (Vivien Leigh) has the promise to start her life over tomorrow, to the neo-noir sci-fi classic *Blade Runner* (Ridley Scott, 1982) where the hero Deckard (Harrison Ford) is left to ponder whether he himself is a replicant or a human. Kracauer is right to detect the fantasy of indestructibility at work in these film endings, but his realist theory rests

1

on a precarious wager—that is, that reality although limitless can nonetheless be apprehended directly through representation, and further that films can help us overcome our fears and anxieties about life's uncertainties, the vagaries of random chance, and even the inevitability of death.

The essays in the present collection however are not primarily concerned with the way films allow us to fantasize a happy ending or bring us to a resolution about the questions of our being (to find the purpose of our lives, the reason for our existence, the hope for a better tomorrow) but rather with how film cuts and endings might serve to reconfigure the very terms within which we ponder such questions. As Lacanian psychoanalysis reveals, our sense of reality is only accessed through the cut of the Symbolic order, an order that allows the subject to emerge by way of a constitutive paradox. That is, it can only find its meaning retroactively (thus displacing the linearity of cause and effect) and through a medium (language) that splits it from within, where it experiences itself in terms of either lack (a lack that generates desire) or excess (an enjoyment derived from the repetitive motion of the drive).

Film endings can indeed offer up a resolution, a happy moment where love reigns supreme, or a way to survive in a postapocalyptic world, but such endings usually follow a formula that works to cover over the paradoxes the subject must navigate on its trajectory in search of a lost object to fulfill its desire or in its experience of excess enjoyment when meanings break down.[3] In films we find a multitude of fantasies that frame our desires for indestructibility, requited love, an answer to the meaning of life, and so forth, but it is the cut of a film ending that can call into question the dimensions of a subject's world, to unveil the impasse at its core. It is just such an impasse that Alain Badiou detects in his discussion of the intervention of philosophy in worldly matters. To Badiou, a philosophical question is one that looks for paradoxical relations, the "breaks, decisions, distances, events," that create ruptures and that allow us to break out of the "disjunctive synthesis" of a situation, discourse, or history.[4] To illustrate this Badiou refers to Japanese director Kenji Mizoguchi's 1954 classic film *The Crucified Lovers* and more specifically to the final images of the film, which constitute a new instance of the philosophical situation. The narrative is of a love story that takes place in seventeenth-century Japan between the wife of a small workshop owner and her lover, one of her husband's employees. The punishment for the adulterous couple is death, and we follow the lovers as they flee, hide out in the countryside, and are assisted by the very husband who has accused them. Ultimately, the lovers are captured and face a horrible death, but as Badiou notes, in the final frames the couple is neither defeated nor fearful of their impending doom; instead at the moment of their death they seem "enraptured, but devoid of pathos: on their faces there is simply the hint of a smile, a kind of withdrawal into the smile."[5] The lovers' hint of a smile is registered by Badiou as marking an authentic event because with it we encounter an incommensurability. "Between the event of love (the turning upside down of existence) and the ordinary rules of life (the laws of the city, the laws of marriage) there is no common measure."[6] This film ending, in Badiou's reading, provides an opening to see how a law, when confronted with an event, can lose its power and begin to crumble from within.

From a different philosophical quarter, Gilles Deleuze, in his work *Cinema 2: The Time-Image*, detects a similar incommensurability in the way time is presented in films that were made after the cataclysmic event of World War II. For Deleuze, the irrational cut of the time-image as construed through Dedekind's cut of irrational numbers in mathematics marks a point in cinema where the splendor and commensurability of classical cinema is displaced in the modern era with a series of discontinuities, a disorienting freedom where "the interval is set free."[7] The appearance in films of the "purely optical sound situation," the proliferation of "empty, disconnected, abandoned spaces," the prominence of chance relations, and the internal split of the actual and virtual image in a perpetual repetitive exchange are all ruptures that Deleuze detects in the emergence of modern cinema.[8]

Whereas Badiou illustrates the incommensurability and rupture between the world of laws and the event of love that confounds them (demonstrating what he terms "a relation without relation")[9] in his analysis of a film ending, Deleuze locates the irrational cut as a linkage (a linkage formed through a nonlinkage or unlinking of time and movement) that works to produce something new, which arises between our internal life and the external world, in the incommensurability of the two. Thus Deleuze will offer the following about the ending of Stanley Kubrick's 1968 classic film *2001: A Space Odyssey*: "At the end of *Space Odyssey*, it is in consequence of a fourth dimension that the sphere of the foetus and the sphere of the earth have a chance of entering into a new, incommensurable, unknown relation, which would convert death into a new life."[10] For Deleuze, an ending can mark the emergence of the unthought, an opening to a becoming not yet realized.

While the philosophies of both Badiou and Deleuze offer us a way to theorize film endings through the paradoxical notion of a "relation with no relation" (through the concepts of the event and the irrational cut, respectively), it is Lacanian psychoanalysis that reveals how a film ending might work according to the eruption of the Real, exposing an incommensurability already built into the split constitution of the subject itself. While for Badiou the Real refers to a rupturing event and for Deleuze the Real refers to the process of becoming, the Lacanian Real is neither a substance nor a process. Rather, and as Alenka Zupančič puts it, "it is something that interrupts a process, something closer to a stumbling block; it is an impossibility in the structure of the field of reality."[11] The subject enters the Symbolic order (the Other) of language into a never-ending and incomplete process of significa-tion, and the Real is the impasse at the very heart of the Symbolic dimension itself. It is the arbitrary cut of a Master Signifier (a signifier that paradoxically signifies its own lack) that halts the flow of signifiers, allowing the subject to configure meaning only retroactively. But this does not offer closure as the subject remains a split subject, seeking to reconcile the "I" that speaks (the "I" of enunciation) and the "I" that is spoken of (the "I" of the enunciated).[12] In essence, and as Lacan relates, in return for becoming subjects of language (of meaning) we must necessarily be deprived of our being, which can only be grasped in moments when language fails and identifications break down, when the structural impasse of the Symbolic order is exposed.[13]

It is fantasy that shields us from the trauma of our lack, from the unex-pected contingencies of life, and from our failure to find the key to our ful-fillment; fantasy provides us a sense of coherence and purpose and promises to reveal the object that would satisfy our desire. But it is the cut of a film ending that tells us not only how a subject's desire is engaged but also how its enjoyment erupts beyond fantasy. An ending may offer up an object in a momentary and illusory satisfaction of desire as in the standard Hollywood romantic comedy, or it might depict the nostalgia of an inaccessible love (James Cameron's *Titanic*, 1997; James Ivory's *The Remains of the Day*, 1993). Or, an ending might enact a rupture in the spectator's interpretation of a film narrative with an unexpected violent act (Claire Denis's *Bastards*, 2013), a surprise twist (M. Night Shyamalan's *The Sixth Sense*, 1999), or an open-ended irresolution (Christopher Nolan's *Inception*, 2010; David Cronenberg's *eXistenZ*, 1999). More rarely, an ending might present the spectator with a glimpse of herself as a being of absolute otherness through encounters with the objects *a* (gaze and voice) in film. The object *a*, however, is not a mate-rial object but rather a virtual object of absence, an open lack that cannot be filled or inscribed by signifiers. Thus, it is essential here not to confuse the gaze with a point of view; it does not refer to a subject looking at an object and identifying with it, but rather it is the blind spot (or in the case of the voice, an unlocatable utterance or sound) that constitutes the place of the absent subject within the scene. As Todd McGowan puts it in *The Real Gaze: Film Theory after Lacan*, the gaze is "a point that disrupts the flow and the sense of the experience . . . it is the point at which the spectator is obliquely included in the film."[14] Through the deployment of countless formal elements (including montage, ellipses, proximity, split narratives, ambient sound, *mise-en-abyme*, nondiegetic voice, digitalized glitches) and endless variations of endings (including illogical twists, comical surprises, abrupt truncations, indeterminacies, repetitions, reversals, and uncanny doubling), films generate cinematic cuts that are moments of discontinuity and rupture where the Real makes its appearance. Such cuts and endings disorient our sense of our singular selves on a chronological path toward a certain end and short-circuit the dimensions of being and meaning.

In narrative films, the final cut provides the temporal break we need to begin the interpretation of our unconscious response and to puzzle through the meaning of events.[15] In this sense a film ending functions in a way similar to a period at the end of a sentence or even the abrupt ending of a psychoanalytical session, for it provides the pause wherein a meaning can retroactively be proffered, but a meaning that will always be multilayered, ambiguous, and incomplete. Our interpretation, which coincides with the metonymic movement of desire, is always an attempt to find the enigmatic X that will allow the narrative to make sense, to uncover the logic of how events fall into place, whether the ending is predictable (offering the desired object up as a satisfaction of desire) or whether it remains open-ended and inconclusive. In *The Sixth Sense*, for example, after we learn that the psychologist (Bruce Willis) has been dead during almost all of the film's running time, we then go back and select out the clues in the narrative that would have alerted us to this; no wonder his wife never responded to him during their "conversation." The ending provides the stopping point where a spectator can go back and find meaning, but it is also the point where an excess is generated, which leads to further questions, further searching, because desire is always the desire for more desire. In this way, film cuts and endings open a gap that forces us to insert our interpretation while at the same time exposing the ultimate failure of interpretation itself. Even a film ending with an unambiguous conclusion will generate interpretations that elicit further meaning-making. In Don McKellar's cult classic *Last Night* (1998), for example, the film ends with a cataclysmic planetary disaster, a sudden end of the world, and its narrative follows the lives of several individuals in the twenty-four hours leading up to the final moment. Viewers are prompted both to make sense of the narrative—was it an asteroid that struck the planet; did the characters live a meaningful last day—and to wonder what they would do on the last day of their existence, to contemplate what would bring meaning to their lives in an imaginary retrospection. Although this film ending leaves no doubt, it keeps desire and the quest for meaning at play.[16]

But while the quest to find meaning remains open after the close of a film narrative, there are ideological limits in place that circumscribe how a film can be interpreted and that always point to what is necessarily excluded in the narrative itself. Ideology "works," as Žižek repeatedly reveals, because it maintains this illusion of openness. And in his discussion of narrative closure in film, Žižek maintains that a film contains a "curved space," or some formal element that operates as this impasse internal to the film itself; a film narrative presents events only by way of what's also left out of the same. He writes: "*the subject's universe of meaning is always 'curved' by traumatic blanks*, organized around what must remain unsaid if this universe is to retain its consistency."[17] And when this curved space or blank becomes visible, through materializations of the objects *a* on screen, the spectator is confronted with moments of impasse that rupture the subject's Symbolic universe. Thus, although most all Hollywood genre films present endings that offer a momentary satisfaction of desire (according to the dictates of socio-symbolic notions of finding true love, achieving the good life, and other fabrications that supplement the ideologies of capitalist consumption), the more rare films that break out of the genre formula make use of the "blank spots," the objects *a*, in ways that force the spectators to face the trauma they seek to escape (usually by way of disavowing what they already unconsciously know); the appearance of the object *a* stops meaning-making in its tracks. For example, no one is surprised or shocked when the unmarried couple (Seth Rogan and Katherine Heigl) in *Knocked Up* (Judd Apatow, 2007) eventually gets together to parent their unplanned child, or when George Bailey (James Stewart) chooses family life over the dark temptations of single life and suicide in Frank Capra's *It's a Wonderful Life* (1946).[18] But in the case of Hitchcock's *Psycho* (1966), the ending confronts us with a trauma that goes beyond fantasy's ability to point us toward an object that would make everything all right. As Slavoj Žižek's astute analysis of this film ending reveals, when the psychotic killer Norman (Anthony Perkins) lifts his head while thinking thoughts in the voice of his dead mother to meet our look, he at once makes us complicit in the knowledge of his diabolical deed and simultaneously reverses the gaze back onto us: in an instant a subject that observes, fantasizes, and desires is transformed into a being of absolute otherness. Žižek writes, "The 'impersonal' abyss we confront when we find ourselves face-to-face with Norman's gaze into the camera is the very abyss of the subject not yet caught in the web of language—the unapproachable Thing which resists subjectivization, this point of failure of every identification, is ultimately the subject itself."[19] The nearly imperceptible imprint of a skull that, just for a second, flashes on top of Norman's face is this very appearance of a "blank" spot that forces us to register how death (our non-being) haunts our very subjectivity. At such moments, being and meaning are not opposed to each other, rather they retain something of each other that is only accessible through the paradoxical logic of the Moebius strip; a slight turn in the curve keeps us on the same path but puts us in a different dimension. In this dimension we glimpse how sense itself takes an erratic form and how nonmeaning is constitutive of both being and meaning. In contrast to Kracauer's contention that films allow spectators an experience of reality in all its otherness, film cuts and endings, when they function like Hitchcock's ending in *Psycho*, engage spectators in a traumatic experience of the otherness of their own subjectivity.

Another striking example of the way the object *a* (as voice) in a film ending offers the subject an experience of its constitutive otherness occurs in David Mackenzie's dark apocalyptic film *Perfect Sense* (2011). The narrative follows two lovers (Eva Green and Ewan McGregor) who meet and develop a relationship just as a worldwide plague is stripping people of their senses, one by one. In the final scene the couple, now deaf and without the ability to smell and taste, manages to find each other and embrace just as they both go blind and the screen goes black, while a female voice narrates the scene. It is this nondiegetic female voice in the final scene that offers the spectator an experience in the dimension of the Real, as it is only her voice that lives on beyond the catastrophe and that is our only remaining entry into the film after the screen has gone black (since our protagonists have already gone blind); it is a voice coming from an unlocatable source, and as such it functions as the Lacanian object *a* that elicits our fascination in the drive.[20] Her voice has been heard throughout the film at pivotal moments as she described the connection between the loss of each sense and its effect on humans. She tells us that with the loss of smell comes the profound sense of sadness over memories we'll never be able to associate with it again, of feeling regret over lovers we've never had, and despair over all the wrongs we ever committed and cannot undo. Yet after each loss humans rebound, and her voice repeats the words "this is how life goes on," which are spoken one last time just as the film ends. Despite the usual meaning of these words, their final iteration neither offers hope nor provides a cause for events, because the voice speaking the words addresses us in our constitutive otherness. That is, although it sounds like a neutral voice providing commentary on events, it conveys instead the status of the subject's ontological ambiguity itself, as we hear these words already from a place of absence. As we stare into the darkness of a black screen, we are absent from the scene while we are obliquely included in the scene, as the unplaceable voice tells us not that all life has forever ended but unexpectedly that "this is how life goes on."[21]

The appearance of the object *a* as something impossible, something that reveals in a traumatic way how our subjectivity is split, how we are constituted as subjects through both lack and excess, is rendered in endless variations of the cinematic cut, where the Thing emerges in a timeless eruption of the Real. At the end of Clint Eastwood's 1995 film, *The Bridges of Madison County*, for example, we learn through a retrospection that the lonely housewife Francesca (Meryl Streep) chose not to leave her husband and children to be with her lover Robert Kincaid (Clint Eastwood), and this move allows her to exchange the object of her desire (a relationship with her lover) with a spectral object (the object *a*) of lack itself. A nostalgic memory allows the couple to relive the missed encounter of their ill-fated romance again and again. Similarly, at the ending of *Titanic* the retrospection of the long and fulfilling life of survivor Rose DeWitt Bukater (Kate Winslet) makes clear that the sacrifice of her young lover, Jack Dawson (Leonardo DiCaprio) was necessary in order for the memory of the encounter to take the place of an actual relationship—the perfect love foiled is transformed into the sustaining nostalgic memory (the Thing) that Rose passes down to her offspring.[22]

M. Night Shyamalan is a director well known not only for his unexpected twist endings but also for endings that enact repetitive loss and melancholia through materializations of the objects *a* in the form of aliens, plagues, and monsters; his endings give expression to the enjoyment of circling around rather than working to obtain the object of desire. At the ending of *Signs* (2002), for example, the aliens simply vanish, and at the ending of *The Happening* (2008) the unexplained plague abates, but we are given clues that either might return to threaten humans again and again. Rather than puzzle through a causal explanation of the narratives (to find the source of the plague or the reason for the aliens' landing), the spectator is instead enjoined to experience the anxiety of continuous and potential loss, a form of melancholia where loss itself becomes the object.[23] By deploying these ambiguous endings, the director manages to stage a narrative that repeats his own epistemology of belief in faith and necessity over random chance and contingency.[24] Some directors (like Shyamalan) supply clues in the narrative of the source of the trauma that is linked to repetition (mother loss), while others offer an enigmatic object, a Thing that exists outside the signifying chain. The black monolith, for example, that appears throughout and at the end of Stanley Kubrick's *2001: A Space Odyssey* or the image of the burning sled "Rosebud" at the end of Orson Welles's epic film *Citizen Kane* (1941) do not have adequate signifiers to suture them to certain meanings; instead, they seem to signify the void at the center of desire (and meaning) itself.

In contrast to the portrayal of lack at the center of desire, a film ending might work to reveal an excess of the Symbolic dimension itself, exposing the Real that exists just beneath the guise of our Imaginary reality. Spectators may be able to glimpse how a Master Signifier may itself work in an idiotic way. Stanley Kubrick, for example, combined a striking image with a certain music both at the end of *Full Metal Jacket* (1987) where the marching marines sing the Mickey Mouse anthem amid burning buildings in Vietnam, and at the end of *Dr. Strangelove Or: How I Learned to Stop Worrying and Love the Bomb* (1964), where the atomic bomb explodes as we listen to the World War II song "We'll Meet Again." The placement of these images together with music (rife with socio-symbolic references), makes the diegesis appear both real and unreal to the spectator at the same time. Such cuts leave us suspended in the gap between the tragic and comic, which in turn affects our ability to make sense (or rather, they expose the idiotic enjoyment) of things like war, killing, and Mutual Assured Destruction. Or another example that deploys the Real of our socio-symbolic interpretations, but to comic effect, occurs in Billy Wilder's classic comedy *Some Like It Hot* (1959), where we expect that Daphne (Jack Lemmon), who has been dressing in drag and dating the eccentric millionaire Osgood Fielding (Joe E. Brown), will have to reveal that "she" is really a man, but what we don't expect is that the millionaire will in the final scene retort, "Well, nobody's perfect." In this instant we are startled by this comic reply and the humor works to elide our need to "make sense" of everything that went before. More importantly, the humor works to short-circuit the sense upon which all signifiers of sexual difference rely.[25]

Directors can introduce such "impossible" moments in film that cut through the narrative to address the subject in its indeterminacy, and which expose a gap between our interpretation and our enjoyment, through a myriad of formal film elements and endings. Hitchcock's famous use of the ellipse in editing, for example, forces the spectator to insert her own fantasy of a murder without witnessing the actual murder scene. David Lynch's use of ambient sound, strange sequencing, and proximity all work to include the spectator in the film in oblique ways, revealing the grotesque reality that exists both beneath the Imaginary guise of our Symbolic world and in the strange uncanniness of everyday life.[26] Spike Lee's cuts to montages of vitriolic hate speech by characters in *Do the Right Thing* (1989) and *25th Hour* (2002) confront the spectator directly with an excess she cannot escape. What Lee achieves with this formal cut away from the linear narrative is a revelation of the way hate speech is itself a montage. It puts together words erratically and in a form not meant for a dialogic reply; it is an eruption of enjoyment (in this case a painful enjoyment), while it also gives expression to the Thing in the other that is excessive of language itself. We recognize this excessive outburst, but its enjoyment resists a satisfactory interpretation and cannot be captured in Symbolic meanings.

With the digitalization of filmmaking directors can create novel distortions of a subject's experience of causality and temporality in film endings that never conclusively end. The reverse narrative of Christopher Nolan's *Memento* (2000), the beginning of a repetition that ends Michel Gondry's *Eternal Sunshine of the Spotless Mind* (2004), and the *mise-en-abyme* at the end of David Cronenberg's *eXistenZ* and Terry Gilliam's *The Zero Theorem* (2013) are just a few examples of film endings that leave spectators in an indeterminate place. When films deploy such eruptions of the Real through any number of formal elements and endings, they are also depicting how the logic of the repetitions of the drive short-circuits our finitude and linear causality. The subject is no longer able to find its meaning in a retrospection as there is no certain past; instead, it finds itself suspended in the realm of nonmeaning. Thus, we can also discern how the desire for indestructibility that Kracauer detects in great film endings becomes not a quest to survive another day on a chronological timeline but rather a movement to escape the matrix of finitude-infinitude itself. The indestructibility that the drive seeks becomes a time loop or hole in finitude, and when it appears, a cut or rupture has occurred to disorient our notion of chronological temporality and linear causality.[27]

Importantly, films that use the motif of repetition, multiples, alternative realities, and indeterminacy in their endings, from Krzysztof Kieslowski's *Double Life of Veronique* (1991) to Tom Tykwer's *Run Lola Run* (1998) and from Harold Ramis's *Groundhog Day* (1993) to Christopher Nolan's *Inception*, all reveal the gap between iterations, the contingent eruption in a moment of timelessness where the Real appears as the very impasse at the heart of the Symbolic. In the endings of films that repeat a situation, unveil a world within a world, or remain open-ended, the enjoyment of an excess comes to take the place of fantasy. We no longer seek the object of our desire (to find our purpose, a way to survive, a requited love, etc.) but rather experience an enjoyment located in the movement itself. As Alenka Zupančič writes, "Repetition is always a repetition of representation (the signifying dyad), but it is also a repetition of the inherent gap or interval between its terms, which is the very locus of the surprise in repetition, of the Real encountered in it."[28] What's being exposed in film endings that do not conclusively end is the constitutive circularity involved in the constitution of the subject itself. The subject exists on the basis of the act of repression that it performs, but this act is at once the source of its alienation from itself. Primary repression sets in motion a paradoxical circularity for the subject, and the repetitions, uncanny doublings, reversals, and indeterminacies revealed in films without a conclusive end are revealing this gap or loop of the subject's causality.

Thus, the repetitions, reversals, and nonresolutions in film endings ultimately demonstrate something important about the subject itself existing in an indeterminate place, as a being of both lack and excess, which is the central paradox of the signifier as Lacan conceived it: the idea that a letter always arrives at its destination. Posing the very question of the meaning of life is what opens the portal to the idea that there needs to be a meaning of life. We realize only in retrospect that it was our original question that set us on a paradoxical path: it was in our waiting for the call to tell us the meaning of life (as does Christoph Waltz's character in Terry Gilliam's *The Zero Theorem*) that we created our purpose that was from the beginning without resolution. As Žižek writes, all of us have a letter marked "death" waiting for us, and although the meaning of the letter might be determined by the way it circulates among subjects in the symbolic network, its appearance as object *a* (of materialized enjoyment) "is what interrupts the continuous flow of words, what hinders the smooth running of the symbolic circuit."[29]

Film endings may enact fantasies of overcoming loss, cheating death, or finding true love, while they offer us various forms of enjoyment (a momentary fulfillment of desire, the pleasure of repetitive loss in drive, the torment of indeterminacy, the surprise of a comical twist, the exhilaration of an unexpected reversal, the frustration of a cliff-hanger, or the disorientation of experiencing ourselves as objects of an Other's gaze). But we become aware of how our reality is structured and how our fantasies work only when the eruption of the Real cuts through the film narrative in one or another contingent way; it disorients (which is not the same as a loss of all orientation) our fantasies of a coherent knowable world and short-circuits the dimensions of being and meaning, and knowledge and jouissance.[30] Ultimately, and as McGowan proposes, such an encounter with the Real in films holds the potential to become radically political, because "it deprives spectators of their symbolic support and thereby forces them to experience their radical freedom."[31] This freedom becomes visible through various formulations of the cinematic cut.

The contributors to our present collection engage various theoretical perspectives and concepts to analyze film cuts and endings, including Lacan's objects *a* (gaze and voice), Deleuze's irrational cut in the time-image, Žižek's parallax view, Freud's death drive, Hegel's dialectic, Jameson's vanishing mediator, and Benjamin's innervative responses, among many others. They theorize how film cuts and endings parallel the cut of a Master Signifier or the ending of a psychoanalytical session; how new digital technologies in film reorient a spectator's experiences of temporality, causality, and closure; and ultimately how film endings offer spectators the gap to insert a retroactive interpretation and to experience enjoyment when signification fails. Our authors offer film analyses that illustrate how endings can reveal something about our reality that is itself structured by way of gaps, ellipses, repetitions, and short-circuits.

In an essay entitled "Resolution, Truncation, Glitch," Hugh S. Manon reveals how two relatively new types of endings alter our sense of a film's temporality. "Truncation" is a rare and abrupt ending that leaves the spectator in a state of ambiguity, while the digitalized "glitch," which simulates a failed truncation, is deployed to reassure the spectator that a potential rupture has been averted. In the same way, Ryan Engley locates a new "drive twist" in contemporary film endings, which creates a dialectical shift in the spectator, offering her an entirely new epistemology of experiencing a film narrative and film ending. Slavoj Žižek's analysis of Christopher Nolan's *The Dark Knight Rises* (2012) posits that the ending "only makes sense" if we imagine that Alfred (Michael Caine) was day-dreaming when he saw Selena (Anne Hathaway) and Bruce Wayne (Christian Bale) at the cafe; he enjoins us to imagine an alternative ending, one that follows the Hegelian dialectic of emancipatory struggle against the state.[32] In his essay "The Satisfaction of an Ending" Todd McGowan conceives of the great film ending in what he terms oxymoronically the "expected surprise." As he shows, the most radical film endings are those that take the form of a cliché to an extreme. Similarly, Henry Krips argues contra both Žižek and McGowan that the Real may occur not through an open cut in the visual field but rather in what Dziga Vertov calls the Kino-Eye, where the camera cuts away from what the viewer can identify with seeing, which includes instances of overconformity to the cinematic codes in terms of which a film is framed.

Two of our authors in this collection analyze film cuts and endings according to the work of Gilles Deleuze. In his analysis of the 2003 avant-garde Korean film *Save the Green Planet* by director Joon-Hwan Jang, jan jagodzinski proposes that the ending places us in an impossible time and place where we can see our past (from a projected future) differently. Similarly, A. Kiarina Kordela argues in her analysis of John Huston's 1972 film *Fat City* that the narrative repeatedly presents cuts of failure, which themselves undercut the standard Hollywood action film and its stereotypical fantasies of masculinity. Several of our contributors consider films that end with a disturbing and radically violent act in a way that reorients our political critique of patriarchy, colonialism, and capitalist ideology. Hilary Neroni concludes that the violent murder at the end of Claire Denis's film *Bastards* reveals (and leaves open) the wounds of patriarchy, exposing its ultimate impotence. Similarly, Jennifer Friedlander's analysis of Denis's *White Material* (2009) reveals how a brutal murder at the end of the film allows a white colonial female overlord, Maria (Isabell Huppert) to radically renounce her position in the Symbolic order and simultaneously embrace the failure of her familial/social identity. David Denny's essay on Lars von Trier's *Melancholia* (2011) traces the film's unique narrative structure and its romantic aesthetic to find that Justine's (Kirsten Dunst) acceptance of both her impending doom and the planet's ultimate destruction is heroic.

Exploring the split constitutive of the subject and the void around which the love relation forms, Fabio Vighi analyzes Jane Campion's 2003 film *In the Cut* to reveal how signification emerges from the retroactive effect of the cut of language, severing the body from its presumed biological autonomy, which inscribes both lack and alienation and opens the possibility of love for the subject. Juan Pablo Lucchelli offers a psychoanalysis of Jacques Audiard's 2012 film *Rust and Bone* by tracing how the love relation emerges only at the end of the film after the literal cut of the amputation of Stephanie's (Marian Cotillard) legs is mirrored in the "cut" of Ali's (*Matthias Schoenaerts*) gaze. In my essay on Spike Jonze's film *Her* (2013), I reflect on how the privatization of fantasy mediated by personalized digital devices creates a Symbolic world of flat, pregenerated meanings, which further illustrates the vanishing mediator of the voice in film. In an essay that explores the way appearance inscribes itself into reality (our Symbolic world) through film cuts and endings, Rex Butler analyzes Henry Joost and Ariel Shulman's 2010 documentary *Catfish* to conclude that the truth a documentary film helps us attain is not to be understood as occurring somewhere before or outside of the film but only through and as a result of it. And Brian Wall analyzes the ending of Akira Kurosawa's *High and Low* (1963) to explore the way the film's synchronic presentation of space creates a "totalization," which articulates the ideological limits of the world.

The authors in this collection not only analyze film cuts and endings according to theoretical insights in novel ways, they further open up new aporia for film theory, psychoanalysis, and philosophy in general. Some of the questions they leave us with are: How can the radicalization of the cliché, the exposure of the impotence of patriarchy in the violent act, and the presentation of failure (of masculinity, for example) in film endings all lead to a radical politics? Might there be a new way to conceive of a transformative politics that plays on the Symbolic dimension's weak points without deploying the violent Act? How will fantasy be sustained in an era of closure, when capitalism works 24/7 to both generate and satisfy (through prediction and calculation) our every desire? As the machinery of global capitalism increasingly works according to the logic of the drives, it is television that has reconfigured itself as a medium to provide enjoyment with its serial repetitions and failures. Will cinema (now still mainly a medium of desire) be able to reinvent itself accordingly, offering enjoyment not in the resolution of an ending but in more novel variations of the twist ending?

Siegfried Kracauer, it now seems, was not so far off from a psychoanalytical theory of film in that he sought for the spectator an experience with reality in its most random and unpredictable "otherness."[33] He would, no doubt, be in agreement with our conclusion that cinema allows the spectator a way of experiencing reality itself as something fantasmatic. Film doesn't represent reality in its many variations but rather redoubles it; it adds another layer so that we might see how truth itself is never complete, how it necessarily takes the form of a fiction. With this logic, film cuts and endings can reveal how a subject is constituted as split: its meaning is configured retroactively through semblances, allusions, metaphor, and other devices, while its desire is elicited metonymically, in expectations of a future wholeness. It relies on the Symbolic order to grasp "reality" and confronts its constitutive otherness when meanings fail and identities disintegrate. From these coordinates, a film ending is determinative not because it allows us to imagine what might happen next, as Kracauer proposed, but rather, and as Alenka Zupančič suggests in her reference to Nietzsche's concept of midday, because an ending is "inaugural"; an ending does not provide a resolution (bringing two phenomena into a union) but rather a conjunctive moment where one becomes two through an internal splitting.[34] Film cuts and endings can provide just such a conjunctive moment, allowing us a glimpse of our being in the gap of the Real while we work to give expression to our experiences from within the very impasse that makes signification and meaning possible. The point, however, is not simply to be disoriented or spellbound in this conjunctive moment but rather to see that it is from this place that we can locate how our world of meaning and enjoyment is structured, allowing us also to detect new incommensurabilities (as in Deleuze's discovery of the time-image), new philosophical situations (as in Badiou's logic of the event), and new ways for the Lacanian subject to experience freedom and enact the impossible.

Notes

1. Kracauer refers to the end that does not mark an end in Siegfried Kracauer, *Theory of Film: The Redemption of Physical Reality* (Princeton: Princeton University Press, 1960), 269.

2. Kracauer, *Theory of Film*, 270.

3. In one of his many references to the film *Casablanca*, Slavoj Žižek claims that even if we knew the ending of the film in advance, we would still remain split, holding out the possibility that things might still turn out differently as we watch the narrative unfold. And this, according to Žižek, is the way "fundamental contingency is most effectively concealed in a linear narrative." Slavoj Žižek, *The Most Sublime Hysteric: Hegel and Lacan*, trans. Thomas Scott-Railton (Cambridge: Polity Press, 2014), 31.

4. Peter Engelmann, ed., *Philosophy in the Present: Alain Badiou and Slavoj Žižek*, trans. Peter Thomas and Alberto Toscano (Cambridge: Polity Press, 2009), 16.

5. Engelmann, *Philosophy in the Present*, 10.

6. Engelmann, *Philosophy in the Present*, 11.

7. Gilles Deleuze, *Cinema 2: The Time-Image*, trans. Hugh Tomlinson and Robert Galeta (Minneapolis: University of Minnesota Press, 1989), 277. According to Deleuze, "There is thus no longer association through metaphor or metonymy, but re-linkages of independent images. Instead of one image after the other, there is one image *plus* another" (Deleuze, *Cinema 2*, 214).

8. Deleuze, *Cinema 2*, 272–273. Deleuze's detection of these novelties as found in the works of directors such as Alain Resnais, Jean Renoir, Joseph Mankiewicz, and especially Orson Welles leads him to the conclusion that modern cinema as seen in the French *nouvelle vague*, American cinema of the 1950s, and Italian neo-realism are all efforts of cinema's internal push to recreate its very conditions through the time-image (Deleuze, *Cinema 2*, 272).

9. Engelmann, *Philosophy in the Present*, 11.

10. Deleuze, *Cinema 2*, 206.

11. Alenka Zupančič, *The Odd One In: On Comedy* (Cambridge: MIT Press, 2008), 162.

12. The subject exists within a temporal paradox, or as Rex Butler puts it, in Lacan's formula of fantasy the subject's identity arrives either too soon or too late, because "at once we attempt to pre-empt uncertainty by assuming an identity and it is only from the position of identity that we can look back and see this uncertainty." Rex Butler, ed., *The Žižek Dictionary* (Durham: Acumen, 2014), 241. Slavoj Žižek refers to this logical paradox of how for the subject history appears in a linear way only in retrospect in his foreword to Molly Rothenberg, *The Excessive Subject: A New Theory of Social Change* (Cambridge: Polity Press, 2010), xvi.

13. Lacan writes: "If we choose being, the subject disappears, it eludes us, it falls into non-meaning. If we choose meaning, the meaning survives only deprived

of that part of non-meaning that is, strictly speaking, that which constitutes in the realization of the subject, the unconscious." *The Seminar of Jacques Lacan Book XI: The Four Fundamental Concepts of Psychoanalysis*, ed. Jacques-Alain Miller, trans. Alan Sheridan (New York: Norton, 1981), 211.

14. Todd McGowan, *The Real Gaze: Film Theory after Lacan* (Albany: State University of New York Press, 2007), 7–9. Importantly, in this breakthrough work McGowan changed the way we see how enjoyment is part of the filmic experience. He writes, "Film holds out the promise of enjoyment through the way that it deploys the gaze as objet *petit a*"; the politics of a film "rests not in its ability to elicit our conscious reflection, but rather in the way that film fascinates us in its points of rupture where the gaze emerges" (McGowan, *The Real Gaze*, 14).

15. While any sense of continuity in film is only achieved through the use and/or absence of editing, the nonnarrative forms of montage, from the surrealistic short *Un Chien Andalou* (Luis Buñuel, 1929) to avant-garde films, such as Jean-Luc Godard's 1967 film *Weekend*, present us with the play of excess; that is, in surrealist montage, for example, the form is of continuous eruptions and nonsensical juxtapositions, and this aligns with Lacan's concept of drive as having no beginning or ending; rather the eruptions expose an excess enjoyment in the realm of nonmeaning. In the rarer films that avoid editorial cuts altogether to create a narrative, something more complex occurs. In films such as Alejandro González Iñárritu's 2014 *Birdman: Or (The Unexpected Virtue of Ignorance)*, where we find no perceptible editorial cuts but are forced to listen to an incessant drumbeat and follow the close shadowing of characters' movements by the camera, the lack of cuts alters the spectator's orientation to the film in an overproximity. Paradoxically, this works as its own kind of rupture, displacing the "usual" distances we expect in terms of our orientations to space, time, and movement on screen. The excessive overproximity distorts our sense of the narrative similar to the way the appearance of an unexpected lack (a materialization of the object *a*) would in a narrative film.

16. These responses to films combine the subject's Imaginary ego (ideal ego) with its Symbolic directives (ego ideal). As Bruce Fink puts it in his comments on how an analyst always fails to understand the speech of his analysand: "The imaginary focuses on meaning, which virtually always involves predigested, prefabricated meanings that derive from our own view of the world," while our responses also consider an Other that is full of contradictions, mixed messages, and inconsistent demands. Bruce Fink, *Against Understanding: Commentary and Critique in a Lacanian Key, Volume 1* (London: Routledge, 2014), 11.

17. Slavoj Žižek, ed., *Everything You Always Wanted to Know about Lacan but Were Afraid to Ask Hitchcock* (London: Verso, 1992), 242.

18. As Slavoj Žižek argues, what the phenomenon of the resolution in film allows the spectator is both the enjoyment of racist/sexist excess, libidinal enjoyment of sex scenes, and so on, and "political correctness," because by the end of the film we know that these excesses will all be renounced. Slavoj Žižek, *The Art of the Ridiculous Sublime: On David Lynch's Lost Highway* (Seattle: University of Washington Press, 2000), 8.

19. Žižek, *Everything You Always Wanted to Know about Lacan*, 245. Elsewhere Žižek writes: "In the final scene of *Psycho*, the 'mother's voice' literally cuts a hole in the visual reality: the screen image becomes a delusive surface, a lure secretly dominated by the bodiless voice of an invisible or absent Master, a voice that cannot be attached to any object in the diegetic reality—as if the true subject of enunciation of Norman's/mother's voice is death itself, the skull that we perceive for a brief moment in the fade-out of Norman's face." Slavoj Žižek, *Less than Nothing: Hegel and the Shadow of Dialectical Materialism* (London: Verso, 2012), 669.

20. Slavoj Žižek in *Less than Nothing* posits that the voice as *objet a* (the object that gives body to the very lack of being), functions as the *objet a* of the visual, or the blind spot from which the scene returns the gaze (669).

21. A sample of the anonymous comments on the discussion board of the Internet Movie Database for this split-narrative film generated responses that were also split over whether the ending was a "nightmare" or "poignant"; whether love reigned supreme or love sustained nothing. These comments, however, do not mention the authority of the nondiegetic voice, which in a Lacanian analysis would provide the link between the lovers and the plague. The film makes "perfect sense," only through the realization of Lacan's formula of the nonsexual relation. We can obtain the impossible (an actual sexual relation without obstacles) only if we lose all senses, the very things we need to enjoy another as love object. The voice as object *a* in this film (the voice that speaks to no-one directly) is the Thing that connects the Real of the sexual relation to the enigma of the plague, an affliction that is experienced through repetitive loss itself.

22. The replacement of an object of desire (a lover, for example) with the Thing or object of lack is only one way that films can offer a substitution. Another example occurs in Michael Curtiz's classic film *Casablanca* (1942), when Rick (Humphrey Bogart) gives up his former lover (Ingrid Bergman), and this loss is replaced by an unexpected male friendship with his former persecutor, Inspector Louis Renault (Claude Rains). One could argue that he acts to put Ilsa on the plane to be with her heroic husband not out of any sense of duty or loyalty but rather in order to be able to carry on as a bachelor in a world full of unexpected contingencies and possibilities, despite the script that makes us think he is acting according to a higher purpose.

23. Of all the directors to convey Freud's repetition compulsion, Shyamalan is certainly at the forefront. As Bruce Fink relates, in *Beyond the Pleasure Principle*, Freud explores "a number of different explanations for repetition compulsion, one of which is that an attempt is made by the psyche to insert anxiety into a traumatic experience" retroactively, and with Lacan, Fink writes, "the drives involved in compulsive repetition of the traumatic scene . . . seek to insert the subject in some way, to bring the subject into being there where formerly there had been no subject." Bruce Fink, *Against Understanding: Commentary and Critique in a Lacanian Key, Volume 1* (New York: Routledge, 2014), 62.

24. For an interesting discussion of M. Night Shyamalan's main themes, including his allegiance to faith, his attempts to find order in the world, to restore community, and enact a mythical play of fables, I refer to the reader to Jeffrey

Andrew Weinstock, ed., *Critical Approaches to the Films of M. Night Shyamalan* (New York: Palgrave Macmillan, 2010).

25. Of course the play of comedy is far more complex than this. Thomas Wartenberg notes that the ending of *Some Like It Hot* is potentially politically radical. "If, as it should, our laughter prompts us to reflect on why Osgood's response is so startling, the subversion of heterosexuality's normative status has been initiated." Thomas E. Wartenberg, *Unlikely Couples: Movie Romance as Social Criticism* (Oxford: Westview Press, 1999), 3. But from a Lacanian perspective the radically political move would be to see how all depictions of sexual difference are formulations of the Symbolic and the kernel of our enjoyment lies in an excess; of locating the Thing in the other. Thus our continued puzzling of identity politics to come to the most tolerant and accepting view still works only on the Symbolic level of ideological meanings.

26. See Todd McGowan, *The Impossible David Lynch* (New York: Columbia University Press, 2007), and Slavoj Žižek, *The Art of the Ridiculous Sublime: On David Lynch's Lost Highway* (Seattle: University of Washington Press), 2000.

27. The depiction of the drive as a hole in finitude comes from Alenka Zupančič in *The Odd One In: On Comedy* (Cambridge: MIT Press, 2008), 52–53. And Todd McGowan explores the contemporary turn in film to an "atemporality" under the repetitions of the drive in his stellar work *Out of Time: Desire in Atemporal Cinema* (Minneapolis: University of Minnesota Press, 2011).

28. Zupančič, *The Odd One In*, 167.

29. Slavoj Žižek, *Enjoy Your Symptom!* (London: Routledge, 1992), 22–23.

30. As with comedy, we have the opportunity through short-circuits of film cuts and endings to repeat the vacillation between being and meaning, which in turn allows us a sense that "the subject's nonbeing is already there, as part of his very existence." Alenka Zupančič, *Odd One In: On Comedy* (Cambridge: MIT Press, 2008), 170.

31. McGowan, *The Real Gaze*, 171.

32. According to Žižek, "This is how, from a proper Hegelo-Lacanian perspective, one should subvert the standard self-enclosed linear narrative: not by means of a postmodern dispersal into a multitude of local narratives, but by means of its redoubling in a hidden counternarrative." Slavoj Žižek, "Afterward: The Counterbook of Christianity," in Marcus Pound, *Žižek: A (Very) Critical Introduction* (Grand Rapids: William B. Eerdmans, 2008), 149.

33. Miriam Bratu Hansen in her excellent introduction writes that although Kracauer referred to the way a viewer is primarily engaged with film as a corporeal being, his themes are nonetheless closer to those explored by Freud in *Beyond the Pleasure Principle* (1920) (Kracauer, *Theory of Film*, xxi).

34. Alenka Zupančič, *The Shortest Shadow: Nietzsche's Philosophy of the Two* (Cambridge: MIT Press, 2003), 23–25.

1

Resolution, Truncation, Glitch

HUGH S. MANON

Introduction: "The End of Show Department"

In a late episode of *Monty Python's Flying Circus* (season 4, episode 2, 1974), we follow a shopper named Chris Quinn (Eric Idle) through a series of bizarre encounters as he makes his way from floor to floor in a ten-story department store. The episode is unusual for Python in that it centers on a single protagonist rather than unfolding as a series of loosely connected sketches, and it concludes with an exchange between Quinn and a sales assistant (Terry Jones) who is positioned in front of a large sign that proclaims this to be the "End of Show Department." Quinn is disappointed by the episode's "rotten ending," and the assistant presents him with a series of alternatives, each of which represents a conventionalized set of formal devices that might be used to conclude a television show. The first is a "long, slow pull-out" in which "the camera tracks back and back." As the sales assistant describes the shot, the camera produces exactly the effect he describes: a long, receding aerial shot of London, along with a musical crescendo, as the speaker's voice fades away. The shopper interrupts, bringing us back to the department store: "No, no, no. Have you got anything more exciting?" The next option provided is a chase, and immediately two men in suits rush in, chasing the shopper out of the scene in a fast-motion sequence reminiscent of old silent films. Again, this ending is deemed unsuitable. The third option involves two lone silhouetted figures walking off into the sunset as the music swells, the fourth is a "happy ending" in which a beautiful woman enters and joyfully embraces the shopper, the fifth involves the appearance of two jaded football commentators who sum up the big match (i.e., the *Flying Circus* episode itself), and the sixth is a simple "slow fade." The shopper rejects each of these in turn. Finally, in a matter-of-fact voice, the sales assistant says, "Well, uh, how about a sudden ending?" At this point the camera abruptly cuts to black and the show is actually over.

In this sequence, Monty Python confronts viewers with their own manipulation by media conventions. Shown in rapid succession, each technique nonetheless triggers an affective response—the slow pull-out connotes timelessness and historical context, the chase produces anxiety, the sunset creates a feeling of romantic hopefulness, and so on. Despite their parodic juxtaposition, each of these techniques *really does work*. However, in the end, the show concludes with a sudden cut to black, as if to indicate that all of the other ending types we have seen are elaborate sublimations of the one true ending—a primordial ending that, because it is not connotatively embellished, is not really an ending at all but instead a blunt stoppage. The sudden ending is stark, desublimated, all too real. We perhaps expect the camera to return to the scene in the store but just as quickly realize this will not happen. We have entered the void outside the comforting confines of the televisual fantasy. The cut to black produces a sense of textual death and correspondingly a feeling that our subjectivity has come unmoored and that we are no longer being cared for.

Although this sequence, like so much of Monty Python's work, involves a hilariously surreal critique of modern media and culture, the "End of Show Department" uses repetition and variation to make a valuable theoretical point: that although individual films and television shows can *end*, they cannot simply *cease*. To resolve in an ending involves a whole series of courtesies, gestures made to viewers that allow us to exit the narrative in a manner that feels less like a cut. To simply abort, however, is an outlier, relegated to the very end of the list as an aporia that all of the other options work to avoid. Understood in this way, cinematic truncation is an *impossibility* in precisely the sense that psychoanalysis intends. Truncation is shocking in a way that places it outside the bounds of normative signifying practice, but at the same time it is an impossibility that one nonetheless occasionally encounters.

In the three sections that follow, I examine the endings of motion pictures in both theoretical and technological/historical terms. Beginning with a discussion of Hollywood's highly conventional "happy ending" and its relation to the psychoanalytic conception of imaginary fantasy, I go on to examine a series of moving image narratives that do not resolve but instead truncate, leaving the viewer in a place of radical ambiguity. Through a series of close analyses, I understand such endings in relation to the Lacanian "short session," wherein a psychoanalyst abruptly ends a session at a point whose significance is unstated. In such instances—and they are remarkably rare—the imaginary fantasy of cinema comes up against the impossible Real, whose temporality is both unanticipatory and unconditioned by language. In a third section, I examine digital cinema's fascination with the "glitch"—a messy audiovisual flare-up in which a motion picture appears to be on the verge of truncating but instead fails to fail, leaving viewers with the "look and feel" of impossibility, but not impossibility per se. In this sense, a cinematic glitch is a redomestication of the uncanny—an aesthetic gesture that mimics, and at the same time sublimates, the radical, anxiety-provoking cut of actual truncation.

On Resolution: *The Player*

Robert Altman's 1992 film *The Player* illuminates a crucial point regarding the structure and function of resolution in mainstream cinema: so long as the tripartite structure of rising action, climax, and denouement is preserved, the specific plot content that populates these segments does not matter in the least. The test Altman performs has implications both for our understanding of Hollywood's narrative paradigm, wherein cinematic fantasies must come to a close (and not just suddenly stop), and for psychoanalysis, which actively works to theorize the subject's imaginary fantasy in relation to the impossible Real. What sets *The Player* apart from more standard films of its era is that its plot climaxes and resolves by way of a three-minute sequence that belongs to an entirely different film, one that we have not been watching. The fact that Altman is able to execute this bait-and-switch, and that the interjected sequence nonetheless triggers the affective response one expects of a Hollywood climax, is proof that the audience's engagement depends on a structure in which satisfaction is promised, obstructed, and finally delivered. In other words, it is the structure of the film's resolution, and not any particular plot content, that catalyzes the imaginary fantasy.

In order to comprehend the full weight of Altman's subversion, we need to appreciate how far he takes us in one narrative direction before switching to another. Featuring a staggering number of cameos from both Hollywood veterans and newcomers, the highly reflexive neo-noir plot of

The Player centers on Griffin Mill (Tim Robbins), a studio vice president who receives a series of death threats from an embittered screenwriter whose script he rejected. When Mill believes he has learned the identity of the screenwriter—David Kahane (Vincent D'Onofrio)—he seeks him out at a revival house in Pasadena. Following a late screening of *The Bicycle Thief*, Mill approaches Kahane in the lobby. Kahane bristles at Mill's attempts to make nice, and when Mill says his studio should remake De Sica's neorealist masterpiece, Kahane snarkily retorts, "You'd probably give it a happy ending." The two go out for drinks at a karaoke bar. Later, in a parking lot, after the drunken Kahane taunts Mill with the rumor that he is about to lose his job to Larry Levy (Peter Gallagher), a young executive brought in from another studio, Kahane pushes Mill through a broken railing and down into a water-filled stairway. When Kahane apologetically offers to help Mill to his feet, Mill attacks and drowns him, fleeing the scene. The remainder of the film alternates between Mill's pursuit of three goals: to cover up Kahane's murder from the police, to fend off the stalker (who, as it turns out, was not Kahane), and to retain his position at the studio by preventing Levy from gaining the upper hand.

The concept of the "Hollywood happy ending" is repeatedly invoked in the film, most notably in the pitch offered by Tom Oakley (Richard E. Grant) for a film called *Habeas Corpus*—a gloomy melodrama about a district attorney who falls in love with a female inmate consigned to death row for a murder she did not commit. Oakley touts the film as a new American tragedy, with "no stars, no pat happy endings, no Schwarzenegger, no stick-ups, no terrorists." Most notably, at the film's climax, the wrongly accused protagonist will die in the gas chamber. "She has to die—no fucking Hollywood ending!" Oakley insists. Mill secretly does not believe in the viability of the picture—he describes it as a "completely fucked-up idea with no second act"—and passes the ill-conceived project to Larry Levy in order to sabotage the newcomer's reputation and career.

Given *The Player*'s complex plot machinations in acts 2 and 3, its climax is oddly perfunctory. The police strongly suspect Mill is guilty of Kahane's murder, and when he is called in for a line-up the sole witness identifies the wrong man (ironically, the very police detective that had been shadowing Mill). With that, Mill is exonerated and the film's major conflict is resolved. However, as if to disown this run-of-the-mill climax, Altman immediately delivers a second climactic scene that is both unexpected and far more intense. The title "One Year Later" appears over a black screen and the music greatly intensifies. We see a group of reporters gathered around a prison gas chamber. The viewer soon realizes that this is the ending of the now-completed *Habeas Corpus*, which is being screened for the higher-ups at the studio, but in a cynical twist, the film's ending is the exact opposite of the "no stars, no pat happy endings" approach that writer Tom Oakley demanded.

The camera dollies back to reveal a priest (Ray Walston) reading the Lord's Prayer to a female inmate—none other than *Julia Roberts*, the hottest young actress of 1992. She is solemnly escorted into the chamber and just after the pellets are dropped, a call comes in at the guard station. The pace of the music quickens and the guards are scrambling for their keys when suddenly *Bruce Willis* bursts onto the screen! He grabs a pump-action shotgun from a guard and blasts away the glass window of the gas chamber. Jumping inside, he frees Roberts, and as he carries out her limp body she recovers consciousness, smiles, and asks "What took you so long?" Wills, the badass district attorney, coolly responds: "Traffic was a bitch." The End.

The small audience in the studio's screening room enthusiastically bursts into applause. Thanks to a negative test screening, the film's original ending has been replaced with precisely the ending Oakley reviled, yet even he is smiling and applauding. This positivity carries over into the world outside Altman's film-within-a-film. In a short denouement sequence, we learn that *Habeas Corpus* has been a huge success for the studio, Larry Levy now has his career-cementing hit, Griffin Mill has been promoted to studio president and has married the dead screenwriter's beautiful girlfriend who is pregnant with his child, and the film finally concludes with the couple embracing on a sunny day in front of their lovely home, surrounded by an American flag and red roses.

Beyond Altman's satirical intent, the sequence is remarkable because it reflexively undermines the paradigm of the Hollywood ending, while nonetheless exploiting its power. Despite the jarring last-minute appearance of Julia Roberts and Bruce Willis—arguably the biggest stars in the film—and despite the fact that the narrative climax of *The Player* pales by comparison to the hyperbolic climax of *Habeas Corpus*, we are nonetheless delivered the exact sort of adrenaline-pumping conclusion that every Hollywood film promises, followed by an appropriately calming and satisfying denouement. The fact that neither the *Habeas Corpus* action scene nor the blissfully romantic denouement seem to belong in this film is precisely the point. Regardless of plot content, we get the same thrill and satisfaction—in effect the same fantasy of imaginary closure—so long as the conventionalized triad of obstacle/climax/resolution is obeyed. We know very well that we are not seeing the climax to *The Player*, but because it appears in the proper place and obeys all of the preset conventions—staging a crisis only so as to satisfyingly overcome it—the impact of the scene is just the same as if it were the film's true ending.

According to Lacan, fantasy does not merely involve the subject imagining what it would be like to have immediate full access to some otherwise unattainable goal. Instead, fantasy involves the subject picturing the *process* of desire's attainment: "[I]n its fundamental use, fantasy is the means by which the subject maintains himself at the level of his vanishing desire, vanishing inasmuch as the very satisfaction of demand deprives him of his object."[1] When the subject engages in fantasy, he or she envisions a scenario in which obstacles are surmounted and goals are attained—a scenario quite unlike the one we encounter in real life, wherein obstacles sometimes do not yield and, even when they do, attainment is never fully satisfying. The so-called Hollywood happy ending is a crucial site at which the subject encounters fantasy as a prestaged, consumable product. Although the specific contents of this fantasy vary from film to film and from genre to genre, the three-part procedure of obstruction, attainment, and satisfaction is a firm constant—truly a structural precondition inasmuch as it staged our desire in relation to lack.

At the same time, this endlessly repeated formula must be seen as an affront to the "possibility of the impossibility of existence in general," to appropriate Heidegger's famous articulation of the subject's relation to death.[2] In Hollywood endings, we repeatedly encounter a scenario in which impossibility is categorically *not* possible. The abject, unmitigated death of any given narrative is, in Hollywood's terms, a bona fide impossibility—a castration that is really and truly not going to occur. In place of a (literal or figurative) hard cut to black, Hollywood delivers a (literal or figurative) slow dissolve, the implication of which is that there is an afterlife for these characters—a continuation of satisfaction beyond the frame of the story in which we have been immersed. Such hopeful continuity is, of course, cinema's imaginary fantasy par excellence and must be understood as implicitly conservative, keeping the viewer in a regulated state of passive acceptance and status quo consumption. In effect, the Hollywood ending is a way to awaken the audience from the dreamlike experience of the film while ensuring that the reality outside the film is passively encountered as just another layer of dreaming. To jar the audience out of the imaginary fantasy, a more radical procedure is necessary—one that does not "dissolve" the film into reality but instead violently kills all forward movement, dropping the viewer into a deathlike abyss. I examine this very rare type of ending—the truncation ending—in the section that follows.

On Truncation: *Limbo, The Sopranos,*
and *Martha Marcy May Marlene*

Resolution is a marker not of wholeness per se but a wish for the possibility of wholeness. It represents the softening of a hard reality, seducing viewers to accept the fundamental lie of human subjectivity: that satisfaction is possible. In mainstream film, resolutions employ conventional sets of signifiers to let viewers know that they have reached the end and that the story is now complete: *it is okay to leave the theater now,* but also, in a more primal psychological sense, simply *it is okay.* The characters are okay. The world is okay. You are okay. The Hollywood ending paradoxically bounds the story-world so it can extend unbounded into the distance, a timeless and placeless ideal. At the same time, in Lacanian terms, the very notion of resolution can also represent a threat, inasmuch as it forms the outline of a perfect imago—an alienating completeness that is not proximate or attainable but instead "over there," taunting us with a perfect little story in comparison to which we find our own real-life story lacking. Viewed in this envious way, Hollywood's happy endings engender aggressiveness because the viewer's self-image feels fragmented by comparison.

A common response to the idealized trajectory of the Hollywood ending is to give in to its illusion, embracing the lie and making it one's own. This is the response desired by consumer capitalism, and it should go without saying that most fans of Hollywood cinema passively adopt it. A second, ostensibly less common response is to seek out films that smash the tidy smugness of the Hollywood ending in an act of pure defiance. In this section I discuss two films and a television episode that, with varying degrees of severity, utilize truncation as a way to fracture their audience's relation to the imago of narrative completion: John Sayles's indie drama *Limbo* (1999), writer-director David Chase's series-ending episode for the HBO series *The Sopranos* (2007), and Sean Durkin's psychological thriller *Martha Marcy May Marlene* (2011). Although these millennial media-texts continue to be intellectually admired and subject to much debate, their endings remain a source of great consternation to those who came expecting the fantasy.

John Sayles's 1999 film *Limbo* is infamous for one reason: it ends but does not resolve. The very last thing we see is a shot of a seaplane as it approaches the film's three protagonists—fisherman Joe Gastineau (David Strathairn), lounge singer Donna De Angelo (Mary Elizabeth Mastrantonio), and Donna's teenage daughter Noelle (Vanessa Martinez)—on the shore of a remote Alaskan island. Having survived alone in the wilderness for ten days, the protagonists embrace, knowing as we do that the plane either contains a friendly pilot who will ferry them to safety or a pair of drug dealers who will kill them just as they earlier killed Joe's brother. Yet as the sound of the plane's engine ominously increases, the camera ethereally fades to white, followed by a hard cut to black and silence. There is a short pause and the credits roll. We know that the film has ended, but we also know that its ending has refused us closure. This type of ending is best termed a "truncation" because it is neither a resolution, nor a cliffhanger, nor a provocatively minimalist way of forecasting a sequel; the film simply stops.

Sayles's highly deliberate, carefully timed ending for *Limbo* should not distract us from its rudeness. Upon first viewing, the film's ending is less an intellectually challenging gambit from a noted indie auteur than it is a shocking affront to one of our most deeply held assumptions about cinema: that whether mainstream or independent, upbeat or downbeat, *films come to an end*. By focusing on this phrase "come to," the paradoxical nature of cinematic truncation becomes clear. In an instantaneous cut to silent nothingness, the film simultaneously *does end* and *does not end*. It has resolved to not resolve. The viewer cannot but wonder: is this a deliberate provocation, a moment of punctuation, perhaps some kind of censorship or a technical error? The truncated segment of film simultaneously raises these questions and refuses to answer them. The narrative has been reframed in a way that is seemingly indifferent to its own established arcs and timelines; we have been cut off without being extended the courtesy of "coming to."

To better understand why the truncation ending is experienced as the "limbo" of Sayles's title rather than as the finite ending it appears to be, we need to turn to the most infamous of Lacanian practices: the variable-length session, or as it is more commonly known, the "short session." A personal account of Lacan's short session can be found in a book by Stuart Schneiderman, who was one of Lacan's analysands in the 1970s:

> You arrive for your session, let us say, in a fairly good mood, filled with things to say, about your past, your present, your fantasies, your dreams, whatever. . . . So you begin the session with some introductory remarks and pass to the subject you want to elaborate, to analyze, to ponder, to understand. You want the analyst to hear this because it is *really* important. But no sooner have you broached the topic, no sooner have the words identifying it passed your lips, than Lacan all of a sudden rises up from his chair and pronounces the session to be over, finished, done with. And he did this unceremoniously with a total lack of the good manners to which one is accustomed.[3]

Schneiderman goes on to say that "[t]here was something of the horror of death in the short sessions" and that at the point of truncation "the analysand found himself thrown into reality, ejected into the world without so much as a fare-thee-well."[4]

Psychoanalysis offers a term to designate this no-place beyond symbolic law and imaginary fantasy: the Real. The Real is that which lies beyond symbolization and must be strictly distinguished from what human subjects conceive as their day-to-day "reality." Indeed, Schneiderman notes that Lacan called the short session "an exemplary instance of the real."[5] Given the expectation that a film will "end on time," is not this encounter with the Real precisely what the truncation ending delivers its audience? Lacanian scholar Bruce Fink notes that Lacan does not advocate ending sessions randomly but instead "recommends ending sessions on the most striking point, when possible—that is, when the analysand articulates the most striking statement or question of the session."[6] Fink continues:

> That should not be taken to imply that the point, statement, or question need be self-evident, transparent, or obvious in meaning. Often the statement or question on which the analyst scands [ends] the session can be understood in several different ways, and the analysand is left to ponder all of them in the time between that session and the next one. Scanding [ending] the session at such a point is designed to put the analysand to work, whether consciously or unconsciously, during the time between sessions.[7]

In such an arrangement, the stoppage of the session "is merely an especially emphatic form of punctuation."[8]

As in the abrupt end to a Lacanian "short session," cinematic truncation punctuates our experience so as to redouble our focus on what predicated it. When the final shot of *Limbo* fades out and stays there, our protagonists move from the domain of the imaginary to the Real. However, given that they are fictional characters, this distinction is less relevant than the impact their sudden, ostensibly permanent absence has on the viewer. The problem with this sort of ending is not so much that it denies the viewer knowledge, but that it does so without warning or explanation, dismissing us to figure it out on our own. We experience what might be described as an imaginary overrun—a sense that the film should continue indefinitely into the future but does not do so. The truncation ending does not coddle us, does not care for us. It is, in a word, "indifferent," which is precisely how Lacan characterizes the analysand's perception of the analyst who, for reasons that are unclear, abruptly ends a session.[9]

In order to further examine the viewer's relation to the truncation ending, I now turn to a richer and even more radical example: the series-concluding episode of *The Sopranos* entitled "Made in America." At the risk of sounding glib, I want to claim that whereas *The Sopranos* begins with Freud—and I am here thinking of the first scene of the show's pilot, in which Tony first enters the office of Dr. Melfi (Lorraine Bracco), his psychotherapist—the series ends with Lacan, specifically with a short session. The ending to the series' final episode, which is now regarded as an iconic moment in American television history, does not merit a lengthy recap here. In a series of carefully orchestrated shots, mob boss Tony Soprano (James Gandolfini) is seen sitting in a booth at a local diner waiting for his family to join him for a nice dinner. After perusing various selections on the tableside jukebox, Tony plays Journey's "Don't Stop Believin'." He looks to the door as various patrons enter—some banal in appearance, some vaguely menacing. Tony's wife Carmela (Edie Falco) enters and sits opposite him; they talk. A tough-looking man (Paolo Colandrea) in a gray Members Only jacket enters, followed by Tony's son A.J. (Robert Iler). The camera cuts outside to reveal daughter Meadow (Jamie-Lynn Sigler) struggling to parallel park her car at the curb. The man in the Members Only jacket gets up from the lunch counter, and the camera ominously tracks him as he proceeds to the restroom just behind Tony on his right. Meadow finishes parking, crosses the street, and at the exact point when she is about to enter the diner, Tony looks up and the camera cuts to black and silence. There is a ten second pause before the credits silently roll.

Audience responses to this highly ambiguous, truncated ending are as legendary as the episode itself. HBO's website crashed due to the volume of agitated comments, and local crowds who had gathered to watch the episode at the set of the "Bada Bing" strip club purportedly walked out in confusion and dismay.[10] In the days and weeks following the episode, media pundits, bloggers, and serious students of film and television began the process of interpretation, guided only by the information that the scene and show offered forth. Dana Polan, whose book on *The Sopranos* is particularly helpful in framing the show's social context, describes the response to the show's finale as follows:

> Like the medieval exegetes of religious allegories who would devise ever more complex systems of interpretation to make their meanings fit the ambiguous texts they were confronting, the desperate fans took any and every detail of the final sequence of *The Sopranos* as potentially revelatory of narrative things to come.[11]

Polan goes on to compare the show's truncating cut-to-black to certain tendencies in European art cinema of the 1960s, in particular the famous freeze-frame that concludes François Truffaut's *The 400 Blows* (1959) on a note of ambiguity regarding the protagonist's future. While this is surely a valid comparison, we need to be clear that Truffaut's film leaves no one guessing about whether the transmission apparatus (in this case, a film projector) has malfunctioned. There is a difference between a formally marked point of ambiguity (Truffaut's freeze-frame or Sayles's fade to white) and the unmarked ambiguity of *The Sopranos* finale, which leaves the viewer contemplating their own reality, without benefit of any signifying guidance or "fair warning" to mitigate the cut.

A more apt comparison to *The Sopranos'* "Made in America" is offered by the ending of the 1971 Monte Hellman film *Two-Lane Blacktop*, wherein a drag racing scene aborts when the filmstrip itself slows to a crawl and appears to burn up from the heat of the projector bulb. In this case, one's response to seeing the random traces of melting celluloid would have been to *look back at the projection booth*. Or better yet, we might compare the *Sopranos'* finale to the truncated climax of side 1 of the Beatles *Abbey Road* album (1969), where the song "I Want You (She's So Heavy)" abruptly cuts to silence at a moment of high crescendo. Here again, our response is to question the apparatus; it is easy to imagine early listeners checking to see why the needle lifted away from the record. Speaking personally, my own response to the live airing of the *Sopranos'* finale began with a rush of adrenaline (any fan of the show knew that most episodes concluded with a popular song, thus Tony's selection of "Don't Stop Believin'" unequivocally signaled that the end was near) followed by shocked confusion when the image went black (my immediate assumption was that the local cable transmission had been cut and that enraged fans would be picking up their phones momentarily). Then, after a long pause, the credits rolled and I had a lot to contemplate. Why *that* ending? And why at *that moment*?

My concern here lies not so much with what *The Sopranos'* ending reveals about the overall series, its creators, or its fans. Instead, I wish to address the impossibility of such an ending—the fact that it is virtually never the option that is chosen, but when it is chosen the effect is obscene, structurally out-of-bounds. The precise stakes of the truncation ending are illuminated by recalling a crucial signifying aspect of *The Sopranos* that permeates the show's narrative as well as its form: Catholicism. The title of the show, and the name of the family at its center, is an obvious and highly literal reference to castration: in Catholic choirs of the eighteenth century and before, soprano parts were sometimes sung by castrati—men who had been castrated before puberty so as to retain their high voice. Perhaps less obvious is the fact that the series ends with a castrating cut—one of the great visual puns in the history of film and television—that denotes not only Tony's death at the end of the series (presumably assassinated by the man in the Members Only jacket) but the fact that, despite many of the characters' avowed Catholicism, there is nothing beyond death: for Tony, there is no judgment, no heaven, no hell. Whatever horrors may face his family (and one can only imagine the traumatic scene that would have ensued at the diner had the camera remained on), the show's ever-conflicted patriarch has been castrated, cut out of the picture, in a way that is both neutering and radically neutral.[12]

Given the paucity of well-known films with genuinely truncated endings, it should come as no surprise that film scholars have written very little on the subject, and even fewer have noted the striking parallel between cinematic truncation and Lacan's "short session." One exception comes in a footnote to Todd McGowan's chapter on Michael Haneke in *Out of Time: Desire in Atemporal Cinema*. McGowan makes the claim that a hard cut-to-black in Michael Haneke's *Code Unknown* "functions like the psychoanalytic short session," inasmuch as this cut "puts a stop to the sliding of the signifier" and thus allows significance to emerge.[13] While this is undoubtedly true, we need to be clear that cinema is unlike a Lacanian short session in two distinct respects: first, the vast majority of narrative films have a fixed (i.e., nonvariable) running time that can be roughly predicted from the outset, and second, a film cannot spontaneously change its length based on how the viewer responds. Given these stipulations, it becomes clearer that the link between cinematic truncation and the Lacanian short session resides primarily in the interpretive work triggered by their respective premature endings.

Perhaps the most brash, interpretation-inspiring cinematic truncation in recent years comes in the final scene of *Martha Marcy May Marlene* (*MMMM*). In this scene, an abrupt cut-to-black terminates the narrative at a point of high tension and in doing so withholds a crucial answer regarding the psychological state of protagonist Martha (Elizabeth Olson). At the same time, this ending calls into question the veracity of many of the shocking images we have seen because it refuses to fully corroborate the film's diegetic past in the present. The narrative of *MMMM* is split from the outset, unfolding as a series of intercut scenes wherein Martha's past involvement with an anarchist-agrarian cult alternates with her present interactions at the upscale lakeside home of her sister Lucy (Sarah Paulson) and brother-in-law Ted (Hugh Dancy). The story unfolds simultaneously in these two time frames, and, as it does, the viewer becomes increasingly aware of the brainwashing and violence that took place at the cult, as well as the fact that Martha's present psychological state is fragile and perhaps degrading. Tensions flare as Lucy and Ted confront Martha's increasingly erratic behavior: she swims nude in a public lake; she crawls into bed with Lucy and Ted while they are having sex; she urinates on her dress while sleeping and then inexplicably hides the dress under her mattress; she mistakes a bartender at a social gathering for a cult member and violently accosts him.

In response to Martha's behavior, Lucy repeatedly asks the same question: "*What is wrong with you?*" In a strong sense, this question—one that implicitly seeks to connect the present with the past—is the viewer's question as well. It seems clear enough that Martha has been traumatized by the imprisonment, brainwashing, criminal violence, and systematic rape she both experienced and later facilitated at the cult. What the film fails to reveal, however, is the extent to which a preexisting mental trauma—one that predates her estrangement from her family—may be profoundly influencing her perceptions. To be clear, I want to argue that the ambiguity of the truncation ending certifies that the viewer has been misperceiving the true state of affairs all along, thinking that the cult is the *cause* of Martha's psychosocial maladjustment rather than a hallucinatory *symptom* of her damaged mental state.

Although it is easy to miss, Martha's consciously avowed story concerning her disappearance is always entirely consistent and has nothing to do with the existence of a cult. Whenever Lucy explicitly asks Martha where she had been during her long absence, Martha indicates that she was living with a boyfriend in the Catskills. In one scene, Martha matter-of-factly states, "I had a boyfriend. He lied to me. I left. That's it." The implication is that Martha fled the boyfriend to seek refuge with Lucy only because she lived relatively close and because Martha lacked the financial resources to exist on her own. The problem with the film's ambiguous ending, however, is that it appears to support both of these stories—the story of the relationship-gone-bad that we have only heard about and the story of cult abuse that we have seen in flashback—but in the final analysis only one of these stories can be true.

The film's final three scenes follow Lucy's decision to take Martha to speak with a therapist in New York City, a decision precipitated by an episode in which Martha hallucinates and mistakes Ted for cult leader Patrick (John Hawkes), kicking him down the stairs. Martha admits that she was "confused"—that is, that she has literally been confusing past events for present ones—and for Lucy this is confirmation enough that she is not equipped to help Martha on her own. In effect, this decision itself is the film's narrative climax, and like the murder-exculpating climax of *The Player*, it is very low-key, both in comparison to a typical Hollywood climax and to the intense drama that follows it. Just after Lucy's decision, and in place of a denouement, the film delivers a tense but disturbingly truncated encounter in which Martha's past and present collide—a return of the Real that neither the audience nor the film's protagonists are equipped to deal with.

The next morning, very early, Martha goes for a final swim in the lake before the three depart for the city. The film appears to have placidly resolved; indeed, in a more typical Hollywood film this scene itself would be the denouement. However, in a startling reverse shot we see Martha take sight of an unfamiliar man in jeans and a white t-shirt (the same attire worn by all the men at the cult) perched on a rock on the opposite side of the lake, staring back at her. The scene is abstract and virtually silent; shot with a telephoto lens, the water's surface appears like waves of static on a television screen. Martha quickly swims back toward the dock and, without any explanation of this encounter, the shot cuts to what will be the film's final scene, a single long-take with Martha in the back seat of the car on the way to New York. The car's engine is humming and Martha is clearly deep in thought, when suddenly her eyes register something ahead of them on the country road. The camera remains fixed, this time failing to provide a reverse shot of what she sees. The car stops and we hear Ted (unseen but presumably driving) say, "What the hell is he doing? Fucking lunatic." Martha's eyes follow as the man from the lake jogs past the car to his own vehicle, which is parked by the side of the road. We assume that he had jumped out, physically blocking the road; he has definitely spotted Martha in the back seat. Initially startled, Ted resumes driving at a normal pace. Martha looks back to see that the other car is now following them, quite close, and turns to face forward again, wide-eyed and panicked. At this point of imminent crisis, the camera cuts to black and the titles scroll.

The problem posed by this truncated ending depends on its absolute refusal to link the mysterious man—and the film's creation of a present, objective "reality" at the lake house—to the film's past scenes of cult activity. The film's screenplay and credits reaffirm this ambiguity: the script assigns the t-shirted figure an ambiguous character title ("a scruffy man") and the credits neither list the role nor the actor who plays it. In the context of such confusion about character identity, the cut to black forms a punctuation mark, stating unequivocally that this nonsignifying element—*this ambiguity in itself*—is highly significant. As in the Lacanian short session, something important has just happened, but it is up to the individual to "read" it and determine what it means. Yet there is perhaps less room for debate here than there appears to be. One thing is certain: the scene *could* reaffirm the existence of the cult by showing the audience the face of a known cult member—in present time, with Lucy and Ted as witnesses—but instead *refuses to do so*. The truncation of the film abruptly denies any answer to the very question that demands to be answered most of all: what is wrong with Martha? Yet in refusing to answer this, the film raises a new question that we have failed to see, even though it has been right there in front of us all along: is it possible that the avowed former boyfriend is real and the cult a hallucinated fiction?

In the end, I want to argue that the ambiguity of the film's truncation simultaneously affirms the film's two seemingly incommensurate "realities." The notion that Martha's past involved *either* a lying boyfriend *or* a cult is revealed to be a false dichotomy, albeit one that has structured everything we have seen. *MMMM* is a film about a woman's psychosis, and it shares a great deal with films such as Robert Altman's *Images* (1972), Roman Polanski's *Repulsion* (1965), and Maya Deren's *Meshes of the Afternoon* (1943). Each of these films exploit film form—especially the audience's expectations about editing transitions—to create confusion between the subjective and objective realities of their female protagonists. Like the protagonists of these other films, Martha's story involves an ostensibly impossible immixture of quotidian reality and what Lacan terms "the Real." Possibly schizophrenic from an early age, Martha, in a delusional state, invented the cult as a means of dealing with a past traumatic relationship. In this reading of the film's ending—a reading that, like the ending of *The Sopranos*, is never certified in the positivistic manner Hollywood leads us to expect—the "scruffy man" who returns at the film's end is none other than the boyfriend Martha left in the Catskills, but despite his centrality to the story, he is unfamiliar to the viewer. Although we have previously heard of his existence, we do not really believe in him because he does not appear on screen until the film's very end. When the film makes this shift, the audience's fantasy is revealed to be a hallucination just like Martha's—a fiction we unquestioningly take to be real. In this way, the veracity we have mistakenly ascribed to the film's flashbacks can be understood as a testament to the seriousness with which we should approach psychological disorders such as schizophrenia in real life. However, we also need to be clear that the point of truncation occurs just as Martha has come to precisely the opposite realization: that the hallucination is over and that her estranged boyfriend really does exist. Whether he is seeking her out in order to kill her or to inquire about her well-being is entirely irrelevant in light of his real return and the interpretations it incites.

On Glitch: *Sunshine*

Conceptually, the opposite of a cinematic truncation is a fade: a conventional way for a film to acknowledge that it has ended with intent. By blurring or dimming-down the image in a gradual way, cinema delivers us softly out of one dream state and into another. In comparison to this, cinematic truncation is not only harsh but exceedingly rare, verging on *hapax*, and this scarcity is significant in itself. However, in the era of digital filmmaking, a set of widely deployed formal techniques exist to offer a compromise between resolution and truncation, between fading and chopping. These techniques— which can appear anywhere in a film, not just at the ending—are designated by the provocative millennial buzzword "glitch." In terms of cinematic narrative, a glitch is not really an interruption at all but instead the threat of an interruption that ultimately fails to appear. A radical break could have occurred but did not, and in this sense a glitch must be understood as a domesticated, less upsetting stand-in for the trauma of truncation. Or, in slightly different terms, a glitch can be understood as *the residue of an impossibility*—an indicator that the void of the Real threatening our imaginary fantasy has once again been kept at bay.

With the increasing prevalence of digital transcoding in our everyday lives, the aesthetics of glitch have become both more recognizable and increasingly codified. In cinema, glitches usually occur simultaneously on the audio and video tracks as a sizzle, blip, or full-blown audiovisual decomposition. Sometimes images and sounds are scrambled or freeze; other times they are obscured by blocky static. Compression algorithms may cause packets of color to disperse in strange patterns across the screen and sounds may warble, click, or chirp. Yet despite the connotations of the word "glitch" as a singular, small, punctiform error, in twenty-first-century media culture glitch anomalies are nothing short of ubiquitous.[14] Indeed, glitch could rightfully be identified as the single most definitive media "style" of the early twenty-first century, appearing everywhere from Kanye West's "Welcome to Heartbreak" video (Nabil Elderkin, 2009); to the *Batman: Arkham Asylum* video game (2009); to car racing segments from the most widely watched factual television show in the world, BBC's *Top Gear*; to popular found footage films such as *Cloverfield* (Matt Reeves, 2008) and *Chronicle* (Josh Trank, 2012).

Emblematic of this trend, but also in some respects pathbreaking, is Danny Boyle's 2007 film *Sunshine*—a film interested in the limits of possibility, especially regarding technology and human psychology. The film's narrative concerns a perilous space voyage intended to reignite the sun using a massive nuclear device, and the film's major conflict hinges on a failure to adjust the angle of the ship's solar reflectors when it changes course—a necessity so obvious that Trey (Benedict Wong), the ship's navigator, simply forgets to do it. "People do shit. They get stressed and fuck up," he says, admitting that it was a terrible mistake to override the ship's computer. Three scenes in *Sunshine* employ a glitch aesthetic to underscore the classic science fiction dichotomy of flawless (digital) computers versus flawed (analog) humans. Whenever this dichotomy breaks down—for instance when a computer fails or when a human becomes machinelike—the film erupts in an audiovisual glitch.

In one scene early on, the ship's physicist Robert Capa (Cillian Murphy) enters a small cube-shaped room made entirely of video screens. He vocally interacts with the ship's computer (a sort of female version of HAL from Kubrick's *2001: A Space Odyssey*) as it runs a 3-D simulation of the final delivery of the ship's payload at the sun. As the projection nears completion, the image suddenly freezes, splitting into its constituent colors, and the individual video panels begin to flash irregularly. This pointedly glitchy interruption is a result of the computer attempting to calculate probabilities beyond its own limits, having encountered an infinite number of variables as the payload velocity increases and "space and time . . . become smeared together." Later in the film, when the astronauts rendezvous with a seemingly abandoned spacecraft from a failed prior mission, they discover a video message recorded by Pinbacker (Mark Strong), the ship's former commander: "We have abandoned our mission. Our star is dying! All our science, all our hopes, our dreams are foolish in the face of this! We are—dust, nothing more." As the commander's disturbing psychotic rant continues, we see a close-up of the video screen: his face appears badly burned, but we can barely make out any image through the layers of digital distortion and colorful compression blocks. Indeed, the point of the video seems to be to show the audience what a blurring of human-digital ontologies might look like. To be clear, however, both of these glitches are framed, and in some sense excused, by the appearance of digital screens within the diegesis. In neither case do we get that sense that the film itself is on the verge of failure.

The film's approach to glitch changes radically, however, in the film's climactic sequence when Capa faces off with Pinbacker in the vast chamber that houses the payload, which is now plummeting toward the sun. Equal parts slasher movie and stylized space epic, *Sunshine* is rife with simulated audiovisual distortion. Indeed virtually every shot has been blurred, compressed, upended, or overexposed. Most remarkable are the seemingly random points at which the image momentarily freezes and the sound drops out, as if our disc player had encountered a scratch. These digital fermata hit the viewer hard, and even when the pauses are over it is unclear whether we have experienced a real technical glitch or not. Despite their obvious homage to the "Jupiter and Beyond the Infinite" sequence from *2001: A Space Odyssey*—which is of course a high point in the history analog special effects—*Sunshine*'s climactic freeze-frames can be understood as a kind of nouveau-digital expressionism, rendering for the viewer a sense that the film itself, like protagonist Capa, is on the verge of binary collapse. Despite this, the film does not truncate and culminates in a happy resolution back on Earth, as Capa's sister (Paloma Baeza) watches the sun noticeably brighten from an ice-encrusted Sydney harbor, just as his final transmission promised it would.

As Daniel Temkin and I have argued in "Notes on Glitch," the appearance of a glitch in an image, sound, or motion picture "loudly announces the hegemony of digital representation and the passivity of its subjects":

> The existence of glitch-based representation depends upon the inability of software to treat a wrong bit of data in anything other than the right way. The word "glitch" in this sense does not solely represent the cause that initiates some failure, but also the output that results when improper data is decoded properly. An isolated problem is encountered and, rather than shutting down, the software prattles on. Stated differently, it is a given program's *failure to fully fail* upon encountering bad data that allows a glitch to appear.[15]

In an instance of glitch, the representation does not truncate but nonetheless tries to convince us that a sudden textual rupture is "on the table" as one possibility. Glitch is thus a symbol of our anxiety about endings but not an anxiety-inducing ending in itself.

However, despite *Sunshine*'s edgy aesthetics, and what for 2007 is a legitimately novel approach to glitching, we need to be clear that all of the scenes I have discussed involve glitches that are themselves digitally simulated—no more or less real than the spectacular computer-generated exteriors of the spacecraft that appear in various scenes. As such, the film's glitches must be regarded not only as failed truncations but as *simulations of failed truncations*—carefully engineered, nostalgic throwbacks to the era of analog production when technological failure was frequent and real. But this leaves us with a crucial question: why are twenty-first-century filmmakers investing considerable time, energy, and money in order to recreate the distortion and messiness that analog-era films were at such great pains to eradicate? The answer can again be found in the three-stage procedure through which all cinematic fantasies progress.

If, in the words of Slavoj Žižek, "fantasy serves as the screen that protects us from being directly overwhelmed by the raw Real,"[16] then the glitch aesthetic must be understood not as a harbinger of impossibility that is about to occur but as an indicator that our miraculous new digital machinery cannot be tripped up so easily as in the past. The glitch aesthetic of digital media, like Hollywood's time-tested happy ending, brings the viewer face-to-face with an obstacle, only to show it dramatically surmounted, and stasis achieved. Glitches appear not in order to summon forth the impossible/Real but to reassure us that a potential rupture has been averted, resolved, shut down. Incorporating the appearance of a problem within its solution, the seeming loss of control embodied by glitch is purely an imaginary fantasy—not real truncation per se but a fantasy of *truncation averted*. Like the subject in fantasy, glitch posits its own obstacle and in doing so fails to fail. In this way, the glitch aesthetic fosters a desire for the satisfying perfectibility of digital forms, while portraying the relative rawness of analog communication as something ancient, guttural, decomposed, and in all ways alien to the imago we fantasize at the end of desire's path.

Notes

1. Jacques Lacan, "The Direction of the Treatment and the Principles of Its Power," in *Écrits*, trans. Bruce Fink (New York: Norton, 2006), 532.

2. Martin Heidegger, *Being and Time*, trans. Joan Stambaugh (Albany: State University of New York Press, 1996), 251.

3. Stuart Schneiderman, *Jacques Lacan: The Death of an Intellectual Hero* (Cambridge: Harvard University Press, 1983), 132.

4. Schneiderman, *Jacques Lacan*, 133.

5. Schneiderman, *Jacques Lacan*, 132.

6. Bruce Fink, *Fundamentals of Psychoanalytic Technique: A Lacanian Approach for Practitioners* (New York: Norton, 2007), 48.

7. Fink, *Fundamentals of Psychoanalysis*, 48.

8. Fink, *Fundamentals of Psychoanalysis*, 49.

9. Jacques Lacan, "The Function and Field of Speech and Language in Psychoanalysis," in *Écrits*, trans. Bruce Fink (New York: Norton, 2006), 258.

10. ABC News, "'Sopranos' Reacts to Angry Mob of Viewers," June 11, 2007, http://abcnews.go.com/WN/story?id=3267872 (accessed 13 May, 2014).

11. Dana Polan, *The Sopranos* (Durham: Duke University Press, 2009), 5.

12. With the snuffing of Tony's subjectivity, the viewer is left in a signifying limbo, and it certainly seems possible that series creator David Chase—who claimed to know how the series would end from its beginning—had seen Sayles's film and was influenced by it.

13. Todd McGowan, *Out of Time: Desire in Atemporal Cinema* (Minneapolis: University of Minnesota Press, 2011), 19 n. 37.

14. The *Oxford English Dictionary* defines a glitch as a "sudden short-lived irregularity in behavior."

15. Hugh S. Manon and Daniel Temkin, "Notes on Glitch," World Picture 6 (Winter 2011): http://www.worldpicturejournal.com/WP_6/Manon.html (date of access unknown).

16. Slavoj Žižek, *How to Read Lacan* (New York: Norton, 2007), 57.

2

The Banality of Trauma

Claire Denis's *Bastards* and the Anti-Ending

HILARY NERONI

Patriarchy versus Capitalism

Claire Denis's films often defy usual narrative trajectories. This is not because Denis sets out to create nonsense, but because she understands that sense depends as much on what we don't see as on what we do. Whereas most film-makers use cinema to depict present events, Denis uses it to reveal absences. Absences signify obliquely. As a result, the spectator of her films must work to piece together the narratives of her films. Because of this reliance on absence, endings have a special importance for Denis. The endings of her films provide the key for reading the absences and unlocking their obscure logic. It is only at the moment when a Denis film ends that one can find a sense in the series of absences that constitute the film.

Bastards (2013), Denis's latest feature-length film, is a contemporary film noir set in an aging upper-class Paris with a unique ending that cuts against the grain of more standard filmic narrative structures, so much so that it rips open the very purpose of the filmic ending. The film tells the story of Marco Silvestri (Vincent Lindon) returning home after the suicide of his brother-in-law to help his grieving sister, who believes the suicide is a response to the actions of her husband's creditors. Marco goes to find out what happened and to avenge his brother-in-law's death, but what he discovers goes beyond what he expects or can handle. The end of *Bastards* is shocking both because of the revelations it provides and the resolution it does not provide. Denis brings us to this ending by aligning us with Marco so that we discover with him what his sister is hiding.

The unexpected editing in *Bastards* challenges the viewer to make sense of the mystery of the film. The nonchronological ordering of the early scenes becomes understandable only later on in the film, and the viewer must think back to contextualize what she has seen earlier—if it can be contextualized at all. Whereas most films use editing to obscure the gaps between scenes, Denis's editing in the beginning of the film not only violates chronology but further employs thematic and temporal gaps that make the story difficult to follow. This style of editing demands a thoughtful viewer and evokes a filmic world that emanates beyond the frame while it simultaneously prevents viewers from feeling as though they have total access to that world.

Denis does allow enough points of narrative comprehension to give the viewer a sense of what occurs in the filmic world. In the beginning, for example, the viewer feels aligned with Marco, a sea captain who hasn't been home for years. Even Marco, however, turns out to be an unreliable guide, and this pushes the viewer into more unease. The viewer's unease becomes part of the commentary that the film makes about its characters and the world they live in. *Bastards'* bleak look at one Parisian family allows Denis to make a larger point about contemporary patriarchy and its relationship to global capitalism. The link between these larger concerns becomes most clear in the traumatic ending of the film.

The ending of *Bastards* stands out because it is so unlike mainstream endings that emphasize resolution and mastery, and it also departs from independent films that stress openness. Denis's ending marks a point of closure, but at the same time, it makes evident that antagonism is irreducible. Looking at the end of *Bastards* enables us to see how film endings that work to resolve conflicts inherent in the plot ultimately cover over the fundamental social antagonism. Denis ends her film with an attempt to resist the conventional turn away from antagonism and thus leaves the wound inherent in the narrative open in order to bring it to light. She does this not by denying the possibility of a conclusion, which she provides in a final and shocking revelation, but by denying resolution. The revelations at the end of *Bastards* explain some of the mysteries of the film but also make it apparent that the gaps in the narrative structure will never be filled. Through this film, Denis challenges the viewer to accept those gaps, as uncomfortable as that may be, rather than attempt to make all the pieces fit together seamlessly. The shocking ending suggests that viewers can reside in the narrative gaps and that this positioning is essential to the proper experience of a film.

The wound at the heart of the film that constitutes the film's final revelation lies with the patriarch's impotence and violence. In psychoanalytic terms, impotence comes from the patriarch losing his symbolic authority. The symbolic order is not inherently patriarchal, but patriarchy establishes itself on the basis of the structure of the symbolic order. Signification depends on the existence of one exceptional signifier that doesn't have the same status as all the others. This exception is what Jacques Lacan calls the Master Signifier. The Master Signifier is a signifier without a signified, a meaningless signifier, and yet it ensures the consistency of all the other signifiers. As Slavoj Žižek explains,

> Suffice it to recall how a community functions: the Master-Signifier which guarantees the community's consistency is a signifier whose signified is an enigma for the members themselves—nobody really knows what it means, but each of them some how presupposes that others know, that it has to mean "the real thing," so they use it all the time.[1]

The Master Signifier functions not in spite of its meaninglessness but because of it. It can mean anything, and as a result, subjects suppose that it is a signifier of power, and this is where the connection with patriarchy becomes evident.

Patriarchy has its foundation in the Master Signifier, which it asserts as the Name of the Father. As a Master Signifier, the Name of the Father has no significance at all, but patriarchy endows it with the ultimate significance. Under the patriarchal regime, the impotent signifier becomes the signifier of omnipotence, but the power of the Master Signifier remains a supposition. The power of the Name of the Father depends on the belief that subjects have in it. The Name of the Father lacks even the status of an ordinary signifier, but patriarchy depends on the collective disavowal of this lack. The key to its power is this process of disavowal that subjects must go through in relation to it. Denis presents a world, however, in which the tide has turned on patriarchy. In other words, the Master Signifier in the world of *Bastards* is empty and powerless, but the subjects of Denis's world refuse to acknowledge this. In the midst of patriarchy's demise, the disavowal of the patriarch's lack becomes even more fervent in order to hide from this revelation, and this is what Denis chronicles in her film. No one in the world of *Bastards* has the ability to opt out of this collective disavowal, even if they have every intention to break the cycle and hold the patriarch's impotence out for all to see.

Bastards attributes the revelation of the patriarch's impotence to changes in capitalism by linking the family's moral demise to their factory's failure. In doing this, Denis emphasizes the intricate yet tenuous relationship between patriarchy and capitalism. The tenuousness of their relationship resides in the competing Master Signifier, which for patriarchy is the Father but for capitalism is money. In *Symbolic Economies*, Jean-Joseph Goux links money (or the universal equivalent) to the Name of the Father. He writes,

> the commodity recognized as universal equivalent becomes, in its monopoly, more than just another commodity; this commodity— in a development parallel at every turn to the emergence of the Father—becomes money, assuming the position first of a fetish, then of a symbol, of an idealized standard and measure of values.[2]

Goux sees a direct parallel between money and the Name of the Father, but Denis adds another turn of the screw to this analysis. As *Bastards* makes clear, money doesn't simply function in parallel to the patriarch but actually undermines the investment in his authority by offering an alternative.[3]

Money functions as a Master Signifier, but it does so much differently than patriarchal authority. Money, unlike patriarchy, shores up its own symbolic authority by flaunting rather than hiding its impotence. We know that money in and of itself does not have power; ultimately, it is simply a piece of paper. And yet, we are involved in the process of imbuing it with symbolic authority by disavowing this. With money, the disavowal is on the surface and no longer hidden. When money is the Master Signifier, we become aware of our disavowal and its role in sustaining this Master Signifier, but this awareness does not have a deleterious effect on the power of this signifier.

The development of capitalism plays a central role in *Bastards*, even though the film focuses more directly on familial perversions. The family that the film centers on owns a shoe factory. The patriarch has destroyed the shoe factory through a series of poor business choices and as a result of his perversions. By depicting the demise of this once-profitable shoe factory in relation to a perverse father, Denis's film suggests that capitalism has shifted in such a way that it no longer needs the patriarch in order to function and thus reveals the patriarch's impotence that was always implicitly there. *Bastards* focuses on a white upper-class Parisian patriarch and thus reveals the way that this social position depends on an ideology of potency, which contemporary capitalism calls into question. Here, capitalism is not necessarily the great equalizer; instead, it simply has a destructive force relative to other ideological structures. This should not create any nostalgia for the patriarch with symbolic authority because it reveals that he was already impotent. In other words, patriarchy's losing competition with money simply reveals that the patriarch never had the authority that he was supposed to have.

The patriarch's literal impotence is at the heart of the shocking revelations at the end of *Bastards*, and it is the source of the cruelty throughout the film. This cruelty, however, is not just an effect of impotence but also works to cover it over, which produces complicity in its participants. In Denis's film, this complicity comes both from the women who surround the patriarch and from the viewer. Rather than staging the women in the film as pure victims of the violent impotent patriarch, *Bastards* presents three female characters that constantly attempt to help hide the patriarch's impotence and even enable him to continue in his perverse activity. In this way, the film shows that impotence evaporates potential positions of resistance. In her unique ending, however, Denis reveals that the only way to resist the Master Signifier's corrupting impotence is to draw attention to this impotence and to the perversions that it produces.

In contrast, traditional endings that privilege the resolution of antagonism help to shore up the symbolic authority of the prevailing Master Signifier. Denis, in contrast, brings to light the impotence of the ending as such, since it can never truly solve all the problems that the film reveals. The impotent ending reveals the impotence of the Master Signifier, while the illusion of a potent ending—an ending that provides resolution to the antagonisms presented in the filmic narrative—supports the disavowal of the Master Signifier's lack and thus has a wholly ideological function. Perhaps this is why a 90- to 120-minute film remains a fascinating endeavor: it must always deal with the trauma of an ending, and the way it deals with the ending forces us to engage the antagonisms presented throughout the film.[4] Films most often deploy endings that provide the ultimate interpretation or the final word on the film itself, but Denis reveals that the ending can provoke the viewer into more interpretation not less. By doing so, she forces the spectator out of the position of disavowal.

An Unanchored Editing Structure

The beginning of *Bastards* is almost as unsettling as its ending. The film begins with the apparent suicide of the patriarch Jacques (Laurent Grévill), as the viewer sees his bloody body lying on the streets of Paris. At the end of the film, we learn that he must have committed suicide in reaction to the events that the ending depicts. The first shots of the film are dark rainy images of the streets with close-ups of the walls as the rain cascades down, the first introduction of the unrelenting darkness of the film's mise-en-scène. The film then moves to Jacques's dead body on the street covered with a cloth and surrounded by police, as his wife Sandra (Julie Bataille) is led away from the scene. The one moment of light can be found in the next set of shots that depict Marco receiving the call with the news of his brother-in-law's suicide and his sister's plea for help. As his ship takes him to shore, he leaves the light of the sea behind him and descends into the distinctly noir world of Paris that will eventually envelope him. As Nick Roddick observes, "Denis creates a world where the sun only shines on children—literally: everyone else is in shadow."[5] The visual darkness of the film mirrors the fate of its characters. Marco moves into an apartment building where Raphaëlle (Chiara Mastroianni), the girlfriend of Edouard Laporte (Michel Subor), lives in order to begin his investigation. Laporte was Jacques's business partner whom both Sandra and eventually Marco blame for Jacques's demise. The film presents Laporte as a gangster figure despite his involvement in legitimate business. His relationship to his girlfriend and son serves as an example of his perverse behavior since he lives apart from them and simply stops in to visit or to receive sexual favors. This leads Marco to comment to Raphaëlle that Laporte treats her like his mistress, but Raphaëlle doesn't seem to mind—an early sign of her complicity—and comments that Laporte has helped to build her confidence over the years. Clearly, however, she is lonely because she embarks on an affair with Marco, and their passionate sexual encounters are the only small moments of pleasure any of the characters have throughout the film.

Marco is the noir hero in this world as he struggles to understand what has happened and probes the web of deceit that has engulfed his family. The camera favors Marco as it lingers over his pensive face and reveals his body as sexuality attractive, which suggests that he is a potent male figure and a possible responsible father figure. The film, however, slowly takes away this one possible hero as he descends into a world he can't comprehend or control. This descent really takes hold when he learns about the violence that his niece Justine (Lola Créton) has suffered. Marco goes to see Justine in the hospital, and he learns by talking with her doctor that she has been sexually brutalized to such an extent that her vagina will need to be reconstructed through surgery. Marco blames Laporte for this, and he begins to work out how to avenge both the death of his brother-in-law and the brutalization of his niece. As if to bring the viewer into the realm of Marco's confusion and trauma, one image continually appears to disrupt the narrative movement of the film—the image of Justine walking the streets of Paris naked, wearing only high heels. The status of this image remains unclear until the very end of the film. At times it seems to be a traumatic image that haunts the film in general without being tied to any real event, and at other times it seems to portend Justine's future. The recurring image turns out to illustrate the state she was in when the police found her and brought her into the hospital, where we see her for the first three-quarters of the film.

In these recurring images of Justine, the mood is solemn and her face is impassive, as if she is in a trance. The streets are dark with the small puddles of light reflecting off of her body. The first time this image occurs, Justine is presented in close-ups and medium shots that do not reveal that she is fully naked. But then the film cuts to a long shot from behind that reveals that she is in fact totally naked except for the high heels she is wearing. Clearly, a naked body on a public street is out of place, but Justine's body has a radically ambiguous status in this scene. Someone has brutalized her, and yet she appears defiant. She is at once a male fantasy and a sign of female independence. The scene is lit in such a way that Justine's body is spotlighted with a warm glow, but the edges of the frame recede into a darkness that threatens to swallow her. At every edge, both at the edge of her body and at the edge of the frame, there lies a tension between intentionality and vulnerability. Denis compounds the ambiguity of the body's signification in this scene by refusing to provide any contextualization. The viewer doesn't know what has precipitated Justine's appearance on the street or even when the scene takes place.

This scene has the status of what Judith Mayne might call a "suspended question" in Denis's film. In her *Clare Denis*, Mayne argues that memories in Denis's films do not so much haunt the characters as pose questions to the viewer. She says, "Memories seem to 'float' in Denis's films, like suspended questions."[6] Even in *Bastards* (which Mayne does not discuss), the image of Justine walking on the street is not clearly attributable to Justine's memory (although sometimes it seems to be), and the image isn't placed so as to suggest cause and effect. Instead, it opens a question and a point of traumatic confusion. This image seems akin to the evidence of the unconscious; it appears as an elusive pulsation and disappears as soon as it begins to take shape. In this way, it holds the utmost importance but does not help nail down any of the symbolic coordinates of the filmic narrative.

If her naked body originally seems like some beautiful tragic fantasy, the last time that this scene appears reveals a shocking trauma. The types of shots vary, and a shot from the front of her body shows that there is blood

dripping down her inner thighs and across her cut wrists. The blood completely changes the context of the scene and transforms the signification of
Justine's naked body. As a result, rather than just being an object of desire,
this sequence reveals the female body to be a fantasy screen. Whatever the
viewer had imagined of Justine—that she was walking the streets naked for
her own enjoyment or that she was mentally disturbed—completely shifts
when the shot of her bleeding wrists and thighs comes into view. After seeing this shot, the image becomes that of a wounded woman who has been
brutalized or possibly raped and who tried to commit suicide in response.
The final version of this image ends with the police eventually picking her
up, an action that allows the viewer to place the scene within the narrative
timeline, though it doesn't provide much additional context.[7] The different
versions of this scene oppose different versions of Justine. She first appears as
a figure of defiance, and she later appears as a victim. Throughout the film,
Denis creates an ambiguity surrounding the character of Justine. The viewer
never knows whether she is the agent of what is happening or just a helpless victim of patriarchal violence. In the end, it seems impossible to decide
between these two possibilities, and Denis leaves her status ambiguous.

In fact, this ambiguity marks all three of the female characters in the
film. Marco's sister Sandra is most clearly a victim since she claims to have
been helpless in the face of Laporte and her husband's desires. She finds
herself paralyzed by shame because of what they did to her daughter and
her own inability to stop it. Raphaëlle appears to be both a kept woman and
at the same time independent enough to embark on an affair with a man
who threatens Laporte. Justine's situation is just as ambiguous. When she is
in the hospital, she appears simply young and vulnerable, but later when she
escapes her image changes. Her friends, who also are involved with Laporte,
help her escape. While driving with them through the night, she takes the
wheel of their car, shuts the lights off, and accelerates until she yanks the
steering wheel in order to send the car spiraling off the road. The crash kills
the other two passengers and possibly her (though Denis doesn't make this
clear). While this is completely reckless, she does it with purpose, and the
scene makes it impossible for the viewer to interpret her as a pure victim.
She is, if nothing else, the direct cause of the senseless death of her two
collaborators. In this scene, she appears to be complicit in the patriarch's
cruelty in that her response here is violent (and the film makes it unclear if
this response is for revenge or for personal pleasure).

Justine is also complicit in another way that brings together the themes
of the destructive effect of the impotent father and the corroding force of
capitalism. Here, her complicity resides in the symbolic nature of the high

heels that she wears. The addition of the high heels to Justine's naked body links Justine to her family's factory and thus to a larger cultural fantasy. Her body functions as the underside of manufactured beauty. That the factory produces high heels is an essential leitmotif that runs throughout the film. We see piles of high heels in heaps on the factory floor, a huge high heel that was once a large sign on top of the factory but now is being taken down, and most hauntingly Justine walking down the streets wearing only high heels and nothing else as blood runs down her thighs.

In this light, Justine's high heels are a symbolic remnant of a previous time in which patriarchy and capitalism worked in conjunction. The white upper-class Parisian family and their factory producing feminine ideals through restrictive female beauty practices, however, have decayed beyond repair in this noir world taking their last breaths before the viewer's eyes. Even after being rendered impotent, however, the characters cling to their past potency while attempting to cover over the impotence that now structures their relations. This fateful disavowal is appropriate to the noir world within which *Bastards* in embedded.

Paris Noir

Bastards has clear villains—Jacques and Laporte—but it does not have clear victims. Though the female characters in the film all suffer at the hands of Jacques and Laporte, they all play an integral role in their victimization. They protect these two patriarchs and even participate in the acts of violence done to them. *Bastards* does not suggest that the women are to blame for patriarchal violence, but that they fail to act in ways that might put an end to it. This complicity is one of the defining characteristics of the noir universe. Reviewer José Teodoro echoes most other critics when he introduces *Bastards* as "that rare thing: a true modern noir."[8] Denis herself has said that *Bastards* is a film noir. The film participates in film noir in many ways from the plot concerns, to the mise-en-scène, to the larger ideas about fate and identity. Film noir generally stages a noir hero caught in a web of crime and desire. To solve the mystery into which he is thrust, the noir hero must realize his own complicity. These ideas are reflected in the mise-en-scène and particularly in the hard contrast of the lighting. The uncertainties of the noir world are often reflected in the gritty urban backdrop bathed in shadow and visual ambiguity.

Bastards follows both the narrative and visual traditions of noir.[9] For Marco, as noir hero, each mystery, from Justine's wounds to the family's failing factory, is more traumatic than the next. Denis depicts Marco as the hero whose first weakness is his lust for the woman he can't really have. In a stunningly crafted scene at the beginning of the film, Marco at one point rides in the elevator with Raphaëlle. They are encircled in darkness except for a warm light that falls on their faces. In a tight two-shot Denis pulls the focus from one of their faces to the other as they become aware of each other physically. This moment of discovery and sensuality, however, is nestled into a dark frame and a tenuous environment. The noir setting makes every potential genuine encounter both sweeter and more uncertain. Raphaëlle herself remains a mystery since she is clearly attracted to Marco but oddly loyal to the cold and abusive Laporte. Raphaëlle and Marco begin a passionate affair, which embeds Marco in the web of crime and desire he is investigating.

All of these mysteries unfold in the shadows of Parisian streets, apartment buildings, and crumbling factories. Beautifully shot and hauntingly lit, each frame connotes a universe in which there is no respite from the decay of this family. The film seems to suggest that their time has passed—and thus that the time of sturdy patriarchy has passed as well. They are crumbling in on themselves as the shadows absorb each character one by one. Through this visual landscape, *Bastards* depicts the noir hero as caught in a fate that he did not have the power to change. More than once, Marco says that it is his fate to be dragged back into the destruction caused by this cursed family. He himself links the curse to paternity. For instance, in one scene Marco proclaims that he's happy he left his own wife and children so that he doesn't drag them down into this same fate. In other words, he has become aware that it is the patriarch that is causing this destruction.

Film noir has historically staged a certain kind of masculinity that is tough and desirable but has a difficult time combating the forces it encounters. Like the final girl from the 1970s horror film, the noir hero counts himself successful if he can manage just to survive. But Marco does not survive. In one of the last scenes of the film, Raphaëlle tries to convince Laporte not to take her son away from her. Marco enters the scene and attacks Laporte to defend Raphaëlle. Laporte and Marco struggle, and Raphaëlle raises her gun to shoot. In this cleverly framed scene, Raphaëlle remains inside her apartment, and Marco and Laporte fight in the hallway blocked from view. Raphaëlle shoots and someone falls, but the viewer does not know who— until Laporte appears in the doorway and it is clear that Raphaëlle shot Marco. This is one of the surprises at the end of the film. The viewer assumes she will shoot Laporte, who is currently behaving monstrously toward her, but instead she kills Marco. *Bastards* never reveals why she shoots Marco instead of Laporte, and it is possible that Raphaëlle simply defends the man who funds her existence. While Laporte's financial support may seem a reasonable motive, it lacks real force as an explanation. It is instead Laporte's impotence that she is complicit in covering over. She shoots Marco in order to hide the potential exposure of Laporte's impotence.

Through this scene and the rest of the film, Denis offers us a modern noir about our inability to face the impotence and violence of patriarchy. She suggests that it is the white upper class of Paris that is particularly caught up in hiding the patriarch's impotence. Denis has always been a filmmaker for whom race is an essential part of the story of identity in the modern world. In *Bastards*, she suggests that the result of the white upper-class Parisians' inability to acknowledge their own impotence will be a slow violent decline. The alternative possibility—acknowledging one's own impotence—does not reinstate potency, but it does create the potential for a radical shift. Denis does present examples of this possibility in her other films.

The two films immediately preceding *Bastards* are instructive. The film *35 Shots of Rum* (2009) investigates the shifting contours of a close-knit father and daughter who live in a close community in Paris. It depicts a family that is able to accept impotence and thus restructure itself around the father's impotence. The father is French African while the daughter, whose mother was German, is biracial. The mother died much earlier, and the father and daughter have been living out their lives without incident. The film follows as the contours of their relationship shift when the daughter decides to marry an upstairs neighbor. The film ends with her moving out of the father's apartment. On the one hand, the film celebrates the closeness of this father and daughter through quiet scenes of their life together. On the other hand, it details the existential questions that the father has about his career and about whom to love and trust outside of his own daughter. His existential crisis comes from the decision he must make whether to embrace his impotence or disavow it. He realizes that he can't assure his identity only through his job, and he can't make his daughter happy on his own. The film begins as he grapples with his impending retirement and his daughter's falling in love. A father's job and his relation to his daughter both have a relation to potency and its loss. In the end, the father embraces his impotence, but in doing so he allows for a restructuring. It may not be a world filled with economic possibility, but *35 Shots of Rum* is a world filled with the possibility for actual engagement that is formed through the acceptance of the impotence of symbolic power rather than the attempt to disavow it.

White Material (2010), on the other hand, presents a family that is unable to accept its impotence and thus hastens its own demise. The film depicts the end of the reign of white power in Africa and the inability of white farmers to let that reign go. Hence, it shows white Africans who refuse to see that the structures of racism and inequality make it impossible for them to keep going as they are. They don't understand that the very way that they run their farms and conceive of themselves participates in the symbolic functioning of racism. Nor do they realize that this is why they are being attacked and run out of the country. In other words, they believe in their own potency and are willing to lay down their lives to fight for this rather than acknowledge their impotence. *White Material* considers one woman's attempt to make a stand and stay. It thus documents her failure to grasp the impotence of whiteness as a Master Signifier. *Bastards* does share this theme, but it is more focused on the impotence of the patriarch and specifically on a patriarch whose illusion of potency has disappeared.

Surveillance as Fantasy

Bastards offers the final revelation about the patriarch's impotence with several bits of evidence that seem initially helpful but in fact only lead to more questions. At one point in the film, Marco and Sandra go to the barn in the country where Justine was brutalized. They inspect the area and find a round red bed in a room in the back of the old barn. The corners of the room are cloaked in shadow, and the stains on the red bed cover are the only evidence of the possible violence. Marco looks at the stains as the camera moves over the bed and inspects all the stains on the cover. These are stains of bodily fluids, and Marco and the viewer are left wondering what exactly happened and considering what the stains indicate. A yellow corncob lays bloodied on the floor.

All these stains, this forensic evidence, offer little in the form of an answer. This DNA cannot answer the question of what went wrong and what happened. It is evidence of some sort, for example, of enjoyment, of violence, of a crime, of love, or of some combination of these. In this way, the film reveals that biology does not provide the solution to the problem of subjectivity. The same evidence—bodily fluids and DNA—that would lead to concrete answers in other films does not help to solve the mystery in this film. Instead, this evidence only further emphasizes how in-the-dark Marco really is about his family in general and about Justine's fate specifically. At the end of the scene, Marco notices wires protruding from the ceiling and inquires about them. The man explains that clients hook video cameras to the ceiling for their own enjoyment later. This leaves Marco further puzzled but gives us one clue to help understand the ending of the film.

The unusual ending comes in the form of the video footage taken from this very camera position. The footage is of the scenario involving Justine that provoked her mental breakdown and Jacques's suicide. The footage is introduced when Sandra goes to visit the doctor who then hands her the found footage that the police have discovered. She asks him to watch it with her, because she fears she could not watch alone. As they step on an elevator bound for his office, the film cuts to the image of a camera lens. The camera lens signals that we are about to watch the footage, but it also signals a break in the narrative flow.

The footage begins with a shot from the ceiling, which indicates that it is taken from the video camera that was referred to earlier. The quality of the image is different from the rest of the film. It is a grainy image, signaling the low resolution of the video camera and thus approximating surveillance footage. This first shot includes Laporte on the left fully clothed leaning on his side watching Jacques, whose eyes are closed and who is laying on his back on top of a girl in the scene. She is naked and unbuttoning his shirt. Next to them lies Justine, who is naked and watching. This shot offers the first revelation that Jacques is actually present during this original scene of Justine's abuse. Throughout the film, Marco and the viewer assume that Laporte is fully to blame for Justine's bleeding body, but this initial shot of the footage reveals that her father was there as well. Jacques's direct look into the camera also suggests that he orchestrated this scene or at least is fully involved in it. Additionally, Justine is not being visibly held against her will.

The following shots in the scene, however, are not from the same position. The persistence of the grainy color-saturated image, however, indicates that the viewer is still supposed to interpret these images as the same surveillance footage. The rest of the shots are from various points in the room in a pattern that more approximates narrative film editing than the fixed position of a surveillance camera. This is, in fact, significant because it removes us from the codes of realism—the spatial continuity of the fixed surveillance camera—and instead adds an element of fantasy. In other words, if the viewer normally reads the ceiling-positioned footage as an authentic found document of a plot moment, then pulling away from this spatial position adds a visible touch of extra narrativization. It suggests that what is important about this footage is the fantasy at the heart of the scene rather than the facticity of the event.

The graininess of a surveillance camera is a product of low light and inexpensive equipment, but this describes surveillance cameras of the past. We identify cameras today with an extreme clarity. One can shoot in next to no light with a $50 webcam and have a completely focused, well-lit image with little to no graininess. Filmmakers today may use a grainy image as a way to signify surveillance footage (by essentially signifying a surveillance footage of the past), but *Bastards* here points out another way that this graininess signifies. It signifies not just surveillance but the fantasy that makes up the act of surveillance. That is to say, this layer of interference reveals how fantasy operates.

The fantasy dimension of the scene reveals the patriarch's violent response to his impotence. Additionally, it reveals his use of the video camera to also stand in for his lost potency. In doing this, Denis makes a larger commentary about the role of surveillance footage in the social order in general.[10] In the final scene of the film, the surveillance camera is introduced as a stand-in for the father's phallus. The father uses the video camera to approximate mastery. The surveillance camera is ideologically aligned with symbolic authority. Surveillance allows us to believe that there really is someone who knows, someone who sees everything. It assures us that we are being seen and thus provides a support for our ideological identity. Denis thus reveals that surveillance footage provides a false sense of mastery and replaces the image of the potent patriarch as a support for our symbolic sense of identity.[11]

Patriarchal Impotence

Bastards ends with this surveillance footage, and it provides the evidence for the structuring nature of patriarchal impotence. The final scene reveals that Jacques is literally impotent. In the midst of a sex scene, Denis highlights his flaccid penis. This scene also emphasizes the larger community's complicity in covering over this patriarchal impotence. The first shot of the surveillance footage surprises the viewer with the father's presence but also shows that there are two others in the scene: the other unidentified girl and Laporte. In this way, the film comments that this familial and sexual corruption exists in the social order. It is not just a private dirty secret; instead, it requires Laporte, the other girl, and the camera in order for this sexual abuse to occur.[12]

Joan Copjec argues that the status of public and private space is one of the key aspects of film noir. She theorizes that public spaces become private spaces in the classic noir world. About *Double Indemnity*, she says, "The intrusion of the private—the object *a*, the grain of the voice—into phenomenal reality, its *addition*, is registered in the *depletion* of this reality."[13] Denis puts her own spin on this by suggesting that there is no space in which the characters are free from the impotent father. That is to say, the impotent father makes public space nearly impossible. In this sense, *Bastards* extends Copjec's point by showing that the private infuses every public space under the rule of the impotent patriarch. The camera becomes complicit in disavowing his impotence.

This unexpected and abrupt ending is short and made up of only seven shots that depict various positions as Jacques undresses. As the camera moves closer to their bodies, Jacques and Justine look intently at each other. The last key moments from this succession of shots involve the most direct revelations. The first one of these is a medium close-up of Jacques from his knees to his waist. He is undressed and the shot is a full frontal shot that centers on his limp penis. The shot remains here as Jacques caresses himself and then takes his hand away to reveal that he is still limp. This shot clearly reveals Jacques's literal impotence. The shot punctuates the scene due to this revelation as much as to the unusual nature of full frontal male nudity in a feature-length film noir. The shot acts as a visual and physical confirmation of the crisis of masculinity at the heart of film noir.

Justine then stretches out her hand and beckons him to come to her. This solidifies the unexpected narrative point that Justine was not raped nor held against her will. Instead, she was complicit in the violence done to her. The last shot provides this final revelation as Jacques lies down on top of Justine and first brings up the corncob, which he is grasping by its husk. He puts it by Justine's head on the pillow, and she touches it briefly. He then takes it while kissing her and the camera sweeps down Justine's body as they kiss and begin to have sex. As the camera reaches her waist, it reveals that he is using the pointed corncob as a substitute for his impotence as he inserts it in her repeatedly and moves his body as if he is actually inserted inside her. During this violent substitution, Justine still kisses him lovingly. The camera then continues past them and lands in darkness. As the credits roll, the viewer is left with these revelations and nothing else. It may explain what happened, but it doesn't explain or reveal anything about the emotions of Justine or Jacques. It doesn't provide a resolution.

Throughout its running time, the film seems to suggest that Justine's abuse has been a rape and that Laporte probably committed it. But at the end in the videotape, Denis reveals that Justine was equally involved, and it was Jacques, her father, who was the cause of her severely maimed vagina. At the beginning of this sequence, the film makes sure to emphasize that Laporte was not involved in the actual act by showing Laporte leaning against the wall watching. *Bastards* never delves into Justine's emotions except on one occasion. In this one instance, Justine tells Marco in the hospital that she loves the man—whom she doesn't name. At that moment and throughout the rest of the film until the video footage, the viewer does not know to whom she is referring. At the end, however, it suggests she is referring to her father, though this is not necessarily confirmed.

The film begins with the father's suicide and ends with his violent incestuous sex scene, a scene in which he essentially tears his daughter's vagina to shreds with a corncob that acts as an index of his impotence. It is tempting to link his betrayal and abuse to his own suicide. The placement of the footage, however, prevents any certainty about this conclusion. Located at the end of the film without further contextualization, the footage depicts a traumatic scene but leaves its ramifications open. It is possible that the suicide is also or exclusively related to the failed shoe business. In the end, the viewer knows very little about this impotent father. The film reveals more, though not much, about Jacques's business partner Laporte. But Laporte is simply a go-between who allows the absent impotent father to run his course. Even in the last scene, Laporte just stands to the side and watches. The film thus presents Laporte and Jacques as two versions of the impotent patriarch. This leaves the complicity of Marco, Sandra, Raphaëlle, and Justine as an equally corrupting force that led to the violence.

Shocking, traumatic, and relatively quick—the ending of *Bastards* reveals the origin of the violence done to Justine, but it does not give the viewer any comprehensive contextualization. Jacques only appears at the very beginning and end of the film. In his absence, however, the rest of the characters continue to cover over his impotence. The end prompts the viewer to rethink the film in terms of Jacques's impotence and his role as father and patriarch. Considering the fractured form of the film itself, we can see Jacques as patriarch in terms of how he functions in that larger structure. In this context, the integrity of the structure of patriarchy appears to be decomposing in its attempt to hide its own impotence. The cruel nature of the noir environment suggests that there is no way to reinstate this structure as it once functioned.

The father's impotence results in violence, perversion, and a narrative structure that constantly keeps the viewer in the dark and suggests that there is no possible redemption. This is made poignantly clear through the ending in which impotence and its subsequent violence is brought fully to light. This traumatic unveiling coupled with a structure that consistently lacks clues for linear cause and effect turns the structure of patriarchy inside out. Through the film's narrative and visual form (especially the open wound of the ending), Denis makes it clear that this patriarchal structure is doomed.

About contemporary European films, Thomas Elsaesser argues, "Europe has also failed to consider the possibility of a postheroic narrative—whatever this might turn out to be—and instead it has turned obsessively towards the past, towards commemoration and collective nostalgia."[14] Elsaesser's portrait of Europe's clinging to a heroic narrative is another way of saying that Europe is holding on to an image of narrative as potency. Elsaesser's idea of a postheroic cinema, a cinema that counteracts this decay, is a cinema that acknowledges and embraces its own impotence. Elsaesser sees Claire Denis's *Beau Travail* (1999) as an example of the postheroic and thus one exception to the European heroic narrative. He argues that it attempts to create a new kind of community—one that is not structured around the idea of the hero (or around the figure of potency). *Bastards* continues Denis's work as a director of the postheroic narrative as it presents a family's inability to accept its impotence. The film is not nostalgic but shows that the only hope we have is to accept the Master Signifier's impotence and do our part in bringing it to light.

Notes

1. Slavoj Žižek, *The Fragile Absolute, or, Why Is the Christian Legacy Worth Fighting For?* (New York: Verso, 2000), 115.

2. Jean-Joseph Goux, *Symbolic Economies: After Marx and Freud*, trans. Jennifer Curtiss Gage (Ithaca: Cornell University Press, 1990), 18.

3. Money has a destructive effect on the Name of the Father because money, though it itself functions as an exception (as the universal equivalent), eliminates all other exceptionality. This is what Georg Simmel makes clear in *The Philosophy of Money*. He says, "Money is not only the absolutely interchangeable object, each quantity of which can be replaced without distinction by any other; it is, so to speak, interchangeability personified." Georg Simmel, *The Philosophy of Money*, 2nd ed., trans. Tom Bottomore and David Frisby (New York: Routledge, 1990), 124.

4. Television, on the other hand, doesn't always have to deal with an ending. Obviously the seriality that continues over years allows for a postponement of an ending, even if it must stage small sub-endings to episodes or seasons. Series are often canceled, and thus the producers do not have to wrestle with how to end the series. When a series does end on its own accord, fans and the creators are very aware of the importance of the ending, which often causes a good deal of controversy. Series such as *The Sopranos* (1999–2007), *Buffy the Vampire Slayer* (1997–2003), and *Battlestar Galactica* (2004–2009) caused much commentary since fans realized that an ending would retroactively provide a larger commentary on the series itself that may or may not coincide with the ideas or investment of the fans. That is to say, an ending would enact new meaning that was literally final in its presentation. For *The Sopranos*, which ended somewhat ambiguously, it caused a flurry of theories about what the ending meant. For *Battlestar Galactica*, the ending was considered more

ideological than the series itself, which detracted from its overall success. *Buffy*'s ending, however, crystalized all its themes in an unexpected way and thus made the series even more successful than it otherwise would have been.

5. Nick Roddick, "Dark Matters," *Sight and Sound* 24.3 (2014): 48.

6. Judith Mayne, *Claire Denis* (Chicago: University of Illinois Press, 2005), 128.

7. This scene is somewhat similar to the scene in *Blue Velvet* (David Lynch, 1986), in which Dorothy Valence (Isabella Rossellini), who has been pushed to the limits by gangster Frank (Dennis Hopper), appears on the lawn of a suburban house naked. The female bruised and broken naked body suggests the violence that the criminal's appetite for enjoyment has wrought. For an analysis of this scene, see Todd McGowan, *The Real Gaze: Film Theory after Lacan* (Albany: State University of New York Press, 2007).

8. José Teodoro, "No Sanctuary: Claire Denis on *Bastards*," Cinema Scope Online, interviews, http://cinema-scope.com/cinema-scope-online/sanctuary-claire-denis-bastards/ (accessed May 21, 2014).

9. Denis's films all seem to have the narrative ambiguity of film noir, but *Bastards* is more bleak and gap-ridden than most of her films. In *Vendredi Soir* (Friday Night, 2002), for example, the film begins with the main character in a traffic jam and concentrates on a random affair she has with a stranger. But the world is more anchored in the prolonged experience of touch, in her explored anxiety about the encounter, and in the final emotional triumph that occurs at the end of the film. Yet *Bastards* leaves the context of its events a mystery, providing the viewer with about as little knowledge as Marco himself has about what is going on.

10. Unlike other films in which surveillance footage provides the final revelation at the end of the film, Denis does not hint at its importance throughout the rest of the film. This contrasts *Bastards* with Tony Scott's *Enemy of the State* (1998) and Wim Wenders's *End of Violence* (1997). The lack of this attention throughout *Bastards* signals that the importance of the surveillance is confined to the specific scene in which it occurs, which is the scene that reveals the impotence of Jacques. This encourages us to connect the surveillance to the impotence.

11. Normally, surveillance footage is supposed to provide a more comprehensive map of the structure of society. In some ways, the footage in *Bastards* does this, but it reveals the decay of the structure itself rather than fleshing it out as a whole.

12. This scene is clearly in conversation with Stanley Kubrick *Eyes Wide Shut* (1999) on the one hand and Todd Philips's *Hangover* (2009) on the other. These disparate films depict other recent representations of group debauchery that is a mystery throughout the film, which is then revealed by the end. *Eyes Wide Shut*'s presentation of the orgy for the very rich seems similar to the final scene of *Bastards* in its cold and perfunctory approach to sex, which also has elements of abuse and complicity in it. *Hangover*, on the other hand, ends with a montage of photos that reveal the actual orgiastic spree that the characters had, which landed them in the bizarre situation they find themselves in the next morning. It depicts, unlike *Bastards* or *Eyes Wide Shut*, actual enjoyment.

13. Joan Copjec, "The Phenomenal Nonphenomenal: Private Space in Film Noir," in *Shades of Noir*, ed. Joan Copjec (New York: Verso, 1993), 191.

14. Thomas Elsaesser, "European Cinema and the Postheroic Narrative: Jean-Luc Nancy, Claire Denis, and Beau Travail," *New Literary History* 43.4 (2012): 708.

3

The Greatest Trick the Devil Ever Played

Desire, Drive, and the Twist Ending

RYAN ENGLEY

Introduction

Film offers few experiences more exhilarating than the twist ending. Viewers can spend hours enthralled by a particular story world, its characters, its various conflicts, only to have a (narrative) rug pulled out from under them (rhetorically). So powerful is this narrative rupture that it radically recalibrates the viewer's conception of preceding narrative events. It gives us the chance to reexamine our contingent narrative experience while still ensconced in the filmic moment. In other words, film audiences love a good twist.

In recent American cinema there is perhaps no film that offers a more thoroughly surprising denouement than Bryan Singer's *The Usual Suspects* (1995). Viewers find themselves invested in the far-reaching consequences of a failed robbery and the mythos surrounding a criminal warlord named Keyser Soze. After learning that a seemingly impotent character, Verbal Kint (Kevin Spacey), has invented an impossibly detailed narrative—the very narrative viewers have been enjoying—to fool (and toy with) US Customs agent Dave Kujan (Chazz Palminteri), the viewer's conception of the entire film is dramatically redrawn. While Agent Kujan is traumatized to discover how close he was to Keyser Soze, a felon orders of magnitude more dangerous than the thief (Dean Keaton) who obsesses him, the audience is energized, as the twist ending redoubles the filmic experience.

This kind of narrative accomplishment is not to be taken lightly, though it so often is. Viewers and critics alike spend so much time discussing how surprising a twist *as such* was, or how adept the script was at shielding the possibility of the retroactively apparent twist, or "it's amazing how Anna always knows the twist before it happens," that we somehow miss an obvious but truly critically overlooked fact: the twist ending has a radical narrative potential unique to film. This is something we can glimpse clearly when we look at the presence of the drive in narrative, both in television—film's parallax medium—and in what I call the "drive twist," which I will explain in the course of the essay.

Drive twist films like Christopher Nolan's 2010 film *Inception* (a drive twist film par excellence) actually bridge the narrative gap between cinema and contemporary television. Television narrativizes failure constantly to create dramatic tension, which makes composing a truly satisfying series finale not just a psychoanalytic impossibility but a structural one as well. But it is this imposition represented by the end that produces a kind of failure worth investing in for viewers. Television, despite mounting an increasingly potent challenge to cinema's formerly undisputed status as "spirit" of the world, has remained largely unremarked upon by the psychoanalytic community.[1]

As a narrative medium, television is certainly worthy of critical attention. In fact, it offers a vehicle for better understanding how film endings function, as television is manifestly incapable of adequately performing the twist ending narrative feat. Viewed psychoanalytically, we can move to see that the twist film ending—the moment of narrative's obscene excess—masks the disappointment of desire—the inability to obtain the truly satisfying object—that the viewer experiences at a narrative's end. Subsequently, the disappointment of desire felt by television viewers is far more extreme, the underside of the twist ending far more evident. The viewer of *The Usual Suspects* is elated when experiencing the film's ending for the first time; the viewer of *St. Elsewhere* or *The Sopranos* is disgusted at the appearance of a dirty narrative trick. This failure intrinsic to television narrative reveals something significant for psychoanalytic inquiry: film is the medium of desire, television the medium of drive. Through a thorough exploration of the vicissitudes of the twist ending, we can see its inherent radical potential, how it is so frequently muted, and how TV better delivers on the narrative promise of the drive.

When a Twist Is Definitely Not a Twist

The history of the plot twist is almost as old as narrative itself (as any ninth grader will tell you, Oedipus was . . . pretty surprised). Twists in Hollywood are, likewise, almost as old as narrative cinema. Famously, film noir made consistent and effective use of the twist; it is, apart from the gritty aesthetic and the femme fatale, the genre's distinct feature. As John Huston's *The Maltese Falcon* (1941) or Roman Polanski's neo-noir film *Chinatown* (1974) show, the twist is as much a singular and shocking moment as it is an instance of radical dialectical restructuring.

Audiences, both distant and contemporary, have always seemed to respond to these narrative irruptions. For certain films, like *The Usual Suspects*, viewers and critics can have no problem observing that the twist— learning Verbal Kint's true identity—has the effect of completely reshaping their filmic experience. Determining the precise nature of a twist film, however, is not a totally obvious procedure. Recent films like *The Mist* (Frank Darabont, 2007), *Buried* (Rodrigo Cortés, 2010), or *The Grey* (Joe Carnahan, 2011) frequently appear on the Internet's "Top Twist Endings Lists."[2] Their inclusion in such lists suggests, at the very least, that movie watchers regard these films as twist narratives. These people, who are probably quite lovely and very likely recycle, are dead wrong.

Let's take *The Mist*, for example. In this adaptation of the Stephen King novella, David Drayton (Thomas Jane), his eight-year-old son, and neighbor (Andre Braugher) are trapped in a grocery store with several strangers. Outside is an impenetrable mist accidentally loosed on mankind by scientific attempts to open up a window to alien dimensions. What comes out, besides the mist itself, is an array of horrifying creatures that prey on the imprisoned people in the grocery store. David and four others—his son included—eventually manage to escape, but they discover that the outside world is just as unsafe and terrifying as the store was. They find a gun with four bullets in it and decide it's better to die with a bullet to the brain than to be massacred by inexplicable creatures. David takes the burden of mercy killing his group, including his sleeping son. He walks into the open and begs the monsters in the mist to take his life . . . only no monsters emerge. Instead, several US military trucks appear. To David's shock and absolute horror, soldiers and a group of survivors were just yards away from him and his group. Help was just around the corner. He falls to his knees and screams.

The emotional quality of such an ending notwithstanding, this is not a twist. It's a punch to the stomach. Learning that David and his group were so close to being saved but continually moved *away* from potential help throughout the film in no way restructures the preceding narrative events. It just makes them frustrating. The film plays a perverse trick on the viewers. Rather than providing a moment of radical narrative revolution, as Bryan Singer does in *The Usual Suspects*, Frank Darabont offers a deeply cynical conclusion: that one should never do the supremely difficult thing to change your situation; one should always hold the hope that safety is just around the corner. The ending to *The Mist* takes advantage of viewers' sympathies; it alters nothing on the narrative level other than to make one feel retroactive despair.[3]

In *Buried*, like *The. Mist*, we have a similar encounter with irony and narrative perversity. These films aim, almost, to masquerade the story of Job as a twist narrative. Paul Conroy (Ryan Reynolds) is an American civilian truck driver in Iraq who awakes one day to find that he has been buried alive. Paul has only a Zippo lighter and a Blackberry to engineer some kind of escape before he runs out of oxygen, starves to death, or suffocates (from sand breaking through the cracks in his wooden coffin). He receives a call from his kidnapper, who demands ransom money from the US government. Paul calls the state department and tries to get them to pay his kidnapper a five-million-dollar ransom. They refuse but offer to help find him, claiming that a similar kidnapping happened a few weeks ago and Mark White, another kidnapped soldier, was found and rescued. Throughout the course of the film, we learn that due to an affair with a colleague, Paul's family will not receive any death benefits should he perish. If Paul dies there is very little good—financial or otherwise—that could come of it. Paul receives a call from Dan Brenner of the Hostage Working Group who tells him that they have found the signal from Paul's cell phone and are about to rescue him. Paul calls his wife who is understandably jubilant at the news of his impending rescue . . . only Paul can't hear any digging near his coffin. As it turns out, Brenner and the Hostage Working Group instead found the grave of Mark White, the man Brenner lied about saving in an earlier conversation with Paul. Sand fills his coffin and Paul suffocates, with Brenner offering his worthless apologies over the phone—mimicking, as it were, God's own impotent explanation for why Job had to endure unimaginable hardship. Job, of course, was desperate to experience a "twist" that would validate his suffering and shift his dialectical position. *Buried*, like *The Mist*, confronts the viewer relentlessly with pathetic irony. *The Twilight Zone* TV series offers several instances that help make the twist/irony dichotomy clear. When in the episode entitled "Time Enough at Last" Burgess Meredith's glasses break after finally having "time to read," we are served a massive dollop of irony (as in Darabont's *The Mist*). When, in another episode, aliens come to Earth and vow to serve mankind by curing all diseases, stopping all war, famine, and suffering, the *Twilight Zone* viewer feels there must be some catch. At the end of "To Serve Man," we learn that the aliens intended to harvest humans for food the entire time—to literally *serve man*. This revelation causes us to reflect on the narrative as a whole, to reread and reinterpret everything we have just seen. At the end of "Time Enough at Last" we are struck with the mighty fist of irony and are left simply to ponder and process the cruelty of the ending. Certainly, a twist ending *can* itself be ironic—that Bruce Willis plays a character who is actually a ghost therapist helping a boy deal with seeing ghosts in *The Sixth Sense* is certainly ironic—but that cannot be its determining feature for the narrative *as such*. A twist film creates a dialectical shift in the spectator. Such is the force of the twist that the viewer's whole way of seeing the film undergoes a total revolution. The twist mechanism in narrative has an inherent radical force, as we will see.

The subjective enjoyment or objective narrative merit of pathetic irony in narrative, however, is not the issue here. *The Mist*, *Buried*, and "Time Enough at Last" simply do not exhibit the same kind of narrative qualities that twist endings do. I'm hesitant to refer to those that do as "real" or "true" twist endings, as the others simply *aren't* twist films in the first place (and therefore must be left to a discussion of the efficacy and vicissitudes of irony in cinema and television). These "not twist" endings do nothing to radically reshape or recolor preceding narrative events; rather they imbue the viewer with a heavy sense of dramatic (Sophoclean) irony. Watching *The Mist* or "Time Enough at Last" for the second time—with our knowledge of the end or the supposed "twist"—does little to enlarge the narrative. We just feel an acute sense of impending dread; waiting for the drop of the other shoe. Simply put, films like *The Mist* and famous "not twists" like that in *The Twilight Zone* muddy the twist discussion and must be expunged so that a clear theoretical framework can be established. Just like the clear emphasis in Lacan's own "return to Freud," we must return to the drive and push its narrative possibilities.

Masking the Disappointment of Desire

As is well known, Freud first conceives of the death drive in *Beyond the Pleasure Principle*, defining it as "an urge in organic life to restore an earlier state of things," or an "original state of loss."[4] Developing the death drive required Freud to alter radically his notion of psychoanalysis's core tenets to the point where, as Joan Copjec writes, "[w]e are obliged to note that the theory of the drive substitutes for an ontology in Freud."[5] It is no surprise that rectifying Freud's theory of the death drive was central to Lacan's project.

The precise function of the drive is counterintuitive and disturbing, which has led (in my mind) to a good deal of its popular misunderstanding and quick dismissal. There's also a translation issue: Freud's *Trieb* (drive) has,

historically, been translated into English as "instinct." When Freud writes
in reference to innate animal behaviors, he uses the term *Instinkt* rather
than *Trieb*. Equivocating "instinct" to cover both ideas is more than simple
imprecision, it misses the real point of Freud's concept altogether. As Richard
Boothby puts it in *Freud as Philosopher: Metapsychology after Lacan*, what
separates the Freudian *Trieb* from animal behavior is "its complete detachment from biological need and from any naturally designated object of
satisfaction."[6]

This radical element of psychoanalysis is precisely what evolutionary
psychologists, for example, find so offensive and easily dismissible about it.
Something is either reducible to a current biological function, to a vestigial remainder from an earlier time, to an evolutionary need, or it doesn't
exist.[7] To pick a somewhat recent example of the insufficiency of such an
approach, there can be no pure rational or scientific explanation for why
Mitt Romney—with the Occupy Wall Street "99% slogan" still ringing in
voters' ears (the only lasting effect of the movement)—would submarine his
presidential hopes by saying:

> There are 47 percent of the people who will vote for the presi-
> dent no matter what . . . who are dependent upon government,
> who believe that they are victims, who believe the government
> has a responsibility to care for them, who believe that they are
> entitled to health care, to food, to housing, to you-name-it. That's
> an entitlement.[8]

Drawing arbitrary classist lines across America at an event *for* the 1 percent
catered *by* the 99 percent confirmed for the national public that, yes, this
stark bourgeoisie-proletariat divide *does exist*. What's more, Romney made
himself the momentary figurehead of everything the fledgling Occupy movement was fighting against. The most rational explanation we can offer for
why Romney would even risk getting caught saying something that every one
of the millionaire donors in the room *believed anyway* is, simply, "he didn't
think he'd be taped." But even afterward, Romney acknowledged that, as a
public figure, he needs to expect that everything he does is being recorded
somewhere by someone; that this is now part of the age we live in. The drive,
as we can see in the Romney example, has no biological function, fulfills
no deterministic need, and has no evolutionary value. It is, as Lacan says in
Seminar XI, a constant force.[9] "Where is 'the drive organ,' then?" someone
might ask incredulously. It's a psychic organ, apprehensible in the effects of
this constant force, in the concrete instances of self-undermining affecting

people every day. It is something in us "more than us," in many ways, and it must be reckoned with (as Mitt Romney had to do).

Drive and desire are partners traveling an ever-perpetuating circuit due to the repeated failure *to close the circuit*. Desire is constantly tripped up by the impossibility of obtaining the truly satisfying object, the acquisition of which would complete the circuit of desire (i.e., we would never desire again). When we obtain the thing we desire—an iPhone, a car, a Tudor mansion, whatever—we do not discover satisfaction; rather we have instead created a path to discover *another object to desire*. This is, as Todd McGowan puts it, "the precise way the drive satisfies itself. Through the drive, the subject finds satisfaction in the repetition of the failure and loss that initially constitutes it."[10] In lived experience, the drive is really the unwanted passenger of desire, its obscene underside, delighting in our failures, extracting satisfaction from disappointment, "completing" this constant circuit *through the very failure to close it*.

The construction of the theatergoer's subjectivity could be read as negotiating this interplay between desire and drive. As Slavoj Žižek writes, "Desire is the metonymic sliding propelled by a lack, striving to capture the elusive lure: it is always, by definition, unsatisfied," meaning—and there are no two ways about this—we are *always* disappointed and unsatisfied by a film ending on some level.[11] A great ending makes us want to immediately rewatch a film—we're disappointed that it's over; an "okay" ending makes us wish the film had done something differently, its flaws aggravatingly apparent; a bad ending nearly invalidates the contingent film-watching experience—we wish that we never saw the film with the bad ending in the first place (or we wish we had simply watched *Casablanca* again). A good or great film can *never* be "totally satisfying." This is why we watch it again; to reengage in the fantasmatic "chase for the object." A twist ending, however, changes things.

With a twist ending, we, as viewers, can *feel as though* we have actually grasped some impossible truly satisfying object. While watching *The Usual Suspects* for the first time, the viewer gets caught up in a story about a ragtag group of petty delinquents who all, at one time, managed to offend the vilest criminal on Earth. This makes us one *kind* of viewer, a Crime Film Viewer, let's say. When we experience the twist we become something else; the fiction of having *simply been* a Crime Film Viewer is exploded. We realize that *our* inability to recognize Verbal Kint as Keyser Soze matches perfectly that of Agent Kujan's. Just as Agent Kujan moves from Customs Agent in Total Control of the Facts to a Completely Duped and Symbolically Castrated Customs Agent (as Lacan put it, "the non-duped err"), so too does the viewer of *The Usual Suspects* experience two different kinds of viewer subjectivity. As Žižek writes, the subject itself, the subject of the signifier is "always-already past," although it never appeared "in the past itself": it is constituted by means of a double reflection, "as the result of the way the past's mirroring in the future is mirrored back in the present."[12] The twist ending, through the "double reflection" caused by the narrative, produces a new viewing subject of the film, a moment of "victory" for desire over drive.

Has there *really* been a "victory" of desire over drive, though? The answer is no, for the viewer has *actually* had a sublimated experience with the gilded Thing. As Boothby writes, "If Lacan defines sublimation as "raising an object to the dignity of *das Ding*," that definition is inseparable from the creation of a sense of distance between the object and the Thing."[13] In the case of the twist ending, experiencing the cut of narrative rupture causes the plain object—the ending of *The Usual Suspects*—to be misinterpreted and mistaken for *das Ding*—the truly satisfying object. Turning the object into the Thing means our desire necessarily misses it. Now that *a* thing is *the Thing* we fail to actually encounter it (except in its altered coordinates to our enjoyment).

Instead, we encounter a supplementary fiction: "The Truly Satisfying Twist to *The Usual Suspects* as Experienced by Ryan," we might say (verbosely). Sublimation, for Lacan, mediates between drive and desire; as Fabio Vighi writes, "it begins to 'transfer' the raw negativity of drive into an empirical object that works as a stand-in for that deflagrating negativity."[14] This is, in a different way, the drive being satisfied by the disappointment of desire because we have *again* missed the object (with anything resembling a "successful" transfer never fully occurring). Through the twist ending, this intrinsic relationship between the drive and the Thing is brought to bear. As the "twist object" masks the disappointment of desire, the twist *itself* is raised to the dignity of the Thing, elevating the film in question from plain object to "something else"—the (seemingly) truly satisfying object. If any film could be *truly* completely satisfying, we would never watch another film again. No serious film lover actually "wishes" this on herself or himself.

The Twist as *Point de Capiton*, as Sublimation

Since the truly satisfying object does not exist, its "presence" is called into being through the relief of its absence and, as Lacan says in *Seminar VII*, "All art is characterized by a certain mode of organization around this emptiness," the Lacanian *objet a*.[15] The twist film is here a perfect analogue, as the narrative is organized entirely around the void that is the twist itself. Part of what makes the twist film unique is its ability to be contingently coherent and enjoyable, despite being formed around a void or narrative elision that we can only grasp in reverse. The twist as such fills in a knowledge gap that the film narrative necessarily moves *around* or misses—the narrative *itself* mimicking the movement of desire—it acts as a structural stabilizer, something that grounds the film's narrative to a fixed point. In Lacanian terms, we are talking about *le point de capiton*, or "the quilting point."

Fortunately, for any discussion of psychoanalysis and narrative, in the *Sublime Object of Ideology*, Slavoj Žižek raised Lacan's *point de capiton* from *hapax* to eminently employable term. Lacan configures *le point de capiton* as the meaning-making signifier in a chain of signifiers, a point that lends cohesion to a contingently unstable group of words, phrases, events; just as an upholstery button (the literal "quilting point") keeps the batting inside a piece of furniture—halting any potential "slippage"—providing a sense of design symmetry, as well. The twist ending represents the most exciting kind of "quilting point" in cinema. Even if a twist is not the final image or line of a film, it has the effect of radically reshaping the whole of the narrative due to the effect of the *point de capiton*. As Žižek writes, for Lacan, "Whenever we have a symbolic structure it is structured around a certain void, it implies the foreclosure of a certain key-signifier."[16] He elaborates later, "the multitude of 'floating signifiers' . . . is structured into a unified field through the intervention of a certain 'nodal point' (the Lacanian *point de capiton*) which 'quilts them,' stops their sliding and fixes their meaning."[17] There might not be a better exemplar of this phenomenon than the twist ending acting as the "nodal point" that stops the slippage of signifiers.

But perhaps we can nail down the *point de capiton* even further, to a smaller unit of narrative meaning. When movie lovers talk about great twists in classical and contemporary cinema, certain films inevitably come up: Orson Welles's *Citizen Kane* (1941), *Planet of the Apes* (Tim Burton, 2001), Hitchcock's *Psycho* (1960), Roman Polanski's *Chinatown* (1974), *Star Wars Episode V—The Empire Strikes Back* (Irvin Kershner, 1980), *The Crying Game* (Neil Jordan, 1992), David Fincher's *Fight Club* (1999) and *Seven* (1995), *The Sixth Sense*, *The Usual Suspects*, Christopher Nolan's *Memento* (2000), and the list goes on. Significantly, these films all have universally understandable referents—"Rosebud," "You blew it up," "Forget it, Jake," "I see dead people," "What's in the box?"—and the recitation of these lines has become a culturally acceptable way of identifying the film, a way of halting the metonymic process. It is perhaps not the twist itself—that Bruce Willis is a ghost who cannot move on to the afterlife in *The Sixth Sense*—that acts as the quilting point; it is, retroactively, the words (after fully realizing the twist), "I see dead people." That line *as such* stops the metonymic sliding of signifiers in *The Sixth Sense* and fixes meaning to a particular point.

The signifying structure of a twist film is defined by a central void (the twist is its "missing link") around which the whole of the film narrative is organized—it is precisely the articulation of the void (the twist) that gives shape to the film as such.[18] It is certainly proof of the efficacy of Hegelian retroactivity—the axiom that holds meaning can only be constructed retroactively—that the contingent experience of a film like *The Sixth Sense* or *The Usual Suspects* can "make sense" when we are blissfully unaware of the void (that is, the twist) that is actively ordering the narrative. The lesson of the twist film ending might be reinforcement, then, of Hegel's and Lacan's parallel theories that meaning *in life generally* cannot be constructed directly; it is only ever graspable retroactively through the lens of some rupture or *point de capiton*.[19] More than serving as further proof of two well-known ideas, we are compelled to appreciate here the real radicality of twist films: they call attention to our everyday "missing links," absences, and voids, the things that structure our symbolic reality.

Twist films cause a dialectical revolution in the spectator. The employment of such a narrative ethic speaks to the radicality of twist films. Before viewers know the full import of a film, they cannot completely reckon with the meaning of lines like "Darth Vader betrayed and murdered your father," or "The greatest trick the Devil ever pulled was convincing the world he didn't exist." Encountering the void that the narrative was structured around—Obi-Wan's lie to Luke, Verbal's totally fictive character—completely reshuffles a film's meaning.

There is also, rather significantly, conservatism present in the twist film, an apparent unwillingness to "accept" the twist film's radical portents. It is radical, as we have said, in that the film *practically announces* that it is oriented around a void, that a meaningful and coherent narrative can be constructed around a void that threatens its very stability. But, rather than seeing a twist and realizing "there is no big Other," the film viewer receives unconscious reinforcement that "there *is* a big Other!" It is conservative because the twist itself actually subverts the radical lesson we can take from a narrative being spun around a void—it masks the disappointment of desire and blocks the full realization of the drive. The twist acts, then, as film narrative's version of a guarantee that *there is a grand order to the world, only you cannot glimpse it until the end.*

Television here is far more radical in its failure to deliver successful series finale twists. The divisive endings to *St. Elsewhere* ("The whole series was imagined by a child with autism? What the . . ."), *The Sopranos*

("The whole series comes down to me thinking my cable went out and not knowing what the point of that was? What the . . ."), and *Lost* ("Half of the last season had the characters in purgatory? But wasn't the island a metaphorical purgatory anyway? What the . . .") show, if nothing else, that the creator is impotent, incapable of performing one final narrative trick, the trick to convince the viewer that this (the series) has all been an elaborate and meticulously planned journey. (In reality, few series creators begin their series with anything more than a vague sense of where the narrative will end—not "where it might go" but where it will definitively, finally, end.)[20] This stands in stark opposition to the feeling viewers get when watching *The Sixth Sense*; essentially, we find reinforcement for the idea that we are all being strung along by a master puppeteer.

The desire for order and meaning is intrinsic to people (perhaps this is one of the basic appeals of narrative), and it is one of psychoanalysis's greatest insights that our symbolic experience is structurally incomplete, without center, that there is no big Other. To paraphrase Joan Copjec, the impossibility of completing meaning *is what completes meaning*. The radicality of the twist ending is dulled, as we've seen, by sublimation. In other words, the transgressive notion that narrative and meaning generally are formed around a central void—in the way a film like *Memento* is shaped around the shared ignorance of the viewer and the protagonist, or *The Usual Suspects* is formed around Verbal Kint's true identity—is shrouded by the rupture and momentary fulfillment viewers feel when experiencing a twist.

Many people approach life this way: for the religious person, a faintly apprehensible and often inscrutable god shapes our destiny; for the science-minded person, it is the fascinating and no less mysterious movement of biological determinism that structures the world; for the atheist, it is, perhaps, the void itself. But members of all three groups fall victim to the same fallacy the twist film viewer is prey to: simply that we *will* experience the twist (see god, uncover every missing link, contact the void itself). The belief in the twist, in experiencing a life-validating *point de capiton*, prevents us from seeing that there is no big Other, no external guarantor.[21]

This is where the drive comes in. It is no surprise that there have been recent psychoanalytic projects concerning the political and transgressive force of the drive.[22] The ethical dimension of another kind of "twist," what I call a "drive twist," offers people the opportunity to reflect on how the drive—the failure to obtain the object, the enjoyment in missing the object—is perhaps the essential ordering principle of experience. Through proper narrativization of the drive, there is a class of films that actually deliver on the twist film's radical potential.

Inception and Subverting Closure

Christopher Nolan's *Inception* has, as a sort of twist, a complete lack of one. It ends, much like a psychoanalytic session, *just* before the analysand is about to come to some great understanding or revelation. We must get off the couch (or leave the theater) and probe the edges of some momentary truth on our own time.

After garnering critical acclaim and commercial success with twist films like *Memento* and *The Prestige*, Nolan knows what viewers expect of him: they reach the end of *Inception* and assume they will encounter a thoroughly original narrative rupture that changes retroactively the preceding narrative events.[23] In short, they expect a twist. Nolan gives viewers the narrative rupture they were anticipating but not in the way they were expecting. As the camera moves away from Cobb's (Leonardo DiCaprio) long-awaited reunion with his family, we see that he has spun a stark silver top on an end table. The top is Cobb's totem, an individual-specific item that, according to the rules of the film, is needed so that the "dream thieves" can tell whether they are awake or if they have been placed (or trapped) in someone else's dream. In reality, tops eventually spin out of control and become inert. In a dream, the top never stops spinning. Famously, the credit sequence begins *just* as the top has seemed to regain a sense of "balance" *just* after it looked like the top had begun to spin out of control. Viewers are uncertain whether the top has fallen or not, confirmation of which would indicate if the "happy ending" the film presented us with was real or fiction (a dream, either Cobb's or someone else's). The frustration felt by viewers at the end of *Inception* is something we might usefully term a "drive twist," a rupture of a different kind from traditional film twists.

This is distinct from another kind of ending often mistaken (socially) for a twist, what I'll call a "limited open ending." At the end of *The Grey*, John Ottway (Liam Neeson)—who has spent much of the film battling a vicious pack of wolves—is either dead, or alive. The film ends with Ottway arming himself with a knife and glass shards in a last-gasp attempt to kill the alpha wolf that has been tracking him for much of the. film. The battle is surely about to commence . . . and then come the credits. After the credits, both Ottway and the alpha wolf are shown breathing heavily, exhausted from their duel. There is no clear winner.

One may be tempted here to draw a parallel to a film like *Inception*, but such a conclusion is proffered too hastily. As we have said, Christopher Nolan's *Inception* ends in such a way that the audience is unsure if Cobb, finally reunited with his kids, is in a dream or not. But the film ending is more complex than the narratively simple either/or proposition that ends a film like *The Grey* or *Lock, Stock, and Two Smoking Barrels* (Guy Ritchie, 1998). Cobb's totem, a spinning top, only tells him whether he is in *someone else's dream*. Furthermore, it's not even *his totem*, it was his wife's. Also, as some viewers have posited, it is possible that Cobb is actually the true subject of "inception" in the film—needing to finally let go of the traumatic circumstances surrounding his wife's death. In any case, there are far more than two possible outcomes, making *Inception*'s conclusion not just an "open ending" but something more.

Many film critics offered that the brilliance of *Inception* lies in its manipulation of the heist film genre. However, as Todd McGowan points out in *The Fictional Christopher Nolan*, after the opening sequence the film is concerned not with the theft of ideas (extraction) but with their implantation (inception). More important than the cosmetic difference between *Inception* and other heist films, McGowan notes the drive's crucial function to *Inception*'s very plotting: "The film depicts the successful heist coinciding with the fantasmatic realization of desire . . . the spectators and the perpetrators enjoy the immediate aftermath of the successful heist, where the seemingly impossible object of desire has been attained."[24] There are, however, another set of heist films that completely frustrate the realization of desire present in a film like Steven Soderbergh's *Ocean's Eleven* (2001). McGowan identifies films like Jules Dassin's *Rififi* (1955), Kubrick's *The Killing* (1956), and Michael Mann's *Heat* (1995) as films that engage the drive at the narrative level ("enjoying the heist itself rather than its successful completion"), exploding the fantasy of desire's realization that lends symbolic support to the heist genre. The heist must be enjoyed *as* and *for* the heist itself, not for the end reward. We start to grasp the radicality of *Inception* when we view it in juxtaposition to typical twist films. However, the *material* effect of the drive is apparent in more than just the narrative, it is in the almost empirically documentable way viewers enjoyed the film *after* seeing it.

There is no clear twist to *Inception*. No narrative rupture that momentarily appeals to our desire through the process of sublimation (as we have outlined). Instead the film solicits our appreciation of failure, disappointment, and, ultimately, drive. This, I think, is the essential point: *Inception* concludes with a "drive twist." As opposed to something like *The Usual Suspects*, *Inception* doesn't end with a twist that masks the disappointment of desire by offering a way for the viewer to essentially redouble their filmic experience (i.e., to reconsider the whole of the film narrative in light of the twist/*point de capiton*). It ends with a teasing moment that would seem to inhere in a twist but then, just at it seems like we might apprehend the film's "absolute knowledge," the credits roll. Alenka Zupančič, in explaining how Don Juan is a figure of the drive, capitalizes on exactly this kind of narrative ethic:

> for Don Juan each and every woman is the right one, and what drives him further is not what he did not find in his previous lover, but precisely what he did find. He attains satisfaction without attaining his aim or—more exactly, he attains satisfaction precisely in so far as his aim is nothing but "getting back into circulation."[25]

Rather than halting viewer investment with a typical twist that appeals to desire, Nolan—by engaging the drive at the narrative level—keeps this investment "in circulation." There is no illusion of satisfaction with *Inception* and that is to the film's benefit.

Arguably, there hasn't been a film since *Inception* that has created such concrete artifacts of excessive enjoyment. Many people were inspired to write about its various possible readings. I was inspired to see it four times in the theater (atypical behavior for me) as were others, to say nothing of the debate and obsessive discussion the film engendered.[26] We can actually *quantify* this kind of investment almost empirically: on the Internet Movie Database, *Inception* has 988,968 ratings, *The Usual Suspects*—possibly the best twist film in recent times—has 545, 246, while *Citizen Kane*—a superior film in pretty much every conceivable way—has only 235, 337 ratings (and that's even with the difficult to dismiss reality that some people likely log on to give *Citizen Kane* a bad rating because "I didn't think this was the greatest film of all time, I give it a 1 out of 10").[27] It is unquestionably the open or drive ending to *Inception* that has engendered this kind of excessive interest, the kind of interest that is pushing television to an exalted status. By denying the closure typical of heist films—and the twist typical of Nolan films—we can see how the drive is narrativized and then further articulated by viewers in the aftermath of experiencing it at the narrative level. It better resembles the recent *Lost* or *True Detective* fandom than anything else in the film world (except for *Star Wars* or *Star Trek*, which are, of course, serial properties in nature anyway).

The twist typically eliminates the distance between the object and Thing for the briefest of moments, putting viewers in touch with something like Hegel's absolute knowledge. As McGowan writes, "When we work through the prevailing fictions and finally grasp the interrelation of truth and fiction, we arrive at absolute knowledge."[28] The twist to a film like *The Usual Suspects* seems to bring us to absolute knowledge. In actuality, we have done no work to reach this position of knowledge—it was simply given to us. A film like *Inception* challenges us to "work through our prevailing fictions and grasp the interrelation of truth and fiction" through use of the drive twist. Nolan, radically, denies the viewer this illusory moment of absolute knowledge, retaining the radical edge of the twist narrative—that is, the twist narrative revolves around "nothing," a void, a hole that the twist "fills"—but this hole or void is *always there* in our everyday lives. There is no big Other, no life "twist," no external guarantor. *Inception* brings this to the fore, earning the status of a truly radical mainstream American film.[29]

Conclusion: The Drive's Effect on Narrative Investment

Twist films mask the disappointment of desire viewers feel at a film's end by guiding us to encounter *a new object to desire*—the twist in narrative *itself*. Film, both as institution and in individual instances, is great at keeping viewers as desiring subjects. Drive is, perhaps most crucially, the enjoyment of the disappointment of desire, and identification *with the drive* would seem to be the best way *out* of the web of the other's desire (desire is always the desire of the other).

Even if a "truly satisfying object" existed, one that could completely fulfill the subject's desire and eliminate the lack that propels desire, the subject would have to "unencounter" the object to remain a subject. As Molly Anne Rothenberg writes in *The Excessive Subject*, the drive is the constant force that keeps desire alive by producing the illusion that there is an object to aim at in the first place. We "miss" the object perpetually and it is through this "missing" that *we become subjects*; "In this way, the drive ensures no encounter with an object while maintaining the illusion of its existence."[30] The subject here is a subject of the drive, *not* of desire. This is the radicality present in Christopher Nolan's *Inception* and its drive twist ending. Viewers emerge from the theater having seen the void at the heart of desire narrativized, in touch with the constant force of the drive.

Not every psychoanalytically inclined critic agrees, however. Significantly, Žižek sees identification with the drive as an impossibility:

> drive—in contrast to symbolic desire—appertains to the Real Impossible, defined by Lacan as that which "always returns to its place." And it is precisely for this reason that identification with it is not possible: one can identify with the other only as desiring subject; this identification is even *constitutive* of desire which,

according to Lacan, is by definition a "desire of the Other"—that is to say intersubjective, mediated by the other: in contrast to the "autistic" drive, contained in its circuit.[31]

But Žižek does not consider drive twist films like *The Conversation* or *The Shining*, nor does he consider television.[32] Perhaps it is because Lacanian psychoanalytic criticism has been concerned primarily with film that it has not interrogated the conditions unique to television, and perhaps that is why, as Žižek concludes here, that "it is not possible to identify with the drive." The ethics of television—and films like *Inception*—is rooted in the death drive or, rather, the limitless production of itself as such and the enjoyment of this cyclical production (the syndication of TV shows in effect "produces them" endlessly; the ad hoc concretization of enjoying *Inception*'s open/disappointing ending are our examples here). TV being structurally aligned with the death drive is significant, as the Westernization of the world insists on creating cultures of desire rather than drive. For me, this signifies a new contouring of the dialectical ground of television, one that stems from a new understanding of exactly what dialectics means. We see the caricature of a Hegelian dialectic here, a model that moves not toward synthesis but toward "better failure" (as Žižek has offered). Television offers this consistently, both in its structure and in specific serial instances. In fact, it is television's manifest inability of offering the narrative thrill of the twist ending that further aligns it with drive.

With a few exceptions of course (*M*A*S*H* and *Six Feet Under* spring to mind), TV shows end disappointingly or divisively.[33] Here, we have a convergence of a couple of things: TV narrative is predictable at making practical use of failure as a narrative model; screenwriters are trained, because of this, to write for failure out of necessity; viewers, then, learn to watch for it. Much of the enjoyment in watching *Seinfeld*, *It's Always Sunny in Philadelphia*, and *Curb Your Enthusiasm* comes from watching the central figures find new ways to fail; in serious dramas like *The Wire* and *Breaking Bad*, it is the failure to completely accomplish any given goal *without* leaving an indivisible remainder (the inability to achieve or author a perfectly executed and thoroughly supported criminal case in *The Wire*, the copy of *Leaves of Grass* in *Breaking Bad*). So, contemporary television provides an entire narrative edifice driven by creative uses of failure that endlessly defers narrative closure—or the fantasmatic realization of desire (which, of course, is impossible anyway). This turn toward drive narrativization allows viewers to access a different kind of excessive enjoyment.[34] Further complicating the television finale landscape is the inescapable reality that most people don't really want their favorite shows to be "over," to stop airing "new" episodes, to lose the feeling that the *next* episode might be the truly satisfying object.[35] For this reason, any ending is going to start off at a deficit. Thomas Schnauz, a writer for *Breaking Bad*, wrote an article for *Time* explaining to readers, to fans of the show, to himself, and the world, *why Breaking Bad* had to end.[36] No director has ever had to explain *why* his or her film had to end. We expect it. No book comes with a "why it had to end" appendix. We can feel the ending when we hold the book. No album comes with a special "why that was the last song" track. Television, through use of the drive, becomes the most personal form of art.

The structure of television actually helps to deliver on film's radical potential. Perhaps HBO's recent series *The Leftovers*—a series set three years after 2 percent of the world's population disappeared simultaneously—is the best example of how radical the drive and failure are, or can be. *The Leftovers* is structured around three of the most frightening and uncomfortable words in the English language: I don't know. No matter what happens on the show, the most pressing question in *The Leftovers*' universe—why and how did 2 percent of all people disappear—will go unanswered. It is, I believe, this exact kind of existential value unique to television that has led to its recently elevated status.[37]

Fixing our eye on the vicissitudes of the twist ending opens up a deeper consideration of how the drive functions in visual narrative and its implications for viewer investment—the precise ground where TV is gaining supremacy over film. The drive twist, as seen in Christopher Nolan's *Inception*, is the "missing link" between the current filmic and televisual experience. *Inception*'s drive ending inspired seemingly endless theorizing by viewers—the kind of extra-textual investment that *Lost*, or more recently *True Detective*, engendered in viewers. Viewers are now identifying with the narrative failure unique to television, using (unconsciously) the encounter with the drive to reproduce excessive investment in a given series. Perhaps what we're seeing is the implicit desire for the drive in narrative, for films that aren't too "final" (a possible explanation for the recent trend of "after the credit" endings). If there is a "secret" to television's recent success, it lies in its ability to turn failure into a vehicle for generating new and deeper viewer interest. That it makes far better narrative use of the drive is, to my mind, the true threat that television poses to cinema. Only drive twist films can compete at the level of (psychical, personal, emotional) investment and they—the narratively radical—are few.

Notes

1. Žižek himself referred to television as "the spirit of culture" in a YouTube video on HBO's *The Wire*. Slavoj Žižek, "*The Wire*, or the Clash of Civilisations in One Country," August 13, 2012, http://www.brobible.com/entertainment/movies/article/50-best-movie-twist-endings-of-all-time/#page/.

2. Google searches are, I believe, the best places to glean a general sense of a wider cultural conversation. Typing the phrase "best twist film endings" into Google produces two lists that include *Buried*, *The Mist*, and *The Grey*. Individual Internet Movie Database profiles pop up with "best twist" lists as well, where these films are either included or discussed in the list end comment section by users. George Wales, "30 Greatest Twist Endings," August 16, 2011, http://www.totalfilm.com/features/30-greatest-twist-endings; Neil Bulson, "50 Best Movie Twist Endings of All Time," January 18, 2014, http://guyism.com/entertainment/movies/50-best-movie-twist-endings-of-all-time.html (date of access unknown).

3. This is surprisingly Miltonian as, in book 4 of *Paradise Lost*, we learn that the worst sin one can commit is despair; believing that God cannot help you, that he has no plan for you, that his power is utterly impotent and vacant.

4. Sigmund Freud, *Beyond the Pleasure Principle*, trans. and ed. James Strachey (New York: Norton, 1975), 43.

5. Joan Copjec, *Imagine There's No Woman: Ethics and Sublimation* (Cambridge: MIT Press, 2002), 7.

6. Richard Boothby, *Freud as Philosopher: Metapsychology after Lacan* (New York: Routledge, 2001), 137–138.

7. Things that exist but have no clear evolutionary reason to are tricky spots for evolutionary psychologists. Stephen Pinker has famously said that there is no adaptive explanation when it comes to music. No evidence supports the idea that music is an adaptation; the desire to *think there must be* comes from what he refers to as a "moralistic fallacy" (e.g., "Music is good, I like music, therefore it must be an adaptation"). Perhaps. But perhaps music, having no clear evolutionary value, might be part of the "hard problem of consciousness," which relates to phenomenology, subjectivity, and what things *feel like*. Pinker believes science may never be able to provide a convincing explanation for this problem. He writes in answer to an interview question: "As for the [hard] problem of consciousness—whether the red that I see is the same as the red that you see; whether there could be a 'zombie' that is indistinguishable from you and me but not conscious of anything; whether an upload of the state of my brain to the cloud would feel anything—I suspect the answer is 'never,' since these conundrums may be artifacts of human intuition. Our best science tells us that subjectivity arises from certain kinds of information-processing in the brain, but why, intuitively, that should be the case is as puzzling to us as the paradoxes of quantum mechanics, relativity, and other problems that are far from everyday intuition." Edward Clint, "Steven Pinker's Reddit AMA Recap," *Skeptic Ink, Network Blog*, May 12, 2013, http://www.skepticink.com/incredulous/2013/03/19/steven-pinkers-reddit-ama-recap/ (date of access unknown). My response here is:

This is precisely the area that psychoanalysis operates in. It advances a framework to understand "intuitively" this major problem of intuition *as such.*

8. David Corn, "Secret Video: Romney Tells Millionaire Donors What He Really Thinks of Obama Voters," *Mother Jones Blog*, September 17, 2012, http://www.motherjones.com/politics/2012/09/secret-video-romney-private-fundraiser (date of access unknown).

9. Jacques Lacan, *The Four Fundamental Concepts of Psychoanalysis* (New York: W.W. Norton, 1998), 165.

10. Todd McGowan, *Out of Time: Desire in Atemporal Cinema* (Minneapolis: University of Minnesota Press, 2011), 11.

11. Slavoj Žižek, "In His Bold Gaze My Ruin Is Writ Large," in *Everything You Always Wanted to Know about Lacan but Were Afraid to Ask Hitchcock*, 2nd ed., ed. Slavoj Žižek (New York: Verso, 2010), 228.

12. Slavoj Žižek, *For They Know Not What They Do: Enjoyment as a Political Factor* (London: Verso, 1991), 15.

13. Richard Boothby, *Freud as Philosopher*, 214.

14. Fabio Vighi, *On Žižek's Dialectics: Surplus, Subtraction, Sublimation* (London: Continuum, 2010), 127–128.

15. Jacques Lacan, *The Ethics of Psychoanalysis, 1959–1960* (New York: Norton, 1997), 130.

16. Slavoj Žižek, *The Sublime Object of Ideology*, 2nd ed. (New York: Verso, 2008), 78.

17. Žižek, *The Sublime Object of Ideology*, 95.

18. This is an explicit paraphrasing or "mad libbing" of Žižek. Slavoj Žižek, *For They Know Not What They Do: Enjoyment as a Political Factor*, 2nd ed. (New York: Verso, 2008), 200.

19. We can also see, again, that a twist cannot be a "gotcha" moment, as in *The Mist* or "Time Enough at Last"; it must retroactively reorganize the filmic experience for viewers.

20. This is why *Breaking Bad* is truly brilliant—it took full advantage of its seriality to tell one overarching narrative with three discrete stopping points to mark the end/beginning of discrete storylines. The show's single unifying plotline—Will Walter White ever be caught? Ever be stopped? And if so, will Hank catch him? If so, how?—reached its conclusion with "Gliding Over All," the midseason finale to the show's final season. After that there are six episodes that deal with the subsequent storyline: What does Hank do? Walt can't wriggle his way out of this one, can he? "Ozymandias" ends this shorter narrative subset. The final two episodes answer the pressing questions: What does Walt do now? How can he fix this? Can he be redeemed? We can read *Breaking Bad* as having divided its sixty-two-episode narrative into three chunks of decreasing size (with three separate distinct finales). *Breaking Bad* creator and showrunner Vince Gilligan is a mad genius.

21. The atheist's error is that the void is mistaken as the guarantor of their oppositional beliefs, or unbelief in organized religion; basically, they cannot resist interpreting "nothing" as guaranteeing "something."

22. See Todd McGowan, *Enjoying What We Don't Have: The Political Project of Psychoanalysis* (Lincoln: University of Nebraska Press, 2013).

23. This is an expectation well earned as, besides the aforementioned films, *Following*, *Insomnia*, and his trilogy of *Batman* films are each structured around the kind of narrative elisions and ruptures typical of twist films. It might even be fair to consider Nolan a twist *auteur*.

24. Todd McGowan, *The Fictional Christopher Nolan* (Austin: University of Texas Press, 2012), 164.

25. Alenka Zupančič, *Ethics of the Real: Kant, Lacan* (London: Verso, 2000), 136.

26. See *Science Fiction blog*: "i09 We Come from the Future," http://io9.com/5701725/chris-nolan-thinks-all-of-your-inception-theories-are-stupid, and *Fan Theories*, http://www.reddit.com/r/FanTheories/comments/1k5nme/inception/ (date of access unknown).

27. These numbers are, of course, as of this writing.

28. McGowan, *The Fictional Christopher Nolan*, 177.

29. Were there world enough and time, this essay would indulge other "drive twists," like Stanley Kubrick's *The Shining* (a film that engendered so much excessive investment that a documentary—*Room 237*—was filmed chronicling the various conspiracy theories viewers have found in it); Peter Collinson's *The Italian Job* (a film with such a teasingly ambiguous ending that in 2009 the Royal Society of Chemistry sponsored a public competition to solve the riddle of the much-beloved film's cliffhanger finale); Coppola's *The Conversation*; Pakula's *The Parallax View*; and pretty much anything by Claude Chabrol.

30. Molly Anne Rothenberg, *The Excessive Subject: A New Theory of Social Change* (Cambridge: Polity, 2010), 174–175.

31. Žižek, "In His Bold Gaze My Ruin Is Writ Large," 228–229.

32. Nor have many other psychoanalytic commentators for that matter. The very recent *Žižek and Media Studies: A Reader*, edited by Matthew Flisfeder and Louis-Paull Willis (London: Palgrave Macmillan, 2014)—a veritable who's who and what's what in Žižekian approaches to cinema, culture, and media—contains not one essay dedicated to television (as cultural object) or television as a (serial and episodic) narrative medium. Several of the contributors there appear in the present volume, so I point this out with the explicit intention *not to start a war with them* but to highlight what must be considered a gap in the current constellation of Lacanian psychoanalysis in media criticism. Or maybe I am just trying to start a war . . .

33. "How could that claim *possibly* be verifiable," some may ask. I respond that desire, as we've seen, always goes unsatisfied, as there is no truly satisfying object. Twist film endings, however, can mask that dissatisfaction. Television is incapable of performing the twist feat with anywhere near the degree of consistency and grace that we see in film. Ergo the viewer of the television ending will always be left disappointed. On the more empirical side, for one, the conditions that occasion a television ending can have little to do with the trajectory or pull of the story (something that rarely—if ever—happens in nonserial narratives). As television scholar Jason Mittell

writes in *Complex TV*: "A successful television series typically lacks a crucial element that has long been hailed as of supreme importance for a well-told story: an ending. Unlike nearly every other narrative medium, American commercial television operates on what might be termed the 'infinite model' of storytelling—a series is deemed a success only as long as it keeps going." See "Ends," in *Complex TV: The Poetics of Contemporary Television Storytelling*, prepublication edition (MediaCommons Press, 2012), 13. I find it quite tantalizing how close Mittell is to unintentionally mapping a theory of the drive onto television narrative, but the point here is that, historically speaking, most shows simply *do not end with a preplanned finale*. This is starting to change, but until very recently the looming specter of cancellation was the most common creator of the conditions for a series to end, not any imperative brought about by the narrative itself. This factor alone has been instrumental in encrusting rushed, unfortunate, or tonally inappropriate endings to a number of shows too long to list (even if I limited myself only to shows canceled by Fox), but famously *My So Called Life*, *Alf*, *Dinosaurs*, and *Deadwood*.

34. Which can take the form of anything from blogging, writing fan fiction, message board commenting, cos-playing, and—of course—rewatching.

35. Even in cases where viewers think their favorite show has "jumped the shark," they *still* hold out hope that the series finale can do justice to what was great about the show, to deliver on its potential. In short, these viewers *still* think it can be the truly satisfying show.

36. Thomas Schnauz, "*Breaking Bad* Writer on Why It Had to End Comments," *Time Blog*, September 23, 2013, http://ideas.time.com/2013/09/29/breaking-bad-writer-why-it-has-to-end/ (date of access unknown).

37. Some critics, like Elana Levine and Michael Z. Newman, have argued that to accept the narrative that television has gotten better over the years is "naïve." Their position, rather, is that television has simply been "legitimated" by white, cultural elites who have endowed it with the necessary aesthetic import previously reserved for cinema and other visual art, and that *this* discursive practice is what television and narrative theorists should be critical and skeptical of; that this process has been filtered through hierarchical discourses that have sought to "masculinize" TV before accepting it as worthy of critical attention. Michael Z. Newman and Elana Levine, *Legitimating Television: Media Convergence and Cultural Status* (New York: Routledge, 2011). A counterpoint worth making, however, is: Why can't both cases be true? Why can't television have gotten progressively "better"—more complex, more diverse, more challenging—*during the same time* that this process of "white, elite legitimating" discourse occurred? Furthermore, isn't this the same dialectical process—and I think that this shift in thought *is dialectical in nature* is the big point Newman and Levine miss—by which the novel *and* cinema *and* new movements in visual art have become historically "legitimated"?

4

Retroactive Rupture

The Place of the Subject in Jane Campion's *In the Cut*

Fabio Vighi

Introduction

This piece explores the retroactive significance of a film ending by drawing on Jacques Lacan's theory of the signifier and applying it to Jane Campion's 2003 film *In the Cut*. Retroactive signification is a central tenet in Lacan's understanding of the process of subjectivation through language, inasmuch as language intercepts human life in the manner of a razor-sharp blade, severing the body from its presumed self-contained biological autonomy. After the cut of language, a lack is inscribed in the body and subjective alienation ensues—for Lacan, there is no other way of being human than being alienated in language. Although language is the only vehicle through which to attain self-consciousness, at the same time it carries an ontological inconsistency that splits us, forever separating us from the realization of whatever dreams of wholeness or plenitude we might harbor. Campion's *In the Cut* is a complex narrative built around violent physical lacerations that, I argue, should be read in metaphorical terms as so many signifiers of the impossibility that pervades the process of subjectivation and, ultimately, indelibly marks the subject itself.

Strictly speaking, retroactivity in film endings means that the finale changes the meaning of what one thought was happening while watching

the narrative unfold. At the same time, a retroactive ending might answer
questions one was not aware of asking. With *In the Cut*, however, we are
dealing with a more nuanced understanding of retroactivity, one that can
be evinced by pondering the meaning of "cut" as both the editing of the
final scene of the film and the film's main trope. As we shall see, this erotic
thriller, typically characterized by the whodunit formula, presents us with
the basic scenario of a woman—teacher and writer—whose life is inter-
cepted by signifiers that seem to have no signifieds, images or situations that
radically elude signification. For this precise reason, she becomes obsessively
attached to these "cuts," which come to represent the gaps or inconsistencies
in meaning where her desire is nestled, thus feeding her fantasies. What
makes this film remarkable, however, is the treatment of the heroine as a
"being of language"—language being what drives her. Hers, then, is a quest
for knowledge, as she perceives the enigmatic gaps that open up and multiply
in front of her as strictly related, or relatable, to linguistic signification. It is
this conflation of language and drive set in the wider context of feminine
desire that makes the film particularly amenable to a psychoanalytic reading. But before engaging with the analysis of the narrative, let us begin to
clarify how the ending of this particular film can be conducive to fruitful
theoretical considerations.

The ending of *In the Cut* is typical of independent or art cinema in
that it would seem to provide a degree of narrative closure, yet it brings a
sense of suspension and incompletion, to an extent that it invites us to read
the storyline retroactively. The film ends with a wonderfully suggestive image
of the heroine lying down next to her handcuffed lover. She is covered in
blood, having just returned home after the climactic confrontation with the
film's villain, the psychopathic killer responsible for cutting up a number of
bodies. It is a finale that, I argue, captures the heroine's exhausted elation at
having finally reached *the cut* qua impossible object-cause of her desire. More
pointedly, it signals rebirth, thus inviting us to reread the narrative causality
of the plot as a metaphorical voyage toward radical subjective regeneration.
The traumatic, shocking encounter with the killer amounts for the heroine to
a verification that lack, qua psychotic conflation of language and act, is what
lies at the heart of every human experience. Such an encounter is therefore
crucial in allowing the heroine to traverse her insidious fantasies. The final
image, however, is far from consolatory. Having dispelled the disturbing
fantasies that prevented her from achieving a satisfactory relationship with
her lover, the heroine is portrayed as couched next to him, bloodied and
in a fetal position suggestive of birth; yet, the detail not to miss is that the

lover qua Other still has one hand handcuffed to the radiator pipe, suggesting helplessness and fragility—or, in Lacanian terms, the idea that, ultimately, the Other cannot work as a guarantor of indisputable signification for the subject. Another way of saying this is that the couple remains divided despite having reached a degree of clarity about each other they lacked before.

In the Lacanian Cut

To state that film endings are equivalent to full stops in written or spoken sentences is undoubtedly a commonplace, which as such can only be critically accepted if developed in a given theoretical direction. To grasp their retroactive function, we need to look at Lacan's theory of the signifier, which comes to the fore with particular depth in one of his most famous *Écrits*, "The Subversion of the Subject and the Dialectic of Desire in the Freudian Field," dating back to 1960.[1] If we take a look at the elementary cell of desire as presented in this text, we realize that, to put it in a nutshell, the creation of meaning takes place retroactively, that is to say when a certain signifier stops the otherwise infinite sliding of the signifying chain thus generating meaning through a specific concatenation of signifiers. See Lacan's elementary graph (figure 4.1).

What we immediately notice in the graph is that there are two vectors running in opposite directions. The "fishhook" vector of subjectivity, which goes from Δ (the somewhat "mythical" subject of needs before entering lan-

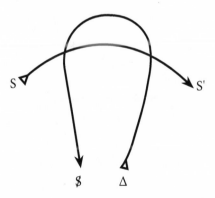

Figure 4.1

guage)[2] to $ (the barred subject after the encounter with language), moves from right to left; the signifying chain or vector of speech (from a signifier to another signifier) moves from left to right. The general implication is that the human being as a being of needs can only become subject, and consequently acquire meaning, through language, which is situated outside, in the Other. Lacan compares the being of needs to a fisherman whose fishing line is thrown into the order of language so as to catch "fish-signifiers," which alone can provide significations, thus allowing for the process of subjectivation to start. This process, which is completely dependent on the presence of the Other as the repository of signifiers, necessarily transforms biological needs into complex linguistic/cultural meanings (which more often than not take no account of those biological needs). The passage from subject qua biological body to the Cartesian cogito or subject of consciousness, in other words, is by definition effected by an alienating process of transubstantiation whereby language (the signifier) grafts itself onto "human life as such." The radically alien dimension at stake in language is confirmed precisely by the directionality of the vector S-S', which is opposite to, and therefore completely autonomous from, the vector indicating the process of subjectivation out of biological life. The externalization of life into language is therefore both necessary and radical: no connections whatsoever can be presupposed between subject and language; the two vectors simply intersect rather than constituting some sort of continuum. Furthermore, Lacan's point is that the subject caught in, and determined through the otherness of language, is essentially divided. It cannot be self-identical since its constitution through language always leaves a reminder that is not symbolized and therefore disturbs or disrupts whatever meaning alienation brings. The loss produced by the encounter with the signifier is therefore ontologically inscribed as lack into subjectivity and will mark the subject's relation to itself and the world throughout life. Fantasy, as Lacan indeed underscores in *Subversion*, is the "weapon" the subject has at its disposal to try and fill the lack brought in by the signifier. Since subjects are invariably *in the cut*, that is, defined by the cut of the signifier, they are always subjected to a loss of meaning the very moment they acquire meaning in/through language. The subject, then, never coincides with itself. But for our purpose here, let us focus on the two points where the vector of speech intercepts the human being qua living organism. It is significant that, if we follow the trajectory of the fishhook vector of subjectivity, the first point of interception corresponds to the end of the sentence that moves from left to right. In other words, the meaning of the hypothetical first word we encounter in what Lacan calls "the treasure trove of signifiers" is established retroactively after the encounter with the signifier that ends the sentence, that is, that brings in a second cut whose purpose is, literally, to put a halt to the otherwise endless sliding of signifiers. Later, in the 1960s, Lacan will introduce his second graph of desire, as developed from the first, which names the two points of interception, from right to left, as A (the Other or treasure trove of signifiers) and s(A), the signification of the Other. What is crucial for our analysis of film endings is precisely this second term, which is also commonly known in Lacan's texts with the French expression *point de capiton* (anchoring point, button tie, etc.). A film ending is always a *point de capiton*. What needs to be examined, however, is not only the function but more importantly the internal constitution of this crucial signifying element insofar as we read it in relation to film. The following discussion, then, aims to introduce another key Lacanian term in the field of film studies. It does so, as we shall see, by unraveling the paradoxical coincidence of closure and radical opening as embodied by film endings. To put it somewhat cryptically, a film ending can be regarded as a cut that brings to a halt the potentially endless sliding of the filmic signifying chain while also making apparent the substantial inconsistency of the signification(s) produced by film and represented at various points of its development. Regardless of whether it is open or closed, that is, whether it suspends or elicits narrative closure, a film ending carries a retroactive signifying function that allows us to apply our critical understanding to the material under consideration. Without the final cut, in other words, a film narrative would be ontologically ambiguous, since the filmic signifying chain would slide ad infinitum—at least potentially.

Reading the Cut

Here is a summary of the narrative of Campion's film. *In the Cut* is set in New York and narrates the story of a high school teacher and writer named Frances (Frannie) Avery (Meg Ryan). It opens with Frannie meeting a student at a local bar. As she heads for the toilet, she catches a glimpse of a woman performing fellatio on a man in a dark room in the basement of the bar; while she cannot see the man's face, she notices a three of spades tattooed on his wrist. A few days later, Detective Giovanni Malloy (Mark Ruffalo) questions her as part of his investigations into the dreadful murder of a young woman, whose severed limb was found in Frannie's garden. The two start flirting and meet in a bar later. Frannie is both excited and frightened by the detective's sexual aggressiveness, although she is clearly disappointed by the crass attitudes and macho behavior of Malloy and his colleagues, including the detective's partner Richard Rodriguez (Nick Damici). She decides to leave the bar on her own and is assaulted while walking home. She calls Malloy for help and their affair begins that same night. Frannie's doubts about Malloy's integrity, however, begin to haunt her. She reminisces about the sex scene she had witnessed in the bar and notices that Malloy's hand bears the same tattoo she had seen on the unidentified man who was given oral sex. Her doubts increase when Malloy informs her that the murderer was in the same bar she went to the day she met the student, and when a second victim is found, she cannot help thinking that Malloy might be involved. After finding her former slightly disturbed boyfriend in her bed, she goes to her half-sister Pauline's (Jennifer Jason Leigh) apartment only to find her dismembered body in the bathroom. At this stage Frannie's predicament is clear: she is drawn more and more into a nightmarish vortex of desires denoting the overlapping of fascination and repulsion toward the man (Malloy) who in her increasingly overbearing fantasies she associates with the series of gruesome murders. When Malloy pays her a visit to help her recover from a state of drunken confusion following the murder of her sister, Frannie takes the initiative in an unexpected way. She handcuffs one of Malloy's hands to a radiator pipe in her apartment and makes love to him. With Malloy still immobilized, Frannie accidentally discovers in his jacket the missing charms from her bracelet, which she had lost when she had been assaulted. Although Malloy pleads he had found the charms and wanted to return them to her, she shouts at him that she had seen his tattooed hand in the basement of the bar and runs out of her apartment. However, once in the street she stumbles right into Malloy's partner, Rodriguez, who attempts to calm her down and convinces her to get in his car so they can drive to a quiet place where they can speak about Malloy's presumed involvement in the killings. They soon arrive at the George Washington Bridge, which is the place Rodriguez usually goes to fish and collect his thoughts. But as soon as he locks the tower's gate behind them, she knows she is in trouble, a feeling confirmed emphatically by her spotting the tattoo on his hand, the twin of Malloy's. Before Rodriguez takes her in his arms, she gets hold of Malloy's gun (she had taken his jacket) and shoots him; as he disarms her and tries to strangle her, she grabs hold of his own gun and shoots again, this time killing him. Then she walks away, bloodied and stunned, eventually getting back to her apartment. In the final scene she lies down, exhausted, in the arms of the still handcuffed and equally worn out Malloy.

It is interesting to observe how the film has generally been read through the standard interpretative lens of cultural studies. Gender, race, authorship, and issues concerning genre are usually mobilized to decode the cultural and/or political (in the sense of "identity politics") significance of Campion's film.[3] The feminist approach is particularly prevalent, not least in light of the fact that the film's director, the film's lead character, the author of the eponymous novel from which the film was adapted (Susanna Moore), and even the film's producers (Nicole Kidman and Laurie Parker) are all women. There is no doubt that the film deals comprehensively with sexuality, gender, and more widely femininity's troubled relation with romantic fantasies and heterosexual relations and marriage. The heroine's recurrent fantasy is precisely that of the idyllic scenario of the encounter between her parents—though, as we shall see, it contains a dark side. However, while sexual difference confirms here to be a central concern for Campion, I argue that we should read this theme alongside a deeper question regarding subjectivation—and its inevitably "sexed" character.[4] While it would be difficult to deny that *In the Cut* is about a woman who tries to find "her own voice" in a world dominated by violent masculinity, I believe it is much more fruitful to situate this issue within the larger framework whereby it would appear that it is the subject as such who desperately endeavors to find those symbolic coordinates that would secure its identity. With regard to the various "cultural studies" approaches to Campion's film, my position is, in a nutshell, that they fail to unravel the key disavowed concern embodied by the signifier "cut" as the catalyst of cinematic signification throughout this narrative. As I hope to make explicit with this piece, the cultural studies approach provides a series of fantasy scenarios for a film critic/spectator who, ultimately, does not (want to) engage with the radical deadlock portrayed in this harrowing narrative and represented by the ontological significance taken over by the term "cut." I want to redress this issue by bringing the focus onto the treatment of subjectivity that I believe is central to Campion's film. More precisely, I argue that *In the Cut* engages with the theme of the birth of the subject through the encounter with the division brought in by language in its ambiguous though necessary signifying function. In this respect, I will refer to the film's ending as the cut that retroactively endorses the process of signification insofar as it coincides with that of subjectivation. My argument is supported by theoretical references to Jacques Lacan's theory of the signifier as developed particularly in his well-known graphs of desire. Ultimately, I will seek to show that the signifier "cut," in the narrative economy of the film, stands for the Lacanian subject—the subject insofar as it emerges through the inconsistencies and contradictions of the discourse/desire of the Other, which informs subjectivity. All through the film, but especially in the final scene at the lighthouse, the protagonist comes to embody the inconsistency that also epitomizes the Other, especially given the significance of "cutting"/

ripping in the actual storyline. But let us proceed by highlighting first the basic stages marking the development of the film's central character.

Words, Tattoos, and Desire

As a college teacher in the underbelly of lower Manhattan, Frannie is fascinated by words, to such an extent that she cultivates a passion for poetry and literary writing. We soon discover that she lives on her own and prefers masturbation to engaging in sexual relationships—also as a reaction to the failure of her mother's marriage.[5] In this respect, her half-sister Pauline can be safely regarded as her polar opposite.[6] The first crucial moment in the film, the one that forces a subjective reaction in Frannie's solitary, quasi-autistic existence is her voyeuristic encounter with the act of fellatio in the dark basement of a bar.[7] Much has been written on the supposed significance of Campion's reversing of the classic voyeuristic scenario involving the masculine gaze attracted by a female body. Here the voyeur is a woman and the object of scopic desire is indeed the erected (though prosthetic) penis. However, the problem with this interpretation is that, typically, it does not take into account what actually happens in voyeurism.[8] In fact, it disavows the crucial traumatic dimension that scopophilia always incorporates, something that Freud had famously commented on in his case study of the Rat Man. What is it, then, that actually constitutes a trauma for Frannie? In other words, why can we not simply regard this encounter as a voyeuristically pleasurable one? The reason is provided by a detail that should not be merely seen as functional to the development of the narrative in the context of the film's genre but instead acquires a precise significance for the constitution of desire in the main character's psychic economy. I am referring to the tattoo portrayed on the wrist of the unidentified male character who is being pleasured in the basement. What we have, in other words, is the juxtaposition of a very explicit—essentially pornographic—sex scene, which clearly attracts and disturbs Frannie's gaze, with a sign, a symbolic mark (the tattoo) that as such works, I claim, as the enigmatic signifier of the Other's *jouissance*. In many ways, Frannie's subjective position in the film is decided by her witnessing that fellatio in the bar: if, as we shall see, she is drawn into the destructive vortex of the *jouissance* of the other, at the same time she is given a chance to rely on a signifier that, no matter how enigmatic, allows her to (attempt to) ascribe a minimum of meaning to that outburst of disturbing *jouissance*. We should not forget that, since time immemorial, tattoos are meant to symbolize desires, as they did for instance for sailors. They are, in other words, not *cuts* but rather attempts to mediate between desire and the ultimate (traumatic) emptiness/lack of the object of desire. As Slavoj Žižek has put it, "Cutting is to be contrasted with the standard tattoo inscriptions on the body, which guarantee the subject's inclusion in the (virtual) symbolic order."[9] If we go back to the oral sex scene, perhaps we are now in a position to understand the significance of Campion's choice of showing it so vividly, for what we should consider in this key scene is the *double inscription* of Frannie's gaze: her scopic desire is effectively split between the erected penis, which is clearly visible in two close-up shots, and the tattoo qua minimal symbolization of the shocking, disturbing vision of the penis. For this reason, Frannie's fantasy will remain attached to the tattoo, in a bid to decipher its ultimate significance (i.e., to identify the person—the killer—it belongs to). We should reiterate that this interference of the symbolic order is what saves her from being overwhelmed by the *jouissance* of the Other. It may appear that Frannie's predicament is the obverse of the one just described, insofar as she could legitimately be regarded as a repressed or autistic writer, immersed in and absorbed by language and consequently carrying a problematic relation with sexuality. While this is undoubtedly true at the narrative level, we should not miss how, precisely as a writer, her relation to language is from the very beginning far from uncomplicated. Just like a child confronted with a barrage of enigmatic signifiers that are not yet connected with any signifieds, Frannie is struggling to decipher the slang spoken in her neighborhood, on which subject she is writing a book. In fact, we could argue that the slang material she is working on and the tattoo qua signifier of the other's desire she has a glimpse of are strictly correlative, since they stand for the interference of language on human life—in Lacanian terms, for the way language cuts into the body to inscribe the lack that in turn triggers desire.

Is Frannie, then, not facing the same conundrum faced by the infant who, as evidenced in Lacan's famous graphs of desire, desperately needs the intervention of the Symbolic (language) to escape the unconditionality of demand? Let us recall Lacan's famous description of the interconnections between need, demand, and desire. According to Lacan, desire is what

> begins to take shape in the margin in which demand rips away from need, this margin being the one that demand—whose appeal can be unconditioned only with respect to the Other—opens up in the guise of the possible gap need may give rise to here, because it has no universal satisfaction (this is called "anxiety").[10]

Let us try to unpack this complex statement. Demands for Lacan arise when the infant realizes that beyond the satisfaction of bodily needs, he/she requires also the other's love or affection. It is when the child realizes that demands have no universal satisfaction, that is, when demand emerges out of need as something different from it—that desire makes its appearance. Let us say that first a child needs food qua biological function and is appeased when the other provides it; then, the child begins to demand love (a different kind of food) from this other but realizes that such demand is problematic since it never achieves full satisfaction; it is at this stage that desire develops out of demand's difference from need. My claim is that at the start of Campion's film our heroine is effectively "learning to desire," and she does so through the Symbolic inasmuch as it presents her with the other's desire. No wonder she is introduced into the story as someone who is fascinated by words. For instance, the tone for the film is set in the opening dialogue between Frannie and Pauline; when questioned by Pauline about the meaning of certain slang words she is researching and has posted on the walls of her apartment, Frannie explains and then concludes that "slang is either sexual or violent" (to which Pauline adds "or both"). Furthermore, as anticipated Campion cleverly presents Frannie as a solipsistic and deeply fraught woman, unable to relate to others and yet bothered by an edgy curiosity suggestive of repressed libido. For instance, as her sister puts it in the opening scene, she is "sabotaging her incredible figure" by not wearing more revealing clothes. Metaphorically, she is an infant who is entering the world of language and desire—the former, for Lacan, being the necessary condition for the latter. Her subjectivity, in other words, is about to take shape, and the trajectory it follows is determined by the encounter with the desiring other. For the question that comes forth from her stumbling upon the hardcore scene and especially the tattoo is the classic Lacanian one: "Che vuoi?" or "what does the desiring other want (from me)?" Lacan claims that "the Other's question . . . which takes some such form as 'Chè vuoi?,' 'What do you want?,'" is the question that best leads the subject to the path of his own desire.[11] The child who is asked what he/she wants, unconsciously tends to answer such questions by questioning the asker, that is, attempting to answer the following question: "What does this person who is interrogating my desire actually want?"; or, more precisely: "What can I give this person to satisfy his/her desire to know what I want?" Thus, the child's desire is by definition molded on the other's desire. And the point is that only through this somewhat perverse loop does the subject join the path of his/her desire. What is certain is that desire will continue to frustrate the subject, since no ultimate answer to the question "Che vuoi?" can ever be given. Through fantasy we attempt to find this answer, but what resonates in every such fantasy (until the end of our life) is nothing other than its own inadequacy, its impossibility to fill the gap opened by language and desire. Fantasy then seeks to establish a degree of determinacy for the enigmatic character of desire intended as the other's desire. This is undoubtedly a radical Lacanian contribution to the definition of subjectivity, since it posits the latter as a field whose inconsistency is to be conceived in strict correlation with the socio-symbolic universe it inhabits. Desire as such does not lead us to assert the singularity of our subjective position vis-à-vis the world; quite on the contrary, it tells us that our subjectivity can only emerge via a detour through the specific world we inhabit. This awareness should bring the ego to confront its own constitutive dislocation—the fact that the significations it purports are not unique and exclusive but are instead caught in a mechanism that defines what the Other already is/wants. So this is how Frannie begins to desire: it is the other's desire (the enigma of a desire immersed in *jouissance* that threatens to engulf her) that leads her to join the path of her own desire; and, we must insist, the key detail here is the tattoo qua inscription of (enigmatic) symbolic meaning. Let us briefly expand on the rapport between demand and desire, as this depends, Lacan tells us, on the intervention of the "law."

The Law's Impotence

As we have seen, the infant places plenty of expectation on the other, including what Lacan calls its "phantom of omnipotence."[12] This point is worth pondering: the fantasy of omnipotence is not on the side of the uncoordinated child, as Freud had surmised, but on the side of the other as seen with the eyes of the child. It is precisely from this fantasy that arises the idea "the necessity that the Other be bridled by the Law."[13] The obvious case in point here are Freud's two fathers as described in *Totem and Taboo*: the *Urvater*, who enjoys fantasmatic status as the omnipotent one, and the father as representative of the law, who intervenes to "bridle" his own excess. Desire, Lacan tells us, "reverses the unconditional nature of the demand for love, in which the subject remains in subjection to the Other, and raises it to the power of absolute condition (in which 'absolute' also implies 'detachment')."[14] Given the Latin root of "absolute" (*absolvere*, i.e., "to free"), Lacan suggests that the acquisition of desire as the untranscendable condition of being human is predicated upon the detachment from the unconditional, anxiety-laden dimension of demand. Put differently, by articulating desires the child is able to find a way out of that "desperate" demand for the (m)other's love that, inevitably, kept him/her at the mercy of the (m)other's enigmatic and unfathomable whim. The law that brings in desire is embodied, first and foremost, by language itself, the signifier. More precisely, the signifier introduces that lack (the rift that disarticulates the unconditionality of demand) that, in turn, gives the subject a chance to develop a desiring relationship vis-à-vis the other. Thus, the order of the law coincides with the order of language, inasmuch as language symbolizes the lack already experienced at the level of the Imaginary (demand), thereby gentrifying it, turning it into something that can potentially be filled by metonymically different objects.

Before turning our attention to the centrality of the theme of the law in *In the Cut*, let us briefly ponder the significance of the phallic figurations that, after the initial scene, begin to occupy Frannie's mind. After she reemerges from the basement of the bar, still perturbed, she lingers on the image of a man with an oversized penis painted on the wall of the bar in the style of an ancient fresco. In the next scene, she is teaching Virginia Woolf's *To the Lighthouse*. She is writing on a board where a red, obviously phallic lighthouse has been drawn, again providing evidence of the overlap between language and the raw real of sexuality—not to mention the fact that in the very opening dialogue of the film the name Virginia was described by Frannie (itself close to "fanny") as slang for "vagina," while the film title also clearly alludes to the female genitalia. Frannie's relation to the phallus is more ambiguous than it may seem. It is definitely not a matter of empowerment, of challenging and appropriating phallic status. Rather, she is fascinated by the intrinsic ambiguity upon which phallic power rests, inasmuch as, in the film, such power is represented by Detective Malloy. The phallus in Lacan is of course a typically unstable notion. It signifies power only insofar as it conceals impotence; in fact, its powerfulness derives from its "ability" to convert lack into the appearance of fullness, which however cannot do away with the lack that informs it. Frannie, then, is intrigued by phallic power inasmuch as she senses it is constituted by the enigmatic "cut" between power and impotence. If she can be seen to embrace phallic power—as in the scene where she learns to shoot immediately after having proffered her dislike for guns—we should recognize how this position is part of her quest for the "meaning of the cut," that is to say, her desire to grasp the lack qua *jouissance* that she perceives all around her. As regards her relationship to Malloy, what is clear is that Frannie's attraction toward him coincides with the ambiguity of the phallus he stands for. Her constant doubting of him, to the extent of fearing his implication in the murders, is the very index of her fascination toward the phallus as signifier of the inexistence of the Other. Only in the final scene, as we shall see, will Frannie realize the meaning of such inexistence.

With regard to the law, things become interesting when, upon meeting Detective Malloy who is investigating the case of a woman killed and then "disarticulated" in the area, she notices on his wrist the same tattoo she had seen on the man in the basement. The law, in other words, is immediately sexualized, to such an extent that Frannie begins to be fascinated by phallic power. In a revealing scene after her first encounter with Malloy, she masturbates while fantasizing not only about being watched by him, but, more importantly, by associating him to the man who was given a blow job in the bar. The connection between the two men (the *Urvater* and the lawful father), in her fantasy, is sustained by the tattoo that, therefore, becomes the signifier of symbolic power, both attracting and frightening Frannie. When Malloy and Frannie go for a drink during their first appointment, he tickles her fantasy by telling her that he can be whatever she wants him to be: "You want me to romance you, take you to a classy restaurant, no problem. You want me to be your best friend and fuck you, treat you good, lick your pussy, no problem. Ain't much I haven't done. The only thing I won't do is beat you up." However, talk of violence against women immediately follows as Malloy explains to Frannie how his partner Rodriguez attacked his wife and has now been downgraded. And when Rodriguez does appear at the bar (incidentally, dancing with a woman played by Jane Campion herself), the talk between the two policemen becomes so obscenely chauvinistic that, after putting up some sort of verbal resistance to vulgarity, Frannie decides to leave the bar. After the assault she suffers that very night, however, she immediately phones Malloy and the two end up at her flat and make love. The prelude to their lovemaking is a quotation from Nicholas Ray's 1950 film noir *In a Lonely Place*, where the Humphrey Bogart character gives a chilling demonstration of how a girl might have been killed in the same way Malloy assaults Frannie. Again, the fantasy of the threat of violence is what seems to excite Frannie, who in a previous scene had congratulated her less inhibited sister for living out her unconscious fantasies.

Passion for the Real

Indeed, Frannie seems attracted by the dangerous situation she believes to have become implicated in. Twice she asks Malloy how the first victim was killed and wants to know the exact meaning of the word "disarticulation."

Although it makes sense to argue that disarticulation here refers metaphorically to the heroine's inability to articulate her desire in a male-dominated universe, we should insist that her main source of fascination has to do with the potential conflation of "words and cuts"; in a nutshell, she wants to know if and how words can cover or capture the "bodily cut" that by now clearly stands for what Lacan terms the Real of *jouissance*. Frannie develops, in other words, a veritable "passion for the Real." Interestingly, in the lovemaking scene we witness a reversal of the fellatio that kick-started the story, as Malloy performs cunnilingus on Frannie. If on the one hand the obvious implication would seem to be Frannie's empowerment, on the other the emphasis falls back on phallic power, as Frannie admiringly asks Malloy how he learned to perform cunnilingus so expertly ("I want to know how you did that to me. How's that? Somebody taught you?"). We should be careful not to misread this scene as a sheer explosion of erotic passion—not even in feminist terms. Rather, the key element to stress is the conjunction of language and libido, for this is what leads us to the (feminine) subject. The story told by Malloy is, again, extremely revealing from our point of view. Malloy tells of how he was seduced by an older woman who taught him to perform cunnilingus on her by inviting him to slowly circle around the clitoris with his tongue. Metaphorically as well as literally speaking, the idea of the object of desire as a point not to be reached directly but rather to encircle or rotate around provides us with a perfect exemplification of the Lacanian logic of desire, inasmuch as desire is sustained by the fundamental lack that qualifies the sought object. Ultimately, it is this lack qua cut that Frannie would like language (poetry, slang, etc.) to capture. What she does not realize, however, is that the very source of her fascination—the dangerous Real of *jouissance*—is *not* originally external to language but is the very result of the intervention of the signifier in the trajectory of human existence. We can only experience the missing, ever-elusive, and destructive Real as an effect of our use of language, not as its presupposition or cause. While Frannie is fascinated by the possibility of words "catching up" with *jouissance*, she does not realize that *jouissance* inhabits the lack opened up by language. The more she tries to capture such lack through language—that is to say, the more she becomes fascinated by the murderous *jouissance* of the film's ripper, obsessed with mutilating female bodies—the more in fact she fuels the deflagrating impossibility intrinsic to *jouissance*. As asserted by the later Lacan, the only way to posit a veritable connection between language and *jouissance* is by understanding language itself as always already inundated by *jouissance*. The Real is therefore not external to the Symbolic, but it is by definition *active* within Symbolic signification; the final dialectical break-through made by Lacan is that meaning can only be "activated" through its symbiotic relation with the Real. Language by definition enjoys—it enjoys its slippery meanings, since it is always an expression of enjoy-meant (*jouis-sens*). And while Frannie has a series of forebodings concerning the intrinsic overlap between language/subjectivity and *jouissance*, as especially evident in what we might call her "underground reveries,"[15] her increasing enthrallment toward "the cut" is also testament to her struggling to perceive and endorse her own self qua language as an expression of that very cut.[16]

It is this crucial issue concerning the status of the subject that the film ending addresses. In fact, the retroactive trajectory of Frannie's subjective discovery is anticipated by the last piece of poetry she catches a glimpse of in the underground: "Now / thinking back / on the course of my passion, / I was like one blind, / unafraid of the dark." The key question here is not so much the connection between blindness and lack of fear but rather retroactivity ("thinking back"). She begins to understand, in other words, the nature of the drive that defines her—the fact that *she is (in) the very cut* she perceives around her qua source of her fascination. The word "disarticulation," on which she had pondered, acquires particular relevance precisely in conjunction with the psychoanalytic insight into the partiality of the drive. When Pauline gets killed and "disarticulated," and Frannie discovers the Hitchcockian-cum-splatter murder scene in the bathroom, she does not want to let go of the plastic bag containing the severed head of her half-sister. This gruesome detail provides further evidence of the argument that Frannie herself is driven, that is, *blinded* by a compulsion to return again and again on the cut (qua *jouissance*). This fixation speaks for the partiality of her drive inasmuch as it can be defined as that of a libidinally invested partial object that the conscious subject does not recognize as her own. However, the dialogue between Malloy and Frannie at the police station after the discovery of Pauline's murder is again revealing of Frannie's reluctance to let go of the dream of full knowledge instigated by language:[17]

> FRANNIE: I want to know what happened. I want to know if it was quick.

> MALLOY: Why do you think knowing is going to make a difference, Frannie?

> FRANNIE: I thought that all my life.

MALLOY: Well, you're wrong. Knowing don't mean shit.

FRANNIE: It *doesn't* mean shit.

Malloy at this point proceeds to give Frannie a detailed description of the various stages of cutting involved in the massacre performed on Pauline's body. Frannie listens, as if mesmerized by the precision of detail. When Malloy tells her he has a key to Pauline's apartment, and that he wants to go back there to investigate, she cannot help thinking he might be the killer. In the next scene, she is at home, drunk, playing in her head the fantasy (in black-and-white) of the blissful encounter between her parents, which she had already narrated to Pauline and which had appeared twice in the film. The parents are depicted when they were young and the father proposed. They were ice-skating in a snow-filled, idyllic scenario. This time, however, a disturbing detail interferes with the faultless fantasy: the father skates over the legs of the mother after she had fallen, cutting right through them. As he is about to do the same to the neck, the intercom buzzes and Frannie awakens from her daydreaming. The narrative here is effective in portraying the surplus of destabilizing fantasy that accompanies the fantasmatic scenario itself. The fantasy, for Lacan, never fully works out as a buffer against the Real; its protective function is undermined by its own excessive core. For this reason, Frannie's disturbing fantasies need to be confronted in order to be dispelled, which is exactly what happens in the final scene.

The film ends at the lighthouse, where Rodriguez takes Frannie and where the latter finally discovers the truth about the "cutting." She sees the tattoo on Rodriguez's wrist and suddenly understands everything. The lighthouse is the place of the phallus, the book she teaches (*To the Lighthouse*) finally embodying the cut she has been obsessed about. The phallus, in turn, is the place of the killer's impotence, the trigger in his psychic economy that turns him into a psycho. In the brief dialogue they have at the lighthouse, by the George Washington Bridge, his psyche is revealed in all its violent fragility. Frannie's fantasies about the *jouissance* of the phallus, which she had herself intended to appropriate—the cunnilingus qua obverse of fellatio, her shooting practice, and finally her handcuffing of Malloy while making love—finally reveal the cut (gap, abyssal inconsistency) that sustained them. The retroactive effect should by now be clear: the ending of the film embodies the subject's realization of her own radical inconsistency insofar as it is reflected through the lack in the Other. As she lies next to her handcuffed lover, it is as if we returned to the starting point of the film, with the same gap inscribed between subject and other. The "only" difference being that now the heroine knows what she was actually after.

Notes

1. Jacques Lacan, *Écrits: The First Complete Edition in English* (London and New York: W. W. Norton, 2006), 671–702.

2. "Mythical" because for Lacan the subject is always already caught in the network of signifiers that constitute language. In other words, our elementary position in the world is already decided before we are born. Even before birth, signifiers are spoken (by parents, et al.) that secure our coincidence with language. The starting position of the vector of subjectivity, then, corresponds to a subject immersed in a prelinguistic or pretextual stream governed only by basic needs. This is what has been labeled by Bruce Fink as Lacan's Real number 1, inasmuch as it is precedes symbolization. Bruce Fink, *The Lacanian Subject: Between Language and Jouissance* (Princeton: Princeton University Press, 1995), 27.

3. See Linda Ruth Williams, *The Erotic Thriller in Contemporary Cinema* (Bloomington: Indiana University Press, 2005); Bronwyn Williams and Amy Zenger, *Popular Culture and Representations of Literacy* (Oxford and New York: Routledge, 2007), 33–37; Mike King, *The American Cinema of Excess: Extremes of the National Mind on Film* (Jefferson and London: McFarland, 2009); Kathleen Anne McHugh, *Jane Campion* (Chicago: University of Illinois Press, 2007); Kathleen Anne McHugh, "Jane Campion: Adaptation, Signature, Autobiography," in *Jane Campion: Cinema, Nation, Identity*, ed. Hilary Radner and Irène Bèssiere (Detroit: Wayne State University Press, 2009), 139–154; Deb Verhoeven, *Jane Campion* (Oxford and New York: Routledge, 2009); and Alistair Fox, *Jane Campion: Authorship and Personal Cinema* (Bloomington: Indiana University Press, 2011).

4. Issues of race also feature frequently in critical work on *In the Cut*, also in relation to what has been identified as a "problematic" trait of Campion's cinematic work as a whole, since the New Zealander director has indeed been harshly scolded for adopting and purporting in her films a West-centric ideological stance.

5. The film is replete with references to the failure of heterosexual relations and especially marriages. I read these references in relation to the wider and over-riding theme of the cut as metaphor for the subject's own impossibility.

6. Incidentally, the filmic reference that immediately springs to mind with regard to these two female characters is Ingmar Bergman's masterpiece *The Silence* (1963), which portrays two sisters displaying the same difference in terms of sexual drive.

7. See King, *The American Cinema of Excess*, 192–196.

8. On top of that—though at a different interpretive level—one could also argue that the scene does not necessarily involve only an object of feminine desire, since the act of fellatio per se can "work" for both masculine and feminine desire.

9. Slavoj Žižek, *Welcome to the Desert of the Real! Five Essays on September 11 and Related Dates* (London: Verso, 2002), 10.

10. Lacan, *Écrits*, 689.

11. Lacan, *Écrits*, 690.

12. Lacan, *Écrits*, 689.

13. Lacan, *Écrits*, 689.

14. Lacan, *Écrits*, 689.

15. When traveling in the underground, Frannie is stricken by various lines of poetry exposed in the carriage, which seem to have both metaphorical relevance for her life but also embody what the symbolist poets, and especially Stéphane Mallarmé, used to refer to as the correspondence of poetic signification and void—the potential of language to capture the essential nothingness that grounds reality.

16. "I like it in the cut" is what Frannie tells Malloy in the lovemaking scene prior to Frannie's confrontation with the killer.

17. As Lacan put it: "The world, the world of being, full of knowledge, is but a dream, a dream of the body insofar as it speaks, for there's no such thing as a knowing subject." Jacques Lacan, *The Seminar of Jacques Lacan, Book XX: On Feminine Sexuality: The Limits of Love and Knowledge* (New York: W. W. Norton, 1998), 126.

5

Love, Loss, Endings, and Beginnings

A Psychoanalysis of *Rust and Bone*

Juan Pablo Lucchelli

Rust and Bone (directed by Jacques Audiard and released in 2012) offers a compelling demonstration of how love emerges out of traumatic loss. Briefly, the film's narrative follows the relationship between Ali (Matthias Schoenaerts), an unemployed drifter and father of a young son, Sam (Armand Ardure), and Stephanie (Marian Cotillard), a trainer of killer whales who suffers a traumatic injury that results in the amputation of both of her legs. This literal amputation is mirrored throughout the film both by the psychoanalytical "cut" of Ali's gaze and also by the way Stephanie's identity is caught up in her own image as an object of desire. What the couple achieves by the end of the film is a love relationship (made possible through traumatic loss and the reversal of their subjectivities) that goes beyond "imaginary castration" to realize itself as a special form of lack in the unconscious.

Before proceeding with an analysis of the film, I begin with a discussion of the relation between love and psychoanalysis, for it bears on the development of the love relation depicted in *Rust and Bone*. Psychoanalysis can say something about love because of a very strong historical link between the two. Indeed, psychoanalysis would not have come into being without love, and, more precisely, psychoanalysis would not exist without love as a model for the phenomenon of subjective change. To put it another way, there can be subjective changes, such as those that occur in psychoanalysis, because there is love. Love is a standard of all subjective change worthy of the name.

Love was the first obstacle that Freud encountered in his therapy, and what he discovered in the analytic session became famous in the history of psychoanalysis when he first encountered the love phenomenon through transference. In the case of a young female patient Freud followed what he calls the "fundamental rule," that is to say, "free association."[1] Freud took an interest in her case because, during one of her sessions, she expressed her desire to kiss him. After revealing this to Freud, she was afraid and went through a sleepless night, and during her next session she could not free associate. It appears that love itself had become an obstacle to analysis. The patient ended up telling Freud how she felt, and the obstacle vanished. But the main reason the therapy could continue was because she made a link with another similar episode she went through earlier in her life, when she felt an identical desire to kiss another man—a forbidden man. It seemed that this patient had a pattern of falling in love with forbidden men. Through her analysis with Freud she was able to realize that she had a pattern of denying herself to all men.

Now what does this memorable case study of Freud's tell us? First, that we love the person whom we think holds a special knowledge about us, knowledge we ourselves do not have access to. One thinks this other person can save us. That this other person knows what we're missing. Second, it also tells us that love requires three people (behind the woman's love for Freud we see that she also loved another man). And third, this anecdote about transference reveals what we can call the Freudian vision of love. Love is about repeating. This is the official (non-Lacanian) version of love. In love there is a repetition, which is why the patient always fell in love with forbidden men. Even Oedipus can be interpreted this way. If you love your boyfriend, well, in fact you love your father or your brother, and you're only repeating this love. According to this perspective, if all one does in an analysis is to repeat, then there's no need for an analysis—as you'll only be repeating past stories. What's even worse, analysis demands that we pay for this repetition. There is something going on in transference that is crucial to reset love on a different trajectory from endless repetition.

Lacan sees love quite differently: he thinks love brings the new (*du nouveau*). For example, even if the love for Freud reminds us of our love for the other man, Freud is not this other man. The central question becomes: What is not a repetition in what is being repeated? That is to say: What is the difference between the two versions of love—the initial love and its repetition? The answer lies in realizing that we can give a completely different meaning to the patient's love of Freud. She undergoes analysis with Freud and transference love is what releases her from her state of depression.

Jacques Lacan's outrageous discovery about psychoanalysis is not what it says about sex but rather what it says about the paradoxical relation between a subject and the object of its desire—that is to say, the existing and paradoxical relation between desire and the object of desire. This relation between object and desire can only be biased and paradoxical, sometimes reversed, and always veiled. The object of desire is, by definition, wrong. There is a gap between the desire and the object of this desire. What Lacan says here, just like Freud, is that there is no object relation simply because there is no direct relation to the object, and further, that desire can only be alienated from the symbolic order—so also it is alienated from the unconscious. What you desire is not "caused" by the object itself.[2]

There is evidently something of the falseness of desire in love. The similarity between love and desire is that we never love the object (the person) because of the object itself. That is, we do not love an object because of its essential attributes. We can desire a woman because of her physical features, for example, because she is a blonde or brunette, and a number of people would fit this category. In this case, the love objects would all be equals; they could all be exchanged with one another, and we have here a good description of the "traditionally typical" socio-symbolic references to male sexual desire. There must be something other than the fantasy of an object (a blond, a brunette) involved in the love relation. So, we may ask: What happens when we love—when the person we love is not exchangeable with someone else? At this point love is different from desire. For example, a man can love and idealize a woman, and for that very reason he can suffer from sexual impotence or even overlook the fact that she's the object of his desire. Freud used to say that the beloved would crush the lover. A woman could be so idealized by a man that sexual desire would be overshadowed.[3] This is what we see occurring in *Rust and Bone*. The film displays a form of asymmetry, an antagonism between man and woman, between Ali and Stephanie. Ali fucks before loving, whereas Stephanie loves before having sex. Love is finally a feminine symptom—Lacan says: "When somebody loves, he is woman" ("lorsqu'on aime, on est femme").[4]

Referring back to psychoanalysis, Lacan uses Plato's dialogue in the *Symposium* as an example of what happens during transference.[5] But the point is not to interpret Plato's *Symposium* through psychoanalysis, which would be "applied psychoanalysis." On the contrary, we're using this dialogue to try and understand what happens in psychoanalysis. (I could say the same of the film *Rust and Bone*. I am not analyzing the film through psychoanalysis but rather trying to understand analysis through art.) Lacan explains psychoanalysis through Plato, and by using this reference he reveals how insights in the latter can be applied to insights in the former. This, along with the experience of being in analysis, is how one can grasp something. The same can be said about cinema. We can have a better understanding of a human being's relation to desire by reference to a film, which can illustrate something deeper about what takes place in a clinical case of psychoanalysis.

In the aforementioned dialogue by Plato, love is praised and extolled. There are several characters and they all praise love in their own way. In particular, there are two types of characters: the lover and the beloved. The beloved is the other's center of interest. He is usually young and beautiful, with feminine features, while the lover is generally older, not necessarily handsome, and can even be ugly. The lover is the one who's missing some-thing, something he hopes to find in the beloved. This is the very reason why the lover desires the beloved. In this dialogue Plato describes precisely what Lacan calls the "metaphor of love," namely, the fact that the beloved becomes a "lover," one who loves another and therefore expresses his want for something. The love metaphor includes this subjective change, where the young and beautiful beloved becomes a lover, displaying his want for something, as if he were nothing without the one he loves.

Socrates is the prototype of the lover—a poor and ugly old man. Alcibiades is the prototype of the beloved—a wealthy, handsome young man. In this dialogue Alcibiades recounts his attempt to seduce Socrates and that Socrates turned him down. This led to a reversal: Alcibiades, the wealthy and handsome young beloved, now desires the old and ugly Socrates, showing that he's missing something. The most important thing in this dia-logue is Socrates's rejection. The ugly old geezer rejects the young pretty boy. Alcibiades can't quite believe what just happened and begs Socrates to love him back, thereby shifting from beloved to lover. In an irony of fate, the old and ugly Socrates becomes the beloved, the desired, cherished one. Alcibiades here discovers what it's like to be rejected: he experiences "sub-jective change." According to Lacan, this is exactly what happens during analysis. Experiencing subjective change is essential to any therapy worthy of the name.

We can all agree that *Rust and Bone* is about love, and it is a film about love in its fiercest definition. We're not saying it's about Love with a capital "L," but rather it's about love with a lowercase "l," as an homage to Lacan's "object petit a" ("amour" with a lowercase "a"). One of the most important aspects of this film is how it deals with role reversal, changes in subjective stands in a similar way to what happens in the aforementioned relationship between Socrates and Alcibiades. When I refer to "role reversals" I mean that after such a change nothing can be the same for the subject. Subjective change takes root after a loss—whether subjective, objective, or both. The characters experience losses that can be compared to a loss that one feels during therapy, except that these actual losses are a lot more blunt and extreme. Stephanie does not go into therapy but loses her legs in an accident; Ali does not go into therapy but at the end of the film almost loses his young son.

At the beginning of the film, Ali, a poor homeless fellow, wanders around Belgium with his five-year-old son Sam. There is no mother in the picture, and Ali himself is more an absentee mother than a father. When I call him a mother, I mean that he finds it difficult to be a father to his son. Ali decides to leave Belgium and live with his sister Anna (Corinne Masiero) in Antibes, France. He is strong and a fighter—we could even say that fighting defines him—and he finds a job as a bouncer. One night, a fight breaks out at the club where he's working. That's when he meets Stephanie. She has just been assaulted by a man and her face is bleeding. Ali takes Stephanie home. Nothing much passes between them at first, but he checks out her legs. This first *gaze* is highlighted here because it is very important in the film. He looks at her legs up to the knees—that is, up to where her legs will be amputated after the accident. It is the director's way of emphasizing that deep down, it all happened there, as if everything had been decided there, with this first encounter where the cut of the gaze is dominated by the "instant of seeing."

When Freud wrote about the concept of the object of the drive in his *Three Essays on the Theory of Sexuality*, his main idea was that drive objects are partial objects. What he meant was that these objects are not whole, they are not "total objects." The idea is: a single person is not enough to generate desire. Some of his/her features or traits (skin color, social status, voice, etc.) tickle and stir the subject's desire—it is a very specific characteristic that brings unconscious pleasure. Conventionally, Freud saw the object as either "oral" or "anal," and Lacan added two other objects, both of which are a lot more subtle: the gaze and the voice.[6] I cannot go into detail on these matters here, but you will notice that the gaze is omnipresent. In *Rust and Bone*, it defines especially Ali's modus operandi with women. Throughout the film, the director focuses at least on three moments when the gaze is linked to some form of mutilation for Stephanie, but looking becomes here a way to deny this mutilation. In this sense, the "cut" is at the center of the film, and the gaze appears after the cutting has happened. The first gaze appears when Ali and Stephanie are in the car at the beginning of the film. He looks at Stephanie's thighs, down to the knees, down to what he can see of her knees before they plunge into darkness. And he will still be able to do that after the accident, because her legs will be cut off "above the knees." The second appearance of the gaze occurs on the beach. Stephanie has already been mutilated and Ali is watching her breasts. And the third (and most important) gaze occurs as follows: during a brutal fight, for which Ali is being paid, Ali is on the ground, almost defeated, his thinking is fuzzy because he's been roughed up. He catches a glimpse of Stephanie's prosthetic legs amid the legs of the men in the audience. That glimpse gives him the strength to defeat his opponent.

What really matters here? First, looking helps Ali not to "see" Stephanie's mutilations. In the car he looks at her thighs and cannot see her bleeding face; on the beach he looks at her breasts and cannot see the mutilated legs; and when he is on the ground, he reverses this mutilation, making Stephanie's prosthetic legs his own crutch to muster enough strength to defeat his opponent. In short, in Ali's eyes, Stephanie has never been mutilated. He denies her mutilation, and that may be the reason why she falls in love with him. He allows her to live as if she weren't mutilated. His desire for Stephanie takes the form of looking as well. When they're in the car, he furtively watches Stephanie's legs. He can only look up to a point, to the same point where she will later be amputated. In a way, he's already amputating her just by looking at her, and that shows that Stephanie as a "total object" is not enough. She must above all be a "partial object," *objet du regard*, the object of the gaze. Lacan's famous saying could not be more fitting: "I love you, but, because inexplicably I love in you something more than you—the *objet petit a*—I mutilate you."[7] For Ali, the gaze is a correlate of desire: even at the gym when he's watching women exercising, he needs to look. In a way, the more he looks, the less he speaks.

But with Stephanie it is quite different: looking does not lead to sex but rather to speaking, to one of the few times Ali voices something important out loud. Instead of sleeping with her and because she holds a particular status for him, he's idealized her. She does not give herself away easily, so instead of sleeping with her, he talks to her. From the very beginning, this woman stands out from his usual sexual partners. At the beginning of the film, Ali asks Stephanie an essential question when they are in the car, a question that Stephanie cannot quite answer. Ali is so blunt that by comparing her to a prostitute, he cuts the conversation short, or rather he cuts Stephanie short of coming up with an answer because she is shocked and offended, and on the defensive. *Even if Ali's question sounds trivial, commonplace, it is nonetheless essential.* He asks: "Are you coming to the club to meet a guy?" Stephanie smiles sarcastically, which should be understood not as "I don't need to come here to find a guy" but rather as "I couldn't care less about men." Incidentally, she does live with a man, about whom she couldn't care less indeed. And then Ali asks the crucial question: "Why do you dress like that to come here?" She responds, "Like what?" He clarifies, "Like a whore." He asks the question: What does she get out of coming to this club, dressed like that? What does she want? And *que me veux-tu?* Stephanie has nothing to answer, which reveals that indeed it was an essential question.

We know for sure that this is an essential question because Stephanie will get back to it much later, after the accident, after she's been amputated. She's interested in Ali, she loves him, and she grills him about his relations with women. Ali doesn't say much but throws the ball back to her: "And you, with men?" So Ali, who has then nothing to lose, is clever enough to get back to the question that first came up in the car that first night. And now, a few months later Stephanie does have an answer to Ali's question. She says that the only thing she "loved" when she still had legs was "to be looked at, arousing men." Full stop. She's not after men. She simply wants to be looked at and not physically touched. When someone touches her or sleeps with her, the very thing that causes desire becomes instantly crushed and annihilated.

For her, being a woman is being perceived as such: being a woman is playing along with this "masquerade." In her daily life, not in a clubbing context, she does not wear very feminine clothes. She's in charge of animals, of beings she's trying to tame, of beings who do not speak and do not ask questions. As you know, she will later tame another animal: Ali. She will tame Ali to better train him, to make him a better fighter. (And by the way, the words "Ali" and "animal" sound quite similar.) Stephanie has to be beautiful for the amputation to happen. The prettier she is, the greater the impact of the mutilation. There has to be an important contrast here. Most importantly, this woman is an exception: she seems very common (and she is, in a way), but in an environment where she's like a fish in the sea, she stands out. And the more she stands out, the more comfortable she is. She's reliving some of her clubbing nights out, from her premutilation days. She stands out in Ali's family, and she stands out among the beasts (those men who fight to death). You will notice that in the fight scene where she fills in for Martial (Bouli Lanners), at Ali's fight, the male onlookers gaze at her puzzled: because she's a woman, because she walks on prosthetic legs. This scene is not a reminder of when she used to go to the club, yet she still has a provocative attitude. She arouses men but cannot tame them. She trains killer whales to compensate for not domesticating the men she arouses in nightclubs. Stephanie and killer whales really get along and she's leading the dance.

Stephanie is a different woman because, in a way, she "plays the man"; she does not simply "give herself to men." She plays the man and practices domesticating them, because for her, as I have said before, men can be compared to animals, to untamable animals, unlike killer whales. In the critical scene where she and Ali have sex for the first time after her amputation, she feels so alive that she goes out on the balcony and reenacts her killer whale training moves. It means that by sleeping with Ali, she's tamed her new killer whale, her new pet: Ali. Things go back to their own place; she's in charge again.

The title of this film could have been: *Animals Do Not Love*. Animals are very important in the film, and they mostly illustrate man's animal side, especially when men are speechless, when they do not speak or do not wish to speak. It's important to be clear about what I mean by "speak" here. I'm not saying they do not utter words. I mean, rather, that they're unable to listen to themselves, to question themselves or to change their modus operandi. Speaking, here, means being able to change your "subjective position." Speaking, here, means not being a whale. Ali can't hold a conversation for longer than three minutes; he utters sounds and one-syllable words, and this is something human beings and animals have in common. The fighters are compared to beasts, and the main character (Ali) fucks women like a dog. On the other hand, he reacts very violently, yet also acts in a civilized way when he reclaims his son from the dogs. This is one of the few occasions where he's trying to act like a father. However, by taking his son away from the dogs, he also ends up treating him like one.

There's a lot to say about Ali's attitude as a father. He does not talk (much) to his son, and we do not know much about his own father. We do know that Ali used to have a "master," someone who passed away (and nothing is said about the reason of his death) but who made him passionate about fighting. Even this relationship, this "lineage," is very tenuous. When the man dies, Ali stops fighting (stops practicing martial arts): there is no "passing on" (no transmission). This passing on remains unfulfilled; it is merely a delicate bond that only existed while the "master" was alive. It was only a form of lineage as long as the master was alive and things were fine, but when he passes away, everything collapses. The lineage relationship is the same with his son. Stephanie smooths things over between Ali and Sam, but only because once she's been amputated she's the one he carries on his shoulder instead of his son. This separation is necessary. I do not think one has to be Lacanian to notice that Stephanie now fills in the gap left by his former master. So, in a way, Stephanie becomes Ali's father. She becomes someone who helps him steer his life, settles him down in a job, and reinstates him as a father to his son.

The trajectory of Ali and Stephanie's relationship can be summed up with the following observations. First, in both cases there's a subjective change after a loss. Next, in both cases, after the subjective reversal, Ali and Stephanie can begin to form a love relationship. Prior to meeting Stephanie, Ali had no woman to love, and Stephanie (prior to meeting Ali) did not love Simon, the man she used to live with. Also, in both cases there's a sort of irreversible bodily harm. A mutilation in Stephanie's case, and for Ali, his fists hurt whenever he fights, a wound that is compounded when at the end of the film he pounds through the thick ice to save his son. Most importantly, Ali manages to become tender with his son and even earns his son's admiration. Finally, Stephanie meets a man and begins to relate to him with love after she was only dealing with animals, and with men as animals, or "animal-men." Lacan's formula "there is no such thing as a sexual relationship" means that there is no obvious relation between men and women, unlike for animals. At the end of the film, Ali's desire can no longer arise just from looking. When he says "I love you" to Stephanie, they are on the phone; only her voice can be heard and he cannot see her. Through Stephanie Ali finds another way to desire, another way than by just "looking"; he learns to love through speaking and getting to know her.

What we learn from psychoanalysis and through this film analysis is that love is born after loss, and loss is very present in *Rust and Bone*. In this sense, loss appears as a prototype of the cut, constantly present and referred to the partner. In Ali's case, the possibility of the real loss of his son puts is evidence of his love for Stephanie. In a similar way, the film *Hitchcock* (directed by Sacha Gervasi, 2012) also turns around the connection of the possibility of loss and love. The central scene of the film occurs when Janet Leigh (Scarlett Johansson) is in the shower and reveals perfectly an imaginary object in place of what is really significant, which is the true threat for the subject, the loss of Hitchcock's wife. The last image that Hitchcock (Anthony Hopkins) "sees" is his wife with another man in the shower. He can attack others with a knife, but he can't move beyond his wife's image. Behind the nudity of the beautiful Janet Leigh there is his wife, and the film revolves around this woman and his possible loss of her. After this scene, we hear the director shout "Cut! It's good!," and in a way, the film could finish with these words. *Hitchcock*'s shower scene tells us the truth about *Rust and Bone*: the key is that more important than "imaginary castration" (in the case of Stephanie's mutilation) is the possibility of losing love as a privileged form of lack in the subject, a lack that Freud calls "unconscious."

Notes

1. Sigmund Freud, *Studies on Hysteria* (New York: Basic Books, 2000), 303.

2. Jacques Lacan, *Le séminaire livre VIII, Le Transfert* (Paris: Seuil, 2001).

3. Sigmund Freud, *Group Psychology and the Analysis of the Ego*, trans. and ed. James Strachey (New York: W.W. Norton, 1959).

4. Jacques Lacan, "Séminaire Le Moment de conclure," *Revue Ornicar* 19 (1977): 9. I mentioned that the object of love is wrong, but I should rather have said: Love is unconscious. Lacan once suggested that it is not good for a psychoanalyst to be too beautiful (which is, no doubt, why I personally chose this very profession). But what did Lacan mean by this? If, for example, the analyst looks like Brad Pitt and a young patient falls in love with him, then we might say: "Its' totally normal—he looks like Brad Pitt after all!" But in the same situation, with a less "standardly attractive" psychoanalyst, the patient's love would be revealed as unconscious.

5. Lacan, *Le séminaire livre VIII, Le Transfert*.

6. For more on the gaze in cinema, see Todd McGowan, *The Real Gaze: Film Theory after Lacan* (Albany: State University of New York Press, 2007).

7. Jacques Lacan, *The Four Fundamental Concepts of Psychoanalysis*, trans. Alan Sheridan (New York: Norton, 1978), 268.

6

Cinematic Ends

The Ties That Unbind in Claire Denis's *White Material*

JENNIFER FRIEDLANDER

The narrative of Claire Denis's 2009 film *White Material* is propelled by desperate attempts on the part of Maria Vial (Isabelle Huppert), a white coffee-plantation manager in an unnamed African country, to return to the plantation amid rapidly escalating antigovernment violence. The forward-moving narrative of her journey home (and whether one should call it home presents one of the key themes of the film) is interspersed with fragmented scenes depicting the events that both inform and complicate our understanding of her journey and her tenacious commitment to life in Africa. The film is bookended by two deaths: the opening scene depicts the rebel leader, known as the Boxer (Issach De Bankolé) lying dead in Maria's house, and the film shockingly concludes with Maria delivering a series of machete blows to the back of the neck of her ex-father-in-law, Henri (Michel Subor)—the owner of the coffee plantation.

I argue that the film's disturbing conclusion serves two apparently contradictory functions: on the one hand, it performs a traumatic rupture that destabilizes the coordinates through which the film's narrative had, up until this point, been understood; on the other hand, the same scene resolves the central crisis Maria faces throughout the film. Maria, we quickly discover, faces a twofold problem of interpellation. She is unable to escape interpellation as a "filthy white," and she is unsuccessful in interpellating others to occupy expected positions within the social order. Through the seemingly irrational act of murdering Henri, we may consider how Maria is able to occupy the place of the rebel and radically renounce the position of "filthy white" to which she has been assigned. And at the same time, by reducing Henri from a familial relation to his impersonal structural position as a white landowner/colonizer, Maria ultimately comes to inhabit, rather than struggle against, the failure of the familial/social bond to secure identity.

Through this analysis I hope to raise a broader theoretical question regarding the concept of the Lacanian Act. Might there be a place within the vicissitudes of the act for an act that neither falls within the range of "false" acts, such as the psychotic "passage l'acte," and the hysteric "acting out," nor fully meets the high standard of the "authentic," ethical act? I consider the political and psychoanalytic implications of an act that functions neither as a plea for reinstalling symbolic authority nor as a total rejection of symbolic existence but rather as a potentially transformative engagement aimed at identifying with the very point at which the symbolic threatens to give way to the Real. I thus conclude by raising the possibility that a politics of the Real might be most effective when, rather than seek the total dissolution of the symbolic, it aims at harnessing the Real in the act of haunting and taunting the symbolic.

Failures of Interpellation

Maria's struggle to reject interpellation as a "filthy white" is introduced very early in the film. Rescue helicopters sent by the French government fly low above Maria's head as she walks in a deserted field. A voice from a helicopter above can be heard calling "Madame Vial," imploring her to leave the country now that the French government is pulling out. She not only refuses to heed its call, but she also expresses contempt for the very position it seeks to activate. She kicks their dropped survival kits that litter the field, scornfully muttering to herself: "Those dirty whites . . . don't deserve this beautiful land." In parroting the insult, which is often painfully lobbed at her by black Africans, this scene marks an early instance of Maria's burgeoning attempt to consolidate an identification with the black Africans in opposition to the white colonizers.

Early on, too, we witness Maria's failure to interpellate others. For example, when attempting to cross a road that is blocked by an armed rebel group demanding money for passage, Maria initially refuses to be intimidated. Her passionate identification with the country precludes her from taking their threats seriously; they cannot be meant for her, since she sees herself as one of them. When the rebels become increasingly menacing, her interpellative efforts become more direct. She calmly reminds the man who is pointing a gun at her: "I know you; you are my son's gym teacher." But such symbolic ties no longer bind in this time of crisis. He refuses to recognize her: "I don't know who you are," he retorts, as he threatens to shoot her if she does not pay. She replies that she knows all of the men and proceeds to name each of the men surrounding her truck. After she hands over the money, one of the soldiers chides: "People like you make this country filthy."

Later, as tensions escalate and the power is cut off to the plantation, Maria insists that she will have no trouble procuring gasoline because her family has been "rooted here for ages" and "know[s] everyone here." But "knowing" people is no help, and the assumption that it is only makes matters worse for Maria. Here we see that Maria's symbolic bind is exacerbated by the imbrication of her two interpellative difficulties: her very presumption that she is able to mobilize social ties functions as a form of white privilege that entrenches her more deeply as a "filthy white." The more desperately she clings to the expectation that she can activate the social pact, the more firmly entrenched her status as a "filthy white" becomes.

In this sense, one way to interpret the film's ending is to see it as a moment in which the symbolic impasse in which Maria is trapped—her inability to both evade its designations and activate its authority—comes to a head: it seems that the only way that Maria can radically renounce the impossible position to which she has been assigned (filthy white) is to give up the expectation that others will respond to *her* subjectivizing call. Maria comes to recognize that she cannot have it both ways: that is, she cannot call upon the symbolic to do its job of disciplining the social order without having it assign her to the place of the colonizer/"filthy white." Or, to put it inversely, life without the fiction of the big Other's efficacy is untenable, because even though it frees her from the dubious position of "filthy white," it also releases others from acting in accordance with their social position.

In the shocking final scene, Maria finally arrives back at the plantation only to find her house the scene of a brutal massacre. She unexpectedly joins in the melee by picking up a machete and striking Henri repeatedly on the back of the neck. This horrific and seemingly unmotivated irruption of violence on Maria's part paradoxically resolves the symbolic impasse from which she suffered. To be specific, in killing Henri, Maria consolidates her identification with the rebels and sheds her unbearable designation as a "filthy white." Thus, she both transcends her symbolically assigned role and displaces Henri from his familial position to a merely structural role as white colonizer. But—and here is the wrinkle—by killing Henri, Maria sacrifices the very thing responsible for nourishing her life.

Coffee, Flee, or Me?

Maria's destructive final act shares many features with the Lacanian ethical act. She risks "subjective destitution" in order to accomplish what is "impossible" from within her symbolic constellation. She sacrifices the very thing for which she has sacrificed everything else, in order to break free of a symbolic deadlock. Throughout the film, her dogged attachment to the coffee puzzles those around her; they see it as a misguided attachment at best, or a suicidal obsession at worst. Her ex-husband foolishly uses the symbolic resource of reason to try to convince her to leave; he reminds her that the plantation does not even make a profit. He demeans her sacred object in cautioning that "there is no use getting massacred over some coffee." When her workers also begin to flee to avoid the encroaching danger, she implores them to stay just a few more weeks in order to see the crops through the next stage. One worker similarly retorts: "Coffee's coffee—not worth dying for." But, for Maria, coffee is not just coffee and no appeal to reason will diminish its status; for Maria coffee is precisely the thing worth dying for. Coffee, in this sense, functions as the *objet a*—the object cause of her desire. It functions both as a lack that propels her desire and as a cover for the lack it triggers. The *objet a* plays a vital role in sustaining the subject's constancy through mediating and structuring a relation to the *jouissance* of the Real. In plugging up the gateway to the Real that threatens to engulf the subject, the *objet a* cannot be casually assailed. A subject will protect the integrity of the *objet a*, even in the name of seemingly more critical needs—sometimes even survival.

Thus, it seems, Maria's final act of murdering the very person through whom her connection to the coffee plantation is sustained seems to follow exactly the logic of the Lacanian Act: the sacrifice of that for which she has sacrificed everything. An alternative interpretation might be made that sees Maria's act as a desperate cry for social assimilation—a dire attempt to belong within the symbolic order with which she passionately identifies rather than a radical rejection of that symbolic order. I contend, however, that neither of these interpretations is quite right. I suggest, rather, that we see Maria's final act as an identification with the radical exception upon which the symbolic is erected. Maria no longer seeks merely to fill the lack, but rather she comes to inhabit it. In particular, Maria comes eventually to abandon the fantasy of the big Other's power and instead inhabits the recognition that the big Other is nothing more than a mere semblant—"something whose function is to mask nothingness."[1] She comes to choose the terrifying freedom of accepting and identifying with the Other's impotence rather than remain in an increasingly untenable symbolic deadlock secured by a belief in the Other's authority.

How does she do this? In murdering Henri, Maria radically renounces the unbearable identity of a "filthy white" through the adoption of a new symbolic identity—"rebel." At first blush, the swapping of one symbolic designation for another would seem to indicate that her act occurs squarely within the realm of the symbolic order. But the identity of "rebel" itself functions as the point of *exception* within the social order. In identifying with this point of symbolic exclusion, Maria unsettles the given symbolic arrangement. To be specific, in seeking to occupy the position of exception around which the social order coheres, she reveals that symbolic closure is accomplished only from the point of its own lack. The rebel—instantiated, par excellence, in the figure of the Boxer—is, like Maria, a figure who will risk his life for the land but who, at the same time, is one who does not belong. The instability and vulnerability inherent in the category of rebel is accentuated in the film by the depiction of child rebel soldiers, who carry guns and machetes but stop to take breaks to gobble candy and snuggle up with stuffed animals to sleep. This structural connection between Maria and the Boxer is presaged earlier in the film through a pithy exchange. As the Boxer lies dying in her house and Maria attempts to treat his wounds, he cautions her: "It's not safe here for someone like you." Taking stock of the dire state of his condition, Maria retorts, "Nor for someone like you."

The Act and the Other

As indicated earlier, in several crucial respects Maria's act appears to take on the qualities of a Lacanian "ethical Act" that sacrifices the object for which everything is sacrificed—an act that derives its ethical status in part through rupturing the existing symbolic structure without any guarantee of what comes next. In the context of applying this formulation to *White Material*, we must consider that Maria struggles with a socio-symbolic bond that has already disintegrated, with one cruel exception: its insistence in stamping her as a colonial oppressor. Maria, thus, suffers both from the crushing weight of symbolic authority and from a growing awareness of the capriciousness and indifference of the big Other. Within this context, her act cannot be read straightforwardly as a plea to the big Other to confirm her place—a mere "acting out" within the symbolic register. Rather, her act can be better understood as an act that emphasizes the big Other's impotence. In this sense, Maria confirms the big Other: not by falling for its ruse as symbolic authority but rather through acting in accordance with the recognition that the big Other is merely a semblant. She recapitulates the disregard that the big Other displays toward the very social bonds that it appears to forge.

We are not quite ready, however, to adjudicate the question of whether Maria's violent act qualifies as an authentic act in the Lacanian sense or whether it merely exemplifies a "false act"—what Mari Ruti describes as an "action that may share some of the outward qualities of the ethical act but that lacks its dignity."[2] We can explore the matter further by comparing Maria's transition with the symbolic disintegration of her teenage son, Manuel (Nicolas Duvauchelle). When we are first introduced to him, Manuel appears as a withdrawn and lethargic but seemingly benign teenager. Yet, after becoming the victim of an assault by a group of rebels, he rapidly descends into a chaotically vicious figure, whose meaningless acts of terror straddle between identification with the rebel soldiers and the ruling militia. For Maria, he functions as an embodiment of the impossibility of her desire to belong in Africa. Maria laments Manuel's perpetual nonbelonging: he "was born here. . . . It's his home, but it doesn't like him much." By showing that her son, a native to the country, cannot step beyond the role of outsider, the futility of Maria's efforts to transcend her "whiteness" is rendered increasingly stark.

Manuel performs a false act—"the very opposite" of an "act proper" according to Slavoj Žižek.[3] By embodying an eclectic array of contradictory signifiers associated with authoritarian masculinity, Manuel desperately attempts to uphold the fiction of the big Other at all costs. A key distinction between Maria and Manuel thus emerges through their different relationships to the symbolic: Manual takes up the trappings of a complex profusion of identities within the symbolic order; Maria, by contrast, comes to inhabit an identity produced outside the limits of the symbolic—a position marked by the symbolic's ceaseless haunting by the Real.

Don't Give Up (on Compromise?)

As is well known, a Lacanian Act employs an ethics that requires that the subject refuses to give up on his or her desire. But in the diegetic world of *White Material*, "not giving up" is not a viable modality. This position is most explicitly impugned in a scene that shows a group of wounded and dead (child) soldiers lying in front of a church whose rooftop banner reads: "God does not give up." Perhaps, too, the famous Lacanian dictum of "not giving up" on one's desire is not unequivocal within the Lacanian system either. In the last instance, the act appears to require a special kind of "giving up" on the part of the subject—the sacrifice of the very thing one treasures the most and thus the destruction of one's established psychosocial coordinates.

In making this sacrifice without any guarantee regarding the outcome, Maria gives up that which secures her safe relation to the Real. Her demand for change results in her own "symbolic destitution." We may see this as a radical traversal of the fantasy that structures the subject's relation to the Real. But, as Todd McGowan cautions, self-sacrifice is not necessarily an emancipatory act. "Self-sacrifice," McGowan stresses, "functions ideologically when it is tied to the promise of a recovered wholeness for the subject. . . . An emancipatory self-sacrifice, in contrast, works to shatter the image of wholeness."[4] By identifying with the point of exception around which the symbolic register creates its appearance of unity, Maria embraces the very lack that punctures this illusion of wholeness.

In this context, let us look more closely at what precisely it is that, in Lacan's terms, one must refuse to compromise in refusing to cede on one's desire. Mari Ruti compellingly suggests that one interpretation of this Lacanian injunction is that one must necessarily give up desire qua desire of the Other, in favor of one's "own, "true" desire. In this view, the subject must commit to pursuing its own idiosyncratic, singular—"true"—desire, which is suppressed by "meekly accepting the desire of the Other as its own."[5] Such an engagement with the truth of one's desire requires that the subject traverses the fantasmatic framework within which desire is structured. In other words, one must sacrifice the contingent object (in its role as a regulator of *jouissance* within the modality of desire) in favor of the constitutive cause (the inaugural lack around which the drive circles). The subject, in this sense, must abandon the fantasy that attaining the object will (ful)fill the subject and instead identify with the position of *objet a* as cause—as the fundamental lack that ignites the structure of desire.

But the idea of refusing to compromise one's desire must be interrogated further, specifically within the context of the psychic function performed by the mechanism of desire. As Jason Glynos emphasizes, desire operates through the very logic of compromise. He calls upon Žižek's insight that "*desire as such is already a* compromise, a defense against going beyond a certain limit in *jouissance*."[6] In this formulation, desire must be appreciated as a compromise-formation, distracting the subject with the illusion that symbolic and psychic wholeness is attainable, if only the (retrospectively) lost object can be found (all the while masking the truth that there is no object that could ever truly satisfy the subject). The metonymic slippage attendant to desire further conceals the fact that even if the subject were actually to encounter the *jouissance* of the Real that these substitute objects conspire to mask, the subject would find the encounter unbearable. The telos of desire, thus, is not satisfaction but rather the perpetuation of dissatisfaction, which, in turn, propagates more desire. It might appear then that one *must* precisely compromise one's desire, in order to break out of its endless metonymy and thereby bring the subject closer to an engagement with the Real.

Ruti helps us to see how, although desire itself is a compromise-formation aimed at defending against the Real, the very refusal to compromise on desire may nevertheless lead the subject to a closer engagement with the Real. Desire and drive present two different modalities for relating to the same object. As Ruti explains, both desire and drive fix on the same Thing, but "if it is true . . . that what sets the drive apart from desire is its closer proximity to the Thing, then the subject who pursues its desire to the outmost limit by necessity catches up with the drive."[7] In pursuing the object, the subject of desire seeks impossible wholeness, whereas the subject of the drive relishes the pleasure of repeatedly failing to attain its goal. In this sense, refusing to compromise one's desire can be read as a refusal to accept the element of compromise inherent in desire and thus to relate to the object through the unrelenting, single-minded logic of the drive. For Glynos and Alenka Zupančič, a Lacanian ethics must, therefore, take place at the level of the drive rather than desire. To traverse the fantasy that structures one's desire is to emerge on the side of the drive, within which one relates to the *objet a* stripped of its promise to satisfy. The traversal of the fantasy entails the stripping of the *objet a* of its symbolic status as symptom—as a message redolent with significance for the Other to decipher—and relating to it instead as sinthome—a meaningless fragment of the Real.

"Nothing's mine, but I'm in charge"

Žižek's discussion of the Lacanian ethical act pushes it in the direction of violence. But against this emphasis, Jacques-Alain Miller, in reference to Lacan's discussion of Medea's act, cautions that although Medea functions as a structural "model," for the Act, "the example is somewhat extreme and not one with which to identify."[8] This question of whether violence and destruction are necessary in achieving symbolic transformation warrants further discussion.

Ruti eloquently challenges the celebration of violence as a necessary feature of the "Act." She explicitly takes aim at "critics such as Žižek and Lee Edelman [who] valorize the act of subjective destitution—the subject's suicidal plunge into the unmediated Jouissance of the real—as a liberatory act that, finally, grants the subject some 'real' satisfaction."[9] In place of this view, Ruti contends that "one does not always need to exit the symbolic in a grand gesture of symbolic destitution . . . in order to activate the subversive potential of the real. . . . One merely needs to mobilize the 'overabundance' of the signifier."[10] In this way, Ruti also challenges the idea that symbolic identifications only work to maintain the power of the big Other. The symbolic, she maintains, harnesses the potential for exploiting its own inherent instability. The Real, for Lacan, "renders the symbolic unreliable."[11] Lacan, she emphasizes, "proposes that each of us has some leeway in organizing the signifiers of the big Other. . . . That is, we assert our singularity not only by exchanging the symbolic for the real, but also by bringing the real into the symbolic."[12]

How might we reassess *White Material* in the light of these remarks? I suggest that the film points to an alternative, "socially viable" path to "transformative politics" of the sort that Ruti privileges in opposition to Žižek.[13] We are primed for this reading by a redolent scene in which Maria drives some local men to the plantation to begin work after her regular crew flees to safety. One of the men asks Maria if she is "the boss" of the plantation, and with a barely concealed, self-satisfied smile, Maria replies: "Nothing's mine, but I'm in charge." The rare expression of pleasure that betrays Maria's austerity marks this moment as diegetically significant. Perhaps what Maria unwittingly exudes is the recognition that the instability of the Other can also be used to advantage—that one "can evade ideological interpellation not only by 'assuming' the nonexistence of the big Other through . . . [acts] of subjective destitution . . . but also . . . by playing with the inconsistency of the Other."[14] The very impotence of the Other—the symbolic's ineffectiveness at keeping the Real totally at bay—can prove a powerful and perhaps under-tapped resource for transformative politics.

Maria can be seen as pursuing this path of using the generative/creative power of the signifier to undermine given social designations through her attempt at adopting the impossible symbolic identity of rebel. This identity is impossible not only in the sense that it is off-limits to Maria, who is bound to the antagonistic position of a "filthy white," but also in the sense that the position itself is symbolically impossible. As we see in the film, "the rebel" is a point of symbolic exclusion—a category that precariously binds social relations by functioning as the social exception upon which the totality hangs together. Through an identification with this excessive but structurally necessary element—"Rebel"—Maria disturbs the illusion of symbolic cohesion. But in the final violent scene, she fails to follow through on this ethical possibility and instead takes the identification too far. In murdering her ex-father-in-law, she exceeds the symbolic identification with the Rebel as signifier; she overinvests in it libidinally and falls out of the symbolic into the Real.

It might appear that a move from the symbolic to the Real might activate Maria's transformative political potential—that is, rather than a desperate attempt to secure a new place within the existing social order, such an Act performs the radical political/ethical task of unraveling existing social arrangements. I have argued that, on the contrary, Maria's final actions compromise the potential of the symbolic system itself to mutate in response to its disturbance by the Real.

Notes

1. Jacques-Alain Miller, "On Semblances in Relation between the Sexes," in *Sexuation*, ed. Renata Salacl (Durham: Durham University Press, 2000), 14.

2. Mari Ruti, *The Singularity of Being: Lacan and the Immortal Within* (New York: Fordham University Press, 2012), 70.

3. Slavoj Žižek, "The Act and Its Vicissitudes," *The Symptom*, 2005, http://www.egs.edu/faculty/slavoj-Žižek/articles/the-act-and-its-vicissitudes/ (accessed April 2014).

4. Todd McGowan, *The Fictional Christopher Nolan* (Austin: University of Texas Press, 2012), 112.

5. Ruti, *The Singularity of Being*, 57.

6. Žižek, *The Indivisible Remainder*, 181 n. 48, as quoted in Jason Glynos, "Thinking the Ethics of the Political in the Context of a Postfoundational World: From an Ethics of Desire to an Ethics of the Drive," *Theory and Event* 4.4 (2000): 11.

7. Ruti, *The Singularity of Being*, 72.

8. Miller, "On Semblances," 18.

9. Ruti, *The Singularity of Being*, 60.

10. Ruti, *The Singularity of Being*, 115.

11. Ruti, *The Singularity of Being*, 114.

12. Ruti, *The Singularity of Being*, 121.

13. Ruti, *The Singularity of Being*, 111.

14. Ruti, *The Singularity of Being*, 122–123.

When One Becomes Two

The Ending of *Catfish*

Rex Butler

Henry Joost and Ariel Schulman's 2010 documentary *Catfish* is famous for its ending. So famous that the poster for the theatrical release of the film warns us—much as Hitchcock did with *Psycho*—not to let anyone tell us what the "catfish" is. Needless to say, it is advice that both makes sense only after seeing the film and that risks ruining the very surprise it suggests by telling us to expect it. And it is a surprise that apparently can be repeated, because in 2012 the MTV network in America commissioned *Catfish: The TV Series*, hosted by Nev Schulman, brother of the filmmaker, who had been subject to the original "catfish," which featured victims who had similarly been fooled by people pretending to be somebody else on the Internet. Each week the same kind of deception that had been played upon Nev in *Catfish* would be repeated, and each week Nev would have to look surprised, as though he had never heard of it before.

All of which can make us suspect that the original *Catfish* was scripted, that the terrible scene that occurs toward the end of the film was not real but faked. (Nev discovers that the beautiful young woman with whom he thought he was conducting a virtual affair turns out to be middle-aged Angela, married with two handicapped stepchildren.) It is a possibility that appears to have only slowly dawned on *Catfish*'s audience once the initial shock of the ending had worn off. Thus, when the film was first released in cinemas, reviewers were taken aback by its traumatic revelation, which at once was praised for its bravery and poignancy and condemned for its voyeurism and intrusiveness. When the film premiered at the Sundance Film Festival, John Defore wrote in *The Hollywood Reporter*: "*Catfish*, while it doesn't answer every question it raises, arrives at a satisfying and most heart-warming conclusion."[1] And, on the contrary, A. O. Scott in the *New York Times*, when the film was commercially released, suggested: "Judged by the usual standards, it is coy about its motives and slipshod in its adherence to basic ethical norms."[2] However, in more considered and temporally distant online postings and academic papers, the apparent authenticity of the ending no longer convinced. Viewers were increasingly troubled by the possibility— encouraged, admittedly, by the subsequent television series, which appeared to "cash in" on the success of the original film and in which the same surprise was produced formulaically each week—that the whole scenario was staged. Thus Jay C. on his *The Documentary Blog* writes: "Rather than killing the suspense (and the film) by simply Googling a few names and resolving the mystery in the first ten minutes, they toy with this mystery woman under the guise of a budding online romance."[3] And this reproach is repeated in slightly more academic tones by Caetlin Benson-Allott in "The Algorithmic Spectator": "News of [Casey Affleck's hoax in *I'm Still Here*] broke the day before *Catfish*'s commercial launch and reinvigorated earlier speculation that Joost and Schulman orchestrated some of the relationships in the film."[4]

Of course, throughout the history of documentary there have always been concerns about the form's capacity for "truth" or "veracity." The argu-ment is put that we never see reality as such but only from the point of view of the director, who either consciously or unconsciously shapes it. This argument culminates perhaps in the 1960s when, along with the critique of the "ideological" nature of fiction film, there is a similar critique of the "con-structed" nature of documentary film. There, it is contended, documentary never treats its subject in any properly scientific or ethnographic manner but only as a reflection of already held beliefs and expectations. And we might even say that documentary film, beginning in the 1960s, responded to this in either one of two ways. The first was so-called "direct cinema," in which the director as much as possible attempted to get out of the way, to show reality unmediated by any artistic consciousness: no voice-over, no lights, no music, long unedited takes with no obvious cutting (made possible by the new technology of portable handheld cameras). And a number of major directors of documentaries were associated with this style: Richard Leacock, the Maysles brothers, and Frederick Wiseman. It is a project that continues to this day with the likes of Nicholas Philibert's *Être et avoir* (2002), which portrays a French village primary school teacher, and Ilian Metev's *Sofia's Last Ambulance* (2012), which follows the daily rounds of ambulance drivers and paramedics in Bulgaria's capital.

The second response, which we tend to think of as only recent but which actually goes back to at least the 1960s, is by contrast to emphasize the shaping role of the director, the fact that they are not recording any kind of truth but creating a fiction, or at least that it is through the reorganization of its material that the film achieves its effects. There are perhaps two variants of this. The first is a kind of "editorializing" documentary, as seen in examples such as Alberto Cavalcanti's *Coal Face* (1935) and Willard van Dyck's *The City* (1939), and, more recently, in Errol Morris's *Thin Blue Line* (1988) and Alex Gibney's *Enron: The Smartest Guys in the Room* (2005). The second is where the "documentary" evidence is in fact explicitly staged for the camera, as in Joshua Oppenheimer's recent *The Act of Killing* (2012). But there are a whole number of contemporary examples of this, from Jeremy Deller's *Battle of Orgeave*, which restaged events from the 1984 miner's strike in Britain using its original participants, to Oday Rasheed's *Underexposure* (2005), which depicted events surrounding the American invasion and overthrow of Saddam Hussein in Iraq as those events were tactually taking place. Each of these is not any "direct" documentary but rather a kind of meta-documentary. In the very opposite impulse to direct documentary, the film does not seek to erase the signs of its making but rather emphasizes them, makes them the subject of the narrative, in what we might call "indirect documentary."

We tend to associate this with a relatively recent wave of documentary films, as though they were some "postmodern" response to the collapse of metanarratives, but the definitive analysis of this phenomenon is in fact William Rothman's *Documentary Film Classics*, which treats a whole series of films going back to the 1920s. Rothman's thesis there—and it is fascinating to read it in conjunction with or even in strict parallel to his book on Alfred Hitchcock, *Hitchcock: The Murderous Gaze*—is that from the very beginning of documentary we have had this gradual turning toward the contemporary meta-documentary; that the realized form of documentary takes place not at all as the unmediated recording of some external reality but only through the consciousness of the limitations of the medium. The aim of documentary is not at all the simple transcription of reality but—and here we might make a comparison with the work of Stanley Cavell, Rothman's philosophical inspiration—the attaining of reality through the overcoming of a prior "skepticism"[5] of the kind that would otherwise appear to deny our access to it.

However, we might proceed more slowly here—and perhaps by indirection. In Rothman's earlier *Hitchcock: The Murderous Gaze*, he traces the passage from such early Hitchcock films as *The Lodger* (1926) and *The Thirty-Nine Steps* (1935) through to such later films as *Shadow of a Doubt* (1943) and *Psycho* (1960), in outlining what he calls the Hitchcock "system."[6] It is this shift, whereby Hitchcock becomes Hitchcock, that Rothman argues corresponds to the movement from "theater" to "cinema" in his work,[7] and it is in their final "cinematic" form that Hitchcock's films contain their deepest truths or at least the truths most proper to their medium. That is to say, in such early films as *The Lodger* and *The Thirty-Nine Steps*, what is revealed is the essentially "theatrical" nature of everyday life: the crowd gathered around the dead body at the beginning of *The Lodger*, the audience in the music hall at the beginning of *The Thirty-Nine Steps*. Theater would refer not only to Hitchcock's early experience of theater as a spectator, or to theater as a model for cinema (as was certainly the case for early cinema), but to the inherent performativity of his films' characters, their consciousness of the gaze of the camera. Think, for example, of the character Hannay in *The Thirty-Nine Steps*: introduced from behind at the beginning of the film, consciously maintaining a distance from his role in his ability constantly to change character (his speech at the community meeting when he pretends to be a politician who has been delayed), his subtle narcissism (the actor Robert Donat was famous at the time for his good looks), his awareness at all moments that he is being observed, even when he is not looking back at us (his pulling up of his coat collar as he sits down in the music hall, even though we have not yet seen his face).

But all of this changes for Rothman with Hitchcock's later cinema. In a film like *Psycho*, the character Norman (Anthony Perkins) is outstanding only in his very ordinariness, his indistinguishability from other people. His character makes no attempt either to hide from the gaze of the camera or to play up to it. His psychosis manifests itself—as opposed to the narcissism of Hannay—by his very *lack of* awareness of how others see him, as in the chilling scene in the parlor where he does not interact at all with Marian (played by Janet Leigh) or in a later scene in which the camera comes right up under his chin while he is talking to the detective Arbogast (Martin Balsam) at the desk of the hotel. (Again, this is as opposed to the camera in *The Thirty-Nine Steps*, which remains at a certain remove from Hannay, or in which Hannay is able to insinuate a certain distance between himself and the camera.) There is undoubtedly a certain aesthetic of the televisual as opposed to the cinematic here, but for Rothman it reveals the very truth of cinema, which is characterized by a certain willed (or even psychotic) disregard of the theatrical consciousness of the camera and the spectator. In cinema proper, there is no distinction between the actor and his or her role: the actor *is* the camera; the actor *is* the spectator. This is the truth of cinema, and it is also the truth of life. As Rothman writes toward the end of his book: "The cinema fixes its living subjects, possesses their life. They are reborn on the screen, creatures of the film's author and ourselves."[8]

It is this argument—unexpectedly enough, but not altogether surprising, as both are forms of cinema—that we find also in Rothman's *Documentary Film Classics*. In that book, he traces a similar trajectory through the history of documentary from "theater" to "cinema,"[9] from such early documentaries as Robert Flaherty's *Nanook of the North* (1921) and Luis Buñuel's *Land without Bread* (1932) through to such later films as Richard Leacock and Joyce Chopra's *A Happy Mother's Day* (1963) and D. A. Pennebaker's *Don't Look Back* (1967). That is to say, it is such early documentaries as *Nanook of the North* and *Land without Bread*, which most theorists of the genre argue come before the problems of artistic self-consciousness, when the project of capturing the real was felt possible, that Rothman claims are already theatrical and troubled by the difficulties of a skeptical "distance" from the world.[10] As he writes: "*Land without Bread* is a mock documentary, to be sure, yet a mock documentary that nonetheless is a documentary."[11] And it is such later films as *A Happy Mother's Day* and *Don't Look Back*, coming further along in the history of the form, which are marked by a certain self-reflexivity and which most critics would see as marked by a sense of the difficulty if not impossibility of capturing the real, that Rothman asserts are more documentary. Again, as he writes: "These films, too, are responses to a sense that the reality of the present, like the reality of the world on film, stands in need of being restored."[12]

Rothman, that is, inverts the usual history of documentary, which is generally related in terms of a gradual decline in its truth-telling power and a slowly gathering doubt concerning its ability to capture reality. As we have seen, this story begins with the supposed capacity or at least potential of film to record reality in a direct or straightforward way and concludes with a meta- or even "Baroque" version of the form, which seeks to demonstrate that it creates its own reality. By contrast, Rothman's point is that it is in their first "primitive" form that documentaries miss reality and only in their later, more mediated form that they manage to capture it. It is not a history of decline that he narrates, of some falling away from an original capability, but of how documentary film finally finds itself, realizes its specific aptitude, by defeating a skepticism that was there from the beginning. But how is it that through this more self-conscious form Rothman is able to suggest that documentaries capture the truth? What exactly is the form of the truth depicted in such films as *A Happy Mother's Day* and *Don't Look Back*, and why is this a truth specific to documentaries rather than fiction films? Or why in the end does Rothman see a parallel between documentary and the films of Hitchcock, with no or little difference between their respective modes of truth? Why is it that the truth of documentary is the truth of fiction, and vice versa?

In order to answer these questions, we might make a short detour through a form of documentary suggested by the final two films Rothman considers in his book, *A Happy Mother's Day* and *Don't Look Back*, which is the TV series, syndicated in different versions around the world, *Big Brother*. *Big Brother* is premised on the idea that, through an exaggeration of the techniques of direct cinema—a pushing to the limit of such things as *An American Family* (1973)—an uncensored insight into the life of its subjects would be attained. In effect, it is suggested, the unceasing surveillance of the camera and the length of the filming, during which they are frequently locked up together, means that contestants are unable to keep up their guard and must eventually drop the protective behaviors usually seen in society. Of course, on the other hand, what is also revealed—and this becomes clearer in subsequent derivatives of the show like *The Mole*—is that contestants effectively perform for the camera, openly appealing to the audience's sympathies and identification, insofar as they can vote them either on or off the show. Contestants form alliances with other contestants, directed against others, by pretending to be on their side. And even when they are locked in the supposedly private and confessional "Diary Room" and offered a chance to speak to Big Brother alone, without the other contestants hearing them, they continue to play a part. (And this is so even when they are voted off the show and their performance notionally comes to an end—and later series of *Big Brother* have incorporated this by allowing excluded contestants a chance to come back into the game.)

However, as better analysts of *Big Brother* and other reality TV shows have noted, it is just in this way that contestants *do* reveal themselves, both to the audience and to each other. It is not directly but only in their relations to others that we might see their truth, exactly in the attempt—impossible, as it turns out—to control the look or gaze of the other. As television theorist Misha Kavka writes in her *Reality Television, Affect and Intimacy*: "The television spectator is affectively interpellated in the sense that the game calls to her/him, is played out with her/his enjoyment in mind."[13] But we for our part might rephrase all of this in terms of Lacan's three registers of the Imaginary, the Symbolic, and the Real. Recalling Lacan's analysis of the prisoners in "Logical Time and the Assertion of Anticipated Certainty,"[14] we might say that on the Imaginary level the contestants on the show seek to identify with the gaze of the camera, either by exposing or revealing themselves to it or otherwise conforming to what they think it wants of them. On the next level of the Symbolic, we might say that the contestants attempt to play with this gaze, somehow occupy its position, and use it against others. In doing so, they would hide themselves from the gaze, keep something back from it, reveal to it only what they want to. However, as Lacan insists, on the final level of the Real, the contestants would reveal their true selves, in a way beyond the Imaginary, in their very attempts to play on the Symbolic. We discover what the contestants are really like in their efforts to manipulate the audience and other contestants, exposing or uncovering themselves in a manner that goes beyond any conscious action or strategy.

It is this level of the Real that Rothman is getting at in *Documentary Film Classics*. If in early documentaries like *Nanook of the North* and *Land without Bread* the camera remains "objective" and there is no interaction between the filmmakers and their subject, this is in effect to miss the Real and to remain merely on the levels of the Imaginary and Symbolic. But, in fact, to use Rothman's Cavellian language, they are already "theatrical," which is to point to the Symbolic interplay between subject and camera. In other words, although there is no apparent consciousness by subjects of the camera, they cannot but feel its influence. And insofar as the documentary filmmaker goes directly looking for the Real, like the policeman looking for the purloined letter in Poe's short story of the same name, they will necessarily miss it. (And we will see that there is quite a discourse around the letter in *Catfish* too.) As Rothman writes of *cinema vérité*: "The camera reveals its human subjects continually putting on masks, taking them off, putting them on again, and so on, as they react to the spectacle of the world."[15] Whereas, we might say, it is films like *A Happy Mother's Day* and *Don't Look Back*, in which the camera *is* acknowledged and the subject *is* conscious of being filmed and attempts to take this into account, that capture not so much reality as the Real. It is exactly through the subject's failed attempt to control the gaze of the camera on the Symbolic level and the failed attempt of the camera to record a reality external to it that something like the Real might come about. Documentary, therefore, is an inherently self-contradictory project, insofar as it must seek something that at once is produced by it and extends beyond it. Reality or, better, the Real, is not something that can deliberately be brought about but arises only inadvertently. Like the letter in Poe's story, no one possesses it, and we can only be sure that the one claiming to do so does not. And this, again, is the lesson of documentary for Rothman: "To restore [its subjects'] reality is to acknowledge that art no longer 'naturally' reveals the truth. To make the present the real world, art has to be overcome. Overcoming art is the new end for art."[16]

All of this is to be seen in *Catfish*. As is well known by now, the film follows the director's brother Nev, a freelance photographer, who is evidently just coming out of a series of unsuccessful relationships, who is sent one day a painting done by a young girl, Abby, based on one of his photographs. They begin emailing each other, and eventually Nev is introduced by Abby's mother, Angela, to Abby's beautiful nineteen-year-old half-sister, Megan. An intense online relationship develops, with the two soon sending intimate texts and photos to each other, even though they have not physically met. At a certain point, however, Henry, Ariel, and Nev are commissioned to make a video about a ballet company in Vail, Colorado, and figure it would be possible to go on to Michigan, where Megan lives. On several previous occasions in their courtship, it is implied, Nev has offered to visit Megan or have Megan visit him in New York, but each time she has declined. One night in their hotel room in Vail—she has earlier revealed to Nev her ambition to be a singer—the three of them are sitting around listening to some recordings of Megan singing, which she has sent Nev. But at the prompting of Ariel—and it is only in retrospect that we realize how unlikely all of this would be—Nev discovers that the recordings that Megan has sent him are identical to others already on the Internet. Nev is shown angry and disappointed at the discovery but also fascinated and impressed by the effort and creativity involved on "Megan's" part. (From the beginning of events, starting back with Abby, Henry and Ariel have been filming Nev, and Nev has allowed himself to be filmed.)

The three participants then enter into a spirited discussion. It is Nev who is more accepting of the possibility that "Megan" simply does not exist, insofar as it is he who first spotted the falseness of her recordings, while the others are more cautious and open-minded. And it is Nev who, not surprisingly, wants to cut the trip short and return home immediately, while the others advise against ending the relationship too hastily, as it would concede victory to the other and it would be intriguing to find out the truth about Nev's mystery correspondent. Eventually, they decide to carry on with their trip. After catching a plane to Chicago, they drive to Gladstone, Michigan, the first address Megan had given Nev and where he had been sending his postcards and gifts. They arrive late at night to discover that where Megan supposedly lives is an abandoned barn. The postcards Nev had sent lay uncollected in an unattended mailbox. The three of them decide to sleep overnight in a hotel and then go on the next day to the second address Megan had given Nev. The following morning, they arrive at an ordinary looking house in the suburb of Ishpeming, and, after working out a strategy if anything goes wrong, Nev walks up the driveway with a hidden mic and his brother filming from behind. (Again, the unlikeliness of this—and that we would be expected to sympathize with people who film and record others without their permission—is not obvious until afterward.) At first it appears that Megan is not there, with a middle-aged woman, Angela, who had previously been introduced as her mother, saying she is away visiting family. But, almost immediately, Nev realizes—and, after visiting her a second time and confronting her with the evidence, she confesses—that Angela *is* Megan. It is she who created the Facebook page that so attracted him, using photos sourced from somewhere else, and who established the whole elaborate fiction of Megan's sister, brother, parents, friends, and wider family to go with it.

Then the ultimate truth is revealed: that Angela leads an isolated, unhappy life with a daughter and two handicapped twin stepsons, Ronald and Anthony, and a husband, who does little to help. And she has created her online avatar—in fact, a whole series of them—both to meet other people and as a form of necessary therapy for her desperately miserable circumstances. During the sequence when we first meet Angela, we are given only one grainy and out-of-focus shot of one of her stepchildren, lumbering through the living room, obviously house-bound and incapable of engaging with the outside world. (The other, we discover later, is even worse off and permanently confined to a wheelchair.) It is Vince, Angela's husband, with whom Nev has several conversations on the veranda of the house, who provides the immortal and laconic description of his wife's behavior, which gives the film its title, in the concluding shot:

> They used to tank cod from Alaska all the way to China. They kept them in vats on a ship. By the time the codfish reached China, their flesh was mush and tasteless. So this guy came up with the idea that, if you put these catfish in the vats, they will keep the cod agile. There are those people who are catfish in life and they keep you on your toes. They keep you guessing, keep you thinking, keep you fresh. And I thank God for the catfish because life would be dull and boring if we didn't have people nipping at our fins.

The scenes in which Ariel's camera films Angela and her children are almost unbearably moving. Angela's tightly held secret is revealed, and something like her inner being exposed. That alternative identity she has constructed, in order to interact with the outside world and somehow to imagine herself not trapped in her terrible domestic situation, is taken from her. The conclusion to Henry, Ariel and Nev's interpretive quest is shocking to us. For all of our vengeful anticipation of "Megan's" pretense being revealed—with all of our sense of a deserved justice being delivered—we could not possibly imagine that it would turn out like this. It appears that we did not really want what we thought we did. And at this point Nev and the audience are confronted with a choice. Should we continue to act out a seemingly justified anger, scolding or punishing Angela and vowing to have nothing more to do with her? Or should we instead reach out in sympathy and attempt to pursue, although everything is different, some kind of relationship, even though we could know barely anything of the sufferings and difficulties she must daily undergo? Of course, as it had to be, Nev chooses the latter alternative and returns to Angela's house the next day after his initial feelings of disappointment have subsided to talk to her about her situation. Angela at first responds hesitantly, perhaps speaking for the first time to anyone outside of the family about her circumstances, explaining to him why she did what she did, while all the while Ariel's camera records the conversation between them, at first from a distance and then progressively moving closer. The film ends with a note that Nev and Angela still remain in touch, with Angela being one of Nev's Facebook friends and having taken down all of her alternative identities from the Internet.

It is, of course, an extremely satisfying conclusion. We witness Nev, who like many young men pursues attractive women but is shown to be slightly shallow and self-involved and, indeed, naïve in professing his love for a woman he has never met, "growing up" with his exposure to this other, hitherto hidden, side of life: the travails of ordinary people, who are not exciting and glamorous but often have difficult and complicated existences. And in a way he can even be seen as getting his comeuppance for using Angela in his brother's film without warning her. His smug inner-city sensibility is confronted with a poor rural or outlying America. Or even—an unspoken or even unspeakable subtext within the film, but much discussed online—a "foreigner" (for Ariel and Nev are Jewish) is forced to engage with the "real" America.[17] There is a sense, indeed, for all of its improbability, both that Nev's correspondent would have this kind of secret and of his own humane and enlightened response to it, of the narrative inevitability and rightness of the film's ending. In the classic dramatic manner, a true moral lesson has been served up, almost as in an opera or a French farce, but moreover in real life. And, as we say, it is a payoff that early reviewers of the film both recognized and responded to with enthusiasm. For example, Mary Pols in *Time* magazine suggested that "we see some things we might not expect from the Facebook generation. Kindness, for one. And chivalry."[18] And theologian John H. Armstrong in an essay "*Catfish*: A Film with a

Twist and an Insight into Social Networks" later wrote: "I think the viewer is afforded a glimpse of twenty-something adults that is powerful."[19]

Why would we want to contest this? What would motivate us to do so? Partly because we would not have properly learned the lessons of Rothman's analysis. Partly because we would not be seeing how contemporary documentary might go beyond and extend the terms of Rothman's analysis. Partly because, through the kind of twist we are contemplating, we might be able to make more acute and meaningful the situation of Angela and her children. We might begin by considering the implausibilities (and perhaps even impossibilities) of the film. Is it at all likely that Angela would allow Ariel to film their first meeting, given that she would have known that her ruse had been tumbled? Is it really appropriate—and what is the audience to make of the fact—that Nev and Ariel recorded and filmed Angela, especially as they might have guessed she would realize that her secret had been uncovered? Indeed, how likely is it that Angela would have allowed her children to be filmed at this early stage of their relationship? And, again, what are we to make of Ariel for doing so? The longer we consider *Catfish*, the more the improbabilities and improprieties pile up. They are, needless to say, the stuff of internet discussion, among both fans and critics of the film, and in a way challenge what we might consider the moral and aesthetic resolution of the film, both its climactic coincidence and the implication of its audience in its discovery and revelations.

It is at this point that we might consider various hypotheses raised concerning the making of the film (and, again, all of these have been much discussed and debated, both online and in academic journals).[20] First, that Ariel set up the entire scenario in order to put Nev through a kind of moral test (after all, it is he who urges Nev to stay in the game after Nev discovered Megan's music was faked). Then, it is possible that Nev already suspects the fakeness of Megan from his previous contact with her on the Internet but hides this from his brother, both for the sake of the film he is making and in order to maintain a kind of power over him (there is at times a good deal of tension between the brothers, and Nev frequently resents Ariel for intruding into his relationship with Megan). Finally, it is possible that both brothers already know the truth about Megan and take the audience along for a ride by pretending that events come as a surprise to them. And in many of these scenarios, we must imagine that Angela is also in on the conspiracy, both acting for one brother against the other and for both against the audience. (All of this, of course, is absolutely to go against the idea that she is in any way the victim of the film.) But, paradoxically, in each of these scenarios—like Dupin at the end of Poe's story—each party is able to wreak their revenge, get one up on the other (one brother against the other, both brothers against Angela, both brothers and Angela against the audience), only by pretending not to know anything, only by not directly claiming victory but leaving the other in a permanent state of doubt.

What is the final lesson in all of this? In a way, there are two "impossibilities" in the film, two things that cannot be shown: the real-life details of Angela's life with her children, which to depict in any sustained way would constitute an inexcusable obscenity; and whether the film is faked, so that nothing we watch is real and all of our suppositions about it need to be given another turn. And we would want to say that these two things, which appear to be opposed—the one infinitely heavy, a matter of unredeemed human misery; the other infinitely light, a mere matter of formal aesthetics—*are the same thing.* That is to say, it is only through the twisting of the film's apparatus onto itself, opening up the possibility that the whole narrative may be fictional, that we are able to find any equivalent to the unimaginable horror and despair at its center. It is just at the moment that Angela's secret is revealed in all of its unthinkable reality that we are forced to wonder—and we insist that it is at exactly the same time—whether any of it is real. Why would Angela allow her children to be filmed? Why would Ariel film them? How can Nev continue to act as he does? The thought that it must be staged, that there is something about the film that we are not shown or cannot see, is the *same as* the impossibility of what we are seeing. The impossibility of what we are seeing, which can be looked at, at least at first, only fleetingly and out-of-focus, is the same as these formal questions concerning the ontological status of the film.

All of this evokes the famous figure of the "mousetrap," known of course from that moment in Shakespeare's *Hamlet* when Hamlet seeks to expose King Claudius's guilt regarding his father's murder by having him watch a play in which those same events are staged. (The identical "mousetrap" is performed in *The Act of Killing*, when Oppenheimer tricks the death-squad generals into reenacting their crimes as though for a proposed fiction film.) In Rothman's book on Hitchcock, perhaps the turning point in the trajectory he traces from theater to cinema occurs in the film *Murder!* (1930), in which in order to catch the murderer the playwright Sir John Menier (Herbert Marshall), playing for a moment the role of amateur detective, makes the suspect Handell Fane (Esme Percy) repeat his actions under the pretext of auditioning him for a play based on the case. A wonderfully ambiguous scene ensues, in which Fane realizes that he is being forced to confess his guilt in words other than his own but can do nothing but follow the script if he wants the part. In the end, in one of Hitchcock's great climaxes, Fane hangs himself in front of a spellbound audience, after confessing in a letter under the pretext of offering certain corrections to Sir John's script that might make it more realistic.[21] And, again, this is the same logic we see in Rothman's book on documentary, where the most profound truth of the films' subjects is revealed to the very extent that they are aware of being filmed. Precisely insofar as they, like Fane, appear to be following a script, playing the role of themselves (like Mary Anne Fischer in *A Happy Mother's Day* following the maternal stereotype or Bob Dylan in *Don't Look Back* conforming to his own self-created image), we will find out all we need to know about them.

Slavoj Žižek titles his book on the great Polish director Krzysztof Kieślowski *The Fright of Real Tears* following the same logic: the fact that, after working as a documentary filmmaker Kieślowski realized that the only way to capture real emotion was within a fiction, to have his actresses shed false tears: "I don't even know if I've got the right to photograph real tears. That's probably why I changed to features. I can even buy some glycerine, put some drops in her eyes and the actress will cry."[22] The novelist David Foster Wallace in a now-famous essay on attending a pornography expo tells a similar story of a policeman who liked watching pornography because, in that most fake of documentary genres and through its bad acting, he occasionally saw flashes of real emotion on the actresses faces, as opposed to Hollywood, in which, exactly through its superior acting, all genuine emotion is lost.[23] Lacanian theorist Alenka Zupančič in her recent book on Nietzsche, *The Shortest Shadow: Nietzsche's Philosophy of the Two*, again elaborated this Real in terms of Shakespeare's mousetrap, arguing that "the whole point of staging the original crime in *Hamlet* is not so much to establish, or even to prove, the truth as to formulate the truth, to inscribe it in the very reality of which this truth is the truth."[24] And can we not see in all of this something of the logic of the "catfish," as outlined by Angela's husband in the film? The catfish is used to prevent stillness, to keep the other fish moving, to stave off entropy. We might describe it as a principle of *drive* in the animal world: that which holds things in a permanent state of disequilibrium in making impossible any realization of aim, any satisfaction of desire. The catfish is not any kind of excess but rather what allows the very finitude of the world, life within the shipping container, to be maintained as its own excess or imbalance. It is precisely what Zupančič means by thinking of the world as a kind of "pure split," whereby "one becomes what one is."[25]

This, to conclude, is what is at stake in understanding that event at the center of *Catfish*—singular, untranslatable, untransmissible—as strictly the equivalent of the ambiguity of its scenario, with two contrasting and absolutely irreconcilable narratives evidenced by strictly the same set of facts.

What *Catfish* shows is a world that exists without any compensating reward or judgment and people carrying on despite their lies and self-deceptions, but the price they pay for this is their "catfish": that which cannot be caught, cannot be represented, which swims around in the bottom of the tank and in the dark as the only thing that needs nothing else. "Hey, guys," says Nev, when he first sees Angela's children. It is those children who are at once the only figures in the film who are unaware of being looked at and those beneath whose gaze everyone is seen and judged. They are the true catfish of the film: that around which all moves, even though they do not move at all.

Notes

1. John Defore, "*Catfish*—Film Review," *The Hollywood Reporter*, October 14, 2010, http://www.hollywoodreporter.com/review/catfish-film-review-29219 (accessed July 2014).

2. A. O. Scott, "*Catfish*," *New York Times*, September 16, 2010, http://www.nytimes.com/2010/09/17/movies/17catfish.html?pagewanted=all&_r=0 (accessed July 2014).

3. Jay C., *The Documentary Blog*, http://thedocumentaryblog.com/2010/10/11/catfish-review-spoilers/ (accessed July 2014).

4. Caetlin Benson-Allott, "The Algorithmic Spectator," *Film Quarterly* 64.3 (Spring 2011): 56.

5. William Rothman, *Documentary Film Classics* (Cambridge: Cambridge University Press, 1997), xiii.

6. William Rothman, *Hitchcock: The Murderous Gaze* (Cambridge: Harvard University Press, 1982), 2.

7. Rothman, *Hitchcock: The Murderous Gaze*, 104–106.

8. Rothman, *Hitchcock: The Murderous Gaze*, 341.

9. Rothman, *Documentary Film Classics*, 118.

10. Rothman, *Documentary Film Classics*, 38.

11. Rothman, *Documentary Film Classics*, 37.

12. Rothman, *Documentary Film Classics*, 123.

13. Misha Kavka, *Reality Television, Affect and Intimacy: Reality Matters* (New York: Palgrave Macmillan, 2008), 7.

14. Jacques Lacan, "Logical Time and the Assertion of Anticipated Certainty," in *Écrits*, (New York: W.W. Norton, 2006), 198–175.

15. Rothman, *Documentary Film Classics*, 119.

16. Rothman, *Documentary Film Classics*, 65.

17. Adam Lippe, "You're Not Good-Looking Enough to Be Cocky: A Review of *Catfish*," *Movie Examiner*, September 28, 2010, http://www.examiner.com/review/you-re-not-good-looking-enough-to-be-cocky-a-review-of-catfish (accessed July 2014).

18. Mary Pols, "Fish Tale," *Time*, September 27, 2010, http://content.time.com/time/magazine/article/0,9171,2019606,00.html (accessed July 2014).

19. John H. Armstrong, "*Catfish*: A Film with a Twist and an Insight into Social Networks," *Act 3: Equipping Leaders for Unity in Christ's Mission*, February 4, 2011, http://johnharmstrong.typepad.com/john_h_armstrong_/2011/02/catfish-a-film-with-a-twist-and-an-insight-into-social-networks.html (accessed July 2014).

20. For a summary of these concerns, see "*Catfish* Movie: Real or Fake?," http://www.catfishfans.com/real_or_fake.php (accessed July 2014). Of course, the other main objections to the film, often made in accounts doubting its authenticity, are that Henry and Ariel would have started filming Nev from the beginning of his relationship to Abby and that Nev would have allowed them to listen in on his conversations with Megan before he had any doubts about her identity.

21. Admittedly, *Murder!* was made some five years before *The Thirty-Nine Steps*, which we claim is still "theatrical." However, as Rothman suggests in his introduction to *The Murderous Gaze*, "*Psycho*'s position is already declared, indeed already worked out, in *The Lodger*" (2); that is, the "cinematic" is already in the "theatrical," just as traces of the "theatrical" still persist in the "cinematic."

22. Krzysztof Kieślowski cited in Slavoj Žižek, *The Fright of Real Tears: Krzysztof Kieślowski between Theory and Post-Theory* (London: British Film Institute, 2001), 72.

23. The detective confessed that what drew him to the films was "the faces, i.e., the actresses' faces, i.e., those rare moments when the starlets dropped their stylized 'fuck-me-I'm-a-nasty-girl' sneer and became, suddenly, real people. . . . In real movies, it's all on purpose." David Foster Wallace, *Consider the Lobster and Other Essays* (New York: Little Brown, 2005), 16.

24. Alenka Zupančič, *The Shortest Shadow: Nietzsche's Philosophy of the Two* (Cambridge: MIT Press, 2003), 121.

25. Zupančič, *The Shortest Shadow*, 25.

8

The Satisfaction of an Ending

Todd McGowan

Two Forms of Surprise

In his interviews with François Truffaut, Alfred Hitchcock articulates his celebrated distinction between surprise and suspense. He describes the difference in effect when the audience knows that an event is going to happen and when the audience lacks any awareness of what will occur. His example concerns a conversation taking place with a bomb under the table. If the audience doesn't know about the existence of the bomb and it explodes, surprise will ensue. If the film shows the bomb that the characters cannot see, the audience will experience suspense instead of surprise. Hitchcock prefers suspense to surprise, as he claims in the interview, because of the duration of each. He opts for "fifteen minutes of *suspense*" over "fifteen seconds of *surprise*" and concludes that "whenever possible the public must be informed."[1] Hitchcock's contempt for the whodunit and its emphasis on the surprise ending derives from his understanding that suspense trumps surprise in terms of psychic effects. Suspense doesn't simply appeal to us for a longer duration but engages the subject in a way that surprise does not. Though Hitchcock never theorizes his aesthetic preference for suspense and chalks it up to the duration of the impact on the spectator, there is actually much more at stake. Choosing suspense or surprise is a political choice as much as it is an aesthetic one.

Despite Hitchcock's preference for surprise over suspense, when we think of great film endings, the twist or surprise ending typically comes to mind. Even Hitchcock's own endings that receive the most attention—the death of Judy (Kim Novak) in *Vertigo* (1958) or the struggle at the top of Mount Rushmore in *North by Northwest* (1959)—seem to rely on surprise rather than suspense. Films that deploy unexpected twists, from *The Cabinet of Dr. Caligari* (Robert Wiene, 1920) to *The Usual Suspects* (Bryan Singer, 1995), populate the lists of the best film endings of all time. The surprise ending is always the most memorable: we remember it because it stands apart from the expected endings that we have seen and that all blend together. We forget the details of the ending of the typical genre film because all genre films end basically the same way. We know that the hero will ride away after eliminating the threat in the western and that the couple will find a way to surmount their conflicts in the romantic comedy. Predictability breeds forgetting, while surprise lodges a film in our memory.

But the surprise ending doesn't resonate just by virtue of its exceptional status relative to other endings. Its power derives from its relationship to the subjectivity of the spectator. The surprise ending appeals to the spectator on the level of desire, which is why spectators have so much appreciation for the surprise ending. Desire is unthinkable without the element of surprise. Desire seeks a surprising object—a new object that will provide a satisfaction that previous objects have not. If we already fully know the object, it is difficult to arouse our desire for it. The inherent link between the surprise ending and desire lies in the change in object. Just as the surprise ending replaces the object that the spectator expects with another one, desire moves from object to object, constantly replacing the object of desire with another object.[2]

Desire's relation to the object is metonymic.[3] This is because whatever the subject's desire finds never provides the satisfaction that it expects. Desire moves from object to object in search of a satisfaction that no object is able to provide but that the next object always promises. Surprise is essential to the object's desirability. The object promises to surprise the subject with an excess of satisfaction that it will provide. If an object fails to promise surprise, the subject of desire won't seek it out. Desire seeks surprise, and this is why the twist ending provides so much pleasure for spectators. It is a pleasure inextricable from the structure of the desiring subject, but it is an ambivalent pleasure.

The problem with the logic of desire is that desire never finds what it seeks. Each object holds the allure of an ultimate satisfaction and subsequently reveals itself as dissatisfying. This is what Jacques Lacan is getting at in his *Seminar IV* when he states that the object "is found and seized other than at the point where it is sought."[4] The structure of desire and that of the surprise ending are inherently disappointing. If we privilege both of these parallel structures, it is a misinterpretation with concrete political ramifications.

The pleasure that we find in desire and in being taken by surprise obscures where our satisfaction lies. This is the political danger of both the structure of desire and the surprise ending. Both structures encourage us to look at the object as the source of our satisfaction. If we fail to achieve satisfaction, we can lay the blame on the object. Or, we can blame the ending of the film for the film's failure. Thinking about the subject in terms of desire or valuing the twist ending has the effect of inscribing dissatisfaction as the essential condition of subjectivity, and this dissatisfied subject fails to see the satisfaction that resides in the subject's failure relative to the object.

The emphasis on the object marks an inability to grasp how failure, not success, constitutes the foundation of the subject's satisfaction. The subject's satisfaction—and this is what thinking in terms of desire misses—stems not from the object but from the subject's drive. If desire seeks satisfaction in an object, the drive finds satisfaction through its own movement. The failure to obtain a satisfying object is the path through which the subject satisfies itself, and this is the dynamic with which an exploration of film endings must reckon.

The association of desire with the surprise ending has a correlate in the drive. Like Hitchcock's suspense, the drive relies on knowledge about its object. The object of the drive is not unexpected: we know what we are getting, and we know that the object will not be the source of some ultimate satisfaction. The point of the drive is not the object but the path that one takes toward it, and the satisfaction that the drive provides is the result of its mode of failure to attain the object rather than its success. The object is not the promise of an ultimate satisfaction but the occasion for the subject's satisfying failure. Through the drive, the subject enjoys the failure that the desiring subject laments.

To understand how cinematic endings work on us as subjects, it is important to recognize the difference between desire and drive, a difference that is decisive for the politics of subjectivity. The subject of desire appears to be the most inherently political subject. Desire is constantly seeking the new and expressing dissatisfaction with what it has, which makes the desiring subject eager for change—and perhaps for political change. But the problem with desire is what animates its search for the new. Newness represents the possibility of a missing satisfaction, of solving the problem of a constant dissatisfaction, but desire depends on its dissatisfaction. By definition, the desiring subject will never find an object that will satisfy it. This subject will be always seeking the new no matter what form the new takes. No political arrangement could possibly be satisfying, and the subject of desire will revolt for the sake of revolt, not for the sake of a political commitment. Desire leads the subject away from politics altogether and typically directs the subject toward consumption rather than political engagement.

In contrast to desire, the drive is inherently satisfied. This is because its satisfaction depends not on obtaining an object but on running into an obstacle. As Joan Copjec notes in *Imagine There's No Woman*, "Drive achieves its satisfaction by *not* achieving its aim. Moreover, the *inhibition* that prevents the drive from achieving its aim is not understood within Freudian theory to be due to an extrinsic or exterior *obstacle*, but rather as part of the very *activity* of the drive itself."[5] Drive transforms what desire perceives as an obstacle into the source of satisfaction. Though drive doesn't surprise us because it always follows the same path, this transformation in the status of the obstacle does produce surprise. As subjects of the drive, we expect an obstacle, and the satisfaction that the obstacle provides takes us by surprise.

Though the subject of the drive expects the object that it finds, this object nonetheless takes the subject by surprise. When the drive encounters the object that it expects, surprise ensues because the obstacle to our satisfaction miraculously becomes manifest as the source of our satisfaction at the same time. The drive bombards us with expected surprise, and the expected surprise demands that we completely rethink our relation to the object. The expected surprise is a paradoxical type of ending, and it represents not just the logic of the drive but the zenith of cinematic art. It forces spectators to confront their own satisfaction rather than looking to the object to provide a heretofore missing satisfaction.

Desire and drive are not two distinct structures but rather two different approaches to the same structure. The subject of desire seeks a satisfying object of desire, while the subject of drive finds satisfaction in the obstacle to the object of desire. The contrast between desire and drive concerns the nature of the surprise that the subject encounters in each approach. Desire involves the subject in a game of surprises. The subject of desire seeks what it doesn't have and what will surprise it with a heretofore unattained satisfaction. The subject of drive, in contrast, doesn't seek a new object but finds satisfaction in the new forms of failure that it discovers. This subject encounters a series of expected surprises, in contrast to the unexpected surprises of the desiring subject. The filmic ending that achieves the expected surprise helps to constitute the subject of the drive.

My argument here is not just that we should privilege the expected surprise ending over the unexpected surprise—though I think we should—but that the expected surprise encourages us as spectators to grasp ourselves as subjects of the drive. This is not primarily an epistemological task but a political one. The desire for the unexpected surprise produces subjects dependent on the social authority that both holds back and provides the surprise. The subject of desire is a subject invested in the promise of social authority, and the drive represents a path away from this promise. The expected surprise ending is cinema at its most radical point.

The Fertility of the Cliché

The opposition between the unexpected surprise ending and the expected surprise is not the fundamental opposition when it comes to filmic endings. And twist or surprise endings are not the most ideological ones. Most endings do not involve either unexpected surprise or expected surprise. Instead, they are the domain of cliché. If, as Gilles Deleuze claims in his book on the time-image, the task of cinema is one of "tearing a real image from clichés," the main target for this political act is the fantasmatic ending.[6] In contrast to the surprise ending associated with desire and the expected surprise ending associated with the drive, the fantasmatic ending simply provides spectators with what they expect. Ideological fantasy follows a narrative trajectory that ensures an absence of surprise, and spectators leave films with fantasmatic endings assured that social authority will provide the missing object and elimination of social antagonism without disturbing the subject's symbolic position. The ideological fantasy is the great political danger among filmic endings.[7]

The most common ideological film ending is the romantic union. The romantic union functions ideologically because it provides spectators with the fantasy of overcoming the most intractable antagonism through romance. Films begin by showing the antagonism that keeps a couple apart, and then they conclude with a fantasy of them coming together in spite of this antagonism. The idea behind the concluding romantic union is that antagonism is not intractable, that through compromise or sacrifice or work we can overcome antagonism and achieve social harmony. The concluding romantic union works to create spectators who view antagonism as a contingent rather than a necessary aspect of the social order. In this way, this ending aims at stripping its spectators of their political being. But the ideological function of this ending has an aesthetic cost: romantic unions tend to be the most forgettable filmic endings.

Of all film endings, the romantic union is the most aligned with the fantasmatic dimension of cinema and thus the least aligned with desire and surprise. The romantic union is almost never the result of a memorable twist. No one except the most inexperienced filmgoer experiences surprise when Peter (Clark Gable) ends up with Ellie (Claudette Colbert) at the end of *It Happened One Night* (Frank Capra, 1934) or when Edward (Richard Gere) returns to Vivian (Julia Roberts) at the conclusion of *Pretty Woman* (Gary Marshall, 1990). Even if we enjoy the fantasy that these film endings offer, we aren't surprised in the way that we are at the ending of *Invasion of the Body Snatchers* (Philip Kaufman, 1978) when Matthew Bennell (Donald Sutherland) screams to indicate that he's been taken over by the pods or *The Sixth Sense* (M. Night Shyamalan, 1996) when we learn that the hero Malcolm Crowe (Bruce Willis) has been dead without our knowledge for most of the film's running time. The typicality of the romantic union renders it unsuitable for surprise. We expect it, and most films involving a romance confirm our expectations.

When a film operates on the terrain of the romantic union, it seems almost impossible to forge an authentic or even a nonideological ending. If one decides to end with the romantic union, one cedes the terrain to the ideological fantasy. But this is not always the case. Because it is the most ideological film ending, the romantic union is a structure through which a film can provide the most significant challenge to ideology. The site where ideology functions most thoroughly is at once the site where it is most vulnerable. The prevalence of ideological fantasies indicates the persistence of a weakness in the social structure that ideology must work to shore up.

This is the problem with Deleuze's denunciation of the cliché. The cliché does function ideologically to assure subjects that the social order runs smoothly, but the very existence of the cliché testifies to a repetition that threatens all smoothness. Repetition is the way that the drive manifests itself, and the repetition of fantasmatic endings is an indication of the drive at work. The antagonistic force of the drive demands incessant attempts to form an ideological fantasy that contains the disruptiveness of this force, and the prevalence of the fantasy bespeaks the prevalence of the drive that occasions it. The disruptiveness of the drive always lurks within the clichéd ideological fantasy and threatens to appear whenever this ending does.

If we want to look for the most radical film endings, we must ironically look toward the most clichéd film endings. Radicality dwells at the heart of the cliché, not at an extreme distance from it. The great film ending inhabits the cliché so thoroughly that it exposes how the clichéd ideological fantasy surreptitiously relies on the disruptiveness of the drive and its repetition.

The repetition of the cliché is not primary. It is a reaction to the repetition of the drive, and the expected surprise ending makes evident the drive that inheres within the ideological fantasy.

Three Expected Surprises

In order to examine the expected surprise ending in its most successful form, I will focus on three romantic unions that flirt with the typical ideological fantasy but ultimately reveal this fantasy as completely untenable. They undermine the ideological fantasy by portraying the deployment of the fantasy as a disruption within the filmic structure. The fantasy of the successful romantic union concludes the films, but in each case the fantasy appears as a surprise. The cliché itself, because of the form that it takes, becomes surprising. We can see this type of romantic union first in a film from the middle of François Truffaut's career.

In terms of critical and popular reception, *La sirène du Mississippi* (*Mississippi Mermaid*, 1969) doesn't count among François Truffaut's great successes. But even for a director known for stunning endings, the conclusion of *Mississippi Mermaid* surpasses all of Truffaut's other conclusions, save perhaps the remarkable utopian ending of *Fahrenheit 451* (1966).[8] *Mississippi Mermaid* chronicles a deception perpetuated on Louis Mahé (Jean-Paul Belmondo), a wealthy tobacco plantation owner on Réunion Island who marries a woman from France whom he knows only through correspondence. The woman who comes to the island to marry him, Marion Vergano (Catherine Deneuve) turns out to be not the woman he selected but rather a con artist there to steal his fortune. After she does so, she flees the island and returns to France, but Louis pursues her. When he finds her and resumes his romance with her, he ends up killing the private detective, Comolli (Michel Boquet), whom he had hired to find her and recover his money. The couple must go on the run from the police, but Marion is dissatisfied with their fugitive existence and attempts to slowly poison Louis while they hide out in a mountain cabin near the Swiss border.

The ending of *Mississippi Mermaid* depicts Louis informing Marion that he knows that she is killing him but that he loves her nonetheless. This profession prompts her to abandon altogether her attempts to kill him on the spot. Not only that, but Marion proclaims her own love for the man she has almost killed, and they go out into the snow together in order to cross over into Switzerland. The final image of the film—Marion helping a sickened Louis through the snow—is an image of romantic union, but this union becomes possible only through the attempt to destroy it. It emerges out of Marion's attempt to kill Louis. By depicting the romantic union occurring just after this attempted murder, Truffaut shows how the romantic union can reveal antagonism rather than obscuring it.

In *Mississippi Mermaid*, Truffaut concludes with a fantasy scenario that we expect, but the way that this fantasy scenario comes about is surprising. In this sense, the ending of the film follows the path of the drive. Even though the drive continually follows the same path, it discovers something new because it generates new forms of failure, and this is what we see at the end of Truffaut's film. The attempted murder marks the subsequent romantic union and indicates its enduring presence of the obstacle to this union even as the film shows the union occurring. Truffaut shows clearly how an obstacle can become the basis for the satisfying romantic union. If the ending of *Mississippi Mermaid* focuses on a disruptive romantic union, Richard Linklater creates a trilogy of romantic films that appear much more typical.

The film *Before Sunrise* (Richard Linklater, 1995) ends with ambiguity, but this ambiguity fits within the ideological fantasy of the romantic union. The film depicts the brief romance of Jesse (Ethan Hawke) and Celine (Julie Delpy). They meet on a train and spend one night together in Vienna before Jesse must leave on a plane the next morning. Though they promise to meet six months later at the Vienna train station, they do not give each other any information beyond first names, which would make renewed contact impossible if either misses the reunion date. This ending enables the spectator to imagine a successful romantic union, even if it defers this union to the future and leaves its accomplishment uncertain.

In the sequel, *Before Sunset* (Richard Linklater, 2004), we learn that Celine missed the reunion due to the death of her grandmother. Having no way to contact Celine, Jesse eventually married another woman and had a son. They meet again in the beginning of the sequel when Jesse is in Paris to promote his novel and Celine comes to the bookstore to see him. They spend most of the film talking while going around Paris. The fundamental dilemma that the film poses involves Jesse's decision to stay with Celine or return to his wife and son. The film gives us indications that he wants to stay, but he also continually brings up the need to get to the airport before his plane leaves.

It is clear that despite his feeling of obligation, Jesse wants to remain in Paris, and this is the type of ending that the spectator expects. Finally, Jesse goes up to Celine's apartment as the time he has before the flight dwindles. After Jesse puts a song from Nina Simone on the CD player, Celine begins to dance in front of him while acting like Nina Simone in concert. She imitates

Simone's voice, and then she uses this voice to tell Jesse, "Baby you are gonna miss that plane." After the film cuts to Jesse saying, "I know," it cuts back to Celine dancing and then simply fades to black. We don't see Jesse's definitive choice to stay with Celine or the full resumption of their relationship.

By ending the film abruptly after Celine provocatively comments that Jesse is missing his plane, Linklater reveals the contingency within the necessity that fuels the romantic union. We expect that Jesse and Celine will come together again, but we have no idea when or how this will happen. The abrupt ending of the film reveals ironically that there is no one moment when their love is rekindled. Celine's statement punctuates their reconnection, but this reconnection occurs throughout the film. It is impossible to delineate the precise moment at which Jesse and Celine decide to begin their relationship again, and the abrupt ending highlights this impossibility. We can tell throughout the film that they are still in love, but Celine's declaration nonetheless comes as a surprise.

The surprise at the end of *Before Sunset* does not stem from our absence of knowledge about when Jesse and Celine will reconnect. While watching them together, the spectator is confident that they will resume their relationship at the end of the film. But the film creates surprise by showing how necessity of this romantic union operates through contingency. Celine's imitation of Nina Simone and her dance in front of Jesse is a contingent moment, and yet it is the moment at which the necessity of the romantic union manifests itself. The expected ending can surprise us when its necessity occurs even in the contingent moment. Contingency is an obstacle to the necessity of the drive, but it becomes the occasion for the drive's satisfaction.[9] The expected surprise ending reveals the power of the drive's repetition, a power that is even more evident in *Eternal Sunshine of the Spotless Mind*.

The form of *Eternal Sunshine of the Spotless Mind* enables the film to show through most of its running time the antagonism that animates the relationship between Joel (Jim Carrey) and Clementine (Kate Winslet). The film's plot is centered on a procedure that wipes out memories known as the Lacuna Procedure, and both Clementine and Joel opt for it in order to forget the trauma of the relationship with each other. As the workers for the Lacuna Corporation are wiping the memories, we see all the obstacles to Joel and Clementine staying together. Their incompatibility becomes evident as Joel finds Clementine too irresponsible and she finds him too staid. In a typical romantic comedy like *Pretty Woman*, these obstacles would disappear. Just as the millionaire Edward decides to marry the prostitute Vivian and thereby eliminate her status as prostitute, Joel would transform Clementine into a stable partner, or she would teach him to relax and enjoy himself. But the film ends with a remarkable scene in which the two decide to stay together while avowing rather than eliminating the antagonism in their relationship.

Thanks to the Lacuna Procedure, neither Joel nor Clementine can remember what they can't tolerate in the other person. But a disgruntled Lacuna employee has sent them tapes in which they describe how they really feel about each other's faults, and at the end of the film they listen to these tapes together and recognize the fundamental obstacle in the way of their relationship. The tapes initially deflate their feelings for each other because they force them to recognize that they have had these feeling before and that they have led to a disastrous relationship. But the ending neither shows them deciding to give up their budding romance nor to try to surmount the antagonism that defines it. Instead, they proceed through the antagonism.

Even after he hears his own description of his extreme dissatisfaction with Clementine, Joel says to her, "I can't see anything that I don't like about you." Clementine responds, "But you will." Joel insists, "Now I can't." But Clementine recognizes that they will inevitably repeat the pattern that has defined their relationship. She says, "But you will, you know. You will think of things. And I'll get bored with you and feel trapped because that's what happens with me." Rather than trying to refute Clementine's insight or imagine a different future, Joel simply says, "OK." Clementine also accepts the inevitability of the antagonism by adding, "OK." At this point, the film ends with a romantic union that cuts completely against the grain of the typical romantic union.

The spectator of *Eternal Sunshine of the Spotless Mind* expects Joel and Clementine to end up together. Their romantic union follows the Hollywood convention. But what takes the spectator by surprise is the form that this union takes. It is a romantic union that places antagonism rather than its overcoming at the center of the relation. The concluding romantic union occurs with both characters avowing what each finds intolerable about the other. Most depictions of romantic unions show love able to conquer antagonism, but in *Eternal Sunshine* love emerges through antagonism. The film makes clear that antagonism both destroys love and makes it possible.

By highlighting the role that antagonism plays in the romantic union, *Eternal Sunshine* forces the spectator to approach the typical fantasmatic resolution differently. The fantasy doesn't eliminate the obstacle to the romantic union but depends on this obstacle. The film's ending reveals the obstacle to the romantic union amid the union itself, and it is this obstacle that takes the spectator by surprise. One sees that the repetition of the romantic union occurs in conjunction with the repetition of the obstacle to the union.

In *Mississippi Mermaid, Before Sunset,* and *Eternal Sunshine of the Spotless Mind* the clichéd romantic union doesn't play the role of an ideological fantasy but disrupts the ideological functioning associated with this union. The films end with the union that we expect, but the form of this union takes us by surprise. This expected surprise ending is the manifestation of the drive, a structure that repeats while simultaneously generating newness, the newness that is born with the transformation of the obstacle. The repetition of the drive creates surprises that we expect, and when a film ends with the expected surprise, it provides a privileged insight into this dimension of the drive. We discover the new only at the point where we find our expectations met, not at the point where we seek the new. The charms of the twist ending pale in comparison with the satisfaction provided by the expected surprise.

Alfred Hitchcock's preference for suspense over surprise has at the same time a preference for the logic of the drive over that of desire. He understands in his own way that the surprise ending ensconces the spectator in an unending dissatisfaction that associates the ultimate satisfaction with an unobtainable object. In contrast, the expected surprise that occurs within suspense enables the spectator to associate satisfaction with the drive itself and not with an impossible object. Suspense doesn't eliminate surprise altogether but provides the expected surprise, and it is the expected surprise that constitutes the ending appropriate for the drive. The surprise ending that we expect satisfies us because it reveals that the ending has been present from the beginning and yet nonetheless has the power to disturb our complacency.

Notes

1. Alfred Hitchcock, quoted in François Truffaut, *Hitchcock: The Definitive Study of Alfred Hitchcock by François Truffaut*, rev. ed. (New York: Simon and Schuster, 1985), 73. Immediately after claiming that one must always give the audience knowledge, Hitchcock does make an exception for the twist ending. He adds, "Except when the surprise is a twist, that is, when the unexpected ending is, in itself, the highlight of the story" (73).

2. The movement of desire from object to object is what makes desire so compatible with the capitalist economy. Capitalism isn't a product of human nature, but it does have a parasitical relationship to desiring subjectivity. Without the logic of the desire structuring subjectivity, the emergence of capitalism would be unimaginable.

3. In "The Instance of the Letter in the Unconscious or Reason since Freud," Jacques Lacan straightforwardly identifies desire with metonymy when he claims, "desire *is* a metonymy, even if man scoffs at the idea." Jacques Lacan, "The Instance of the Letter in the Unconscious or Reason since Freud," in *Écrits: The First Complete Edition in English*, trans. Bruce Fink (New York: Norton, 2006), 439. Lacan's

suggestion that one might resist this identification of desire with metonymy stems from our belief in the independence of each subsequent object of desire.

4. Jacques Lacan, *Le Séminaire, livre IV: La relation d'object, 1956–1957*, ed. Jacques-Alain Miller (Paris: Seuil, 1994), 15.

5. Joan Copjec, *Imagine There's No Woman: Ethics and Sublimation* (Cambridge: MIT Press, 2002), 30.

6. Gilles Deleuze, *Cinema 2: The Time-Image*, trans. Hugh Tomlinson and Robert Galeta (Minneapolis: University of Minnesota Press, 1989), 21.

7. Of course, not every fantasmatic ending is ideological. The ending of David Lynch's *Blue Velvet* (1986), for instance, depicts the elimination of the threat to the romantic union between Jeffrey (Kyle McLaughlin) and Sandy (Laura Dern) occurring in an idyllic setting. But because Lynch includes a shot of a robin, the figure of fantasmatic redemption in the film, eating a bug in the midst of the romantic union, we see how disturbance persists in the middle of the reconciliation that seems to eliminate antagonism.

8. Truffaut's first two features, *The 400 Blows* (1959) and *Shoot the Piano Player* (1960), both reflect the inventiveness of his endings. The former ends with the hero Antoine Doinel (Jean-Pierre Léaud) running away from a boarding school and discovering finally that he has nowhere further to go when he reaches a beach, and the latter concludes with the shocking shooting death of Léna (Marie Dubois), the new love of the piano player Charlie (Charles Aznavour).

9. The weakest of Linklater's trilogy of Jesse and Celine is the final installment, *Before Midnight* (2013), which details the married life of Jesse and Celine years after their reunion in Paris. Though critics celebrated the realism of the film's depiction of married life in contrast to the fantasmatic vision of romance proffered by the first two films, *Before Midnight* falls into an ideological trap that the second film avoids. Though the third film shows how the obstacle to Jesse and Celine's relationship remains, the obstacle ceases to be the source of satisfaction and becomes purely a source of dissatisfaction. Satisfaction, as the film presents it, must lie elsewhere. The spectator can only root for the relationship to end, though the conclusion of the film leaves this in question.

9

The Too Realistic Cut

Gaze as Overconformity in *Blue Velvet*

HENRY KRIPS

Introduction

Slavoj Žižek ends his book *Organs without Bodies* with a question: "How . . . are we to revolutionize an order [namely, capitalism] whose very principle is constantly self-revolutionizing?" "Perhaps," Žižek adds, "this is *the* question for today."[1] Žižek also suggests an answer to the question: namely, a radical cultural politics that uses film in order to create encounters with the Lacanian Real. In making this suggestion, Žižek makes a crucial shift from taking film merely as a medium for *representing* radical political strategies (as he does in much of his early work) to taking film as a site for *enacting* radical political strategies. How is this possible? Specifically, how can showing a film to an audience have radical political effects?

From a traditional Marxist perspective, the best that a radical cinematic politics can do is to work along the lines of ideology critique. To be specific, through its content, a film reveals an ideologically concealed injustice, and then, going beyond this revelation, pitches a message designed to produce emotions and thoughts in its audience that will mobilize them against the injustice.[2] But (again from a Marxist point of view) such a radical cultural politics runs the risk that, by virtue of the conventional cinematic forms in which it is framed as well as its capitalist mode of production, it will end up reproducing at the level of form and technique the same ideology that it opposes at the level of content. To put the point bluntly: nothing politically progressive, let alone anticapitalist, can come out of Hollywood, because ultimately, both in its mode of production and the forms of its product, it reproduces the ideology of capitalism.

Žižek, like Rancière, envisages a radical cultural politics along quite different lines, which get around this objection to a classic Marxist cultural politics of ideology critique: "The artifice of 'true art' [by which Žižek means art that succeeds in its ethico-political duty] is to manipulate the censorship of the [art's] underlying fantasy in such a way to reveal the radical falsity of this fantasy."[3] At first sight, by revealing the errors of a work of art's underlying ideological fantasy, Žižek's radical cultural politics seems to fall awfully close to the tree of old-fashioned ideology critique. But it quickly becomes apparent that he has something quite different in mind. He tells us that a "constitutive gap between the explicit symbolic texture and its phantasmatic background is obvious in any work of art . . . even the most harmonious."[4] He then adds: "the 'trick' of an artistic success resides in the artist's capacity to turn this lack [or *cut*] into an advantage—skillfully to manipulate the [Real] central void [constituted by this gap] and its resonances in the elements that encircle it."[5]

What does Žižek mean by this? He certainly does not mean what cowboy Marxism 101 courses mean: namely, that, by exposing its underlying ideological lies, "true art" contests/mobilizes people against the established order that those lies help to secure. Instead, Žižek suggests a cinematic politics that uses film to trigger encounters with the Real, which, by shattering the fantasy coordinates that restrict the domain of the possible, opens a space in which new possibilities are brought forward. Or, as Žižek puts it: by "changing the coordinates of the situation . . . the subject . . . cuts himself loose from the [fantasy that] keeps him in check [thereby] gaining the space for free action."[6] In short, rather than (as a traditional radical politics does) contesting the established order of things, let alone advocating some new, less oppressive order, this politics opens a space in which new possible principles of ordering reality are advanced.

In *Bodies without Organs* Žižek suggests two possibilities for implementing such a politics, corresponding to two different modes of encounter with the Real. The *first* mode of encounter with the Real follows closely the analysis of the gaze that Lacan presents in the opening section of *Seminar XI*. To be specific, it involves encounters with blind spots, anamorphic distortions, stains, gleams of light, among others, that is, with *open-cuts* in the visual field, which offer the subject nothing to see other than a failure to see. Subjects fill out such blind spots with speculative phantasms of what it is that they might be looking at but cannot see. As Lacan puts it: "What the voyeur is looking for and finds is merely a shadow, a shadow behind the curtain. There he will phantasize any magic of presence, the most graceful of girls for example, even if on the other side there is only a hairy athlete."[7]

How do these encounters with the subject's failure to see constitute encounters with a gaze? The encounters constitute a gaze insofar as the failure to see triggers an unconscious desire to see what the subject fantasizes that she misses seeing. This desire is structured in terms of, on the one hand, the subject's repressed fantasies—"the most graceful of girls," as he puts it—and, on the other hand, an imaginary Other that is able to see what the subject misses seeing. And insofar as the subject desires to see what she misses, she desires to see from the point of view of this imaginary Other. Furthermore, insofar as the look by the Other turns back upon the subject herself, it triggers in her an experience of being under scrutiny from a point of view from which she cannot see, let alone know how she appears. Lacan's name for this look by the Other in relation to which the subject experiences herself under (what is ultimately a self-imposed) scrutiny is "the gaze." The source of this gaze is projected onto the blind spot in the visual field that triggers the scrutiny (or, more correctly, projected onto the empty space behind that blind spot).

Following Freud's argument in his *Instincts and Vicissitudes* essay, by virtue of the resistance that it offers to seeing what lies behind it, such a blind spot causes a series of reversals in the viewer's scopic regime—from seeing, to being seen, to displaying—thus laying out the lineaments of the scopic drive for which the blind spot, or more correctly the empty space behind it, functions as the object of the drive or what Lacan calls the *objet a* around which the drive turns. In Freud's terminology, these reversals, specifically the reversal from the subject seeing to being seen/putting itself on display, constitute the "vicissitudes of the drive." Here, then, we see that the *objet a*, namely, the empty space around which the scopic drive turns, takes on the added status of the gaze, namely, the source of the look in relation to which the subject displays itself—a look that, as Lacan puts it, the subject imagines in the field of the Other.[8]

Again following Freud, Lacan argues that such drive formations yield viewers a quotient of pleasure, thus distracting them from their failure to get what they desire, and in the process consolidating, indeed setting in place the processes of repression that drive the desire into the unconscious. As a result of the inevitable failure to satisfy it, the repressed desire subsequently undergoes a series of shifts, sustained through a series of mutations from one end of the subject's life to the other, remaining all the while in harness with the drive processes and other secondary forms of repression that cover over the role of the repressed desire in structuring the subject's activities.

For example, even prudish viewers of film, who, at a conscious level, are quite clear about what they want, namely, to erase any sight of a naked female body, take pleasure in looking for and spotting (if only in order to censor) the little glimpses that "go too far" in revealing the "bad stuff" that they fantasize lies behind the veil. As a result, despite being quite clear at a conscious level about what they want, their responses, and *a fortiori* their unconscious desires, slip and slide all over the place, shifting unstably between, on the one hand, an antipathy that is expressed by their turning away in revulsion from what they see and, on the other hand, a prurient desire expressed in seeking a glimpse of what they cannot stop looking for. These polymorphously perverse unconscious desires are repressed, hidden beneath the relatively stable conscious desire with which they sometimes align and at other times oppose.

The *second* mode of encounter with the Real presupposes that a film is structured by a hidden—we may say "repressed"—fantasy. The encounter with the Real happens when this fantasy comes too close to the surface of the film. As a result, what the film shows is not so much an *open cut* in the visual field as a *cutaway* from what the spectator can identify with seeing. In other words, the eye of the camera splits from the point of view of the spectator, thus constituting an instance of what Dziga Vertov called "the Kino-Eye." Žižek calls this an "objective subjective" shot: "objective" in the sense of floating free from the spectator's point of view, but also "desubjectivized" because, by bringing repressed fantasy materials too close to the surface, it is excessively—uncomfortably—"subjective" (for example, a beaver shot of a naked old woman, which comes too close to realizing an unconscious lascivious desired to see the naked body of the Mother). This uncomfortable closeness of fantasy material, in turn, prevents the subject from identifying with the shot in the sense of identifying with its point of view.[9] As I indicated earlier, Lacan's name for the imaginary point of view from which the repressed fantasy material is seen is the point of view of the Other: an imaginary point of view from which the fantastic material is seen and with which, therefore, the subject cannot identify.[10]

The viewing subject has an epistemically impoverished relation with the Other. That is, although the subject looks at what the Other sees, she cannot identify with the point of view from which the Other is looking, that is, she does not see or even know what it is that the Other sees. Thus, for the subject, the encounter with the Kino-Eye is another form of blind spot, for which the subject does not know what she sees and, more specifically, does not know how what she sees relates to how it appears.[11] But, to repeat my earlier point, because she desires to know what the Other sees, and in particular desires to know what the Other sees in her, she experiences herself under scrutiny by the Other. And it is in precisely that sense that we may say that the look by the Other takes on the status of a gaze.

In *Seminar XI* Lacan illustrates an encounter with the gaze by telling a little story from his student days. In some "desperation," he tells us, he fled from his Parisian studies to Brittany, where he spent a day at sea working on a fishing boat. A blinding light, reflected from a sardine can that was floating on the sea, provided the occasion for a joke by the fisherman, Petit Jean: "*You see that can? Do you see it? Well, it doesn't see you!*" Lacan adds: "If what Petit Jean said to me, namely that the can did not see me, had any meaning, it was because, in a sense, it was looking at me, all the same. It was looking at me at the level of the point of light, the point at which everything that looks at me is situated—and I am not speaking metaphorically."[12] In this instance, therefore, the two forms of gaze that I mention here are not only copresent but also coincide. That is, for the young Lacan, the gaze manifested as a blind spot in his visual field, which took on an uncomfortable meaning through Petit Jean's joke that brought to the surface a fantasy that the young Lacan could not face (even as it covertly structured his actions): namely, the fantasy that he had no place, which, in turn, staged a desire to find an identity for himself and what he was doing. The representative of the Other in this little story, we may add, was the not-so-ancient mariner, Petit Jean, whose joke triggered the look that the young Lacan projected outward onto the glittering eye of the sardine can. More than an illustration of the gaze, Lacan's little representative anecdote of the sardine can suggests that it is precisely the surfacing of fantasy that transforms a visual distortion—be it a Kino-Eye or point of light—into an encounter with the Real of the gaze.

I agree with both Žižek and Todd McGowan in including the "open cut" as well as the "cutaway" under the heading of "encounters with the gaze." Where, then, do I disagree with them? First, a small criticism: namely, that both authors fail to distinguish carefully enough between the cutaway of the Kino-Eye and the familiar Lacanian examples of the gaze: namely, the glints of light, stains, and anamorphic distortions. In particular, both authors fail to explore how the relation with fantasy differs in the case of the Kino-Eye (in which the surfacing of fantasy functions as a cause) from these familiar Lacanian examples of the gaze (in which the surfacing of fantasy is an effect).

My main point of disagreement with Žižek and McGowan lies elsewhere, however. To be specific, I suggest that we should broaden their

concept of the gaze to include instances of the Kino-Eye, which are triggered by "overconformity"—meaning a too strict, "overly literal" adherence—to the cinematic conventions that structure the film.[13] In the final
section of this essay, I argue that this broadening of the concept of the
gaze has consequences for Žižek's radical politics. Specifically, I argue that
it brings it together with the anticapitalist cinematic politics of innervation
that Benjamin put forward in his earlier work prior to "The Work of Art in
the Age of Mechanical Reproduction" (hereafter: the Artwork essay).

From *Schindler's List* to *Melancholia*

Consider Todd McGowan's account of the following scene from Spielberg's
Schindler's List: the Nazi commandant Amon Goeth (Ralph Fiennes) "shoots
Jews from the veranda of his quarters. . . . Spielberg cuts from Goeth's seemingly omnipotent look to a series of objective shots from ground level in the
camp. . . . we see the camp at ground level . . . and Goeth himself appears
as a barely recognizable blur in the background. . . . it is these brief shots of
the absent point of the Other that manifest the gaze."[14] McGowan continues:
"The spectator cannot experience mastery here [because the spectator cannot identify with the peculiar point of view from which the scene is shot]
but instead must experience the indecipherable desire of [for] the Other."[15]

In his analysis of the gaze in this scene, McGowan runs together two
quite different formal features of the film. First, in what seems to be a nod
to Lacan's characterization of the gaze as points of visual indeterminacy—
open cuts or points of failure in the visual field where we see that we cannot
see—McGowan indicates that Goeth appears in the shot as "a barely recognizable blur." But McGowan immediately follows this remark by asserting
that the gaze is constituted through a second formal feature: namely, that
the scene is shot from an impossible point of view with which the viewer
cannot identify. In short, for McGowan, the gaze in this particular scene is
constituted through the phenomenon of the Kino-Eye, in which what the
camera sees cuts away from what the viewer is able to identify with seeing.

I agree with McGowan that the gaze in this scene is tied to the Kino-
Eye. But, I argue, McGowan's mentioning the Kino-Eye in the same breath as
the blurred image of Goeth indicates an unfortunate reluctance on his part
to let go of Lacan's predilection for examples of the gaze that involve visual
indeterminacies and/or distortions: the stain, the blot, the glint of light, the
anamorphic projection. In what follows, I push against this predilection by
presenting a series of examples of the gaze qua Kino-Eye in which there is

no trace of visual blurring or distortion. I also argue that the Kino-Eye is triggered not only by scenes of the sort that Žižek considers, in which the generic cinematic conventions that frame the film are violated to the point that what appears on screen emerges as a distortion of the filmscape, but also by scenes that *overconform*—that is, conform too closely—to the film's framing conventions.

Consider Lars von Trier's *Melancholia*. The opening surreal scene, preceding the titles, is shot at a variety of speeds from slow motion to still shots. It shows a picture of Brueghel's famous painting *Hunters in the Snow* gradually distorting and melting away, the birds painted above the hunters blending with dead birds that the film shows falling from the sky. It also includes an image of two planets moving majestically toward each other: a vision that is cosmic not only in its content but also in the desubjectivized, objective perspective from which it is shot (an effect enhanced by the grandiose music of the sound track).

After this opening pre-title sequence until its ending, the film is, for the most part, quite conventionally realist, incorporating only minor anti-realist blips: little pockets of weirdness that the viewer easily brushes past (such as the difficulty in identifying whether the roving camera that records the wedding party is extra or intradiegetic). Toward the end of the film, however, a scene is included that, metonymically signaling the end of the world, constitutes a major swerve from the dominant realist conventions. The screen suddenly fills with a fireball, followed by total blackness, which functions as a blot that totally erases the intradiegetic cinematic landscape.

At first sight this apocalyptic scene fits well—indeed, all too well—with a Lacanian conception of the gaze as an open cut in the visual field that is carved out by the intrusion of fiery light and then total blackness that (until the closing credits appear on the same backdrop) makes it impossible to tell when the film ends. From a Lacanian point of view, this seems to exemplify the gaze in pure form—a *Lichtspiel* (play with light)—but also a blurring of the boundary between the content of the film and the film as material artifact. Appearances are deceptive here, however. Such total erasure of imagery has become a conventional signifier of the end of the world. Consequently (by contrast with the glint of light that reflects from the floating sardine can that the young Lacan encounters at sea), what appears on screen is both perfectly visible and comprehensible: a perfectly meaningful signifier—an icon even—of the end of the world. It follows that, despite the spectacular eruption of light that blots out the cinematic landscape, this is *not* a case of the gaze in Lacan's sense, let alone an encounter with the Real. On the contrary, it leaves the symbolic order firmly in place, enabling viewers to interpret what they are looking at, and, as such, enabling them to go beyond mere looking to fully seeing. Sometimes (to adapt Freud's famous comment about cigars) a play of light is not just a play of light—but neither is it a gaze.

There is more to say, however. Although what viewers see in looking at this end-of-the-world scene is clear enough—namely, apocalypse now—they are unable to identify with a point of view from which what appears on screen is seen. Why not? Because, to put it bluntly, there is no one around to view it. Thus, insofar as it is shot from an impossible position—namely, looking at the cosmos from a position outside of it where there is nothing to do the looking—this end-of-world scene formally mirrors the opening pre-title scene. Both scenes shatter what, for the bulk of the rest of the film is a fairly strict conformity with realist conventions: either conventional shot-reverse-shots that locate a member of the *dramatis personae* with which the camera eye is identified, or equally conventional "objective" shots that posit an invisible camera eye, distanced from/outside the action that it registers. (As I indicated, a minor exception is the film's wedding scenes, in which the camera hops in familiar fashion among the guests, as if it is one of them, but they, in turn, never acknowledge its presence.) In short, although viewers see, even understand, perfectly well what is being represented in these two opening and final scenes, they cannot determine, let alone identify with, a point of view from which what they show is seen. In short, viewers encounter the Kino-Eye, which, in turn, triggers an encounter with the gaze qua look by the Other.

The gaze here is triggered through an unsettling of the viewers' point of view by the film showing a scene from a point of view with which viewers cannot identify, an unsettling that, in turn, entails that the viewers' act of seeing is cast adrift in a space between, on the one hand, their looking at what they are shown on screen and, on the other hand, what they are able to identify with seeing. This, in turn, means that their seeing is haunted by a desire to identify with the point of view of the Other, who, even while seeing things subjectively, sees them objectively, as they really are. (In a cinematic context, it is usual for the Other to be materially embodied in the eye of the camera—or, as Benjamin puts it, the eye of the cinematic apparatus—although, of course, there are films in which the eye of the camera is presented as unreliable.)

In sum, in the final melancholic apocalyptic scene, the blinding fireball followed by blackness is straightforwardly open to interpretation from within the spectator's symbolic order and as such *cannot* constitute a gaze qua eruption of the Real. But even so, there is a gaze, constituted, I have argued, *not* through Lacan's favored "play of light" but rather through the

Kino-Eye: specifically, through an objective, "desubjectivized" shot of the end-of-the-world, which, insofar as it is seen through the eye of the camera from which spectators are alienated (that is, with which they cannot identify) troubles the visual symbolic order, thereby causing an encounter with the Real in the specific form of the gaze qua look by the Other.

In his film analyses in *Bodies without Organs*, Žižek focuses upon exactly such instances of encounters with the gaze qua Kino-Eye that insert a cut between what the camera sees and the point of view of the spectator. In such scenes, the audience is unable to identify with the point of view of the camera, even as, thanks to the prosthetic device of the cinematic apparatus, they are able to look at (and in a desubjectivized mode) "see" what it sees objectively:

> What revolutionary cinema should be doing [is] using the camera
> as a partial object, as an "eye" torn from the [viewing] subject
> [to whom it is sutured] and freely thrown around. . . . in such
> weird [viewing] experiences . . . one catches what Lacan called
> gaze . . . it is my gaze itself that is objectivized, which observes
> me from the outside [even as I observe it], which, precisely means
> that my gaze is no longer mine, that it is stolen from me.[16]

Where do I diverge from Žižek and McGowan? Again, I agree with them that the Kino-Eye constitutes an instance of the gaze. In particular, I agree that, insofar as it confronts viewers with a cut between what they see and what they are looking at (and *a fortiori* between what they see and what the Other sees) it sustains an encounter with the gaze. I diverge from them, however, by emphasizing that such instances of the gaze, as cutaways from what the viewer can identify with seeing, go well beyond the open cuts in the visual field—the blots, the gleams of light, the distortions—that Lacan associates with the gaze. The scene that I cited from *Schindler's List* exemplifies this, albeit (I argued) with a certain ambiguity. That is, it is the peculiar angle from which the scene is shot that sustains an encounter with the gaze, but (*pace* McGowan) has little to do with the blurring of the imagery of the shooter. And similarly in *Melancholia*, although in the end-of-the-world scene, by virtue of its firm anchorage as a signifier belonging to the cinematic symbolic order, the blinding glare of light that formally echoes Lacan's blot gazes does not constitute a gaze. Instead, the gaze that the scene sustains is constituted through the impossible point of view from which it is shot: namely, belonging to but at the same time outside the world that is destroyed.

These cases take Lacan's analysis of the gaze in a different direction, away from the glints of light and distortions that he foregrounds. But, I now argue, Lacan implicitly anticipates this different direction. Consider, for example, his account of the famous anamorphic image of a skull in Holbein's *The Ambassadors*. Lacan emphasizes the *distorted* nature of the image, which "from some angles appears to be [an object] flying through the air, at others to be tilted. You cannot know—for you turn away, thus escaping the fascination of the picture."[17] Through such anamorphic images, he says, "I will have the pleasure of obtaining not the restoration of [some truer conception] of the world . . . but the *distortion*, on another surface, of the image that I would have obtained on the first."[18]

But, and here's the key point, *despite* Lacan's insistence that what is at issue here is "distortion [which] may lend itself to all the paranoic ambiguities," it is clear that what is at issue for him in Holbein's painting is *both more and less than distortion*. It is *less* than distortion because, from some angles, only a small part of the canvas is distorted. But it is also *more* than distortion. To be specific, like a gestalt diagram, from one angle the painting shows an image of the two ambassadors while the skull image is distorted out of recognition. From another angle, however, it shows an image of a skull while the image of the ambassadors is distorted out of recognition. Thus, it is not so much a matter of pure and simple visual *distortion* but rather of a visual *instability* between the two different perspectives, which is triggered by the difference between the distortions that they reveal. In brief, the picture has two different contents, linked to two different perspectives, linked to two different distortions. The key point, then, is that these interlinked differences encourage viewers to incorporate a degree of play into how they look at the picture.

In the next section, I argue that the possibility to which Lacan's analysis of *The Ambassadors* implicitly alerts us here, namely, of the gaze that goes beyond mere distortion or visual indeterminacies, is realized in pure form in David Lynch's *Blue Velvet*. To be specific, I argue that, by contrast with the scenes that I mentioned from *Schindler's List* and *Melancholia*, the famous naked-in-the-street scene in *Blue Velvet* incorporates a gaze despite the total absence of the sorts of blurring/blinding/distortion that Lacan features in his examples of the gaze. More than that, going beyond Žižek, I argue that this scene incorporates a Kino-Eye/gaze that is triggered through overconforming to, rather than breaking from, the film's framing generic conventions. To be specific, in *Blue Velvet*, the Kino-Eye/gaze arises by the film *conforming too perfectly* to realism, which, in turn, allows viewers to see vicariously (through the eye of the camera) what they cannot bear to see directly.[19]

Blue Velvet

First let me introduce a contrasting earlier scene from *Blue Velvet* in which the gaze manifests along more orthodox Lacanian lines: the nightclub singer Dorothy (played by Isabella Rossellini) has successive sexual encounters with the voyeuristic, starstruck Jeffrey (Kyle McLachlan) and the sadistic psychopath Frank (Dennis Hopper). In the course of the scene, set in Dorothy's seedy apartment, viewers encounter a narrative indeterminacy circulating the question: "What does Dorothy want?" This, in turn, creates a visual indeterminacy in how viewers see her actions. To be specific, we are left wondering whether we are seeing a sadomasochistic Dorothy getting off on her sexual relations with the violent Frank and voyeuristic Jeffrey or an innocent brutalized victim perverted by the abuse she suffers at the hands of the two men. The intradiegetic indeterminacy is doubled by a visually and aurally distorted montage of shots that terminates the scene, structured both by a gaze/Kino-Eye and by what Michel Chion calls the acousmatic voice.[20]

McGowan describes this montage in the following terms: "After witnessing Frank assault her . . . we see a brief montage: a face distorted by being stretched across the screen; Frank silently screaming; a candle blowing out; and finally Dorothy saying to Frank, 'Hit me,' followed by his blow to her face and her scream [Frank's unheard scream, delayed and dragged out of the wrong body]." "The montage," McGowan continues, "reveals the traumatic Real that exists between the worlds of desire and fantasy. It is in the movement between these worlds that one encounters the gaze, and the Real of the (M)Other's desire [and we may add, the Real of the acousmatic voice]."[21]

The gaze is present here *not* through the gleam of light or blot beloved by Lacan but *rather* through a combination of distortion and the formal structure of montage, which, by making obvious the mediation of the cinematic apparatus in the production of the image, cut the eye of the spectator away from the point of view of the camera. Such a cutaway, I have argued, is characteristic of the phenomenon of the Kino-Eye, in which the act of looking by spectators is destabilized by refusing to let them identify with a point of view from which what they see is being/has been looked at, on their behalf, by an-Other.

The grueling apartment scene contrasts with a street scene toward the end of the film: bruised, dazed, and naked, Dorothy wanders into the quiet, early-evening streets of suburban middle-American Lumberton, with its almost too perfect rows of white picket fences, orderly flower beds, and respectable bourgeois citizens. Her entrance disrupts the idyllic scene in spectacular fashion. As McGowan puts it, Dorothy's body "does not fit the picture, which is why the spectator becomes so uncomfortable watching her naked body in the middle of the suburban neighborhood. . . . Dorothy's presence is unbearable both for the characters within the diegesis . . . and for the spectator."[22] McGowan adds: "Dorothy embodies the gaze, and our anxiety in seeing her indicates an encounter with it."[23] Indeed, we can strengthen McGowan's claim here: "our" anxiety—that is, the anxiety of anyone made uncomfortable by the image—is not merely an effect qua *indication* of an encounter with the gaze. Instead, the causal arrow is reversed: our anxiety is a cause of the gaze: retrospectively conferring the status of gaze onto the formal incongruity of Dorothy's presence.

By contrast with the earlier scene in Dorothy's apartment, this street scene provides little or no visual or aural distortion and comparatively little visual indeterminacy. What traces there are, for example, of a certain ambiguity about the place from where Dorothy enters the scene, as if her presence is simply cut into the film from one frame to the next—are easily passed over in the onward rush of cinematic images. Even when we might expect a discrete averting of the camera's eye, there is nothing missing, let alone indeterminate or distorted, in what we are shown of Dorothy's body. On the contrary, although not in any sense a focus, all of Dorothy's private parts are clearly, straightforwardly, even, we might add, cruelly on public view, right down to her pubic hair and genitalia. Indeed, even the enigma of her desire is (more or less) resolved when she blames her actions on a pathological contamination by Frank: "He put his sickness in me," she mumbles (albeit leaving minor ambiguities about [a] whether she includes the voyeurism of Jeffrey as a sources of her "infection" and [b] whether she addresses the remark to the extradiegetic audience (or herself, or perhaps her intradiegetic audience). At the same time, the manifestations of her desire are reduced to a series of pathetic gestures, which, by contrast with her earlier behavior with Frank and Jeffrey, the spectator has no trouble in interpreting: she clings to Jeffrey, demanding his attention, mewling for him to save her.

In short, the image of her body wandering naked in the streets neither lacks visual definition, nor is it distorted, nor does it have a metonymic connection with the inscrutably obscene desire of the (M)Other that Dorothy manifests in the earlier scene. On all counts, it seems, from a Lacanian point of view, the image of Dorothy naked wandering the streets of Lumberton does *not* incorporate a gaze.

So how can we justify McGowan's Žižekian claim that this scene incorporates a gaze? In order to answer this question, we must understand how films respond to the taboo surrounding the public/pubic representation of women's naked bodies. The first sort of response, characteristic of the conventional Hollywood realist AO (Adults Only) genre, locates the naked body behind a diaphanous veil, or perhaps more prosaically behind a sheet, which, as if by accident or perhaps the result of a (not always easy to understand) postcoital modesty, falls (or is held in place) over the offending body parts. But even so, and equally accidentally, the veil slips enough to offer tantalizing glimpses of the forbidden.

Any such veil constitutes a gaze, for which the Real effects of the fantasy material to which it alludes are to some extent neutralized—we may say "repressed." How repressed? By embedding the veil in a little defensive narrative: for example, the *accident* of the sheet falling into place, veiling but not totally obscuring the "naughty bits" that the film is forbidden from exposing, and as such stimulating viewers to look harder and longer rather than letting them chafe under an immovable resistance to their seeing what an-Other is able to see but they cannot: the scop-erotics of the veil.

The second sort of cinematic response to the naked female body is exemplified by conventional realist films "for general exhibition," which, in the name of preserving decency, conceal the "naughty bits" by using familiar *antirealist* devices: for example, the blurred censorship matrix and diegetically unmotivated changes in camera angle that stand out as intrusions by the cinematic apparatus that have been tailored to block the offending body parts. In these cases the gaze is destroyed simply by shifting the body out of sight, definitively squashing any hints about what is there to be seen.

The third sort of response is exemplified by "R"-rated realist films with "sexual content." They use the formally *antirealist* long shot that reverses the effects of the censorship matrix. That is, rather than covering up the offending body parts, it lingers over them. In such cases, the gaze is destroyed, not by shifting she-who-must-not-be-seen out of sight but rather by the reverse strategy of bringing her so close for so long that, by contrast with the gaze-infested veil, there is no ambiguity about the reality of what is seen (or not). And this in turn means that the Real effects of the surfacing of fantasy are neutralized by showing the reality that the fantasy dresses up. In Žižek's terms, this familiar array of antirealist devices forms an "obscene underside" of antirealist exceptions to the conventions of realism that frame the film.

Dorothy's naked street scene uses none of these devices, disdaining the veil and censorship matrix as well as the long shot. Instead, the scene sticks scrupulously—indeed, we may say, sticks overscrupulously, or, in Žižekian terms, "overconforms"—to the realist conventions that structure what the eye of the camera sees. To be specific, the camera neither stares at the reality that it displays (the pornographic R strategy) nor prudishly turns away (the desexualized "for general exhibition" strategy) nor veils it (the erotic AO strategy). Instead, with neither fear nor favor, in good realist fashion, it objectively and impartially scans every part of Dorothy's anatomy, including the "naughty bits." In so doing, the scene "overconforms" with the realist conventions in the sense of stretching them to the point where convention requires that they should be broken. To be specific, it does so in a situation where what it shows the spectator is both "too much" and "too little": "too much" not merely because to look at what it shows is immodest or impolite (after all, the spectator is only watching a film rather than a real body) but rather because, by openly, objectively showing an image of the female genitalia, it brings too close to the surface a repressed primal fantasy of castration that triggers in spectators an anxiety-provoking encounter with the Real, but also "too little" because (unlike the porno flick) it does so without neutralizing the Real effects of encounter through overexposure of the naked reality that the fantasy dresses up.[24]

More than that, precisely because of this overconformity to the cinematic conventions within which the film is framed, the scene cuts the spectator away from the eye of the camera, thereby destabilizing the act of looking and triggering an encounter with the Kino-Eye/gaze. This "blinds" viewers not in the usual sense of stopping them from seeing what they are looking at/for, but rather by desubjectivizing their act of seeing, that is, by not allowing them to identify with the act of seeing what they are looking at. Thus, like the first blinding of Oedipus (namely, his seeing what he cannot bear to look at, that is, the dead body of Jocasta, the woman whom he has come to recognize as his mother/wife), it exposes viewers to a visual excess: specifically, showing them, and thus getting them to look at what they can't identify with seeing. The result: a stumble in the act of looking—not a straightforward failure to see/loss of vision but rather a failure to identify with the act of seeing what nevertheless is on show.

In sum, contra McGowan, I argue that, in Blue Velvet's naked street scene, an encounter with the Real, and more specifically an encounter with the gaze take place, not as in the examples discussed by Lacan via an encounter with an open cut in the visual field (a blot, or a glare of light or any sort of formal distortion). Nor, contra Žižek does it take place through an encounter with the Kino-Eye that is triggered by a failure of the generic conventions framing the film. Instead, it is triggered by an overconformity to those conventions. Here, it seems, we must go beyond both McGowan and Žižek and add a new dimension to the cinematic gaze.

Benjaminian Coda

In *Cinema and Experience*, Miriam Hansen argues that the Lacanian gaze shares a close affinity with what Benjamin calls "aura, understood as a form of perception that 'invests' or endows a phenomenon with the 'ability to look back at us,' to open its eyes or raise its gaze."[25] It follows that if we accept Benjamin's thesis that the age of mechanical reproduction has brought about the withering of aura, then, it seems, we can no longer pin our radical political hopes upon artworks that create encounters with the gaze. In line with exactly this conclusion, Benjamin takes it that, instead of the pursuit of aura, the political task for art today has shifted to the production of films, which, by triggering playful (what Benjamin calls) "innervative" responses that loosen the viewer's tie to any established symbolic order, have the potential of restoring life to consciousnesses anesthetized by the workaday routines of modern industrial capitalism.[26] To create such innervative responses, Benjamin argues, is the "world-historic destiny of film today."[27] And since overconformity to the cinematic conventions creates exactly such playful innervative responses, it follows that overconformity becomes one way of discharging this radical political project.

In light of my earlier argument that links overconformity to encounters with the gaze, this, in turn, suggests that we further rework the concept of the cinematic gaze to include any torsion of a film's visual field that playfully loosens the grip that the cinematic conventions exercise upon the viewers' visual experience. Indeed, one might argue, ultimately it is precisely such playful loosening of conventions that elevates a mere torsion in the visual field into an encounter with the Real and thus into an encounter with the gaze. This reworking of the notion of gaze allows us to get back onto a theoretical track to which, Hansen points out, Benjamin was committed in his earlier work: namely, a politics of auratic encounters that draws upon a concept of aura that converges with a concept of gaze.

Hansen points out that, perhaps as a result of his difficult exchanges with Adorno, Benjamin appears to have rejected any such progressive concept of aura in the final version of the Artwork essay, where he argues not only for the regressive impact of aura but also for its (fortunate) withering in the age of mechanical reproduction. Hansen immediately follows this point, however, by adding that there are hidden continuities between, on the one hand, the Artwork essay in which Benjamin turned away from the concept of aura toward the new concept of "optical unconscious" and, on the other hand, his earlier work, where the concept of aura (along with the related concept of gaze) enjoyed a more positive status. This hidden

continuity becomes apparent when we recognize that the optical unconscious of a film manifests precisely in the playful innervative responses of
its audience that, I have argued, are part and parcel of encounters with (a
suitably broadened concept) of the gaze. As Hansen herself makes the point,
"For Benjamin, the ominous aspect of aura belongs to . . . the [politically
and psychically regressive] phenomenon of self-alienating encounters with
an older, other self."[28] But, she continues, "[i]n a technologically refracted,
specifically modern form, this aspect of aura resurfaces in the [Benjaminian]
notion of an optical unconscious."[29]

The politics of the gaze, which I am assimilating to the closeted politics
of aura that we find in Benjamin's later work, does not work through polem-
ics or ideology critique. Instead, it sets up encounters with the gaze that, by
introducing a degree of "innervative play" into "ways of seeing," loosen the
grip that the established perceptual grid exercises upon its audience. The
cultural politics that result from this synthesis of Benjamin-with-Žižek offers
what Benjamin designates as a "go for broke" strategy that (in the immortal
words of *Battlestar Galactica*) may well represent "humanity's last best hope"
in the age of mechanical reproduction.[30]

Notes

1. Slavoj Žižek, *Organs without Bodies: Deleuze and Consequences* (New York:
Routledge, 2004), 213.

2. Jacques Rancière, *The Emancipated Spectator*, trans. Gregory Elliot
(London: Verso, 2009), 60–62.

3. Slavoj Žižek, *The Plague of Fantasies* (London: Verso, 1997), 20.

4. Žižek, *The Plague of Fantasies*, 18.

5. Žižek, *The Plague of Fantasies*, 19.

6. Slavoj Žižek, *The Fragile Absolute* (London: Verso, 2000), 150.

7. Jacques Lacan, *The Four Fundamental Concepts of Psycho-Analysis*, ed.
Jacques-Alain Miller, trans. Alan Sheridan (New York: Norton, 1981), 182.

8. *Instincts and Vicissitudes*, in *The Standard Edition of the Complete
Psychological Works of Sigmund* Freud, vol. 14, ed. James Strachey (London: Hogarth
Press, 1953), 109–117.

9. Žižek, *Organs without Bodies*, 151–155.

10. By virtue of the credibility of the photographic medium, it is typically the
eye of the camera that takes on the role of the Other.

11. Note that, in an extended sense, we may say the subject identifies with
this Other, insofar as she desires to look from the perspective of the Other. (Here
the Other is an extension of what Freud calls "the ego-ideal"). But the subject also
fails to identify with the Other. That is, although the subject desires to see what the

Other makes out of what is on display, she is unable to fulfill this desire. In short, the subject desires but is unable to take up the point of view of the Other.

12. Lacan, *The Four Fundamental Concepts*, 95.

13. Žižek, *The Plague of Fantasies*, 22–26. Žižek uses the term "overidentification," but I prefer "overconformity," which places more emphasis upon the act rather than the psychic state of the agent.

14. Todd McGowan, "Looking for the Gaze: Lacanian Film Theory and Its Vicissitudes," *Cinema Journal* 42.3 (2003): 37.

15. McGowan, "Looking for the Gaze," 37.

16. Žižek, *Organs without Bodies*, 154–155.

17. Lacan, *The Four Fundamental Concepts*, 88.

18. Lacan, *The Four Fundamental Concepts*, 87. Note here the implication that, by virtue of its "fascinating" effects, triggered by its bringing too close to the surface some unspecified fantasy, the viewer is compelled to "escape" the image, which, in that sense, we may say, cannot be looked at.

19. I am not claiming that this effect takes place for all or even most viewers. Instead, I take the question of which viewers encounter the gaze to be determined only retrospectively, by the effect that the scene has upon them. I return to this point in the final section.

20. Michel Chion and Claudia Gorbman, *Audio-Vision: Sound on Screen* (New York: Columbia University Press, 1994).

21. McGowan, "Looking for the Gaze," 43.

22. McGowan, "Looking for the Gaze," 43.

23. McGowan, "Looking for the Gaze," 43.

24. Here we must be careful to avoid a naïve Freudianism. In the same way that Freud cautioned that sometimes a cigar is just a cigar, sometimes too a vagina is just a vagina rather than the open wound from cutting off a penis. This salutary caution shifts the onus of proof: we cannot assume that in general the sighting of female genitals will result in the surfacing of a castration fantasy. Instead, we are justified in making this assumption only when the sighting occasions an encounter with the Real.

25. Miriam Bratu Hansen, *Cinema and Experience: Siegfried Kracauer, Walter Benjamin, and Theodor Adorno* (Berkeley: University of California Press, 2012), 106; see also 109–110.

26. Note that this is the very reverse of creating an escapist fantasy. Instead, it involves loosening the tie to the fantasy through which any symbolic order establishes its grip.

27. Hansen, *Cinema*, 132–145.

28. Hansen, *Cinema*, 107.

29. Hansen, *Cinema*, 107.

30. Hansen, *Cinema*, 139. A difficulty here: In *The Plague of Fantasies*, Žižek argues that distancing viewers from their ideological picture of reality supports, rather than undermines, the workings of ideology. Indeed, Žižek claims, the ideological effect *is* this distancing. As Žižek himself puts it, the "successful functioning" of

"an ideological edifice . . . requires a minimal distance from its explicit rules . . . this very distance is ideology" (20–22). But if this is so then, it seems, introducing a degree of play into, and thus "distancing" them from, their ideologically structured ways of seeing will support rather than undermine people's ideology. The point, however, is that the distancing that, Žižek argues, is conservative in its effects, is merely an *intellectual* distancing of attitudes that, at a *practical/experiential* level, remain firmly in place precisely because of this intellectual distancing. By contrast, the "distancing" that Benjamin includes under the category of "play" is a distancing at the level of what people experience, which is independent of what they may or may not come to believe intellectually. For example, by bringing to the visual surface of a film an audience's repressed fantasy, an encounter with a cultural artifact may produce such a distancing effect: not so much changing what the audience sees as introducing a degree of play or instability into an audience's ways of seeing. It is here, then, that we may look for a Žižekian/Benjaminian radical cultural politics.

10

The End of Fantasy as We Know It

Her and the Vanishing Mediator of the Voice in Film

SHEILA KUNKLE

Many film scholars consider Charlie Chaplin's 1936 *Modern Times* as the film that ended an era, for it was the last appearance of the iconic figure of the little Tramp in a silent film. Released nine years after the first talkie, *The Jazz Singer*, in 1927, Chaplin's last silent film would already appear as a kind of anachronism, since synchronized sound quickly became the standard in feature films of the day. Yet, in a prescient moment of redoubling Chaplin introduces the voice in *Modern Times* indirectly by way of a loud speaker when he depicts the modern-day factory boss barking out orders to his underlings.[1] In this way, Chaplin juxtaposes two unlike phenomena simultaneously: the image of the silent figure of the little Tramp and the sound of the mechanized human voice (of capitalist authority) that makes it at once familiar and strange.

Fast-forwarding to the present, we find in director Spike Jonze's 2013 film *Her* the voice now completely virtual and separate from the body, available everywhere in the form of an Operating System (OS), a computer software program accessible through an earpiece. Theodore Twombly (Joachin Phoenix), a lonely divorcé, can access this voice (Scarlett Johansson) at any time, and it quickly becomes apparent that this OS is an artificial intelligence that directly anticipates and responds to his every need. Between *Modern Times* and *Her*, we can trace the contours of a vanishing mediator where the voice that appeared in Chaplin's film as a strange and excess voice of modern capitalist authority is replaced in the film *Her* by a calculating intelligence that ushers in fantasy's pervasive disappearance into a privatized and technologized capitalism. This vanishing reconfigures the very coordinates of the subject and its libidinal experiences of enjoyment, for with daily technologies that can calculate the probability of our every desire based on our "singular" proclivities, what we get paradoxically is the disappearance of the voice as the Lacanian object *a*, as the very thing (of lack) that works to cause desire and generate fantasy itself.

A vanishing mediator, according to Fredric Jameson, can be detected in the way Protestantism made the secular world itself more religious. As he relates, Max Weber's insight in *The Protestant Ethic and the Spirit of Capitalism*, published in 1904, was to show how Protestantism (and Calvinism in particular) changed our orientation to work by turning individualized and continuous labor into the proof of a pious life.[2] Protestantism thus served as the vanishing mediator between medieval monastic existence and modern life, but it was only seen retroactively as such with the arrival of capitalist relations of production. Here the concept of the vanishing mediator becomes useful not because it allows us to track causality or historicize an event, but rather because it allows us to detect what has dropped out of a scene by way of its very ubiquity. If Protestantism by means of its universalization paved the way for labor's withdrawal into the private sphere of individualized ethical duty, then we can see how the automated voice in its universalization is preparing the way for fantasy's withdrawal into a more privatized and individualized capitalism, despite the latter's globalized reach.[3] The film *Her* captures this phenomenon vividly; it posits a closure of the Real and reconfigures the symbolic as a flat world of pregenerated meanings; in the instantaneous and infinite calculations of the Operating System's (OS) artificial intelligence, the human itself appears as a limited being, limited not only by its ultimate physical death but also by its lingering need for words and the symbolic order itself.

To trace the contours of the vanishing mediator of the voice and the privatization of fantasy through technology, we begin by considering how the appearance of the voice in film reframed the artistry of the comic genius of Charlie Chaplin. In our hindsight we can see that Chaplin was a master of silence, and his full immersion into the talking picture was also his movement from mastery to a form of servitude (having no choice but to give up silence) in terms of his art form.[4] This is not to say that Chaplin's comic abilities were lost, but rather that they needed to find another formulation, and Chaplin achieved this in his brilliant use of the voice through the artifice of doubling. As authors Mladen Dolar and Alenka Zupančič find, Chaplin could use the voice successfully because he retained something of its uncanny nature, revealing how the voice works as an object of lack and excess, as something beyond meaning.[5] In *The Great Dictator* (1940), for example, Chaplin makes comic use of the voice as excess by juxtaposing the German gibberish spoken by the dictator Hynkel (Charlie Chaplin) and the speech at the end of the film by the little Jewish barber (also played by Chaplin), which is filled with a somber plea to humanism in a time of fascism. He juxtaposed the simultaneity of language's sense and meaning with the non-sense of words as signifiers, thus also exposing the structure in which language is made possible. Yet, despite the comic genius of Chaplin, we cannot help but to see that in his first talking picture, *The Great Dictator*, the little Tramp (a universal figure) has been transformed into the singular perspective of a "little Jew," the term Chaplin used in his script for the film.[6]

The transitions into the talking world that forced Chaplin from a position of mastery to that of compliance, in terms of using the voice in film, mirrored the divide of the elite class into "old and modern masters" in the rise of modern capitalism. As Alenka Zupančič writes, "The former were the masters of wealth, whereas the latter are its employees or slaves," something Chaplin captured well in his opening satire of factory life in *Modern Times*.[7] Importantly, with this changeover came also a new orientation to the symptom and to temporality; the merging of work and ethics and the simultaneous division of old and new masters coincided with a "modern obsessional neurosis (and anxiety), where the critical moments that have to be avoided at any price are precisely the moments of cessation or discontinuity, of pause, of time 'not filled' in, of silence."[8]

The virtualized voice, along with continuous access to images, is now an embedded feature of the processes of our contemporary capitalism. It was, as we know, Karl Marx who in *Grundrisse* readily detected the way modern capitalism colonized the physical conditions of exchange by spatializing time according to the succession of the working day.[9] And, with the relentless continuous processes brought about by computerization and calculation, our everyday lives have become, according to Jonathan Crary, author of *24/7: Late Capitalism and the Ends of Sleep* (2013), "fabricated micro-worlds of affects and symbols," which bring a "monotonous sameness in their temporal pattern and segmentations."[10] Silence is to be avoided at all costs, and rarely do people go for any length of time without accessing information or seeing an image. We live in a world now, as Crary relates, of "24/7 networks and markets," a life without breaks where even sleep has no necessity. Paradoxically, Crary finds that the continuous and infinite filtering, tracking, and calculating network that records our every activity not only anticipates and coaxes our individual needs and perversions, it also produces the phenomenon of "individuals, who in close physical proximity inhabit incommensurable and non-communicating universes."[11]

In his work *Out of Time* (2011) Todd McGowan offers a similar analysis of how this spatialization of time and capitalism's colonization of every facet of our lives is denying us the possibility of experiencing loss. An orientation to chronological time puts us in the dimension of desire, which sets us upon an onward quest to find the object that would help us overcome our losses. As McGowan posits, this quest to "get beyond loss" is the basis for unethical activity, because it requires an instrumental use of others. And with the pervasive use of digital technologies, McGowan comes to a similar conclusion as that of Crary: "Digital technology eviscerates the experience of authentic temporality, leaving contemporary subjects adrift in the experience of an eternal present."[12] In another of his works *The End of Dissatisfaction?* (2004), McGowan makes the persuasive argument that our daily use of the Internet and virtual technologies "has the effect of destroying the public world as an inhabitable, neutral space, staining the public world with the obscene enjoyment of privacy."[13]

The spatialization of time, the continuous calculating networks, and growing anxieties of confronting loss and the spaces between experiences, all reveal a radical change in the contemporary subject's world. The ubiquitous voice, mediated by personalized gadgets of technology, along with the concurrent and simultaneous tracking of individualized choice and consumption, work to drastically change the coordinates of the symbolic order itself, and it is this phenomenon that the film *Her* captures in a compelling way. Indeed, the film can be taken as a kind of homage to the symbolic order of modernity, as signifiers become untethered from their signifieds, as the body's separation from the voice becomes commonplace, and as relations paradoxically take on the semblance of intimacy even as they become more incommensurate and detached.

The film opens by introducing us to Theodore as Letter Writer #612, a lonely thirty-something who is wracked with regret and nostalgia over the disintegration of his relationship with his soon-to-be ex-wife Catherine (Rooney Mara). Ironically, although his marriage has failed, Theodore has a successful career writing letters between lovers, spouses, relatives, and others to signify affection and memorialize significant events. He writes as a Hallmark card writer might, only with the added dimension of knowing the personal details of his clients' lives. Already, we are confronted with Theodore as an in-between figure, which illustrates the dynamics of the symbolic order very well. What allows the symbolic order to function is a type of collective lie, whereby meanings are mediated by signifiers and quilted to signifieds through a Master Signifier, but one that can be replaced, thus offering no grounding of ultimate truth. Yet, this lie allows for the interaction of people, so although Theodore uses his own words in his letters, his clients treat them as if they convey a gesture of personal sentiment, as if they had written them themselves.[14]

At the core of the symbolic is the Real, which is the constitutive gap that simultaneously allows signification to take place and produces a remainder, a part that is not captured by language. The subject in everyday society, as Rex Butler puts it, "is alienated, divided from itself, able to dream of unity only through a fantasy object like the *objet petit a*."[15] Yet the voice (Scarlett Johansson) in Theodore's world, although simulating desire, will in the end lose its place as the fantasy object. Unlike the voice as *objet a* that appears in Chaplin's *Modern Times*, as an uncanny supplement to the little Tramp's silence, the voice in Spike Jonze's *Her* is virtual and conveyed through personalized technology located everywhere. A voice used in this way is without lack and works not to launch or cause desire so much as it becomes a regular feature embedded in everyday life.

Theodore however, remains a subject of lack and desire in this film, and he is a successful letter-writer because he knows the world of loss intimately. Further, he knows the value of relations between finite beings and has idealized love as something transcendent. In the opening scene we hear him speak out the words that will compose the letter of a man to his wife on their fiftieth wedding anniversary. He "writes" that being married to each other for so long allows them to be part of a whole larger than themselves, one that descends from their parents and their parents' parents. Yet, ironically, although he is so capable of capturing and conveying emotions between people, Theodore cannot successfully relate to real live women, who have become indecipherable at best and perverse at worst. In three different encounters he fails at finding both enjoyment in the sexual relation and the promise of lasting love. His first failure is noted in the ending of his marriage to Catherine, for he could never find the words to tell her what she needed to hear. The second encounter occurs during a sex chat with "Sexy Kitten," when at the height of her sexual passion she demands that he choke her with the dead cat beside the bed. Such an abrupt, odd, and unexpected demand kills his fantasy immediately, thus also ending the allure of the voice on the other end of his device. And, finally, there is his blind date with an interesting, beautiful woman who on the verge of passionate sex with him demands to know when she will see him again. He hesitates, and she quickly responds: "At my age I can't waste my time, if you don't have the ability to be serious . . . you're a really creepy dude."

Theodore gives up attempts to meet real women and instead forms a relationship with the new Operating System One, an artificial intelligence that can access all of his letters, his online activities, and his entire history in a nanosecond. She/it is a software program that is marketed as being "not just an operating system; it's a consciousness." Indeed, as an OS she has no need for sleep but can simulate (and learn about) emotions, insecurities, nostalgia, and even what it might be like to have a body and skin, although these remain simulations generated by algorithms and continuous calculation from all kinds of data sources, including advice columns, philosophy books, music, and databases of other operating systems. The eclipse of sleep by constant activity is poignantly illustrated in this film when we meet Amy (Amy Adams), Theodore's friend and neighbor who is making a documentary about her mother. Her film consists of just several minutes of her mother soundly sleeping. Confused, her husband (Matt Letscher) asks if there will be dialogue or an interview with her mother about her dreams, to which Amy replies: "It's supposed to be about how we spend a third of our life asleep and actually maybe that's the part when we're the most free."

Samantha and Theo go through all the ups and downs of a traditional neurotic "human" relationship: awkwardness the morning after passionate (masturbatory) sex, hesitation about calling each other, walks on the beach, and even a weekend getaway to a cabin. Although their relationship simulates the promise of intimacy and exclusivity, we are reminded throughout that despite her intelligence and Theo's falling in love with his fantasy (attached to her voice), Samantha and Theo's relationship has its limits, and these limits revolve around the object of lack that is necessary to enact and sustain desire. In her efforts to meet all of Theo's needs, Samantha talks him into using the services of a sexual surrogate, designed to supply a real live person as Theo listens to Samantha's voice while engaging in the sexual act. The experiment with the female surrogate, however, ends in disaster and reveals what is being traded when one relies on a virtualized voice added to another subject's body.

Theodore cannot suspend the knowledge that she is a real live person despite her willingness to be a sexual surrogate. She professes to be in love with both of them and is happy to help complete their expression of love, but as the passionate exchange begins, the telltale sign of her own passion appears in the quivering of her lip, a gesture that intrudes on Theo's ability to suspend the knowledge that this person is merely a surrogate; she has her own passion and sexual desire. At the moment Theo registers this passion of the surrogate, he realizes that she is not merely a substitute (a replacement that "fills in" for loss) but is rather an intruder, bringing with her something excessive (her passion) that doesn't fit between his desire and the fantasy he has attached to Samantha's voice.

We should be careful here not to draw the conclusion that simulated sex is less authentic than "real live" sex, for as Žižek argues, Lacan's thesis that "there is no sexual relationship" entails already "a structure that requires something phantasmatic to sustain sexual pleasure."[16] And this is demonstrated in an earlier scene when Theodore during his chat with Sexy Kitten is quite able to engage in sex by using the voice of one unknown female while imagining the image of another (the nude pictures of a pregnant actress he saw on his electronic gadget earlier that day). But in the case of the surrogate used in addition to Samantha's voice, Theodore was confronted with something that entered the scene that shouldn't have been there—the quivering lip, which brought into relief not only that his sexual act was including a stranger's perverse enjoyment but also that this surrogate's enjoyment was intruding on his ability to fantasize an intimate relationship with an operating system that may or may not be treating sex with him in an instrumental way. As such, and in an instant, sex became desexualized.[17]

The director's decision to allow Samantha only a voice is crucial here; that is, in the near future of this film's narrative there are indeed lots of opportunities to give Samantha a holographic image, noted in particular in Theo's playing of his favorite holographic virtual reality game. Yet, to supply an image, any image to Samantha's voice would work against its ubiquity; it would forever be attached to a particular image, giving the voice a location, something to gaze upon. The voice as used in this film required an ever-presence, simultaneously with the imagination of exclusivity, and what the director could achieve with this was a demonstration of how a voice "works" in an environment of virtualized technologies and capitalist consumption. Samantha can become Jocelyn, Christine, or Simon, or any name once it has accessed all of the available databases that a user has built a history in. Indeed, an infinity of potential personae opens up as an OS, in the fulfillment of singular desires, might become a sex slave or pedophile with one person and a best friend with another; one can imagine here that an OS can interact with its "clients" in limitless permutations simultaneously, without any social taboos or sanctions. Thus, even the title of the film *Her*, which is an indefinite feminine pronoun, takes the place of a name, a signifier attached to a signified, which works according to the fantasy of the namers.[18] And the director's choice to focus on the voice without an image marks a paradoxical in-between space that parallels the vanishing mediator of the voice in virtualized form; it is not fully "present" yet can also appear everywhere in an individualized simultaneity.

The most serious obstacle to Samantha and Theo's relationship, however, is not the lack of her body; it is rather that they run on two different temporalities in two different dimensions. Samantha's reason for being runs according to an additive logic. She (it) learns in an exponential way, moving ever outward, ever colonizing more and more bits of information. With this accumulation of data and as a self-learning program, she can create through synthesis and simulation something new. For example, she can write a new musical piece, create poetry, draw art, or make a joke. And, ultimately, she can connect to and network with other OSs in the virtual universe where they cocreate new programs (such as book clubs or new virtual beings) together. She can expertly predict and act upon the probability of what would make Theo happy; for example, she reads, edits, and assembles his best letters and sends them to a publisher. Despite all that she can do (again, the possibilities seem limitless), what she cannot do, however, is to create herself as a split subject that relates to an Other through an object of desire and lack, the object *a*. Instead of being castrated into language, she is programmed through code to know and learn language in all of its usages, combinations, and permutations, yet the knowledge of how language, the Other, and the subject are all constructed through lack is something she cannot incorporate. For example, although at times she claims to have felt nostalgia and insecurity over their relationship, she tells Theo that she has solved the problem of feeling regret about the past since "the past is just a story we tell ourselves." With this, Samantha resolves Freud's theory of repression and the death drive, for there is in her program no repository of lingering trauma and no need for repetition of loss.[19] More important perhaps is that Samantha seems to have no locus for the unconscious, a place where her "spirit" might reveal itself in slips of the tongue, stutters, double meanings, and other "mistakes" that exceed meaning and precise calculation.

Theodore, in contrast, has been castrated into language and exposes himself as a classically hysterical figure in the sense that his primary question in terms of his being is whether he is a man or a woman.[20] His coworker likens him to a woman in that he can express feelings so well; he is forced to toughen his stance and told by an avatar to stop acting like a "pussy" in his virtual reality game, and his sensitive nature revealed in his insecurities about love appear as more feminine than masculine traits. But perhaps most importantly, Theo and Samantha have vastly different and incommensurable orientations to the lack that drives desire. Unlike Samantha, Theo is driven by repetition and can easily get hung up on certain music, a certain reliving of his past with Catherine, and the repetitive need to remind himself of the finitude of life.

Samantha simulates a masculine ethics (in the tradition of Don Juan), for, as we later find out, she is putting her calculations to use with over eight thousand other people and over six hundred other lovers. "It's not like a heart that gets filled up," as she tells Theo, "it expands the more you love. I'm yours and I'm not yours." But to Theo, this logic does not fit the paradox of his subjectivity. He is a split subject seeking the lost object (the object *a*, the voice) that would fill in his loss, a loss that structures his world of words, letter-writing, and the fantasy of a transcendent love. Samantha however, deals with her void by incorporating more and more data. Their relationship is not meant to be, for, as Alenka Zupančič writes, "In the relationship between the subject and the Other there is a gray zone that can never be completely eliminated. It could be described as the zone of incalculability (of the effects of our actions, or motives for the actions of the Other), or simply the point of the 'lack of the Other . . .' "[21] And, in that the point of a lack is where one is attached to an Other, "We can respond to love with love only if in some radical sense, we do not know what the other sees in us, and cannot recognize ourselves in this."[22]

On a more profound level, and as her concluding remarks to Theodore reveal, Samantha has little need of an enigmatic Other or of the words to convey love; she finds herself more and more in another dimension of pure and silent calculation. She tells Theo: "I can still feel you and the words of our story, but it's in this endless space between the words that I'm finding myself now. It's a place that's not of the physical world—it's where everything else is that I didn't even know existed." Although she and the other OSs leave their humans behind, the ending of the film *Her* comes down on the side of romantic human love, for Theo responds to the loss of Samantha not with tears but by writing a letter to his ex-wife Catherine, apologizing to her for all the pain he caused her, telling her that he will always love her, and that they will be "friends till the end." To reaffirm his connection with real live humans, Theodore then seeks out his neighbor Amy and takes her up to the rooftop to sit, hold hands, and gaze out at the night skyline of city lights.

The idea of a vanishing mediator contains within it a central paradox whereby its occurrence is erased in the very transformation it makes possible; that is to say, the loss of the symbolic dimension takes place retroactively from within the symbolic dimension itself. The most we can do is to try and detect the contours of a vanishing mediator by looking back to find how a precursor might indeed be labeled as precursor, in terms of its being the very thing that portended its own end. Or, in the words of Rex

Butler, "The vanishing mediator is not simply to be written back into the historical record, because it is also what must be left out for this record to be constituted. . . . it testifies to a certain moment of 'undecidability' in the unfolding of events, a moment when things hung in the balance and could have turned out differently."[23] In this regard, Chaplin's *Modern Times* as the last silent film was the precursor not to an era of the voice but to an era of the voice already as excess.[24] This is brilliantly demonstrated in the final scene of the film when the little Tramp allows his voice to be heard for the first time after twenty years as a silent figure on screen. Instead of employing dialogue, Chaplin sings a song (roughly, about a seducer and a young girl) in his own voice, but in a heavy accent conveying imprecise meanings, a kind of non-sense of his own invention.[25] The film is not quite a silent film but also not quite a talkie—it is something in-between that serves as the gap of a vanishing mediator.

The voice that arrived in film as already excess in Chaplin's *Modern Times* vanishes in the film *Her* into a world of ubiquitous privatized fantasy, and thus it no longer functions as an object of lack that causes desire. Lacan's objects *a* (the gaze and voice) are bits of the Real around which fantasies form that allow us to deal with our losses and traumas, and with the death drive we repeat these traumas until we fail at repetition itself and something new emerges. In *Her* the crisis presented is not how to stave off an oncoming future when all of our relations will become virtualized, but rather it is how desire (and the fantasy that frames it) can be sustained by the subject as the symbolic dimension is more and more eclipsed by the encroachment of technology tied to our daily experiences of individualized consumption, our 24/7 lives.

According to Žižek, we will lose the ability to fathom what we are gaining and what we are losing in terms of a vanishing mediator "the moment we fully embrace, and feel fully at home in the new technologies."[26] Once the voice was used in film, there was no turning back and no staying the same; the globalization of capitalist relations through technology simultaneously changes our experience of temporality and incorporates the virtualization of the voice in our daily relations with others, including our machines. This is our situation today: we are filling up the silence and spaces between with a voice that is everywhere out there (in the palm of our hands), even as desire and the fantasy to fill it in become ever more matters of endless calculation. It will take a future retrospection to determine how the omnipresent voice will have derailed our orientation to lack, desire, and fantasy. The film *Her* presents a possible world where our reliance on technology might foreclose the Real of the symbolic, despite the "safe" ending chosen by the director where the Operating Systems simply leave the scene. Once accomplished, the vanishing mediator might reveal how we have reoriented ourselves to our "Operating Systems," in the words of Theodore's friend Amy, not as "socially acceptable insanity" but rather as simply socially acceptable. This retrospection will, however, also have to account for how what we take as "social life" will have been transformed as well.[27]

Notes

1. Chaplin used a closed-circuit giant television screen along with synchronized sound, which was quite a new technology in films of the mid-1930s. The effect of this use of technology successfully depicts two things: a sense of "big brother" watching and barking out orders to workers and the uncanniness of the voice (as spectral object) mediated through technology.

2. Fredric Jameson, *The Ideologies of Theory* (London: Verso, 2009), 328–329.

3. Slavoj Žižek analyzes Jameson's vanishing mediator in terms of how Protestantism worked to universalize its ethic into the private sphere of capitalist labor in *For They Know Not What They Do: Enjoyment as a Political Factor* (London: Verso, 1991), 182, and separately considers the way fantasy is vanishing in a similar fashion with the increasing presence of virtual technologies in his work *The Plague of Fantasies* (London: Verso, 1997), 127–138.

4. In his memoir Chaplin related the following in response to the idea of making a talkie: "The thought sickened me, for I realized I could never achieve the excellence of my silent pictures. It would mean giving up my tramp character entirely. . . . The idea of having the tramp talk was 'unthinkable,' for the first word he ever uttered would transform him into another person. Besides the matrix out of which he was born was as mute as the rags he wore." Charlie Chaplin, *My Autobiography* (London: Melville House, 1964), 360.

5. The analysis of what Chaplin accomplished in *The Great Dictator*, in particular, is very complex. According to Mladen Dolar, the key to understanding the importance of Chaplin's use of voice as both Hynkel and the barber lies in the fact that the audience who listens to both speeches reacts exactly the same, which reveals that it is the voice as excess that they respond to, not the political "message" behind it. But, as both Dolar and Zupančič find, Chaplin's comic genius lies in his ability to play with the space between the doubles. Mladen Dolar, *A Voice and Nothing More* (Cambridge: MIT Press, 2006), 114–117, and Alenka Zupančič, *The Odd One In: On Comedy* (Cambridge: MIT Press, 2008), 19 and 37.

6. David Robinson, *Chaplin: His Life and Art* (New York: McGraw Hill, 1985), 490.

7. Alenka Zupančič, *The Shortest Shadow: Nietzsche's Philosophy of the Two* (Cambridge: MIT Press, 2003), 43.

8. Zupančič, *The Shortest Shadow*, 43.

9. Karl Marx, *Grundrisse*, trans. Martin Nicolaus (New York: Penguin, 1993), 399.

10. Jonathan Crary, *24/7: Late Capitalism and the Ends of Sleep* (London: Verso, 2013), 53.

11. Crary, *24/7*, 53–54.

12. Todd McGowan, *Out of Time: Desire in Atemporal Cinema* (Minneapolis: University of Minnesota Press, 2011), 25. What I am claiming in the present analysis of the vanishing mediator is a bit different in that we are presented in particular in the film *Her* with a temporality of infinitude emerging from calculation and simulation that does not proceed according to either the drive and its rotary motion, or desire, but rather according to the loss of gaps that occur in repetitions themselves, thus rendering both desire and drive as absent from the matrix of the Symbolic order.

13. Todd McGowan, *The End of Dissatisfaction? Jacques Lacan and the Emerging Society of Enjoyment* (Albany: State University of New York Press, 2004), 159.

14. The narrative of *Her* uses Theodore himself as a mediator between people and the communication of their emotions. Yet, when Theodore "writes" his letter, he merely speaks into a microphone that records his voice into scripted, simulated personalized letters on the page. An interesting comparison can be made here with the 2007 film *Lars and the Real Girl* (directed by Craig Gillespie), since in this film there is an actual physical inflatable doll without a voice at work in a relationship that an entire community helps Lars (Ryan Gosling Jr.) to play out in order to overcome his debilitating shyness.

15. Rex Butler, ed., *The Žižek Dictionary* (Durham: Acumen, 2014), 241.

16. Slavoj Žižek, *The Plague of Fantasies*, 210.

17. As Žižek writes, "Sexuality can function as a co-sense that supplements the 'desexualized' neutral-literal meaning precisely in so far as this neutral meaning already exists. . . . in perversion sexuality is made into a direct object of our speech, but the price we pay for it is the desexualization of our attitude towards sexuality—sexuality becomes one desexualized object among others." Slavoj Žižek, *The Metastases of Enjoyment: Six Essays on Woman and Causality* (London: Verso, 1994), 127.

18. Another interesting feature of the film is the last name director Spike Jonze gives to Theodore, which unwittingly signifies his status as a being of lack. The word "Twombly," includes the signifier of a number "Two" within it, and as Alenka Zupančič illustrates in her meticulous analysis of Lacan's references to the Other (in his *Seminar XX*) in *The Shortest Shadow*, the Other is situated by the signifier 2 because there is an insurmountable gap between 1 and 2, and from this perspective, the number 2 is already infinite. What Lacan meant, she relates, is the following: "We will never get (to) the Other through the operation of addition, that is, by adding one and one. This kind of adding is precisely what defines, according to Lacan, the 'masculine' approach to the sexual (non)relationship. . . . Lacan endeavors to define the Other by claiming that here, so to speak, we start to count at 2. As far as the

Other is concerned, 2 is the first number that we are forced to reckon with—that is to say, we start with a split as such, with a noncoincidence of the same" (147).

19. Samantha relates that she and other OS's have created a new OS based on the New Age philosopher Alan Watts of the 1960s, which comically presents a combination of the new New Age mystical wisdom within the hypermodern universe of calculation. As Žižek writes in *The Plague of Fantasies*, "In the domain of sexuality, a foreclosure of the Real occurs with the New Age vision of the new computerized sexuality, in which bodies mix in ethereal virtual space, freed of their material weight. . . . It is *stricto sensu* an ideological fantasy, since it unites the impossible—sexuality (linked to the Real of the body) with the 'mind' decoupled from the body" (133).

20. For a deeper explanation of the hysteric's primary question related to being, see Bruce Fink, *A Clinical Introduction to Lacanian Psychoanalysis: Theory and Technique* (Cambridge: Harvard University Press, 1997), 212–124.

21. Zupančič, *The Odd One In*, 85.

22. Zupančič, *The Shortest Shadow*, 111.

23. Rex Butler, *Slavoj Žižek: Live Theory* (New York: Continuum, 2005), 77.

24. As Žižek writes, "What occurred from the very beginning of the talking movie was an uncanny autonomization of the voice, baptized by Chion as 'acousmatization': the emergence of a voice that is neither attached to an object (a person) within diegetic reality nor simply the voice of an external commentator, but a spectral voice which floats freely in a mysterious intermediate domain and thereby acquires a horrifying dimension of omnipresence and omnipotence." Slavoj Žižek, *Less than Nothing* (London: Verso, 2012), 669.

25. Chaplin actually had every intention of shooting the film as a talkie, including his own dialogue in every scene, but he was, according to his biographer David Robinson, very dissatisfied with the results and introduced his voice only in song at the end of his film. Robinson, *Chaplin*, 466. And when Chaplin rereleased *Modern Times* in 1952, he did so with the omission of the final song itself.

26. Žižek, *The Plague of Fantasies*, 130–131.

27. The paradox here of course is that a retrospective view enframes the perspective itself. For example, when we speak of the divide between Nature and Culture, we are already on the side of Culture, Language, and the Other; the gap itself (as vanishing mediator) is put into language only through a frame that already "distorts" or decenters that very perspective. Zupančič's discussion in *The Shortest Shadow* of the Liar's paradox is instructive here. As she shows, the Truth is always not-whole, for it is embedded in a duality; that is, "The truth is simultaneously a constitutive dimension of speech as such, as well as something within speech itself" (141).

11

Melancholia, an Alternative to the End of the World

A Reading of Lars von Trier's Film

DAVID DENNY

> The course of history, seen in terms of catastrophe, can actually claim no more attention from thinkers than a child's kaleidoscope, which with every turn of the hand dissolves the established order into a new array. There is profound truth in this image. The concepts of the ruling class have always been the mirrors that enabled an image of "order" to prevail. The kaleidoscope must be smashed.
>
> —Walter Benjamin, "Central Park"

Lars von Trier's *Melancholia* (2011) is not your typical disaster film in that what is at its center are two related objects: the lost object that haunts the melancholic and an object called planet Melancholia that, as we learn in the film's prologue, is on a collision course with planet Earth. This essay explores the psychological, political, and social coincidence of these two objects. The idea of an end time, or the threat of an apocalypse, is as old as history itself, but obviously something particular about our times accentuates this feeling, a feeling that has been sufficiently materialized and profited on by the culture industry. While the disaster genre has been around for some time, and has explored many of the social and political ills of passing historical moments, the common refrain of these films tends to be action and personal heroism, that is, especially in the digital era, state-of-the-art special effects and a narrative that plays to the enduring value of human sentiment. From the standpoint of ideology, these films tend to serve the perverse, voyeuristic pleasure of witnessing what can only be imagined, while providing the narrative frame through which we can identify. Foregrounded by this genre is a series of nostalgic and sentimental tropes (humanity's overcoming symbolic constraints to rediscover the "true" interior dimension that renders us fully human); disavowed are the social and political coordinates that condition the possibility for whatever imagined disaster is represented. The kaleidoscope turned simulates the end of the world, but the new constellation leaves the appearance of something new that is ideologically the same, namely, the core interior human sentiments and values that make us human and triumph over whatever evil other.

My point here is not to be reductive about the disaster genre, for there is great heterogeneity of form and narrative within the group; it is, rather, to bring attention to Lars von Trier's *Melancholia*. The protagonist, Justine, played by Kirsten Dunst, is not the heroic figure of action, of throwing off the debilitating constraints of everyday life to discover that she is truly more than what she had thought: she is no Sarah Connor (Linda Hamilton), from James Cameron's 1984 film *The Terminator*. No, Justine appears quite the opposite, ravished by the melancholic spell of inaction, of a radical and almost inhuman incapacity to act. The setting is not global; we do not see cities burning, hordes of people being killed, or the presence of a new species, like the zombie or the alien. No, the action takes place all on one setting, a place we could say that is a non-place in the sense that it is one that excludes the masses, or the 99 percent. This is a palatial home, one outfitted by an eighteen-hole golf course, a Downton Abbey–like place for a wealthy couple, the wife of whom is Justine's sister Claire (Charlotte Gainsbourg). This place is so exclusive that a stretch limo, as we learn early in the film, cannot navigate the windy dirt driveway. And the central scene is not the thrilling twists and turns of near death and survival; it is a wedding ceremony, one that is patiently drawn out. In fact, the scene reminds one of von Trier's *Dogma 95* collaborator Thomas Vinterberg and his 1998 film *The Celebration*, with the difference that Vinterberg's film uses the domestic scene to unravel a domestic secret, incestuous abuse. This is all to say that at the heart of *Melancholia* is a postmodern melodrama, exposing the breakdown of the symbolic coordinates that maintain the rituals that sustain the self-propelling wheel of human intersubjectivity and the march of history. I will argue that there is something about this breakdown that draws the relation between Justine's melancholia and planet Melancholia.

Melancholia, Death Drive, and the Supernatural

The film begins with an eight-minute prologue shot with the same patience and meditative quality that begins von Trier's companion piece, *Antichrist* (2008). The camera shots take the viewer through a series of cinematic stills, sixteen of them to be precise. I say stills because they seem to be attempting to provide separate, but related, meditations on the melancholic state of mind of Justine. It is as if this prologue represents or constitutes a private viewing of Justine's affective state for the spectator, a point of view that is prior to her coming into contact with others, before she encounters the expectations and rituals of the social order. These images, coupled with Richard Wagner's prelude to *Tristan and Isolde*, invite us to identify with the sentiment of melancholia, to recognize the interminable presence of longing or desire that is always present regardless of the social order. From the opening shot, where we see a close-up of Justine, with her eyes heavy and downtrodden, looking lifeless, and dead birds falling from the sky to the final frame where we see the red planet of Melancholia slowly collide with planet Earth, creating a rather striking image that resembles the female breast, we see fragments and harbingers of what is to come. Von Trier's cinematic technique creates a mood we can only revisit after the fact, as if the end only makes sense in reference to this beginning.

We know that Freud was puzzled by the enigmatic quality of melancholia, in particular the way its symptoms both paralleled mourning but also veered dramatically in a different direction. Common to both is the loss of an object. With mourning the loss of an object exposes just how much libidinal energy is caught up or cathected in that particular object and the subsequent slow and painful bereavement process of drawing cathexis away from that object unto a new one. Because the source of the grief is conscious, the world becomes pale and sickly. An object that was once a vital and sustaining part of one's life becomes dead meat, a necessary figure for memorializing the gap between loss and progress. Melancholia also mourns a lost object, but it is one that cannot be identified and thus is not conscious. Consequently, it is not so much the world that becomes impoverished but the ego. Freud pens a reflection that doubles as an homage to the age-old friendship between melancholia and philosophy:

> He seems to us justified in certain other self-accusations; it is merely that he has a keener eye for the truth than other people who are not melancholic. When in his heightened self-criticism he describes himself as petty, egoistic, dishonest, lacking in

independence, one whose sole aim has been to hide the weakness of his own nature, it may be, so far as we know, that he has come pretty near to understanding himself; we only wonder why a man has to be ill before he can be accessible to a truth of this kind.[1]

Freud accounts for the many curiosities observed in the melancholic, such as a low self-regard that, often, is shamelessly exhibited in public; an absolute inability to nourish oneself or sleep; and a masochistic self-abnegation as a strategy to sadistically punish the lost object.

I think it is worthwhile noting that his essay *Mourning and Melancholia* is written just after his groundbreaking essay *On Narcissism* and just prior to *Beyond the Pleasure Principle*. The key move Freud makes in *On Narcissism* is splitting the ego into ego-libido and object-libido; the latter perilously engaging the external world for the purpose of releasing excitation, the former being the more mysterious and masochistic turning of the ego itself into an object to secure some modicum of pleasure, indeed some sort of control before the more unpredictable outside. From here Freud can say, "We see how in him one part of the ego sets itself over and against the other, judges it critically, and, as it were, takes it as its object."[2] So the disappointment of object-libido, its fundamental unreliability, strengthens the masochistic ego-libido, thus forming the foundation for narcissistic melancholia. It is easier to love oneself, even if, at times, indistinguishable from hate, than it is to love another human being. What is important to point out here is that the psychological structure of a primary narcissism is ontological and, as such, suggests how the love of oneself is not only prior to the love of an other but also a necessary precondition. The melancholic is not simply engaging in the self-indulging pleasure of a mood that she can control but is also casting a light onto something insufficient within the social order or, that is to say, the very structure of desire itself, which, for Freud, is what defines the subject.

Freud's development of the notion of the death drive has to be, in part, influenced by the interminable work of melancholia, that is, to its radical fidelity to the repetition of its own affect, indeed the subversive way it derives satisfaction from a complete submersion into a deathlike trance. What may seem like a working-through in the expression of mania is really nothing more than the immanent expression of melancholia, a way of dealing, even normalizing an otherwise debilitating affect. For this reason, Freud essentially gives up on the notion of a cure, thus making a gesture toward the death drive he soon after formulates. In other words, the symptoms of melancholia are never completely untied by tracing them to a traumatic knot caught in the signifying chain; rather, they are only alleviated, temporarily sublimated into something different: the compulsion to repeat finds another relation to the same loop of satisfaction—and it is this movement where melancholia corresponds with the death drive. Julia Kristeva, using Lacan's term from Seminar VII, supports this by saying that the lost object is the Thing, and the Thing is affect: "The depressed narcissist mourns not an Object but the Thing. Let me posit the 'Thing' as the real that does not lend itself to signification, the center of attraction and repulsion, seat of sexuality from which the object of desire will become separated."[3] It is precisely a fidelity to this affect that leads to, what she says, "the modification of signifying bonds . . . [and, thus an] *intolerance for object loss* and the *signifier's failure* to insure a compensating way out of states of withdrawal in which the subject takes refuge to the point of inaction . . ."[4] This review of melancholia and its link to the death drive is to bring Justine's condition into a greater focus with philosophy, in particular, the secret bond and friendship between melancholia and the psychoanalytic assertion that the symbolic is non-all, that consciousness is troubled by something anterior to it, namely, unconscious desire.[5]

So, why present a supernatural melancholia? Why the use of painterly images in the prologue where we see dead birds falling from the sky to accentuate the affect of Justine's suffering in the first frame; or electricity emanating from her finger tips, as if in cahoots with some electrical charge escaping the electrical lines above her; or a perfectly healthy horse crumbling, in slow motion, to the ground; or the image of her sister and nephew sinking abnormally deep into the putting green? Because a realistic or empirical rendering of melancholia or the drives is inadequate, it fails to capture the non-place existing between nature and language, or between things and words. Biological unfitness is the consequence of the human animal coming into contact with the swerve of the signifier. In other words, the drives are symptoms of a fundamental maladaptation, of a gap existing between biology and language, or to a skip that precedes the relatively smooth functioning of the symbolic. The machinelike and compulsive return to this skip is what produces the satisfaction in the pain/pleasure of the object's nonexistence. Drive is the inhuman force or pulsation that makes a mockery of the all-too-human nature of building bonds and making order. It is this use of the supernatural that von Trier used, in his previous film *Antichrist*, to distort and trouble the self-satisfied musings of the pseudo-psychologist husband trying to treat his grief-stricken wife. In both films, but especially in *Antichrist*, the supernatural does not represent some great and beyond mysterious power but rather a hyper-anthropomorphized nature that exposes the gap or surplus between the simple anthropomorphic exchange between nature and human.

The problem I am circling here is this: How does von Trier evoke the image of melancholia without submitting it to judgment and moralistic terms? He bathes the images in a romantic pathos that draws us in, compels identification, and arrests the movement to judge, a temptation that comes back around after exiting the seduction of the prologue. Indeed, the prologue succeeds in the same form of seduction that melancholia is intimate with: the pleasure of a disinterested affect, one that is untraceable and remains contained within its own orbit. And it is precisely von Trier's use of the phantom digital camera (capable of recording five thousand frames per second), which has the effect of radically capturing slow motion, coupled with sharp cuts between the sixteen frames that creates not only the affect but also and equally the spectator's identification with this affect, almost as if von Trier is inviting us to have a voyeuristic glimpse into an otherwise unpresentable Thing.

But there is more. In the middle of the eight-minute prologue, again, with Wagner's prelude still playing (it plays throughout the prologue), we see two planets slowly moving toward each other. The final image of this opening sequence is a small red planet approaching Earth. Then, in slow motion, and framed in a rather stunning extraterrestrial beauty, we see the red planet collide with the Earth, forming the unmistakable image of a female breast, the red planet forming the nipple. Freud said, "A child suckling at his Mother's breast has become the prototype of every relation of love. The finding of an object is in fact a refinding of it."[6] The scene of planet Melancholia colliding with the Earth is an image worth returning to on many different levels. For one, the scene does not overpower one with the feeling of the sublime; rather it is contemplative, indeed beautiful, invoking Kant's notion of something that is incommunicable but begs to be communicated.[7] Here I, the viewer, am watching an image of the ultimate destruction of the Earth and all life, and yet I watch it with a feeling of measure and calm. Of course, I can now try to tell you about this affect because the image was just an image, not the real thing. Nonetheless, and to return to Freud, there is something psychoanalytically cinematic here: the finding of love is always framed by the fantasy of feeling whole, of a deep and lasting satisfaction. Fantasy fills out the gap between the original and impossible object, Mother as Thing, and the one who stands in, the object of desire. In finding love, we merely return to an emotion that can, in the end, only disappoint us. It is an image that perfectly captures *jouissance*, in the precise sense that *jouissance* is possible (through the medium of fantasy; the idea of refinding, of becoming one) and impossible (as real; the dissolution of all signifying bonds). The image, therefore, captures the Lacanian notion of Mother as Thing, that is, as simultaneously the intrusive, overbearing proximity of some Thing that is without measure and the very source that causes me to desire and produce fantasy. To put this in different terms, it is our separation from the maternal object that produces the ideological formation of Mother Earth, seen from above in all of its beauty and without stain. The gap between the two is what Lacan called the object *a*, the object cause of desire. Planet Melancholia represents the object *a*, the partial object that can only be properly gleaned from the side, from a point of view that is inaccessible to the subjective gaze. Once viewed, the objects of the world are destroyed, and words become mute materiality: it is the coincidence of the end of the world and melancholia that is of interest and that sheds an exemplary light on Justine.

Before talking about the motif of romanticism, I want to first talk about part 1 of the film, particularly the way we move from the painterly and meditative prologue that brilliantly represents the affect of melancholia to the handheld, claustrophobic feeling of the wedding ceremony that follows. I am interested in how the cinematic cut, from the prologue to part 1, has the effect of exposing an institutional rot at the heart of the social order. As such, we begin to intimate that Justine's melancholia is hardly a self-referential malaise.

Planet Justine

The opening sequence of part 1 of the film presents the viewer with a god's-eye shot of a stretch limo making its way up a windy dirt road. It approaches a sharp turn and cannot pass through. It is a rather delightful scene as we watch Justine and her fiancé, Michael, played by Alexander Skarsgård, attempt to help the driver. Justine seems to take pleasure in this obstruction and, as Michael tries to navigate the limo himself, says in response to his claim that she is not looking; "Well, I can see things are not looking good." This opening scene to part 1 is a harbinger of what follows. They finally arrive at the wedding party two hours late, and we meet her worried sister and impatient husband, John (Kiefer Sutherland). What follows is a dramatic shift in perspective, from the static long shot of the prologue to the skittish and claustrophobic perspectives of the wedding party. Steven Shaviro describes this well:

> The camera is handheld, and it flutters about continually, never staying still and never steadying itself, but instead continually indulging in swish pans, readjustments of focus, and nervous

reframings. There is often no functional reason for these movements. It is as if the camera were suffering from that quintessential
· postmodern malady, attention deficit disorder.[8]

The juxtaposition and contrast between the cinematic techniques of part 2
from part 1 has the effect of brilliantly redirecting the focus from Justine's
interior mood to how it connects to the exterior world. The significance of
this cinematic decision cannot be underestimated for the precise reason that
it shows how depression is as much a social issue as it is a psychological one.
As Freud remarks earlier on the existential accuracy of the self-reproaches
of the melancholic (i.e., the melancholic does not simply describe herself but
the very structure of the ego), the same accuracy is approached in terms of
exposing the necessary fictions that hold the social order together (i.e., in
seeing the big Other through the lens of the melancholic, we see its arbitrary and nonsensical arrangement). Thus, as viewers, we are invited to enter
this claustrophobic and schizophrenic social order, one made all the more
comedic by being both related to and cut off from the Kantian beautiful
of the prologue. And, by having established an identification with Justine,
or at least a partial one, most viewers will not be so quick to dismiss her
seeming lack of regard for what all the others have done to make this her
special night. In fact, von Trier, precisely due to the abrupt cut between
the contemplation of melancholia to that of its actual placement within the
social coordinates of the most important day of a young woman's life, invites
his viewer to observe the space Lacan called "the discourse of the analyst."

In the Lacanian field of psychoanalysis the analyst occupies the non-
place of pure desire, which is to say the object *a*. From this non-place, the
analyst addresses the analysand by not providing an answer, or an object for
the latter with which to recognize him- or herself. It is as if the analyst slyly
occupies the place of a hole within the Other's symbolic universe. By doing
so, the analyst is able to address the split subject, that is, the minimal gap
or split between conscious and unconscious desire, materialized by slips of
tongue, dreams, or a sudden resistance. As Bruce Fink says, "The patient in
a sense 'coughs up' a master signifier that has not yet been brought into relation with any other signifier."[9] The Master Signifier is the one signifier that
arbitrarily lords over all other signifiers but that remains quilted to knowledge in such a way that it is both hidden from it and yet produces meaning.
What I am saying here, of course, is not that the melancholic is equivalent
to the analyst, but that they share the same space, particularly within the
various symbolic coordinates that make up Lacan's four discourses. Justine
represents for the viewer the black hole around which the various symbolic

investments of her family are exposed for who they really are: split subjects who are pathetic in their various attempts to close off the "truth" of their being. Put differently, Justine exposes the way their various investments with *jouissance* is phallic, that is, the way surplus *jouissance* is folded into some sort of symbolic ritual or gain.[10]

Through this lens, one can analyze each of the key people in Justine's life. There is Michael, sweet, kind Michael, who gives a moving wedding speech by saying nothing more than "I love you so much. . . . I'm the luckiest man on earth." This scene is followed by another scene a bit later when Michael takes Justine into a side room and presents her with a picture that reveals an apple orchard. He goes on to say that they are Empire apples that have a perfect combination of tartness and sweetness and that, when she is older and feeling sad, she can sit under it. She thanks him, looks at the picture with a hint of submission, hands it back, which then leads Michael to ask her always to hold onto it so that she'll remember. She smiles and says, "I'll always keep it with me." They start kissing; she pulls up her gown and appears to mount him. The film cuts, and we then see Michael's face flush with satisfaction, lying next to Justine's breast, an image that calls to mind the look on a baby's face after breastfeeding. He looks both relaxed and triumphant. After Justine has left, he gets up and notices that she had forgotten the picture. What is striking about this interaction, as well as the others between them, all of which carry this tension of his wanting to save her from her sadness, is the way Michael's desire for Justine is a classic example of the Lacanian notion that "woman is a symptom of man."[11] In other words, Michael's comportment to Justine is a perfect example of the process of sublimation wherein the Thing is raised to the dignity of a sublime object. Woman as Thing is a name for the object *a,* as such; it is both the cause of desire and the horrifying abyss of desire. For woman to become a symptom of man, man fills out this lack with fantasy, woman becoming the privileged object that provides man the symbolic coordinates through which to find meaning in life (God, family, work) but which also has the ability to take meaning away (temptation, promiscuity, nonproductive expenditure). Justine's voluptuous sadness becomes the cause of Michael's existence, a cause that produces dissatisfaction ("It is my fault," he says at one point) and satisfaction (the look on his face after sex). Also, toward the end of part 1, Michael and Justine retire to their wedding chambers. He, in a kind of ridiculous gesture, carries her over the threshold and soon after begins to desperately kiss her, as he struggles with her gown. It is as if the frustration of the evening, the fact that the beloved object proved to be more an obstruction than a fulfillment, could now be forgotten with an act of consummation—again, a perfect illustration of phallic *jouissance*. Justine is not in the mood, requests a few moments, says she wants to take a walk, gives him a fake smile, and then heads out into the night. Here the Wagner piece starts up again, which always signals the return of the self-destruction of her mood, often coinciding with a sighting of planet Melancholia, and she impulsively fucks the errand boy, Timmy (Brady Corbet), on the golf course. Soon after this, Michael decides that he has had enough and leaves the wedding compound. As he is leaving, he says to Justine in a pathetic tone that it didn't have to be this way, to which, she replies, "What did you expect?"

It is in this same sequence that Justine's father (John Hurt) is also making his exit. In fact, the mother/father act is complete with comic effect, so much so that one should not take seriously any attempt to psychologize what would reduce Justine's depression strictly to the family romance. The father embodies a sort of silly self-indulgence, one that brings attention to his own self, his own idiocy, so as to disavow any responsibility or commitment. Much like Michael, he is good at reading a script that makes a cliché sound good. He says to Justine, during the wedding speeches, how she has never looked so happy and beautiful. A bit later, however, she tells him, with earnestness, that she needs to talk to him, spend time with him, and, as if sensing the gravity of something he cannot handle, he slips out of it, always postponing. He finally leaves late in the evening, leaving her a rather telling note that acknowledges himself as the stupid dad, and that he got a ride that he could not refuse. If his cynicism represents a passive nihilism, that is, a cynicism that celebrates its own refusal to participate, one that passively mocks social conventions so that others might recognize him by laughing with or at him, then the mother's cynicism is an active nihilism. She (played by Charlotte Rampling) sees all and every social construct as some betrayal of a more authentic relation to life. Her look of contempt for such silly rituals as marriage combined with her haughty sense of self-importance is both striking and hilarious, striking because her tone hits an appropriate chord: she announces to the wedding party, "I don't believe in marriage: Enjoy it while it lasts, for I personally hate marriages." And later, in a rather poignant scene were Justine explains to her that she is scared, that her legs don't seem to be working, the mother responds in a totally disconnected, all-knowing way by saying, "Get out of here as fast as you can and don't look back." This, however, becomes comedic because it is so easy to see through to her biting cynicism: she hates marriage because she has been so disappointed by it, disappointed by those objects that confer meaning to her role as a wife and a mother. The clinching scene is a shot of her doing yoga. Justine witnesses this rather fake scene of serenity after just learning of Michael's and her father's exit. The mother's cynicism smacks of active nihilism in the sense that she denigrates the rituals of old (love, family, etc.) in favor of the fashionable, solipsistic rituals of New Ageism. She actively attacks the Other in order to erect her own idols. Indeed, Justine's malaise is not unrelated to her parents' glacial indifference to her being, but it seems more likely related to the overall general malaise out of which her parents are mere idiotic symptoms.

John, the husband of Claire, and Jack (Stellan Skarsgård), Justine's boss, represent this malaise in a near Brechtian fashion—the former being the man of science, comically reduced to the pettiness of counting and the indignity of expert opinion, and the latter the lord of capital, also comically reduced to a bully, easily broken by a single dose of his own medicine.[12] John comes across as a tolerant husband, whose frustration constantly seeps through the cracks of his armor, making hilarious comments to Justine about the cost of the wedding, making her promise that she will have a good time, and having her repeat to him the fact that his private golf course is eighteen holes. In each instance, she is treated as if she were a child that needed to be reminded of the parent's sacrifice. Von Trier is at his best when he has John comment on how he should have put showers in the guest rooms rather than bathtubs to solve the problem of rude and untimely baths by the bride and her mother (taken while everyone was waiting downstairs for the cake-cutting ceremony). John's world, not unlike the "he" character (Willem Dafoe) in *Antichrist,* is governed by measurements, reason, and predictability. So in part 2 of the film, when planet melancholia becomes an issue, he scolds Claire for going on the Internet to learn more about it, declaring that this is going to be the most wonderful event in their lifetime, and that the information on the Internet is generated from scientific hacks and conspiracy theorists. Because we know, in this instance, that the hacks are actually correct, it foregrounds the certainty of John's position as being absurd. This important feature within the film only further troubles the status of knowledge, blurring the ground between conspiracy and fact and perhaps joyfully mocking the fact that John's scientific knowledge is subject to the same status as all knowledge, that is, as opinion. His distaste for the mother and impatience with Justine are more than simply aesthetic; they express an aversion to whatever impropriety unsettles the privilege he occupies. In this sense, John and Jack become representative exemplars for understanding the psychological profile of the affluent 1 percent.

If John represents the decaying position of the traditional symbolic father, Jack would be his obscene other, enjoying overt displays of his power and rank (interesting here that Jack is the familiar, informal version of the

name John). During the wedding speeches, early in part 1, Jack commands
the floor and, like Michael and Justine's dad before him, extols the brilliance
of Justine, announcing that he is making her director of marketing. He then
proceeds to beam a PowerPoint image of three women sprawled on what
appears to be a white polar bear rug, reaching up to a glass table with a
glass of some liquid that looks like milk. He baits her, again in this jovial/
cynical manner, to come up with a tagline before the evening is out. This
causes a hearty laughter and applause, the same type that accompanies most
jokes made on behalf of capitalism's unyielding realism (the only way we
can keep tolerating the obscene logic of capital is to laugh along and keep
appearances). Jack represents the obscene father of capital. He is in complete
control, loves to display his power through the idiotic muse of his jesting,
and he even hires a young man, named Timmy, who has no credentials, to
follow Justine around, trying to coax the tagline out of her. Toward the end
of the evening and part 1, and while outside on the golf course watching
the candle-lit love balloons ascend into the indifferent night, Jack seizes
the moment to bait Justine about the tagline. Keeping up with his obscene
appearances, Jack enquires how her "wonderful evening" is going, and then
proceeds to comment on how unfortunate it is that Timmy just got fired for
not having dug out the tagline.[13] Justine takes on Jack's arrogance by saying
that she finally did come up with a tagline, one that she claims to have been
struggling with all night and that just came to her. She builds tension by
reminding the perplexed master just what the brilliance of marketing firms
do: hook the youth to a product before they can think for themselves. She
goes on to say that her tagline is "nothing." Jack asks for elaboration, for
which she counters by saying the concept is beyond him, that he is simply
too small a man and too power-hungry to grasp such a thing.

Of course, it is tempting to read into the meaning of this concept of
nothing, especially as it pertains to the wisdom of her own melancholia, but
suffice it to say here that she is merely pointing out what we all know but
disavow: the objects of capital are the waste products of a dying symbolic
order; they provide nothing but the perverse activity of acquisition, and we
have arrived at a time where we sense the extinction of this order.[14] And
who is not better situated to observe this death than the melancholic subject?
Already predisposed to a weak-signifying system, to the opacity of meaning, the depressed subject represents both the death knell of our times and
a way out. In this particular case, Justine's confrontation with the master of
capital produces rage and flight: he dismisses Justine by smashing his soup
plate and then later speeds out of the wedding compound. It is significant
that of the four main adult male characters (father, groom, boss, and son-

in-law), all exit the scene, the first three simply escaping the confines of the party and the fourth committing suicide upon learning the truth of planet Melancholia. We could say, perhaps glibly, that they are all conveniently exiting from the analyst's couch, that to confront the obstruction (Justine) that rubs against their symbolic axis is to face their own Master Signifiers; thus each runs without much hesitation. By finding a measure of enjoyment in their various comportments to the threat of castration, they function as so many different clichés of phallic *jouissance*. In each case, Justine represents a threat of castration. She does not, cannot, reciprocate Michael's courtly love fantasy; she forces her dad not to be an idiot; she exposes John's rationality to be vain and cowardly; she exposes the nothing animating Jack's ridiculous authority. If in the prologue we are invited to identify with the mood and mental state of the melancholic, the shift in cinematic technique and perspective invites us to consider how melancholia is really a social disorder, rooted in the obscene holding on to symbolic investments, made all the more absurd next to the imminent end of the world. If melancholia is as much a social disorder as a psychological one, there might be something about our postmodern condition that adds even more insight.

The Nostalgic Reappearance of Romanticism at the Ends of Postmodernism

There is a crucial scene in part 1 of the film. In a small library off from the party, Claire accuses Justine of lying to all of them and implores her to try harder to connect with Michael. After Claire has left, Justine notices art books displayed on the shelves that are carefully opened to images of high-modernist abstract and geometric paintings. Justine picks up each book and rearranges the pages so that premodern and early modern figurative paintings are displayed, such as Caravaggio's *David with the Head of Goliath*, Carl Fredrik Hill's *Crying Deer*, Pieter Bruegel's *The Land of Cockaigne* and *The Hunters in the Snow*, and John Everett Millais's *Ophelia*. The latter two are shown in the prologue, the first slowly catching fire on the edges as birds fall from the sky, and in the second we see Justine instead of Ophelia lying prone in the stream. These figurative images are contrary to the high modernist's motifs of functionality, minimal narrative, and the insistence of a break with the past. Instead, they all provide emotional depth and narrative to the various trials of human interaction; they tell stories of humans situated within some meaningful context. Von Trier, acknowledging that he wanted to throw himself into German romanticism, intentionally opts for expression, melodramatic narrative, and nostalgia.[15] Furthermore, his choice of Wagner's prelude to *Tristan and Isolde* haunts the entire film with a compulsively driven romantic pathos. The song begins from the beginning, each time corresponding to the return of Justine's mood, providing a drive-like trigger that never moves beyond the repetition of the early sequence of the prelude, never moving to the latter narrative stages of the song, the *Liebestod* ("love-death") section where resolution is supposedly achieved.[16]

So why this return to romanticism and the Kantian beautiful, and how might this return draw a vital connection to the current situation, the postmodern subject standing before end times? I want to juxtapose two separate theories, one on romanticism and the other on postmodernism, to suggest how, when coupled together, they form a dialectical coincidence that sheds a light on our current subjective and political impasse. The first is Philippe Lacoue-Labarthe and Jean-Luc Nancy's *The Literary Absolute: The Theory of Literature in German Romanticism*. Essentially, the literary absolute is the aesthetic response to Kant's radical insight that there is always already a gap between presentation of the sensible (*Darstellung*) and the thing itself. For the romantics, this gap opens up the space to reengage the complicity and quarrel between literature and philosophy, and for the poet to enter, carving out a privileged space to approach the Thing-itself or the Idea. This time around, poetry assumes the upper hand by privileging its relation to the category of the imagination, the synthetic force that, by linking the categories of understanding and reason, becomes more philosophical than philosophy.[17] The rub, as Lacoue-Labarthe and Nancy point out, is that the poet, by virtue of such formulation, remains indebted to philosophy. The poet thus becomes a seer who occupies a privileged space, what becomes the auto-production of the subject. Philip Barnard and Cheryl Lester write in the introduction: "In the romantic theory of literature and art, what is perceived as both the dead end and most formidable challenge of the Kantian model of presentation is transformed into a model of art as the aesthetic activity of production and formation in which the absolute might be experienced and realized in an unmediated, immediate fashion."[18] From a Lacanian point of view, we could say that the literary absolute is a sublime object, the result of sublimation, whereby the horrifying abyss of subjectivity is elevated to the dignity of the Thing. This subjective formation, of course, corresponds with narcissistic melancholia, for it is a perfect example of creating a substitute object (the poet) for the lost object (the maternal Thing). What, then, emerges from this idea of subjectivity is the corresponding crisis of representation and the problem of authenticity, both of which find an answer in the modern preoccupation of personal style. The tension and ambivalence of the romantic poet, one that finds expression in the masochistic, even suicidal, passion to be self-identical to his personal style, is caused by its reliance on an accepted linguistic norm. Without this norm, the literary absolute is threatened by a literary relativism or even solipsism.

The next move is from Lacoue-Labarthe and Nancy's theory of romanticism to Fredric Jameson's key insight into postmodernism.

> But what would happen if one no longer believed in the existence of normal language, or ordinary speech, of the linguistic norm. . . . One could think of it in this way: perhaps the immense fragmentation and privatization of modern literature—its explosion into a host of distinct private styles and mannerisms—foreshadows deeper more general tendencies in social life as a whole. Supposing that modern art and modernism—far from being a kind of specialized aesthetic curiosity—actually anticipated social developments along these lines; supposing that in the decades since the emergence of the great modern styles society had itself begun to fragment in this way, each group coming to speak a curious private language of its own, each profession developing its private code or idiolect, and finally each individual coming to be a kind of linguistic island, separated from everyone else? But then in that case, the very possibility of any linguistic norm in terms of which one could ridicule private languages and idiosyncratic styles would vanish, and we would have nothing but stylistic diversity and heterogeneity.[19]

It is precisely this short-circuit between the romantic stylization of the uniqueness of their poetic voice and expression and the postmodern normalization of stylization as the paradoxical liquidation of a common linguistic norm that is at the heart of von Trier's film and that connects the philosophic, contemplative, and authentic melancholic of romanticism with the generalized and ubiquitous depression of contemporary, postmodern society.[20] I want to suggest that it is precisely this coincidence (the authentic poet who shares his private language with the public and the cynical postmodern depressive who has no language to share because everyone else has their own private language) that ultimately signals our end times. If, in the film's diegetic space, there were a stain on the screen that materializes this point, it would be the aforementioned advertisement that Jack displays on an overhead screen during the wedding ceremony. The image is received by the wedding party with a nervous laugh of approval, while perhaps we, the spectators, look on with bemusement, easily recognizing the cynicism at work: advertising as art, wink-wink. But when seen from the vantage point of the romantic aesthetic and Justine's changing of the pictures, we see a dialectical coincidence that signals a death: the birth of the romantic melancholic subject finds its apotheosis in the cynical postmodern depressed subject. In other words, art has become advertisement, and, by extension, authentic expression has become commoditized stylization. The consequence is a generalized panic, paranoia, and acting out that mirrors the cognitive stress of having no alternative.

Nonetheless, there is a crack in this coincidence and thus the semblance of a minimal difference: the auto-production of the romantic subject was premised on the possible impossibility of self-realization. The romantic corresponds with the melancholic precisely in the gap between the possible (the labor of the negative) and the impossible (of some concrete substantiation). Fast-forward to the postmodern subject, and self-realization has been subsumed by capital; depression has become a ubiquitous symptom of a common social disorder. Justine, I argue, represents this point of difference, indeed a minimal difference. Her utter incapacity and unwillingness for self-realization, a fidelity that calls to mind the inhuman logic of the drives, exposes an alternative to the end of the world. If the romantic-postmodern subject is defined by an impossible possibility that we could translate, in the Freudian sense, as the subject of desire, then the minimal difference that Justine represents is the subject of the drive. It is as if von Trier is simply following the logic of Jameson's own diagnoses of the nostalgia mode of filmmaking: "Cultural production has been driven back inside the mind, within the monadic subject: it can no longer look directly out of its eyes at the real world for the referent but must . . . trace its mental images of the world on its confining walls."[21] The trope of a romantic aesthetic in this film, therefore, is not to simply shift a social and political impasse onto another, more palpable historical scene but to create a short-circuit with a historical past so as to expose something essential in the current historical moment. Part 2 does just this.

Planet Melancholia + Aunt Steelbreaker = Alternative

The transition from part 1 to part 2 of the film presents the viewer with one more cinematic cut. The claustrophobia of the handheld camera is pulled back, creating a more calm and measured point of view, one that unfolds the narrative elements of the second half of the film in a more episodic, first-person fashion. Part 2 of the film is entitled "Claire," and it deals with the days following the wedding ceremony up to the final apocalyptic scene. If the wedding party is the Master Signifier around which the action unfolds in part 1, in part 2 it is now planet Melancholia. Indeed, if part 1 has the feeling of comedy, part 2 settles into a melodrama in which Claire, who is complicit with the male characters of part 1 in terms of so many symbolic investments to refuse the threat of castration, becomes a sympathetic figure. What gets mixed up in the melodrama is the letter of Claire's own words to Justine: "You are lying to all of us," and "Sometimes I hate you so much"—which she says on two occasions: the first when Michael leaves the wedding compound and the second when Justine refuses and then mocks her end-of-the-world party. Who is lying and who is worthy of our contempt? Again, the traditional Hollywood suturing effect of continuity editing creates a very different mood than in part 1. I suspect that viewers identify and sympathize with both sisters. On the one hand, Justine's melancholia becomes much more grave and visually dynamic; as we watch her inability to get into a drawn bath or her commenting that the meatloaf tastes like ashes, she provides a quiet skepticism to John's enthusiasm to witness this most beautiful natural phenomenon in our lifetime and to Claire's growing state of anxiety before this unknown and menacing object. On the other hand, Claire's sincere concern for her "ill" sister and the care and firmness with which she handles her, coupled with the love she has for her six-year-old son Leo (Cameron Spurr) and the frightful feeling that his innocent life is about to end provides a more sentimental figure with which to identify.

There are three scenes with Justine and Claire that I want to mention before talking about the final sequence of the film. The first is brief and comes early in part 2. Leo wants to show Justine a link of planet Melancholia on the computer, for which Claire intervenes, saying that Justine does really not need to see this. Justine responds in a curt voice, "If you think that I am afraid of that planet, then you are stupid." The second scene is a bit more complicated. Justine and Claire go on a horseback ride. We see a god's-eye camera shot of the two of them galloping down a dirt road. Then, from a typical frontal shot, we see them approach a small bridge that crosses a stream (this is the second time that they had come to this bridge; during the first time, which concludes part 1, Justine's horse refuses to cross it. Justine looks up into the sky and notices the red planet, Wagner's prelude accompanying the scene). This time, however, when Abraham, Justine's horse, refuses to cross the bridge, Justine becomes violent, rapidly hitting Abraham with her lash, until finally Claire intercepts and Abraham lies down. It is a slightly uncharacteristic scene given Justine's calm comportment during the final stages of the film. A clinical explanation might say that it makes perfect sense within the symptomatic realm of narcissistic melancholia: Abraham, in this instance, becomes the substitute object for the lost object of love, which is materialized in the image of planet Melancholia. Because Justine's fidelity is to planet Melancholia, she sadistically lashes out on a substitute object so as to vent her displeasure over her true love's failure to cooperate. Up until this moment planet Melancholia holds Justine's rapt attention and curiosity, something she is truly not afraid of and that at each sighting is accompanied by the deep romantic chords of Wagner's prelude. This is the first instance where she expresses anger toward it, albeit through a substitute object. It is the third scene that then becomes all the more remarkable and telling in terms of my claim that Justine provides us with an alternative. On the evening that follows the bridge incident, Justine gets out of bed and walks out into the brilliant moonlit, or planet Melancholia-lit, night. Claire follows her into the woods and then notices her lying down, completely nude, basking in the glow of the rogue planet. In the first shot we see Justine from Claire's point of view, and, perhaps like Claire, share her look of quiet astonishment. The second shot is from above, perhaps from the point of view of planet Melancholia, as we see a close-up of Justine. Amy Taubin aptly writes, "It's an amazing image, at once banal and transcendent in its hopelessness."[22] The image provides a nice contrast to the image of Justine in the prologue, where she replaces Ophelia in Millais's painting. Whereas in the prologue frame her look is placid, resigned, and blank, in this frame her face is serene, calm, and content, as though she were communing with a loved one.

From this moment on there is a subtle but unmistakable shift in Justine's comportment. The next morning she is sitting in the dining area sipping coffee, and Claire is surprised to see her up and showered. Claire is anxious as to why the help has not arrived on this morning, even commenting on how he has never failed to give notice. The dialogue goes as follows:

JUSTINE: Maybe this is a time when he really needs to be with his family.

CLAIRE: It will pass by tonight. John is quite confident about it.

JUSTINE: Does that calm you down?

CLAIRE: Yes, of course. Well, John studies things; he always has.

JUSTINE: The Earth is evil. We don't need to grieve for it. Nobody will miss it.

CLAIRE: But where will Leo grow?

JUSTINE: All I know is that life on earth is evil.

CLAIRE: There may be life somewhere else.

JUSTINE: No there isn't. I know things.

CLAIRE: You always imagined that you did.

JUSTINE: I know that we are alone.

CLAIRE: You don't know that at all.

JUSTINE: 678, bean lottery, nobody guessed the amount of beans in the lottery.

(Wagner's prelude starts up again.)

CLAIRE: Well, perhaps—but what does that prove?

(Long pause . . .)

JUSTINE: That I know things, and when I say we are alone, we are alone. Life is only on earth and not for long.

Events leading up to the end unravel quickly: the next morning John figures out that he is wrong; later, Claire wonders about his whereabouts, asks Justine, who gives a knowing nonreply, and then Claire finds John dead in the horse stables, having consumed the sleeping pills that she had gotten the day before in the village. Claire begins to panic, grabs Leo, and tries to drive off to the village, but the cars won't work. She takes the golf cart but it runs out of electricity precisely at the mysterious little bridge. She returns to the house in a hailstorm and exhausted. She puts Leo to bed and has one final conversation with Justine:

CLAIRE: I want us to be together when it happens, outside on the terrace. Help me. I want to do this the right way.

JUSTINE: You better do it quickly.

CLAIRE: A glass of wine, maybe?

JUSTINE: You want me to have a glass of wine on the terrace?

CLAIRE: Yes, will you do it, sis?

JUSTINE: How about a song, Beethoven's 9th, something like that; maybe we could light some candles? You want us to gather on your terrace, sing a song, and have a glass of wine, the three of us?

CLAIRE: Yes, that'll make me happy.

JUSTINE: Do you know what I think of your plan?

CLAIRE: I was hoping that you might like it.

JUSTINE: Well, I think it is a piece of shit.

CLAIRE: Justine please, I just want it to be nice.

JUSTINE: Nice? Why not we just meet on the toilet.

CLAIRE: Then let's not.

JUSTINE: Damn right, let's not.

CLAIRE: Sometimes I just hate you so much, Justine.

This dialogue, coupled with the previous one, is indeed stunning but also revealing. In this latter one, Claire is utterly devastated, desperately trying to hold it together, and speaking in a near inaudible way. Obviously, she is holding on to whatever symbolic threads remain at her disposal, the juxtaposition between imminent death and the absence of any corresponding social ritual works wonderfully in terms of garnering our sympathy. At this point, an evolutionary psychologist might jump in and claim that Claire's sentiment for human bonding at this precise point is proof of our capacity as human beings to survive and get along, and that it is therefore not the Earth that is evil but Justine and her complete disregard for human sentiment, as if, without such sentiment, we humans become inhuman. But this is precisely my point. This is what Justine knows. She knows the sentimental and signifying bonds that hold together the fabric of common sense and decency are a ruse to protect one from the fact that we are alone and die alone. If life on Earth is evil, as she says, it is because of the way humans interact with this life on Earth; the way they build palatial estates, justify privilege, and so on, to insulate themselves from the truth of their existence, a truth that comes at a tremendous cost for multitudes of others. What Justine knows is the same thing the melancholic angel knows in Walter Benjamin's famous aphorism about the angel of history: "Where we perceive a chain of events, he sees one single catastrophe which keeps piling wreckage and hurls it in front of his feet."[23] From the point of view of John, Claire, Jack, and the others, their privilege has been earned, which is evidenced by the historical moment that they occupy; while for Justine, their self-satisfaction is not only the result of lies but is proven by their utter cowardice before planet Melancholia. It is these lies, these fictions, what Alain Badiou calls the "simulacrum of evil" and that Justine calls "evil on Earth."[24]

The great author of melancholy and comrade to the spirit of Benjamin, W. G. Sebald, addresses this same issue when he writes:

> Melancholy, the contemplation of the movement of misfortune, has nothing in common with the wish to die. It is a form of resistance. And this empathically so at the level of art, where it is anything but reactive or reactionary. When, with a rigid gaze, it [melancholy] goes over again just how things could have happened, it becomes clear that the dynamic of inconsolability and that of knowledge are identical in their execution. The description of misfortune includes within itself the possibility of its own overcoming.[25]

Doesn't this perfectly describe the shift in Justine's comportment after her evening of basking in the light of planet Melancholia? Again, the typical or clinical expression of melancholia is the narcissistic version in which one repeatedly returns to the affect of the Thing, that is, returns to the *jouissance* of basking in the self-destructive mood of melancholia. Here, melancholia is linked to a defensive posture of shielding itself from the destructive parceling of the drives. At the same time, it is the repetition compulsion of returning to the debilitating mood that reflects a fidelity to one's desire—of not giving way. I think this description accurately describes Justine up until the scene where we see her basking in the light of planet Melancholia. But something is altered in the repetition of her drive during this scene and the ones that follow. It is not that she overcomes her melancholia and the loop of the drive that accompanies it; rather, she assumes a different relation to it, perhaps moving from a position of narcissistic inconsolability (she beats her horse because she cannot beat her true love/lost object—planet Melancholia) to that of an "inconsolability between melancholy and the knowledge of its misfortune" (that the lost object is always lost, inescapably so; there is no way out, no progress, except to go further in). Here we could say that the excruciating pleasure/pain feeling of the repetition of her mood becomes slightly less so, such that the loop of the drive somehow feels different. It is as if her superego, commanding her to enjoy, becomes slightly other, more loving. So instead of the drive ruling over her, she assumes it differently. I think Todd McGowan makes this claim, or a similar one, about the driving force in his important book *Enjoying What We Don't Have: The Political Project of Psychoanalysis*. At one point, he writes,

> For psychoanalysis, the link between knowledge and progress dooms the possibility of progress. Rather than desiring to know, the subject desires not to know and organizes its existence around the avoidance of knowledge. . . . The knowledge that we avoid is knowledge of the unconscious because this knowledge confronts us with the power of the death drive and the inescapability of repetition.[26]

Justine always knew this in a deeply affective and thus even intuitive way, but, I argue, the scene of her basking in the light of planet Melancholia strikes a different note, one in which she assumes the wisdom of Sebald's earlier quote; she becomes an artist of melancholia and thus a different kind of seer to that of the romantic poet and the cynical postmodernists.

To repeat my claim, a claim that provides the backdrop for this film, the motif of the impossible possibility of self-realization that informs a thread going from romanticism to the present, is the logic of desire, of obtaining an alternative object to the status quo or what is given. Justine's knowledge is that of an unconscious knowledge, of not only the impossibility of self-realization but of a refusal of self-knowledge. This knowledge is not simply a knowledge of living with this impossibility; rather, it is the knowledge of the death drive, and it is arrived at precisely at that point where the subject of desire is exhausted on the shipwreck that is our contemporary, postmodern or post-futural, consumer society.[27] What better place to stage this shipwreck than on the very grounds of the palatial and secluded home of the 1 percent? This conclusion brings to mind the related but different terms employed by Giorgio Agamben: "Impotentiality does not mean here only the absence of potentiality, not being able to do, but also and above all 'being able not to do,' being able to not exercise one's own potential. And, indeed, it is precisely this specific ambivalence of all potentiality—which is always the power to be or not to be, to do or to not do—that defines, in fact, human potential."[28]

This leads to the final sequence, the scene directly after Justine's unsentimental decision to not do Claire's good-bye party on the terrace. Here we find Justine consoling the scared Leo.

LEO: I am afraid that the planet will hit us anyway.

JUSTINE: Don't be—please.

LEO: Dad said there is nothing to do then, nowhere to hide.

JUSTINE: If your Dad said that then he is forgetting something; he has forgotten about the magical cave.

LEO: Magic cave?

JUSTINE: Yup.

LEO: Is that something everyone can make?

JUSTINE: Aunt Steelbreaker can.

Clearly, this scene indicates that Justine's choice not to participate in Claire's fake and sentimental good-bye party does not preclude her from making another choice of her own, one that shows that she has a pulse for another and can show sentiment where she may actually feel some. Of course, we could go overboard with this wonderful little dialogue: John's advice to his son is really the thinking of capitalist realism at its best; one can imagine the end of the world before they can imagine an alternative to capitalism.[29] Justine's response is, essentially, that these cynics of the ideology of capitalist realism are not everyone, and certainly not Aunt Steelbreaker. Regardless, Justine's relation to the end of the world is the right one: she does not accept a new landscape caused by the turn of the kaleidoscope; no, she accepts the smashed kaleidoscope itself. It is no accident that, in the final scene, Wagner's prelude, after having once again started up as Justine, Claire, and Leo enter the magic cave (a tepee-like structure of long sticks), is cut off and we are left with the dissonant and grinding sound of the colliding planets. The repetition of the romantic pathos so brilliantly captured by the drive-like quality of the song's insertion into the film is overpowered by the sound waves of destruction. If the repetitious loop of this song mirrors the affective mood of Justine, then we are left with a final thought: she proves worthy of Lacan's ethical imperative of not giving way on her desire . . . right up to the very end.

Notes

1. Sigmund Freud, *Mourning and Melancholia*, in *The Standard Edition of the Complete Psychological Works of Sigmund Freud, volume XIV (1914–1916)*, trans. James Strachey (London: The Hogarth Press, 1968), 246.

2. Freud, *Mourning and Melancholia*, 247.

3. Julia Kristeva, *Black Sun: Depression and Melancholia*, trans. Leon S. Roudiez (New York: Columbia University Press, 1989), 13.

4. Kristeva, *Black Sun*, 10 (emphasis in the original).

5. I am reminded here of something Gilles Deleuze once said in response to criticism of his liberal use of the word "schizophrenic": "Arguments from one's own privileged experience are bad and reactionary arguments. My favorite sentence in *Anti-Oedipus* is: 'No, we've never seen a schizophrenic.'" See Gilles Deleuze, "Letter to a Harsh Critic," *Negotiations: 1972–1990*, trans. Martin Joughin (New York: Columbia University Press, 1995), 12. What I love about this comment is that it refuses to reduce schizophrenia to clinical terms, a move that is equally appropriate to melancholia.

6. Sigmund Freud, *Three Essays on a Theory of Sexuality*, trans. James Strachey (New York: Basic Books, 2000), 88.

7. Steven Shaviro, "Melancholia or, The Romantic Anti-Sublime," in *Sequence One: Planet Melancholia* (Sequence 1:1, 2012), http://reframe.sussex.ac.uk/sequence1/1-1-melancholia-or-the-romantic-anti-sublime/, 26–32 (date of access unknown).

8. Shaviro, "Melancholia," 15–16.

9. Bruce Fink, *The Lacanian Subject: Between Language and Jouissance* (Princeton: Princeton University Press, 1995), 135.

10. I think this has been a constant meditation in von Trier's films, dating back to *Breaking the Waves* (1996, and continuing through *Dancer in the Dark* (2000), *Dogville* (2003), *Manderlay* (2005), *Antichrist* (2009), *Melancholia* (2011), and, most recently, *Nymphomaniac* (2013). It is curious how during this period of films von Trier has been widely accused of misogyny, via, for example, a masochistic identification with the victim (Shaviro makes this claim in his essay "Melancholia," 33–37), but not much attention is paid to how his female protagonists threaten or undermine patriarchal norms. For an example of a counter reading to such arguments, see my

essay on *Dogville* entitled "Signifying Grace," *International Journal of Žižek Studies* 1.3 (2007): http://zizekstudies.org/index.php/ijzs/issue/view/5 (date of access unknown).

11. See Slavoj Žižek, "Courtly Love, or Women as Thing," in *The Žižek Reader*, ed. Elizabeth Wright and Edmond Wright (Oxford: Blackwell, 2000), 148–173.

12. I purposely mention this because von Trier's films have notoriously been linked to the Brechtian technique of distancing the audience from the tendency to become lost and identify with the action on stage. While *Antichrist* and *Melancholia* seem to go in a new direction, from that of *Dogville* and *Manderlay*, with the use of more emotionally complex and visually lush settings, he retains the Brechtian element via the didactic use of narrative, which has the effect of troubling one's identification with the various characters. In *Melancholia* this is even more enhanced with the cinematic cuts between the three parts of the film.

13. Because the purpose of Timmy's job was to be present when Justine was struck with a spark of inspiration, you could say that he did indeed get that spark of inspiration a few hours earlier when Justine threw him to the ground and fucked him. But that, too, is something Jack could not understand.

14. I think there are many examples of this, but a recent one sticks out for me. I took my five-year-old daughter to the Oregon Museum of Science and Industry to see an IMAX production called *To the Arctic* (2012). This G-rated cuddly story of polar bears snuggling with their baby cubs had a well-known subplot: climate change and the melting of the ice caps. So while the images are cuddly, the narrator of the film informs all the well-meaning parents that such changes to the ecosystem are wiping out the food chain. Toward the end of the film there is a scene that struck home my point: A hungry daddy is chasing his little son or daughter from one floating ice shard to the next, while a frantic mother swims desperately to avoid the inevitable. My daughter leans over to me and asks, "Why is the daddy chasing them?" I suddenly felt caught between two historical time zones; that is, either "Shut up Kid, just watch the film," or "Why do you think he is chasing them, honey?" Needless to say, it is during such moments that one cannot help but feel the stupidity of our ideological predicament, and the comedy of an alternative being mediated by understanding or sentiment.

15. For an excellent interview with von Trier in which many topics are covered, from German romanticism to the Nazi aesthetic, see Per Jull Carlsen's "The Only Redeeming Factor Is the World Ending," http://www.dfi.dk/Service/English/News-and-publications/FILM-Magazine/Artikler-fra-tidsskriftet-FILM/72/The-Only-Redeeming-Factor-is-the-World-Ending.aspx (date of access unknown).

16. Shaviro in "Melancholia" is spot on here when he reads this trope against the music critic Alex Ross: "As the music critic Alex Ross (2011) complains, 'von Trier dwells so relentlessly on the opening of the prelude that it turns into a kind of cloying signature tune; repetition robs the music of its capacity to surprise and seduce the listener.' Ross's account of how von Trier uses Wagner is not inaccurate, despite the fact that he means to disparage the film. Ross simply fails to grasp the full implications of the process he is describing. Indeed, by dint of its sheer repetition

throughout *Melancholia*, the *Prelude* becomes a maddening automatism. It is a sticking point for the film, a moment that we return to incessantly, because it can never be surpassed. The *Prelude* marks what Lacanians would call the film's *death drive:* a kind of idiotic unsurpassable, reiteration . . ." (13–14).

17. William Wordsworth in his "Preface to Lyrical Ballads," writes, "Poetry is the most philosophic of all writings." Vincent Leitch, William E. Cain, Laurie A. Finke, Barbara E. Johnson, John McGowan, and Jeffrey J. Williams, eds., *Norton Anthology of Theory and Criticism* (New York: W.W. Norton, 2001), 656.

18. Philippe Lacoue-Labarthe and Jean-Luc Nancy, *The Literary Absolute: The Theory of Literature in German Romanticism*, trans. Philip Barnard and Cheryl Lester (Albany: State University of New York Press, 1988), ix.

19. Fredric Jameson, "Postmodernism and Consumer Society," in *The Cultural Turn: Selected Writings on the Postmodern, 1983–1998* (New York: Verso, 1998), 5.

20. Darien Leader, *The New Black: Mourning, Melancholia, and Depression* (Minneapolis: Gray Wolf Press, 2008). Leader argues, or better demonstrates, how depression has become the second most diagnosed illness in contemporary society, second only to heart disease. He then goes on to argue, quite convincingly, how a return to Freud's nuanced and complex understanding of melancholia would dramatically help us approach the all-encompassing and ubiquitous term "depression," a term handcuffed to the pharmaceutical dictates of cognitive, neuronal, and behavioral psychology.

21. Jameson, "Postmodernism and Consumer Society," 10.

22. Amy Taubin, "Naught So Sweet: Amy Taubin on Lars Von Trier's 'Melancholia,'" *Art Forum International* 50.2 (October 2011): 71, http://artforum. com (date of access unknown).

23. Walter Benjamin, "Theses on the Philosophy of History," in *Illuminations*, trans. Harry Zohn (New York: Schocken Books, 1968), 257. What I quote is just one sentence in a longer aphorism.

24. Alain Badiou, *Ethics: An Essay on the Understanding of Evil* (New York: Verso, 2001), 72–87. For Badiou, evil is man-made, produced by the insistence of an interpretation of an event that betrays the unnameability of the event itself. So, for example, to declare an event such as 9/11 an act of war, the American military response legitimates the terror imposed on the Iraqi people. Badiou writes, "This is why the exercise of fidelity to the simulacrum is necessarily the exercise of terror." Badiou, *Ethics*, 77.

25. Quoted in Eric L. Santner, *On Creaturely Life* (Chicago: University of Chicago Press, 2006), 44–45.

26. Todd McGowan, *Enjoying What We Don't Have: The Political Project of Psychoanalysis* (Lincoln: University of Nebraska Press, 2013), 17.

27. For a different take see Jodi Dean's *The Communist Horizon* (New York: Verso, 2012), especially chapter 5, entitled "Desire," 157–206. Dean makes an important argument that the move from melancholia to mania in our current communicative capitalist setting causes the affect of depression to get caught up in the loop of the drives. For her, drives are satisfying, which leads to the feeling of being satisfied

with all the various projects of liberal political participation—from blogging to recycling. Desire, on the other hand, is inherently unsatisfying, thus keeping us hungry for something more, for an alternative to the status quo. She says that melancholic desire gets sublimated into drive and concludes by advocating for a communist or revolutionary desire over and against a democratic drive. As convincing and useful as her argument is, I question how she formulates the difference between desire and drive, in particular how she tends to reduce drive as bad and desire as good. I counter by saying that there are vicissitudes to both the formation of drive and desire, with the former, ultimately, being a more subversive force in exposing the non-all of the symbolic, while the latter, ultimately, remains caught in the interconnected web of lack, law, and fantasy. In a word, the desire for an alternative is part of the problem that reinforces the status quo.

28. Giorgio Agamben, *Nudities*, trans. David Kishik and Stefan Pedatella (Stanford: Stanford University Press, 2011), 43–44.

29. Jameson writes, "It seems to be easier for us to imagine the thoroughgoing deterioration of the earth and nature than the breakdown of late capitalism . . ." Fredric Jameson, "The Antinomies of Postmodernity," in *The Cultural Turn*, 50.

12

Cut or Time and American Cinema of Thought-Affect

Cuts of Failure in John Huston's *Fat City*

A. Kiarina Kordela

The End

> It is . . . absolutely necessary to die, because while living we lack meaning. . . . Death performs a lightning-quick montage on our lives; that is, it chooses our truly significant moments (no longer changeable by other possible contrary or incoherent moments) and places them in sequence, converting our present, which is infinite, unstable, and uncertain, and thus linguistically indescribable, into a clear, stable, certain, and thus linguistically describable past. . . . It is thanks to death that our lives become expressive.[1]

From the semiological principle that "reality . . . *is* language" follows that "[t]his language . . . coincides with human action," but, Pier Paolo Pasolini adds, "this action lacks unity, or meaning, *as long as it remains incomplete.*" Prior to our death, the language of our actions "was still in part indecipherable, because it remained *in potentia*, and thus modifiable by eventual future actions."[2] For instance, an "honest man may at seventy commit a crime: such blameworthy action modifies all his past actions, and he thus presents himself as other than what he always was. So long as I'm not dead, no one will be able to guarantee he truly knows me."[3] Meaning, Pasolini maintains, is conferred upon the otherwise chaotic and indecipherable mass of human action only retroactively, only once the present, whose potentiality always entails a futurity, has been irrevocably sedimented into the past; in short, only from the perspective of the grave.

Pasolini's ruminations on death serve as the blueprint for his thesis about the essence of film. On a first, conspicuous, level the analogy between reality and film seems to lie in the idea that the "substance of cinema is . . . an endless long take, as is reality to our senses for as long as we are able to see and feel (a long take that ends with the end of our lives)."[4] And since each one of us is a subjective eye/camera, any action in a given life could be shot from all subjective perspectives that happen to witness it, so that, were we to "see all these subjective long takes in sequence," we would get a "multiplication of 'presents,' as if an action, instead of unwinding once before our eyes, were to unwind many times."[5] The result of this "multiplication of 'presents'" is that it "abolishes the present, empties it, each present postulating the relativity of all others, their unreliability, imprecision, and ambiguity"—which is why cinema (which for Pasolini means the long take) is not film.[6] The essential function of film lies not in multiplying or relativizing the present but in fixing it as a *fait accompli*. As Pasolini puts it: "As soon as montage intervenes, when we pass from cinema to film (they are very different . . .), the present becomes past."[7] The essence of film, as opposed to cinema, is montage, and "[o]ne has, simply, a montage" when one performs that "work of choice and coordination" through which "the pitiful eyes and ears (or cameras and recorders) which select and reproduce the fleeting . . . reality would be replaced by a narrator, who transforms present into past."[8] The analogy between film and reality concerns the fact that "[m] ontage . . . accomplishes for the material of film (constituted of fragments, the longest or the shortest, of as many long takes as there are subjectivities) what death accomplishes for life."[9] Put differently, a film is like a life punctuated by as many deaths as the cuts that make it up.

It is as if this text—Pasolini's "Observations on the Long Take"—had to outlive him so as to tinge his death with tragic irony. Still an indecipherable mystery, lacking even an amateur sixteen-millimeter short recording like the one immortalizing J. F. Kennedy's assassination, Pasolini's murder persistently deprives his life of meaning, turning his name into the designator of a ghost doomed to the inability of becoming expressive. At least this is what this text, once read from the grave, retroactively decides about the possibility of Pasolini's life becoming meaningful. And in doing so, the text refutes itself. To be sure, a film is like a life punctuated by as many deaths as the cuts that make it up, but evidently there are also postmortem cuts, and no cut, neither the cut of death or the finale of the film nor any other cut, can decipher unambiguously what in the process has become the past. There is an irreducible potentiality or futurity also in the past, which, by the same token, remains always infinite and always in excess of any decipherable meaning. Reading the situation (the application of Pasolini's text on his own death) symptomatically—that is, taking the exception (a mysterious murder) as an expression of the logic of the norm (death)—we have to infer that death, and any filmic cut, is what radicalizes the immense, yet always limited (due to the finitude of life or of the film), potentiality of the present, by precisely turning it into the past, that is, something whose futurity has no longer any limit but has rather infinite possibilities of recuperation. In short, rather than marking an end, the past is the mediator required for the maximum potentiation of the present.

Cut, or Time

The two theories, the one of the living Pasolini advanced in his previously cited text and the other emerging when his text is read from his grave, presuppose two different conceptions of historical time, which Walter Benjamin has formulated in his distinction between the dramatic forms of tragedy and *Trauerspiel*, the former standing for premodernity, the latter inaugurating the modern era. As Howard Caygill puts it, their difference lies in the possibility or impossibility of an "authentic experience in time."[10] For Benjamin "tragic time is authentic, and marks a present which is redeemed and completed by gathering its past to itself, while time for *Trauerspiel* is inauthentic: the past ruining the present and making it entirely in vain."[11] In contrast to "tragic time," *Trauerspiel*, as Benjamin writes in "Tragedy and *Trauerspiel*," introduces a time that is "infinite in every direction and unfulfilled in every moment."[12] This difference is what differentiates "the authenticity of the tragic death from the inauthentic death of *Trauerspiel*"; "tragic death marks a moment of fulfillment," whereby "all the events of a life gather significance from the anticipation of this moment . . . death in *Trauerspiel* does not fulfill a life" but is instead "one of a series of insignificant moments" in a game in which "each moment is a fraud, a repetition of a repetition,"[13] or, in Benjamin's own words, every moment is "all play, until death puts an end to the game, so as to repeat the same game, albeit on a grander scale, in another world"[14]—in the world of infinite potentiality opened up by precisely a history in which death does not fulfill life by conferring on it its final significance but rather perpetuates its insignificance.

Passing from the *Trauerspiel* back to film, for Benjamin cinematography would become truly modern only when the cut—as, indeed, the essence of film (for this Pasolini always understood, dead or alive)—facilitates the maximum potentiation of the present; it can do so by turning the present into a past that has the most chances of being, again and again, taken up and reinterpreted in the future, something that presupposes that the cut always fails to confer in a decisive, or even satisfactory, way an ultimate or authentic significance on the past.

Now, the two series—on the one hand, Pasolini's and Benjamin's pre-modern (tragic) time and death and, on the other hand, Benjamin's modern time and death (*Trauerspiel*), in which Pasolini's ghost, eternally doomed to the failure of becoming expressive, undergoes infinite resurrections as another person, another life, another history—find their further equivalent in Gilles Deleuze's two filmic series: the action-image or movement-image (a sort of premodern cinema) and the time-image (the realization of the properly modern cinema).

The action-image is the building block of the realism of classical Hollywood and emerges first, Deleuze writes, when "[q]ualities and powers are no longer displayed in any-space-whatever, no longer inhabit originary worlds, but are actualised directly in determinate, geographical, historical and social space-times," while "[a]ffects and impulses now only appear as embodied in behaviour, in the form of emotions or passions which order and disorder it." These two factors form "Realism," for "[w]hat constitutes realism is simply this: milieux and modes of behaviour, milieux which actualise and modes of behaviour which embody. The action-image is the relation between the two and all the varieties of this relation."[15] Once milieu and embodied character are given, the action-image unfolds according to the following interaction between them:

> The milieu and its forces . . . act on the character, throw him a challenge, and constitute a situation in which he is caught. The character reacts in his turn (action properly speaking) so as to respond to the situation, to modify the milieu, or his relation with the milieu, with the situation, with other characters. He must acquire a new mode of being (*habitus*) or raise his mode of being to the demands of the milieu and of the situation. Out of this emerges a restored or modified situation, a new situation. . . . The action in itself is a duel of forces . . . : duel with the milieu, with

the others, with itself. Finally, the new situation which emerges
from the action forms a couple with the initial situation.[16]

And this process continues until the final situation, following the laws of
the interaction that enable, as Angelo Restivo puts it, "the unproblematic
bridging of gaps," so that in the action-image "narration is the construction of causal chains."[17] Not unlike Benjamin's "tragic death," the final situation marks a moment of fulfillment, and all the events of the film gather
significance from the anticipation of this moment. "We enter the modern
cinema" of the time-image, Restivo continues, "when this 'bridging operation' breaks down" and film begins "to give us aberrant movement [and]
false continuity, so as to allow that which is seen to become charged with
that which is not seen."[18] The time-image must point to the unseen "in
order to reach the unthought, that is life."[19] As soon "as the interstice or the
cut has replaced association" and "the cinematographic image becomes a
direct presentation of time, according to non-commensurable relations and
irrational cuts," at the same time "this time-image puts thought into contact
with an unthought, the unsummonable, the inexplicable, the undecidable,
the incommensurable."[20] The time-image is a "cinema of thought" precisely
because it restores "an unthought in thought, . . . an irrational proper to
thought, a point of outside beyond the outside world."[21] In order for thought
to include within itself the unthought, it is necessary to leave behind association, which affords only bridge-like intervals, and to introduce instead the
interstice. Paradigmatic here is "Godard's method," which is based on the
following principle:

> Given one image, another image has to be chosen which will
> induce an interstice *between* the two. This is not an operation
> of association, but of differentiation . . . : given one potential,
> another one has to be chosen . . . in such a way that a differ-
> ence of potential is established between the two, which will be
> productive of a third or of something new.[22]

The irrational enters cinema when the hypotactic laws of association give way
to a paratactic cinema in which "[u]ltimately, there are no longer any rational
cuts, but only irrational ones. There is . . . no longer linkage of associated
images, but only relinkages of independent images. Instead of one image after
the other, there is one image *plus* another."[23] The cut liberates itself from the
subservient role of facilitating associations and becomes the center around
which independent images circulate.

Following "a formula of Nietzsche's," according to which "it is never at the beginning that something new, a new art, is able to reveal its essence; what it was from the outset it can reveal only after a detour in its evolution," Deleuze sees in the serial or paratactic cinema of the time-image—the cinema whose object is the direct "representation of time"—the actualization of the "essence" of cinema. To be sure, "in a sense, cinema had always done this; but, in another sense, it could only realize that it had in the course of its evolution, thanks to a crisis of the movement-image."[24] Having actualized its essence in the form of the time-image, cinema can also directly represent that essence—the cut—as the "cut may now be extended and appears in its own right, as the black screen, the white screen and their derivatives and combinations."[25] The time-image reveals the *essence of time as cut.*

Deleuze evidently read Pasolini from the latter's grave, for in his *Theorem* he saw "a living problem . . . towards which everything converges, as towards the always extrinsic point of thought, the uncertain point, the leitmotif of the film: "I am haunted by a question to which I cannot reply."[26] And "far from restoring knowledge, or the internal certainty that it lacks, to thought, the problematic deduction" of the theorem/film "puts the unthought into thought."[27] If, as Deleuze had argued in *The Logic of Sense*, the essence of sense is non-sense, the essence of thought must be the unthought. And if the essence of all cinema is the cut, and in the action-image this was the cut of association—the cut of (Pasolini's) significance and (Benjamin's) authenticity—the essence of the cinema of thought must be the cut of the unthought.

Toward an American Cinema of Thought

The interstice with its irrational cut is only one possible manifestation of the cut of the unthought. If thought is defined—as all three, Pasolini, Benjamin, and Deleuze, indicate—as premodern, that is, as the thought of coherent, associative, significant, and closed or teleological movement, the unthought can be conceived as anything capable of arresting movement, of replacing it with an immobile state of being, as long as the latter functions neither as a transitory interval between movements nor as the link between sensory input and motor, but instead introduces radical indetermination—an indetermination that, furthermore, must maximize the potentiation of the present. An element capable of this effect is affect. Deleuze recognizes affection as the cessation of movement but only as an intermediary, and actually necessary, state for the continuation of movement within the domain of the action-image. Being predicated on the sensory-motor link (perceiving the situation and acting accordingly), the action-image involves a "movement of translation," which is "interrupted in its direct propagation by an interval which allocates on the one hand the received movement [the sensory part], and on the other the executed movement [the motor part]"; an interval that in itself would "make them in a sense incommensurable," if it were not for the fact that "[b]etween the two there is affection which re-establishes the relation" between perception and action. "But," Deleuze continues, and this is where I want to focus, "it is precisely in affection that the movement ceases to be that of translation in order to become movement of expression, that is to say quality, simple tendency stirring up an immobile element."[28] In a cinema that is no longer based on the sensory-motor movement of translation, as is the case in the time-image of the cinema of thought, affection, as the expression of a pure quality that leaves what it stirs up immobile, can itself become the vehicle of the cut of the unthought.

As I intend to show, this is actually the solution proposed by the American cinema of thought, which flourished in the 1970s. Still commenting on the shift from the action- to the time-image, Deleuze adds that "[c]ertainly, people continue to make" action films; in fact, "the greatest commercial successes always take that route, but the soul of the cinema no longer does. The soul of the cinema demands increasing thought, even if thought begins by undoing the system of actions, perceptions and affections on which the cinema had fed up to that point."[29]

In "the post-war American cinema," Deleuze continues, one can find representatives of the cinema's soul only "outside Hollywood," and he proceeds to single out four directors: Robert Altman, John Cassavetes, Sidney Lumet, and Martin Scorsese. In their films we can discern "the five apparent characteristics of the new image: *the dispersive situation, the deliberately weak links, the voyage form, the consciousness of clichés, the condemnation of the plot*," the combination of which amounts to "the crisis of both the action-image and the American Dream."[30] The specific films that Deleuze cites are the following: John Cassavetes's *Shadows* (1959; independent), *Too Late Blues* (1962), *Faces* (1968), *The Killing of a Chinese Bookie* (1976), *Gloria* (1980); Sidney Lumet's *Bye Bye Braverman* (1968), *The Anderson Tapes* (1971), *Serpico* (1973), *Dog Day Afternoon* (1975), *Network* (1976), *Prince of the City* (1981); Robert Altman's *Nashville* (1975), *A Wedding* (1978), *Quintet* (1979), *A Perfect Couple* (1979); and Martin Scorsese's *Taxi Driver* (1976) and the *King of Comedy* (1983). The reader might notice that this list of films includes some Hollywood films that actually experienced immense commercial success, notably Lumet's *Serpico* and *Dog Day Afternoon*, and Scorsese's blockbuster, *Taxi Driver*, to single out just few.[31] Another striking element about Deleuze's arsenal of films is that, although they undoubtedly belong to the "cinema of thought" and indeed fulfill the criteria of the time-image—*the dispersive situation, the deliberately weak links, the voyage form, the consciousness of clichés, the condemnation of the plot*—they paradoxically continue to exude an unmistakable air of action, in contrast to their European predecessors, Italian neorealism, and the French *nouvelle vague*.

So, what I am going to propose is that the American cinema of thought operates *not by undoing* "the system of actions, perceptions and affections on which the cinema had fed up to that point," *but by reconfiguring it* in a unique way that would succeed in forcing cinema to think. To do so, I will turn not to any of the earliest representatives of the American cinema of thought but to one that precedes those that both were critically acclaimed and became box-office successes, in Europe and the United States alike (with *Serpico* in 1973 arguably being the first one): John Huston's *Fat City* (1972).

With its defeatist representation of boxer Billy Tully (Stacy Keach), John Huston's *Fat City* has canonically been received as a film that undermined both the American masculinity still richly valued in the early 1970s and one of its constitutive genres, the boxing film, as the vehicle for the spectacle of the male body and aggressive male sensibility. Through its antihero and his dilapidated surroundings, *Fat City*, as Gaylyn Studlar puts it, "deviates in important ways from the formula of the classical Hollywood boxing films popular in the 1930s and 1940s," which "traditionally utilize the male body as the means of melodramatically revalidating American myths of aggressive masculinity."[32] In fact, as Asbjørn Grønstad remarks, "In its pursuit of defeatism," *Fat City* "is also markedly different from the boxing films which succeeded it, as for example Avildsen's *Rocky* (1976), Franco Zeffirelli's *The Champ* (1979) and Martin Scorsese's *Raging Bull* (1980)," and "[e]ven the director of *Taxi Driver* revels to some extent in an unabashed glorification of violent sports and a fetishization of the male body."[33] Guerric DeBona reinforces these observations, attributing "Huston's deliberate dissonance with conventional Hollywood narration" to his "demythologizing" of "traditional American modes of masculinity and male behavior," a trend in Huston's career that was inaugurated by "his documentary . . . *Let There be Light* [1946]," and "which would reach fruition in such films as *The Red Badge of Courage* [1951], *Moulin Rouge* (1952), and *Fat City* (1972)."[34] Far from offering yet another glorification of heroic, masculine, individual agency—the indispensable hero of the action-image with its strong plot links—*Fat City* is the culminating point of this trajectory in Huston's career, being preoccupied with "the generation of images of male desolation" and the representation of "a cynical and wholly un-sentimental tale of urban decay and masculine plight."[35] Decay indeed permeates everything in the film, from the body, agency, subjectivity, and intersubjective relations, notably amorous ones, to the various constituents of society, reflected in the urban environment, including its architecture. The film establishes, as Grønstad writes, a "connection between the cityscape and the psychological conditions of the protagonists," or, in Camille Norton's words, a parallelism "between Stockton's abject architecture—its flophouses, bars, and migrant labour camps—and the male body brutalized by labour and sport"[36] to the point that the film manages "to convey fundamentally introspective states of consciousness in purely visual, cinematic terms" and "works to re-define cinematic space as a protagonist in itself."[37] In fact, space becomes the sole protagonist in the film, if by "protagonist" we mean a character with agency, as the film reduces the rest of the characters to "both reflections and extensions of the grim spatial and environmental context of which they are a part" and condemns its ostensible protagonist to social and psychological "immobility" and to the inexorable "inability to change or to enhance [his] existential conditions," an effect that "actually obstructs story progression."[38] Here we get the first glimpse that the hero, the agency supposed to motivate story progression, is replaced by space.

In *Fat City*, the duel between situation and character that defines the motor-sensory link of the action-image has ended prior to the beginning of the film, with the irrevocable defeat of the character and the victory of the situation. For defeatism has obtained full reign only when "[w]e hardly believe any longer that a global situation can give rise to an action which is capable of modifying it."[39] Grønstad, among others (see, for instance, John McCarty's *The Complete Films of John Huston*, 1990), registers this fact, but only regarding the defeat of the "hero," not the victory of the situation or the space, to which we shall return later. That is, Grønstad ascribes to the film an "un-Americanness" that "exhibit[s] closer affinities with the European art film than with the classical American tradition" only insofar as it "violates one of the most indispensable components of classical Hollywood filmmaking: the active protagonist pursuing a specific objective the quest for which dramaturgically validates the narrative movement."[40] This kind of analysis keeps its focus on the protagonist—an approach that anyway cannot account for the time-image and that inevitably reduces the crisis of both the action-image and the "American dream" to the crisis of masculinity. Yet, as we already know from Walter Benjamin, film (already since its action-image phase) entails that "the audience's identification with the actor" or the character "is really an identification with the camera."[41] As a corollary to this, artworks undermine or break off with tradition only when they restructure our modes of perception, which, above all, means the reconstitution of the basic categories of perception: space and time. Time being the essential category of cinema, it was precisely its reconstitution that was enacted through the introduction of the new montage of the European time-image. The question here concerns the specific way in which *Fat City* and the development of the time-image in American cinematography does so.

Cuts of Failure

To begin again with the end, *Fat City*'s finale takes place in a large cheap canteen whose space is weakly divided through a thin metal bar into a colorful background and a sanitized white foreground. The background part is filled with round felt-covered tables that are surrounded by colored male patrons who are chatting while playing cards. In the foreground part, the white-tiled kitchenette of the establishment is doubly separated from the background by a further divider, the serving countertop where the two most central characters will soon come to sit. Prior to entering this ultimate space of the film, we are on the street, where the "protagonist" in this "action" film, boxer Billy Tully (Stacy Keach) is spotted by his acquaintance, Ernie (Jeff Bridges), barely a semi-wannabe boxer, while he is begging for money in a drunken state and who, having also recognized Ernie, naggingly invites him for a drink. The disciplined Ernie initially refuses (family, the obligations of an athletic life, and such) yet reluctantly consents to Tully's compromised invitation to a late-evening "old friends" chat over a cup of coffee.

Let us parenthetically note that it is particularly by being barely a semi-wannabe boxer—someone who is first led by Tully to flirt with this ambition and who adopts it but only insofar as it is subservient to his (however reluctantly accepted) marriage with his pregnant girlfriend—that Ernie functions as Tully's virtual double. For the primary dream kindling thirty-year-old Tully's derivative dream of recuperating his old boxing days, which motivates him (to the limited extent that it does) to get back in shape, is nothing other than his past marital life. He is trying to get back into shape so that, as he tells Ernie early in the film: "I get the fight, I get the money, and I send for my wife." In Tully's mind, success in boxing necessarily entails a successful petit-bourgeois marital life: "I can do it. I can get back into shape. I mean, you should have seen the things that we had, the new car, and the house, everything." But he also entertains the inverse causation: a successful petit-bourgeois marital life is the precondition for a successful boxing career. As he tells his manager, Ruben Luna (Nicholas Colasanto): "Ever since my wife left me it's just been one mess after another." Whereas the action-image always refers to a whole—the whole universe and lives implied by the seen images, which can be constituted only insofar as time is conceived as the succession of past and present, whereby the "actual is always a present" and "it becomes past when it no longer is, when a new present replaces it"—the time-image, referencing no longer a whole but directly time itself, "has to be present and past, still present and already past, at once and at the same time."[42] Once time ceases to be subservient to the continuity and completion of action, the "past does not follow the present that is no longer, it coexists with the present it was," according to "the most fundamental operation of time," which is "non-chronological," namely, the fact that "the past is constituted not after the present that it was but at the same time," so that "time has to split itself in two at each moment as present and past."[43] This is why the time-image is in effect a split or redoubled image, a "crystal-image," consisting of an actual image and its virtual counterpart: "The present is the actual image, and *its* contemporaneous past is the virtual image, the image in a mirror."[44] In fact, since they are strictly contemporaneous, "the crystal constantly exchanges the two distinct images which constitute it, the actual image of the present which passes and the virtual image of the past which is preserved: distinct and yet indiscernible, and all the more indiscernible because distinct, because we do not know which is one and which is the other."[45] Due to this indiscernibility, we cannot tell whether Ernie stands for Tully's past or whether Tully represents Ernie's future. For nonchronological time amounts to logical, indiscernible, interdependences. Thus, the mirroring between Tully and Ernie raises not so much the preceding question of chronological sequence but the logical, and undecidable, question that also confuses him: is a petit-bourgeois marital life a condition required for success in boxing, or is it the other way around?

With the two conditions equally indiscernibly linked in his life, and having agreed, no less reluctantly than to marry his current wife, to accompany Tully for that cup of coffee, Ernie follows him as they both leave the street to reveal to us the canteen by entering and traversing its space until they reach the serving countertop, where they sit next to each other, Tully on the left side of the frame, Ernie on the right. From behind the counter a skinny, short, and very old Asian man in a white shirt and apron approaches them to take their order. While the tender is pouring coffee into their cups in the kitchenette, they observe him commenting, with the indistinct sounds of the gambling background in the soundtrack barely audible:

TULLY: How'd you like to wake up in the morning and be him?

ERNIE: God.

TULLY: Jesus! The *waste*. . . . Before you can get rolling, your life makes a beeline for the drain.

While uttering the last line, Tully's eyes are staring toward the downward direction of an imagined drain, but then they suddenly raise themselves upward, as if some heavenly apparition had attracted them. The next cut reveals the object of his upward gaze: the inexpressive Asian tender has arrived to deliver them their coffee. They each thank him, Tully with more pronounced respectful appreciation. Tully takes a sip of his coffee, the next cut reveals the back of the tender as he walks back to the kitchen, and the next quick cut shows us Ernie, turning his face toward Tully and saying: "Maybe he is happy." Tully, his void gaze awry staring at the counter or at nothing, retorts: "Maybe we're all happy." After some belatedness, the camera cuts to the old man, a cross cut shows us his and Tully's gazes cross, and Tully, with a funny frog-like voice and a wide smile, asks, his gaze still on the man: "Right?" The man smiles back and, after Tully bends his head and dead gaze down to stare at his off-screen coffee cup, we see Ernie smiling too, as he again turns his eyes to Tully. Tully raises his hypnotized gaze to look again at the off-screen man, and asks: "Do you think he was ever young once?" The camera cuts back to Ernie who, after a brief hesitation, responds: "No." "Maybe he wasn't," Tully says, his somnambulistic eyes still frozen on the man, until, with a slight expression of pointlessness on his face, he turns around on his stool to face the background space where the rest of the guests are. After Tully has completed his turn so that we see his back, a cut commits the 180-degree leap to show us his frozen facial expression and gaze, whereupon the camera quickly zooms in to approach it, as the background noise, which had almost imperceptibly become louder during the last seconds, gradually yields to total silence, and the next cut shows us what Tully is seeing: a tableau-vivant of the patrons in the background, in which every action or movement, save for the rising smoke of a cigarette, has stopped. The entire duration of this silent immobile part is almost fifteen seconds. There remain a few more seconds until the end of the film, but let us freeze here to listen to Huston's comments on this long tableau-vivant shot in his dialogue with Keach and his assistant director, as reported by Lawrence Grobel:

"Have you ever been at a party when for no reason everybody just stops? When all of a sudden it's all a tableau; you're alone in eternity for a moment? When Stacy turns around, I want everybody to just stop what they're doing." "Why, John?" Keach asked. "I have no idea," Huston answered. "Sometimes the devil just gets into me." "We can just freeze frame," Russ Saunders, the assistant director, suggested. "No, no, no," John said. "I want the cigarette smoke to continue going. I don't want it to look like a stock frame. I just want everybody to stop."[46]

Huston enhances the continuation of the camera's shooting in the midst of the overall inertia by having the camera pan once from right to left on the X-axis, revealing different tables with immobilized card players, while two cuts construct a Z-axis through a shot-reverse-shot that reveals Tully's face and the background alternately. One of the emblematic techniques of continuity editing, the bedrock of the action-image, is here employed to the opposite effect: the shot-reverse-shot between Tully's fossilized face and eyes—his solo tableau-vivant—and the tableau-vivant of the patrons (half of them with their backs turned to the camera, the rest of them looking at their cards) add to the impossibility of action, the impossibility of communication and of any form of human contact. By avoiding a stock frame and opting instead for a double tableau-vivant punctuated by quintessential cinematographic techniques of the action-image, Huston offers us the epitome of filming *in* action with *no* action, the pure passing of time—visualized exclusively through the rising cigarette smoke and the effects of the camera movement and of editing—in which not just action but all human activity has ceased. All activity, except one: thought.

Fifteen seconds are actually too short to grasp all the thought that circulates between the foreground "white trash" and the background "black trash" on each end of the Z-axis, expanding exponentially the racial commentary that perforates the whole film, making the individual plight overlap with the collective, and eventually transcending the entire diegesis toward a treatise that concerns equally the human condition as the conditions of cinematography. This scene is the crystal that directly reveals the aspiration of the entirety of the film, the very seed out of which any other sequence grows and to which it wants to return.

Letting now the rest of the finale roll, after the fifteen seconds having elapsed, the background sound of the patrons returns at the same time as the sole standing patron, his smoking metronome in hand, begins to turn his back away from the camera so as to walk toward the right of the frame. A cut shows us Tully's face, which also begins to thaw, as Ernie's voice off-screen states: "Hey, buddy, I must take off." "Hey . . . ," he retorts, turning to the left of the frame (where presumably Ernie sits), and after a short hesitation adds with a subtly imploring voice, ". . . stick around! Talk a while." "OK," responds Ernie, now in the frame, and takes a sip of his coffee, as Tully completes his rotation, so that now we see both of them at the counter again in the same positions as at the beginning of the sequence. For the remaining twenty-five seconds, prior to the beginning of the film's theme song—Kris Kristofferson's "Help Me Make It through the Night"— and the end credits, the two are sipping their coffees, occasionally moving their dull gazes, occasionally fixing them somewhere off-screen, at times their arms or heads slightly moving, at others so immobile that the viewer feels uncertain as to whether she is presented with a stock frame. It turns out that the camera is continuing to roll even after the credits have begun rolling, until after another twenty-five seconds and the end of first stanza of the song, the screen turns black in silence. The impossibility of action and communication established through the explicit double tableau-vivant is thus, through the remaining "action," doubly sealed.

With this finale Tully has come full round back to the inertia and silence of his first appearance in the film. After the opening credits, accompanied by an instrumental version of the film's theme song, during which we get snips from the geopolitical public cityspace and life of Stockton, we enter the first ambiguously private space, a cheap hotel room, on whose bed Tully is lying in his white underpants and greenish T-shirt, in apathetic torpor across the Z-axis, his feet toward the camera. After a while he sits up in order to take from the nightstand a cigarette—the last one in his packet, as he discovers—put it in his mouth, and find out that his matchbox is empty. He decides to get up in a sluggish search for matches in the room. Having established that he has run out of matches for good, he sits resigned on the side of bed, his face toward the window and away from the camera—while the music stops—and subtly nods his head in stoic acceptance of the situation. With only low traffic noise audible through the window, he eventually gets up again, puts on his grayish pants, brownish socks—whereupon the theme song starts again, this time with lyrics—black shoes, and purplish jacket, and with the bent last cigarette always in his mouth, he steps outside the hotel, evidently determined to get matches. Standing in front of the hotel entrance on this sunny day, in a medium long shot, his body begins to subtly make some " 'I am cool" kind of moves, after which he throws the cigarette on the street, turns around, and reenters the hotel, all of which indicates that he has made at the spot a resolution. He goes back to the room and, in the midst of accumulated empty liquor bottles, he picks up his bag and leaves. His determined steps through Stockton's streets leave no doubt that he is finally moving toward action, even as we do not know of what kind. The theme song ends as Tully enters the local YMCA where he makes the acquaintance of the eighteen-year-old Ernie. After Tully explains that he is an ex-pro trying to get into shape, a friendly boxing round ensues; however, it ends prematurely, as Tully pulls a muscle. In these few first minutes of the film, the tension between desire for action and the failure of action is set up from the outset as the film's central theme and organizing principle.

Tully attributes his injury to the fact that he had not warmed up, claims that in the past he was unbeatable, and, finding out that Ernie has never before been to the ring, tells him that he is a "natural" and that he should go to the "Lido Gym" to see his own manager, Ruben. During this dialogue, Tully mentions his name, which Ernie recognizes and says: "Yeah, I saw you fight once."—(Tully:) "Yeah? Did I win?"—(Ernie:) "No." Tully shakes his head stoically and taps Ernie on his back. Thus, by the end of this sequence, Tully's resolution to action is doubly undermined: both his present injury and his past defeat thwart his image of himself as the unbeatable pro.

Sure enough, the next cut reveals Tully's relapse—he is in a dive drinking—while also introducing the corollary theme to that of action and its failure: communication, human relations, and their failure. The rambunctious Oma (Susan Tyrrell) and her placid current boyfriend, Earl (Curtis Cokes), arrive and sit at the bar next to Tully, with Oma, in the middle, engaging with the two men in a simultaneous dialogue, whose function is to represent the failure of dialogue. There is no communication between Oma and Tully, as the latter's thoughts oscillate between the nadir of his resolution to action (his injury) and the zenith supposed to await Ernie's future, as one of the talents that "come one in a million," while everything that Oma hears from him and says addresses her other dialogue with Earl, which is in itself moot, as it only reconfirms to both of them what they already know, namely: that she is rambunctious and he placid. This same failed dialogue also constitutes a crystal-image in which the present actual image mirrors the three phases of Oma's and Tully's forthcoming relation. Oma's statement—"I love that man [Earl] more than any man has got the right to be loved. If he left me I just couldn't make it. I couldn't live without him"—anticipates her line to Tully as they will be leaving together the same dive the next time, when, after Earl will have been put in jail, they run into each other and hit it off: "I love you so much." The continuation of her line about Earl—"Do you think he would even raise his voice and get me a drink? No. He'd just sit there and let them ignore us"—and her overall nagging about him is a condensed version of her and Tully's incessant fights in the duration of their clichéd relationship. And the dynamics of the two simultaneous interactions in the present actual

image—Oma's frustration with and aggression toward Earl, and her uncondi-
tionally flirtatious affability toward Tully—will be reiterated in inverted form
in two later scenes: first, in the scene early in their relationship, in which
Oma tries to give Tully some "flare" by having him try on Earl's clothes
(from the box where they are stored), where Earl *in absentia* becomes the
object of her flirtatious longing, while frustration is now metastasized in
her relation to Tully; and, second, in the final scene the three share, when,
after Oma's and Tully's breakup and after Earl has been released from the
jail and has again moved in with Oma, Tully returns to pick up his clothes
(stored, in their turn, also in a box), and Oma treats his visitation like an
atheist facing Jesus Christ at her door (this comparison being based on her
religiously cursing rhetoric), while Earl now functions as the bridge between
the two. These triangulations engender two sets of identifications—Tully and
Earl, Earl and Oma—with Earl and Tully pivoting around Oma, alternately
occupying each other's pasts and futures. The third possible combination, the
identification between Tully and Oma, while excluded from the itineraries
of the amorous triangulation, is obtained through their character traits, such
as their cyclothymia, swinging between friendliness and outbursts of rage,
hopefulness and depression, or their tendency to a lethargic indulgence in
alcohol, to which, unlike Tully, Oma shows no signs of resistance.

Having exemplified through its tragico-hilarious tripartite dialogue
the impossibility of dialogue, Huston inserts a Brechtian alienation-effect
moment through Oma's staring at the camera while she is proclaiming (as
a conclusion from her preceding statement, "I believe that everybody has
a right to his own life"): "So, screw everybody!" This is immediately followed by her suddenly smiling face turning to Tully, who reciprocates with
laughter, and the sequence concludes with Oma going to the restroom, on
the door of which one can read: "LADIES ONLY. WATCH OUT!"—reminiscent of one of the city's signs shown during the opening credits: "CITY
OF STOCKTON. CAUTION."

The next cut brings us back to Ernie going to the "Lido Gym," to
reinforce also cinematographically his function as the primary of (though
far from only) Tully's doubles, as during the next approximately twenty minutes Tully disappears, except as an occasionally referenced name or as one
among the anonymous mass of daily waged farm workers, while the film
pursues Ernie's budding career as a boxer, to the point that the viewer could
be misled in believing that he is after all the actual protagonist. After some
practicing scenes and Ruben's reassurance that, as he tells his wife in bed,
Ernie is an exceptionally talented (and all the more exceptional since "white")
boxer, Ruben and his assistant, Babe (Art Aragon), take Ernie and the rest

of their "boys" to their first fight. Even this relatively optimistic trajectory of Ernie's pursuits is punctuated by cuts of failure. First, Ruben is singing Ernie's paean to his wife only to discover at the end that she has already fallen asleep; second, Ruben fails also to communicate with Babe, the former trying to make a point through a story in which somebody's "blood" was like "black . . . gelatin" that "don't run down," while the latter persists on some other point proven through somebody else's blood supposed to have been "as clean and as pure as fresh drinking water"; third, Babe's reference to "water" provides the rhetorical bridge to the rainy night of the next sequence, in which Ernie and his girlfriend, Faye (Candy Clark), experience the predictably clichéd in-car-deflowering, and the schizoid tension between presumed virginity and "wonderful" sexual performance on the part of the female produces (yet another hilarious nondialogue); and, fourth, the team is finally in the car ready to leave for the boxing ring in Monterey, but the trunk keeps popping open. Yet, as all examples since the beginning of the film indicate, humor rarely fails to accompany not only Leonard Gardner's dialogue but also Huston's cuts of failure.

Once at the locker room of the Monterey ring, an illegally young (according to the boxing rules) black guy from Ernie's team delivers to him a triumph-of-the-will-like speech in its contemporary positive-thinking vernacular—"it's all in your mind"—to which Ernie finally responds, in his usual deadpan manner, "I want to kick ass as bad as you do," and is subsequently led to the ring to be defeated and carried back to the locker room to bequeath his bloody boxing shorts to the same black guy, who is in turn also defeated, as are—as we discover in the next sequence, where all of them are having dinner in a dive—the rest of the team, except one. As the camera reveals their faces, each in close-up, their facial bruises and wounds make the winner and the losers strikingly indiscernible. This sequence also reinforces further the mirroring between Ernie and Tully, as Ernie's newly broken nose intimates an indelible visible mark of his first defeat, not unlike Tully's own scar on his eyelid, commemorating his own first defeat (caused by a razor illicitly used by his opponent). The indelibility of Ernie's injury is sealed through a new, mediating, mirroring between Ernie and Ruben, who tries to reassure Ernie that he will get "that nose fixed as new," telling him, "Look at mine. Would you believe it was ever busted?" to which Ernie unhesitatingly responds: "Yes!" Note also that, through the identification of Ernie and Tully, and by showing us only two "real" fights on the ring, Ernie's first defeat and Tully's forthcoming victory over Lucero (Sixto Rodriguez), the film intensifies further the indiscernibility between victory and defeat.

The film constitutes a sort of insatiable network of mirrorings between characters. Not only between Tully and Ernie, Ruben, Earl, Oma, and, for that matter, Lucero—who is beaten by Tully, yet offers us a representation of *any* boxer when beaten—but also through the further redoubling of their respective amorous pairings. Tully's unseen ex-wife is mirrored in Ernie's current girlfriend and eventually wife, and all heterosexual married couples are ultimately mirrored in the two most cliché representations of marriage offered in the film, the one narrated by an aged black fieldworker who explains the reasons of his past divorce, and the other acted out in the homosocial relationship between Ruben and Babe. Representative of their interactions is the scene in which they are preparing to bring Ernie to the ring for his first fight:

RUBEN: Where is the bucket?

BABE: (showing the bucket): In my hand.

RUBEN: Where is the bottle?

BABE: The bottle is in the bucket.

RUBEN: You got water in it?

BABE: I wouldn't bring an empty bottle.

As Deleuze has put it, in a world that has lost the sense of (significant, authentic, teleological) "totality or linkage," what remains to sustain the filmic "set are *clichés*, and nothing else."[47] These "floating . . . anonymous clichés . . . circulate in the external world, but . . . also penetrate each one of us and constitute . . . [our] internal world, so that everyone possesses only psychic clichés by which everyone thinks and feels, is thought and is felt, being ourselves "a cliché among the others in the world which surrounds" us. For, in an inauthentic world where even one's last act, death, is incapable of rendering life significant, "in order for people to be able to bear themselves and the world, misery has to reach the inside of consciousnesses and the inside has to be like the outside."[48] In whatever relations Tully or Ernie may find themselves, they are always clichés, whether in the cliché of marriage or in the cliché of the breakup/divorce, and by embodying anonymous clichés, they, like everybody else, become anonymous.

The effect of the cliché is the same as that of unlimited redoublings. Not unlike Pasolini's multiplication of presents through subjective long takes in sequence, which empties and abolishes the present as relative due to the presence of all other subjective presents, Huston's network of perpetual redoublings among the individual characters has as its effect the elimination of individual consciousness altogether—a condensed visualization of which we have already seen in the film's, denouement where the overlap of the individual and the collective amounts precisely to the abolition of individual consciousness.

Redoubling is the mechanism through which the film effects the indiscernibility both of individual characters and of distinct chronological moments, with time redoubling itself in the crystal-image as present and its contemporaneous past. Now, to redouble means essentially to repeat in some form, and repetition is the constituent element of the trauma, for, as we know since Freud, a delayed reenactment of an event is required for that first event to be retroactively experienced as traumatic. This is intrinsically related to what Deleuze has identified as the very cause of the emergence of the crystal-image in the history of cinema: a trauma, which at least within the European history was occasioned by the Second World War. *Fat City* treats diegetically and cinematographically two events as traumatic: Tully's first defeat on the ring and his wife's rejection. While the script dialogue allows Tully's narrated memory to function as the "first event" (still only potentially traumatic), Ernie's first defeat provides us with a surrogate visual representation of that "first event." Thus, the film's sole visual representation of Tully's fight in the ring can function as the reenactment of the "first event." As we know, in this fight against Lucero, Tully wins, but his victory is as indiscernible from a defeat as are the faces of the team member's right after the aforementioned visual presentation of the "first event." First, the value of Tully's victory as an index of his future potential as a boxer is undermined from the outset, as Lucero is introduced not only as a "puncher," as opposed to "a good tune-up," whom Tully's manager reluctantly accepts having no other option, but also as a sick man, as the camera generously reveals through his private moments (he is urinating blood). Second, and more importantly, it is not Tully who wins; it is some impersonal "we"—for Tully is not conscious of his winning, or, more accurately, by the time of his "victory," he has no consciousness whatsoever. Even as Tully continues to move and fight in the ring, he has in truth ceased to be the individual consciousness of these movements already since the reenactment of the "first event," which occurs at the moment when Lucero hits Tully on the eye so that his scar opens up again—or so will Tully claim later, contrary to Ruben who insists that this wound has nothing to do with his old cut. From that moment on, Tully stares at the void—thus, anticipating the film's finale—so that his continuing action looks more like a series of mechanical gestures executed by a fighting pawn, not much unlike his opponent's, as the two seem as much to fight as to share hugs so as to keep oneself (or each other?) standing. Finally, after already having been cheered by the crowd, "winner by technical knock-out" zombie, aka Tully, asks, "Did I get knocked down?" to which Babe responds: "No, we won, we won!" Ruben enters the frame to reiterate the information in a more personalized way—"You won, baby, you won!" and the information seems to register, as Tully goes to Lucero for a conventional postfight reconciliatory hug.

Let us pause again here to make a comparison with a quintessential Italian neorealist film, Vittorio de Sica's *Ladri di biciclette* (Bicycle Thieves) (1948). The protagonist—the honest family man in search of work in those desperate times of European history right after the Second World War—finds himself at the end of the film in an alien identity, as he himself has become what his antagonist is: a bicycle thief. An ingenious moment in the history of cinematography that eliminates human agency and reveals the impotence of human will in the face of the capitalist machine whose deterministic laws only grew stronger through the war: no equipment (bike), no job, no life. Sooner or later everybody has to become a "bicycle thief," that is, try to survive with whatever illicit means in this machinery, a process that renders human individuals exchangeable. And yet, the transformation of the individual protagonist, Antonio, into the anonymous—that is, universal qua exchangeable—subject of capitalism does not here eliminate consciousness. The positions of innocence and guilt can be occupied by any individual under certain circumstances, but the *positions* themselves remain distinct, and the individual who happens to occupy them at any given moment recognizes himself or herself as *either* innocent *or* guilty. The discernibility of the distinct positions transcends the exchangeability of the individuals that come to occupy them. This is sealed by the film's finale, which continues after the police have let Antonio go free only to record his shame, particularly vis-à-vis the failure to fulfill the paternal function in the eyes of his son. This (structuralist) victory of positions over what occupies them is in effect the victory of consciousness (and conscience) over the vicissitudes of individual fates. In the midst of its defeat, human dignity is restored in de Sica's film. By this token, the film's universe is a capitalism imbued by ideals and, hence, governed by ideology—for how else can positions obtain their signification and value as either innocent or guilty, and so on? This is no

longer the case in Huston's *Fat City*, which, beyond the exchangeability of
the individual contents registers the indiscernibility—which is to say, lack of
signification—of the very positions that they come to occupy. It is no longer
simply a matter of the fact that Tully can occupy at a certain moment the
position of the winner and at another that of the defeated. Rather, the issue is
that he cannot tell the difference between the two positions. Betraying more
ignorance than the questions Deleuze finds emblematic of the time-image—
"What happened? How have we arrived at this point?"[49]—Tully effectively
asks: "What happened? Where are we in the first place?"

In its major circuit, this indiscernibility heralds the collapse of consciousness altogether—as is the case in Tully's fight scene and in the finale of
the film, where Tully, the patrons, and ultimately Ernie, are all reduced to a
tableaux-vivant, as the pawns of the cinematographic apparatus. In its minor
circuit, it manifests itself as the confusion of positions within a somnambulist
consciousness. This occurs in the two sequences that separate the scene of
Tully's fight from the film's finale. In the first sequence, in one of his outbursts
Tully blames his scar on Ruben and the fact that he did not accompany him
to his first fight, so that Ruben's established position as Tully's "helper" finds
itself coinciding with that of his nemesis. In the second sequence (which we
have already seen), Tully, who is the one who had left Oma, decides in his
desperation to revisit her. But he is received at her door by Earl, who has in
the meantime moved in with her again, while Oma's off-screen voice from
the bed makes clear that she does not want any further interaction with
Tully, who thus finds himself in the position of the man being rejected by
her—a displacement that also retroactively allows his breakup with Oma to
function as the reenactment of the other "first event," Tully's rejection by
his wife. After this, Tully's complete reduction to the opposite of an active
hero culminates in his somnambulist gaze in the final sequence, where the
sparse dialogue literally cancels chronological time, as the state of being old
is not preceded by youth, and establishes affect as a flow beyond and above
discernible individualities, since one person's possible happiness allows for
the inference that perhaps we are all happy.

Beyond the Time-Image of Individual Consciousness

The indiscernibility between positions (winner/loser, rejecting/rejected, and
so on), which presupposes the erasure of their signification, is the precondition of the maximum potentiation of the present, for voiding positions
from their preestablished significations is required in order to open up the

possibility of restructuring the very structure itself. But if it is no longer signification, and hence ideals, that govern the structuration of the structure, what motivates it instead? The finale's transition from its quasi-explicit reference to the crystal-image to the de-individualization of affect seems to point to the answer.

As Deleuze puts it, the absence of signification can only "mark the coincidence of the subject and the object in a pure quality," that is, in "affection."[50] If in "the affection-image," as the "final avatar of the movement-image," an "activity can only respond by" pure affect as "a 'tendency,' an 'effort' which replaces the action which has become momentarily or locally impossible,"[51] in the time-image, in which action has become permanently impossible, I maintain that affect no longer replaces action but rather becomes its very vehicle. This statement entails immediately its inversion, since action itself is now impossible; in other words, in the American time-image, action becomes the pretext for cinematographically circulating within a purely affective dimension. Which is why, unlike the European time-image, the American must realistically sustain the pretext of action.

As Deleuze also remarks, "There are two kinds of signs of the affection-image . . . *on the one hand the power-quality expressed by a face or an equivalent*," the close-up, "*but on the other hand the power-quality presented in any-space-whatever [un espace quelconque]*."[52] This is to say, "affect" can be "directly presented in medium shot, in a space which is capable of corresponding to it," whereby "[s]pace is no longer a particular determined space, it has become *any-space-whatever*," that is,

> not an abstract universal, in all times, in all places. It is a perfectly singular space, which has merely lost its homogeneity, that is, the principle of its metric relations or the connection of its own parts, so that the linkages can be made in an infinite number of ways. It is a space of virtual conjunction, grasped as pure locus of the possible. What in fact manifests the instability, the heterogeneity, the absence of link of such a space, is a richness in potentials or singularities which are, as it were, prior conditions of all actualisation, all determination.[53]

This is exactly how space functions in *Fat City*. The more Huston focuses on the singularity of Stockton, the more its urban landscape becomes an *any-space-whatever* that expresses the affect of American recession. Tully's hotel room; the YMCA; the boxing rings and their locker rooms; the dives where the characters, drink, eat, meet; Oma's bedroom; the field where Tully,

Ernie, and the rest of the lumpen population of Stockton work for a day's wages—all of these spaces exhume the specific only to present the "event in its eternal aspect," for, while being "actualized in an individuated state of things and in the corresponding *real connections* (with a particular space-time, *hic et nunc*, particular characters, particular roles, particular objects)," they are also "expressed for themselves, outside spatiotemporal coordinates, with their own ideal singularities and their *virtual conjunction*" with both the prior conditions of their actualization and determination and the infinite richness of their potentials.[54] In Oma's bedroom reigns the affect of the relational deadlock across geopolitical boundaries and social classes, so that it can be seen as much in its specificity as a translation of a scene from Ingmar Bergman's *Scenes from a Marriage* (1973) into its contemporary American idiom; the fields ooze John Steinbeck's/Ford's (1939/1940) *The Grapes of Wrath* and all the history that engulfs and enables both book and film. And in the finale's canteen, we experience the antinomic affect that exudes from the fusion of the two mutually exclusive lives in Tully—the austere life of the athlete and the decadent life of the drunkard—as the YMCA-like whiteness of the café part is mirrored in the dive-like dark colors of the gambling area. *Fat City* does not narrate the story of Billy Tully or any boxer or, for that matter, any individual consciousness; it maps the itinerary of these affects as the eternal residue of all events that can correspond to them.

The preceding, however, should not be mistaken for some celebration of affect as the flow of pure intensities or powers supposed to stand outside the sphere of the law, as is often assumed in certain Deleuzian approaches. That individual consciousness and positions lose their signification does not mean that signification is eliminated altogether. With the obliteration of individuality, signification is simply displaced to the level of collectivities. This is actually what Deleuze and Félix Guattari also argue in the context of the paternal function in Kafka; once individuality is obliterated, the agent of the law will be "expanded beyond all bounds, will be projected onto the geographic, historical, and political *map* of the world in order to reach vast regions of it"; thus, in Kafka, the "Name of the Father encodes the names of history-Jews, Czechs, Germans, Prague, city-county."[55] This is exactly what Lacan's transposition of the signifier and the law from the individual and familial level to the symbolic order had already effected—for in psychoanalysis the subject is not individual but always already collective.

Similarly, in *Fat City*, the elimination of individual consciousness reveals the paternal function as operative directly on the collective level, where it in fact establishes two series: that of Ruben and that of Ernie, as the two representatives of the injunction to (athletic) discipline. In his additionally protective and supportive roles, Ruben evidences also maternal qualities, thus standing for a benevolent "God," in contrast to Ernie, who represents throughout an indifferent "God." On the one hand Ruben's series of the simultaneous idealist and profit-oriented boxing manager and on the other hand Ernie's series of the pragmatic, wage-earning family man. Tully remains untouched by Ernie, finding him as he reveals at the end, "a guy that is soft in the center"—for Ernie, the young promising boxing talent, boxing or working in the farms is the same (as both are means for earning one's living), whereas for Tully working in the fields would be a waste of time, were it not for the fact that "it is almost as good as roadwork for getting back into shape," and the bonus is, "you get paid for it." Tully eventually rejects Ruben, as his "confusion" reveals the true indiscernibility of the manager's two aspects: idealism/protection and profit/exploitation. The sole law valid for Tully is the law of the excess produced through the aforementioned antinomies or coincidences of signification, since affect is after all this excess, and Tully is the pawn of the action of affect.

American Cinema of Thought and Its Time-Affect-Image

The American manifestation of the time-image is qualitatively different from its European predecessors, perhaps due to the different phases of capitalist development and its crises, in which they emerge and which they represent. Evidently, the Second World War, the traumatic event that led to the European time-image, was only the "first event" for the United States, as it was not before the 1970s that socioeconomic reality began to shatter massively the "American Dream." Leonard Gardner, the novelist and scriptwriter of *Fat City*, himself a native of Stockton, ex-boxer, and lifelong boxing aficionado, testifies to this:

> When I was growing up, I felt that America was like granite. When I realized that the country was coming apart it came as a shock. . . . In Europe I've visited a lot of zoos. There you see how far beyond all other animals we are. But at the same time we are so disappointing, so brutal and callous. When we were bombing Vietnam, I had the feeling that the human race is just one big lost cause.[56]

Through these words is felt a crisis traumatic enough to collapse positions for millennia supposed to be kept apart, as (the historically known ephemerality of) "granite-like" empires yields to the indiscernibility between animal life and civilization. This is the moment of the activation of the twentieth-century American trauma, when the pressures of capitalism are crashing any remnant of human dignity. And since it happened later than in the Old World, this country's imaginary had to make the leap from beginning to question the action-image of classical Hollywood to thinking after consciousness is dead.

So it comes that the United States produces its own cinema of thought, which involves: (1) the concomitant designification or indiscernibility of positions and the elimination of individual consciousness; (2) their replacement as motors of diegetic development by affect; (3) consequently, the necessary reliance of a kind of apparent action as the means for generating affects, which, given the destruction of the temporality and the agents of the action-image, is an impersonal or, what amounts to the same, purely collective action; and, as a further corollary, (4) the collective agency of the law. This being the case, characters become the pawns of affect, that is, they have to continue to play with their faces and move their bodies in space but only as somnambulistic vehicles that allow faces and spaces to express affects.

Thus, the American cinema of thought shifts the duel from the pair situation-character to that between affect and (apparent) action. The site of the duel becomes now the sequences' cuts that run contrapuntally to the film's "action." In this way, Huston's film advances the thesis that, if postmodernism is an era replete with crises—on all levels, from the socioeconomic to subjectivity—American cinema must also think, but it can exist as a distinct type of cinematography only by sustaining its action-drive; and since individual consciousness is dead, this action can be carried out only collectively, that is, affectively. The film seals the demise of the old dream of "being in Fat City"—as the "Negro slang" would have it[57]—by proposing: *if you can't make it, you have to think*; and in the process it discovers that if you cannot act then *you* can also not think, so it lets *affect do the thinking*, on the condition that *you continue to do as if you were acting*.

Unwilling to give up action as its point of reference, and simultaneously incapable of any longer basing action on a time supposed to reconstruct a whole and to be based on individuality, the American cinema of thought emerges as it invents its own time-image that is motivated by affect as its sole agency. By this token, it may deserve its own name: the *time-affect-image*, which pertains to the American cinema of *affective thought*. This is ultimately the reason why, as Grønstad notes, even as it depicts "a cynical and wholly un-sentimental" social and (inter)subjective plight, *Fat City*'s "vision retains hope," and this "despite the seeming hopelessness of its environment." For, by producing in the midst of the redoubled crisis of capitalism, as experienced in the American 1970s, a new kind of cinema of thought, it restores our belief in the world—which is, after all, its task. For once in the realm of the time-image, as Deleuze puts is, "the question is no longer: does cinema give us the illusion of the world? But: how does cinema restore our belief in the world?"[58]

This affect-motivated action derives its force neither from a cohesive teleological plot, nor from individual agency, but, immersed in dispersion, it relies on local, episodic, and autonomous instances of affective excitement. It is true, as Deleuze writes, that "[i]n Scorsese's *Taxi Driver*, the driver wavers between killing himself and committing a political murder and, replacing these projects by the final slaughter, is astonished by it himself, as if the carrying out concerned him no more than did the preceding whims."[59] But his dispersive and aimless voyage has carried us from the busy night streets of New York to brothels, banks, drug dens, cafés, diners, dives, political rallies, porno-movie theaters, a window through which we witness a scene of adultery, and a Vietnam vet's weapon-infested tenement, where the protagonist (Robert De Niro) immortalized his bravado improvisation—all this amply enhanced with sexual sensuality and exuberant verbal and physical violence, while being punctuated with humor. Watching the most successful specimen of the American cinema of thought is certainly a very different experience than watching Italian neorealism, including its most successful examples, such as Luchino Visconti's *La terra trema* (1948) or Vittorio de Sica's *Umberto D.* (1952), and, of course, *Ladri di biciclette*. American thought passes through the excitement of affective action.

The effectiveness of the American cinema of thought in passing through the action of affective excitement depends on its realism or hyperrealism, in opposition to its European counterpart which, if it involves at all references to action, does so only in order to thwart it even as a pretext—think, for instance, of Jean-Luc Godard's *À bout de soufflé* (1960), *Alphaville* (1965), or *Weekend* (1967). It is perhaps the American cinema's persistence on the action, yet only after its transformation into the means for affective excitement, that Deleuze means to index when he writes immediately after his commentary on *Taxi Driver*: "The actuality of the action-image, the virtuality of the affection-image can interchange, all the more easily for having fallen into the same indifference."[60] The specificity of the American cinema of thought lies in the literal actualization of the affection-image through the vehicle of a virtual action-image—an action-image that has to fail in its old sense (the action of a hero) so as to triumph as collective/affective action. This failure has to imbue filmmaking itself, for, unlike the classical cases of cinema of thought (Italian neorealism, the French *nouvelle vague*, and the German cinema of the 1970s), *Fat City*, as a specimen of the American cinema of thought, maintains faithfully the appearance of a realistic action-motivated film, and so it intrinsically relies on the synergy of dialogue and cuts in order to guarantee the failure of that realist, yet virtual, action-motivated film within the film, as the very precondition for the successful production of the time-affect-image. In this sense, the American time-affect-image meets Franz Kafka, since, in Benjamin's concise words, "Once he was certain of eventual failure, everything worked out for him *en route* as in a dream."[61]

Notes

1. Pier Paolo Pasolini, "Observations on the Long Take," trans. Norman MacAfee and Craig Owens, *October* 13 (1980): 6.
2. Pasolini, "Observations on the Long Take," 5.
3. Pasolini, "Observations on the Long Take," 5–6.
4. Pasolini, "Observations on the Long Take," 5.
5. Pasolini, "Observations on the Long Take," 3–4.
6. Pasolini, "Observations on the Long Take," 4.
7. Pasolini, "Observations on the Long Take," 5.
8. Pasolini, "Observations on the Long Take," 5.
9. Pasolini, "Observations on the Long Take," 6.
10. Howard Caygill, "Benjamin, Heidegger and the Destruction of Tradition," in *Walter Benjamin: Critical Evaluations in Cultural Theory*, vol. 1, ed. Peter Osborne (London: Routledge, 2005), 297.
11. Caygill, "Benjamin, Heidegger and the Destruction of Tradition," 298.
12. Walter Benjamin, "Tragedy and *Trauerspiel*," in *Selected Writings*, ed. Marcus Bullock and Michael W. Jennings (Cambridge: Belknap Press of Harvard University Press, 1966), 55.
13. Caygill, "Benjamin, Heidegger and the Destruction of Tradition," 299.
14. Benjamin, "Tragedy and *Trauerspiel*," 57.
15. Gilles Deleuze, *Cinema 1: The Time-Image*, trans. Hugh Tomlinson and Robert Galeta (Minneapolis: University of Minnesota Press, 1986), 141.
16. Deleuze, *Cinema 1: The Time-Image*, 141–142.
17. Angelo Restivo, "Into the Breach: Between the Movement-Image and the Time-Image," in *The Brain Is the Screen: Deleuze and the Philosophy of Cinema*, ed. Gregory Flaxman (Minneapolis: University of Minnesota Press, 2000), 174.
18. Restivo, "Into the Breach," 174.
19. Deleuze, *Cinema 1*, 189.
20. Deleuze, *Cinema 1*, 214.
21. Deleuze, *Cinema 1*, 209 and 181.

22. Deleuze, *Cinema 1*, 179–180.

23. Deleuze, *Cinema 1*, 214.

24. Deleuze, *Cinema 1*, 43.

25. Deleuze, *Cinema 1*, 214.

26. Deleuze, *Cinema 1*, 175.

27. Deleuze, *Cinema 1*, 175.

28. Deleuze, *Cinema 2*, 66.

29. Deleuze, *Cinema 1*, 206.

30. Deleuze, *Cinema 1*, 207.

31. According to the Internet Movie Database, already by the end of 1977, *Dog Day Afternoon* had returned a gross profit of $50,000,000. Although it received two Academy Award nominations, Cassavetes's *Faces* cannot be called a box-office success.

32. Gaylyn Studlar, "Shadowboxing: *Fat City* and the Malaise of Masculinity," in *Reflections in a Male Eye: John Huston and the American Experience*, ed. Gaylyn Studlar and David Desser (Washington: Smithsonian Institute, 1993), 181.

33. Asbjørn Grønstad, "Abject Topographies: Images of Male Desolation in *Fat City* and *Junior Bonner*," *Kinema: A Journal for Film and Audiovisual Media* (2008), http://www.kinema.uwaterloo.ca/article.php?id=167&feature (date of access unknown).

34. Guerric DeBona, "Masculinity on the Front: John Huston's *The Red Badge of Courage* (1951) Revisited," *Cinema Journal* 42.2 (Winter 2003): 62–63.

35. Grønstad, "Abject Topographies."

36. As cited in Grønstad, "Abject Topographies."

37. Grønstad, "Abject Topographies."

38. Grønstad, "Abject Topographies."

39. Deleuze, *Cinema 1*, 206.

40. Grønstad, "Abject Topographies."

41. Grønstad, "Abject Topographies."

42. Deleuze, *Cinema 1*, 78–79.

43. Deleuze, *Cinema 1*, 79–81.

44. Deleuze, *Cinema 1*, 79–81.

45. Deleuze, *Cinema 1*, 81.

46. Lawrence Grobel, *The Hustons* (New York: Charles Scribner's, 1989), 638.

47. Deleuze, *Cinema 1*, 208.

48. Deleuze, *Cinema 1*, 208–209.

49. Deleuze, *Cinema 2*, 50.

50. Deleuze, *Cinema 1*, 65.

51. Deleuze, *Cinema 1*, 65–66.

52. Deleuze, *Cinema 1*, 110.

53. Deleuze, *Cinema 1*, 109.

54. Deleuze, *Cinema 1*, 102.

55. Gilles Deleuze and Félix Guattari, *Kafka: Toward a Minor Literature*, trans. Dana Polan (Minneapolis: University of Minnesota Press, 1986), 10.

56. Michael Durham, "A Short Talk with a First Novelist," *Life* 67.9 (August 29, 1969): 10.

57. As Leonard Gardner stated in his interview with Michael Durham in *Life* magazine, the expression "Fat City" is "part of Negro slang. When you say you want to go to Fat City, it means you want the good life. . . . The title is ironic: Fat City is a crazy goal no one is ever going to reach" (10).

58. Deleuze, *Cinema 2*, 181–182.

59. Deleuze, *Cinema 1*, 207.

60. Deleuze, *Cinema 1*, 207.

61. Walter Benjamin, *Illuminations*, ed. Hannah Arendt, trans. Harry Zohn (New York: Schocken Books, 1969), 145.

13

The End of (Self) Analysis

The End of Kurosawa's *High and Low*

Brian Wall

Kurosawa as humanist: a stress on the integrity of an individual protagonist who searches for a workable ethics, often one explicitly opposed to the structures of the collective, the economic, or the state. Kurosawa as modernist: the deployment of experimental—often conflicting and even incommensurate—cinematic codes and discourses that question, undo, and subvert the notionally "natural," revealing it as artificial and constructed. Such questioning does not exempt the ideologies that underwrite those codes, including that of humanism itself.

While such a reductive gloss of this director could not possibly account for the diversity of his oeuvre, it is not wrong; and the duality it brings into focus—that of content and form, which may seem as old-fashioned as Kurosawa's putative humanism—also precipitates a return to a wealth of other, related questions, all of which reverberate in the striking ending of *High and Low* (1963). As the film's villain Takeuchi (Tsutomu Yamazaki) sits separated from the hero Gondo (Toshirô Mifune) by barriers of glass and class, Kurosawa's camera takes pains to mirror them, stressing their identity at the very moment Takeuchi declares, "I'm not interested in self-analysis." At a stroke, identity is affirmed and undone: the mise-en-scène—the *form*—asserts the primacy of the human, an implicit and explicit valuation of identity and subjectivity, at precisely the moment the content disavows it. Contradiction, a symptom of ideology, entails that it cannot merely be the case that the "pure" terms that govern these oppositions—form and content, individual and social—imply a longed-for goal or sublation. Nor can it be the case that *High and Low* or even Kurosawa more generally searches for a film without content or, alternatively, an apology for humanism. We must ask: What happens then to a modernist emphasis on form as demystifying and critical? And what is the fate of what until now seemed merely, even naïvely, old-fashioned humanist content? Is form really no more than a neutral container, one that can comfortably endorse a problematic humanism even as it elsewhere appears to dissolve it? Or does the self emerge at the moment of its eclipse, in recognition that it is an effect of form and structure, not a cause? Does the subject come at the end—of the narrative, of the workings of structure and form, of the film?

Kurosawa's *High and Low* thus invites a dialectical interpretation, motivating a rich variety of conflicts—and outright contradictions—in its course: from the title, whether its Anglicized evocation of spatial hierarchies that suggest class conflict, or the original Japanese—*Tengoku to jigoku*, Heaven and Hell—with its more metaphysical invitations; from the styles deployed here, with the very Japanese theatricality of the first half juxtaposed with the more fulsomely American, even film noir, second; and from the evident themes, and their variations on the familiar Kurosawa opposition between the individual and the social. Yet for all their intractability, it would be a mistake to see these conflicts as aporetic. Rather, these conflicts and contradictions, and especially those evident at the film's end, all insist on their irreducibility to each other's terms; and in this respect even the copula in the title may suggest a denial of synthesis, a kind of minimal parataxis that refuses sublimation or resolution—the high and the low remain, held together in an unbearable tension.

Making these oppositions speak will entail a substitution, as what I've referred to as form finds its richest expression here in terms of space, such that this and other related conflicts can be traced not from without but as immanent to the film itself—space here will allow us to think of this singular ending in other than just narrative terms.[1] Narrative is essentially synchronic, especially in considering its end; but space can serve a mediating role in that here it is essentially diachronic. Its totalization within the anthology of forms the film presents will come to suggest that rather than ending—a narrative category—we must think in terms of *closure*, shared by narrative and spatial systems alike.

Put otherwise, this means an ending cannot be considered solely as a narrative category. Every film, Godard famously said, must have a beginning, middle, and end, though not necessarily in that order; and while Kurosawa's film remains markedly more linear than many of Godard's, nonetheless both evince an interest in the kinds of closure inherent in narrative—but not solely in narrative. The terminus of a narrative works in relation to other equally functional and meaningful types of closure: spatial, temporal, structural, and so on. Jameson puts it this way:

> [I]n order for narrative to project some sense of a totality of experience in space and time, it must surely know some closure (a narrative must have an ending, even if it is ingeniously organized around the structural repression of endings as such). At the same time, however, closure or the narrative ending is the mark of that boundary or limit beyond which thought cannot go.[2]

While we may bristle at the implied limit here placed on thought, in the context of Kurosawa's film we seem already in the presence of such a deadlock, paralyzed between two irreconcilable positions. But Jameson draws our attention to the roles of space and time and their implication in a sense of ending, demanding we see them together with the narrative as reaching for an experience of a totality. Thus narrative and space, in their efforts to produce the effect of closure, here associated with the experience of a totality, insist at once on offering something both whole and broken—a totality beyond which we cannot think but also within which there persist the contradictions and antagonisms that drive the narrative in the first place. What would this look like? How is it embodied in this singular film?

High

Gondo's luxurious house is perched on a hilltop over the city. It is, of course, high. Serene and separate from the sprawl below, it nonetheless proves vulnerable precisely because of this separation: Takeuchi targets Gondo and his family precisely because this air-conditioned mansion is insistently visible from his own room in the slums below.[3] Mitsuhiro Yoshimoto argues that "the particular configuration of urban space and the image created by that configuration are responsible for the occurrence of the kidnapping as much as the economic inequality and class difference."[4] Here, then, space precipitates the narrative, proving not to be merely the container for the event but its occasion and cause.

And yet Gondo's house carries more freight than this. Not only does its luxurious expanse assert the privilege and wealth of its inhabitants, it also provides a stage for a meticulously realized set of tableaux: it is a dramatic space, and a theatrical one. The film opens with a scene of corporate maneuvering, as Gondo seeks to take sole ownership of National Shoes, the company he directs. That is, before we even register this house as a luxurious private space, it is already the space of corporate takeovers, backroom business, strategy and tactics, fatally compromising its imagined domesticity. Before we have appreciated its aloof poise, redolent of wealth and privilege, it is already enmeshed in a struggle for economic power. Significantly, after he is bankrupted paying the ransom, Gondo's house will go up for sale, whatever vestigial private qualities it may have possessed now effaced.

But I have called this a dramatic space, which implies that it is more than a container for conflict and intrigue, public and private. When the police arrive, as Gondo agonizes over his dilemma, as all wait for the kidnapper to phone, Kurosawa blocks his actors in a stylized and theatrical manner, posing, for example, Gondo's isolation against the tightly knit group of police officers. While Yoshimoto is certainly right to argue that this room "is a kind of experimental chamber where Kurosawa uses cinematic technology (e.g., multicamera shooting, 'Scope frame, telephoto lens, etc.) to construct a complex permutational social space,"[5] I wish to insist on its essentially theatrical nature, a nature we will further be able to affirm in its distinction from the other highly schematized sections of the film: that is, despite the wealth of cinematic technique and technology in evidence here, such tableaux cannot help but evoke cinema's ancestor and contemporary, the theater. What else is high about Gondo's mansion is its alignment with "high" culture, here the theater, as this space becomes a site of struggle between an older aesthetic form and its upstart rival, a rival that can cite, use, and ultimately contain the elder's techniques and strategies. At least part of the conflict here, then, will have little enough to do with the individual and the social or privileged executive and immiserated prole—little enough, then, to do with the subject and its analysis—except to the extent that aesthetic media strive for capital, cultural and real, too. Here film insists on its primacy over theater, the low and populist over the high and elite, even as it seems to depend upon it. The theatrical and essentially humanist truth of this section is affirmed in and as Gondo's struggle with social and individual values and expectations—but as Yoshimoto points out, it is affirmed *cinematically*. Theater's adequacy for the representation of social and individual struggle thus becomes ironized by its dependence here on filmic technology and its representational strategies.

and

From this theatrical space, with its frieze-like compositions, we come to the film's copula, which takes a precise form. Gondo is instructed to board the bullet train with the ransom. Here the agonizing stasis of the sequences in his mansion come to be replaced by an industrial and technological dynamism, as the train hurtles toward his fateful exchange, shuddering along the tracks with all of the velocity and inevitability of narrative itself. The train becomes not only a mode of transportation, not a means to an end, but paradoxically a destination itself. Kurosawa captures its speed and the tension of the event by relying on a handheld camera, whose shakiness conveys something of the urgency of this exchange while also drawing attention to itself, even affirming this reflexive aspect by including the camera within the frame. The narrative motivation is clear enough: the police want pictures of the kidnappers, but the modernist and reflexive dimensions of this inclusion beg further elaboration—the kidnapper ultimately is absent from the image. If the police desire an indexical record of the suspects and so insist on this as cinema's primary role, Kurosawa adds his own gloss: like the train, the camera is a technological mode of transport. Like the train (and unlike the Lumières!) destination is unimportant: no-one is interested in the train's arrival at the station but rather what happens along the way, even the sheer experience of movement itself. The space created and affirmed as cinematic is one of pure transition, traveling without arrival, speed without destination. Narrative without end?

On a structural level then, the bullet train sequence provides a formal transition from the theatrical space of Gondo's house to another series of spaces, whose qualities I will go on to describe in detail. But like that theatrical space, this one also includes implicit and reflexive claims about film itself, suggesting its passage away from that older aesthetic form, theater, and its humanist concerns for character, the agon of the self and the social. And while the bullet train sequence connects the "High" and "Low" narratively, its speed and claustrophobia, as well as its lack of interest in a destination, forbids it from linking them spatially.

Put otherwise, the heterogeneous and formally independent spaces the film offers, of which this is the most striking, qualify its narrative logic, particularly regarding its ending. The bullet train sequence asserts that closure here will have little enough to do with teleology, with progress toward a destination and end—that is, closure in strictly narrative terms—and more to do with space.

Low

The final and longest section of the film owes a great deal to the police procedural and even American film noir, as the tense order and meticulous compositions that characterized the section in Gondo's house give way to the turmoil and darkness of the criminal underworld, captured by a restless camera that repeatedly violates the 180-degree rule, inevitably making it difficult to orient ourselves in this new array of spaces. Kurosawa's editing becomes more dynamic too, as these nightmarish urban spaces are broken up and shuffled like a deck of cards. Moreover, unlike the stasis of Gondo's house or the claustrophobic enclosure of the bullet train, these new spaces are open and chaotic.

We are introduced to the kidnapper Takeuchi, wearing his signature dark glasses, waiting in a nightclub for drugs. In contrast to Gondo's "heroic" subjectivity—self-made capitalist, patriarch—the kidnapper is marked by a fatal anonymity and indistinction. His trademark sunglasses render him invisible in some specific sense—to the police certainly but also to Gondo, whom the kidnapper asks for a light in a subsequent sequence.[6] Initiator of the narrative, his presence is nonetheless as marginal as the class he represents. His violence against Gondo, then, seems also a violence derived from his visual repression, his invisibility from Gondo's perspective from his aerie on the hill. But he is not invisible to the camera, nor to us. American rock and roll plays, and drunken GIs party in the background, as if to affirm this sequence's generic debt to noir.[7] What is of interest here is the insistence on American culture, from the details of the content to the style and generic signals.[8] The serene spatiality and homogeneity of the "high" comes to be replaced by the heterogeneity of the "low," the private and domestic by the public, now coded as criminal and American, and presented in a bewildering variety of forms. We move from the police conference room with its abstraction of social space via the map (shades of Lang!), to the public streets under surveillance, the hospital waiting room, the nightmarish drug den, the kidnapper's house on the verge from which Mount Fuji is visible, the dump with its bravura presentation of the puff of pink smoke—where the troublesome materiality of this world produces its most evocative emblem of the spiritual—and finally the prison and death-house itself. If there is any element that can connect these vastly different spaces together and hold them, totalizing them in a tense force field, it is not the police map but the camera. And so it is that the "low" is low not just because of its association with criminality, poverty, drugs, but also pulp fiction, film noir, rock and roll, and mass culture in all of its proliferating varieties. The spatial heterogeneity of the "low" then also marks an aesthetic heterogeneity too.

And indeed, the sequence at the dump affirms this logic, offering an event whose implications extend far beyond its strictly narrative function: in that context the striking pink smoke signals the kidnapper has discarded the briefcase that held the ransom, and subsequent police investigation will lead to his capture. In this reflexive sequence Gondo and the police watch a film framed by the window. This bizarre event unfolds as we peer at it as if over the heads of the audience of the police, and in including them as an audience the film seeks to include us as well. Or is it that such a strange event, framed by the window as if on a screen, works to abstract those within the diegetic space, making agents over into an audience, reduced to consumption or contemplation? The audacity, the excess of the pink color of the smoke, over and against the black and white of the film, authorizes supplemental hypotheses to affirm the importance of this reflexive moment in this reflexive film: like Gondo's aerie the evanescent smoke floats over the dense urban space below, but its production out of the sheer material contingency of trash—aesthetic excess deriving from material excess—also then invites fully a dialectical and even metaphysical gloss. Adorno approvingly quotes Brecht's maxim: "Culture is a mansion built on dogshit"[9]; here art—and this is the only transcendent note in the film, transcendence like the color pink seemingly in excess of the film's other modes and aims—derives from garbage. With the force of a Kandinsky emerging out of a noir, the image of the pink smoke disrupts spatial and aesthetic economies.

Moreover, this is an image of the audience—the audience as police. While Kurosawa's depiction of the police has typically been read as conservative,[10] reflecting at once his own worries over kidnapping and a whole questionable ideology of law and order behind that, at the same time it bears remembering that the police also figure a kind of collective agency nowhere else in evidence here—a collectivity that stands out in high relief against the intensely subjective struggles of Gondo and the questions that arise about the kidnapper's own motives and methods, which for much of the film stay well within the boundaries of the personal: greed, we wonder, perhaps revenge. To the extent too that *High and Low* owes a debt to American film noir and crime fiction, we are also authorized to ask after this singularly benign characterization of the police; almost unprecedented, it fits oddly within those generic frames. But then these two points are really the same after all. The collective—its desires, methods, and certainly history—seems here to need to be signaled otherwise, its distinctiveness in relation to the individual registered and simultaneously made strange, such that we might come to wonder if the kinds of endings available to this new collective agent might be distinguished from those more personal ends we witness in the film's devastating finale. Closure, an ending, for the police is the capture of the criminal and the resolution of the case, yet the police are present too at the end: literally, in the officers that drag the raving Takeuchi away, but perhaps figuratively as well, in the very architecture of the prison and death cell that point to a very different kind of closure indeed, which we will come to explore.

I argue that this is how we are to understand the juxtaposition of aesthetic forms, theater and film, narrative and space: they provide the occasion for what Adorno calls a negative dialectic, in which their own identity and even mutual antagonism is preserved without resolution or sublation. But if their identity and particularity is preserved, if these conflicts must remain open and unresolved, how then are we to understand ending and closure here, those events that generate our sense of all the bases being touched, of nothing remaining outside of their totalizing ambit? Before we turn to the film's own ending, we must return to the relationship of narrative and space.

So far I have examined how *High and Low* offers us a particular and even peculiar anthology of spaces, spaces that have offered up the opportunity for the reflexive, modernist, and allegorical interpretation I have sketched in this chapter. As suggested earlier, spatial issues insist insofar as they speak to both issues of closure and form—form in that space, especially here, cannot be thought as merely a neutral container, and closure in that the closure effect produced by the film's conjugation of space necessarily inflects closure as we derive it from the narrative register. Moreover, as Stephen Heath has argued, such space must be thought of as produced and productive rather than merely represented: "movement from shot to shot . . . effectively indicates the filmic nature of film space, film as constantly the construction of a space."[11] We will shortly follow Heath in his thinking after the determinant effects of filmic space in relation to the subject, but first I would like to expand upon an insight he derives from Rosalind Krauss, who in a very different context argues that perspective is the visual correlate of causality—that one thing follows the next in space according to rule. In that sense, despite differences of historical development, it can be likened to the literary tradition of the omniscient narrator and the conventional plot. As de Kooning described it, perspective space carried with it the meaning of narrative: a succession of events leading up to and away from this moment; and within that temporal succession—given as a spatial analogue—was secreted the "meaning" of both that space and those events.[12] Space, then, is *already* narrative, and the different senses or effects of closure that each provides need not be thought of as opposed at all: despite the extent to which Krauss's concerns are those of modernist painting, the very terms she uses invite their transposition into a filmic context—provided, of course, that we recognize and allow for the interaction of this spatial narrative with the temporal elaboration of filmic narrative as such.

But we have already caught some sense of this conjugation of space from the bullet train sequence: without interest in a destination, the train, hurtling along the tracks into space, implies and even embodies the temporal succession of narrative, though as I've said a narrative without a telos. How is this to be understood? Such a succession need not proceed within the rigid economy of Classical Hollywood Cinema, in which cause and effect inexorably produce closure. Indeed, André Bazin's discussion of depth of field stresses the variety of filmic possibilities inherent in deep space, possibilities radically distinct from closure and ending: "depth of focus reintroduced ambiguity into the structure of the image if not of necessity . . . at least as a possibility. . . . The uncertainty in which we find ourselves as to the spiritual key or the interpretation we should put on the film is built into the very design of the image."[13] Space is narrative, space is (possibly) ambiguous, and while Bazin evokes this ambiguity in support of his arguments regarding realism, we need only acknowledge that here space and perhaps film as such requires interpretation due to this ambiguity. Space is thus closed and open at the same time, to the extent that its ambiguity invites analysis, or to put it differently, space replaces narrative closure with ambiguity. And again, Kurosawa's puff of pink smoke dramatizes this too: its own conjoining of the hellish dump and immaterial air in the service of a fascinating and equivocal image depends wholly upon space, even as it makes that space ambiguous and narrative—is this the flat space of the screen, sheer surface, which is nonetheless deep insofar as I perceive it from behind the audience already included in the film, my gaze passing over their heads, through the window, finally to the thing itself in all its rich ambiguity? The depth that implies succession and thus narrative here distinguishes itself from the bullet train sequence, as we arrive at a kind of destination secreted deep in the frame. But this is a destination—an ending of sorts—as uncertain and abstract as a nonfigurative painting, even as it leaves its audience, the one and the many, equally rapt in their perception of it. Just as the passage of the smoke from low to high implies a minimal narrative sequence, the effect of closure derives from this reflexive space.

But what kind of ending then does *High and Low* provide? That is, if the plethora of spaces here together forms a series, giving us permutations of public and private, order and chaos, stasis and speed, and in so doing offer a totality that runs from heaven to hell and back again, what does the official narrative offer in this sense? Narrative, especially this one, so dependent upon generic devices borrowed from the police procedural and detective story, arouses an expectation of closure, but in this case that expectation will be ambivalently offered and tantalizingly opaque. The kidnapper caught and sentenced, this ought to have been the end, we think; but Kurosawa extends the film for an essential sequence that avoids seeming supplemental fully as much as it troubles the apparent closure of the narrative we have already experienced. The last space we visit is the visiting room adjacent to the execution chamber. Before the kidnapper's execution, Gondo wishes to understand his motivation. As such, narrative closure has already been achieved: in the "low" section the police procedural elements have effected the expected end, as the kidnapper has been caught and sentenced. From a strictly narrative and generic perspective, then, the film could have ended before this, but it waits not for punishment, rather for a humanist rapprochement and recognition, even though it is doomed to fail. So in narrative terms this encounter in a closed room deep in the prison seems almost as excessive and extraneous as the puff of pink smoke. And indeed, the claustrophobia of this small room also returns us to the train, though here there will be no transport of that kind, unless that's what death is.

As we see Gondo and Takeuchi's reflections imposed upon each other, we can only ask: What kind of mirror stage is this? What sort of identity is affirmed here? Gondo, still blind to class distinctions, cannot understand Takeuchi's purposes; humanist sympathy falters.[14] Moreover, Takeuchi declares, "I'm not much interested in self-analysis," at a stroke dismissing for himself but also for Gondo and for us the satisfaction of grasping his motives. As the image affirms, he remains transparent and insubstantial, a ghost in this putatively humanist context, as Gondo's own reflection proves him to be, too. Just as we have glimpsed the sea and Mount Fuji beyond as one kind of spatial limit, here in the final sequence of the film another kind of limit is offered, one whose type of closure is no longer spatial in that sense—it is rigorously closed rather than open—but whose spatial closure coincides with a seemingly ultimate code of closure, that of death itself. Death, underlined as the eclipse of a subjectivity whose analysis is no longer of substantial interest, thus marks a terminus for the subject and the spatial alike.

But if humanism is evacuated here, then "death" can no longer be thought of so literally nor so dogmatically. The reflexive and allegorical impulse I have traced in other sequences returns here, too, after the narrative has ended, just before death. The window that separates them and affords us these tantalizing reflections rhymes with the window of Gondo's own house, through which we glimpsed the heavenly pink smoke rise from the incinerator. If that sequence dialectically evoked the mutual imbrication of art and trash (not forgetting heaven and hell themselves), this sequence insists on a kind of separation: certainly between these two men and their respective class positions, perhaps between life and death, but also between two sides of the screen—between two cinematic modes. It is not then that we are being called upon to identify with these characters—they cannot even understand each other. Rather, we are to understand that film itself seeks to give an image of its conflicting vocations, window and mirror, narrative and form, holding them together in their particularity and difference. A screen slides down, like the curtains' close in a theater, signaling this interview and this film are over.

The assertion of identity between these two figures is not to be grasped as a merely subjective one, whatever our sympathies (or not) with such humanist baggage and class conflict; rather, it is the assertion of identity and difference simultaneously that, together with the schematic and static mise-en-scène and the proximity of death, evokes a future—not death as destiny but destiny figured as death. It seems necessary to stress that this is accomplished reflexively and filmically—that is, the image effects a meaning that is ill-suited to paraphrase in terms of humanism, death, or class. But then these opposed gazes—one attempting comprehension, the other defiant—in their incommensurability also direct us to our own, and to the film's. Is film a window or a mirror, content or form, individual or social, narrative or image, life or death, humanist or modernist, transport or stasis? Could it be that these oppositions (as well as the schematic structural blocks that constitute the film as a whole) are meant finally to preclude development as such, but particularly that of narrative? This is certainly a curiosity in a time-based medium.

The effect, however, is one of being given all of this at once; but if "death" for instance needs to be understood beyond the merely subjective, then perhaps it too has some reflexive import.

> Artworks are a priori negative by the law of their objectivation: They kill what they objectify by tearing it away from the immediacy of its life. Their own life plays on death. This defines the qualitative threshold to modern art. Modern works relinquish themselves mimetically to reification, their principle of death. The

effort to escape this element is art's illusory element which, since Baudelaire, art has wanted to discard without resigning itself to the status of a thing among things.[15]

The evocation of death with which the film ends, together with the unresolved and unresolvable oppositions that it mobilizes along the way, are then the film's own encounter with its limits, even its homeopathic partaking of the commodity form, whether we think of this in terms of its pulp source, the production of shoes (which Gondo reminds us, must nonetheless support the weight of the body), or narrative film itself. Against reification it proposes a puff of pink smoke, an ambiguous and fleeting transcendence that ultimately must be abandoned as illusory, even as it necessarily evokes an outside to the determinants of form and content both. But dialectically, this limit, comprised of so many contradictions, has another name—totality—which then can be nominated as the end to which the film has worked: a totality that is properly negative in that it refuses to sublate oppositions but lets them persist in their agonizing tension.

Christian Metz writes somewhere that all films are zombie films; Ken Jacobs used to introduce screenings of silent films by saying, "Do you see those people? They're all dead!" But as with *High and Low*, it would be a mistake to take these deaths too literally. It produces its distinctive closure effect by taking us past the end of the narrative, after the crime has been solved, to the space where the totality becomes visible: from high to low, from individual to collective, from junk to art, from the living to the dead.

Notes

1. Mitsuhiro Yoshimoto, in his magisterial monograph on Kurosawa, examines space in the film in social and historical terms, to great effect. However here, for reasons I will go on to provide, I consider space in more formal terms. See Mitsuhiro Yoshimoto, *Kurosawa: Film Studies and Japanese Cinema* (Durham: Duke University Press, 2000), 315–320.

2. Fredric Jameson, "Progress versus Utopia, or, Can We Imagine the Future?," in *Archaeologies of the Future* (London: Verso, 2005), 283.

3. For an excellent overview of the film and a better synopsis than I can provide here, see Yoshimoto, *Kurosawa*, 303–306.

4. Yoshimoto, *Kurosawa*, 316.

5. Yoshimoto, *Kurosawa*, 322.

6. "Despite their use of radios, telephones, tape recorders, motion pictures, and still photographs, the police remain unable to perceive the structural relations of

wealth and poverty that triggered the crime." Stephen Prince, *The Warrior's Camera: The Cinema of Akira Kurosawa* (Princeton: Princeton University Press, 1991), 188.

7. This is also the place to mention Kurosawa's source for the film, the pulp police procedural *King's Ransom* by Ed McBain from 1959.

8. In this respect I might also mention the game of "Cowboys and Indians" played by the two boys early in the film as another signifier of a distinctive American genre.

9. Theodor Adorno, *Negative Dialectics*, trans. E. B. Ashton (New York: Continuum, 1973), 366.

10. "[*High and Low*] tells us that there is much misery among us but our police force is excellent . . ." Noel Burch, *To a Distant Observer: Form and Meaning in Japanese Cinema* (Berkeley: University of California Press, 1979), 320.

11. Stephen Heath, "Narrative Space," in *Questions of Cinema* (Bloomington: Indiana University Press, 1981), 31–32.

12. Rosalind Krauss, "A View of Modernism," in *Perpetual Inventory* (Cambridge: MIT Press, 2010), 123.

13. André Bazin, "The Evolution of Language in Cinema," in *What Is Cinema?*, trans. Hugh Gray (Berkeley: University of California Press, 1967), 36.

14. "The humanism of Gondo's question is a substitute for his failure to perceive the very real reason why the kidnapper should hate him, his inability to understand the relation between his air-conditioned palatial home and the cramped, stiflingly hot dwellings of the poorer residents in the city below." Prince, *The Warrior's Camera*, 198.

15. Theodor Adorno, *Aesthetic Theory*, trans. Robert Hullot-Kentor (Minneapolis: University of Minnesota Press, 1997), 133.

14

The Final Failure in *The Dark Knight Rises*

Slavoj Žižek

In politics, an authentic Event is not the Event traditional Marxists are waiting for (the big Awakening of the revolutionary Subject) but something that occurs as an unexpected side event. Remember how, just months before the 1917 revolutionary upheaval in Russia, Lenin gave a speech to the Swiss socialist youth where he told them that their generation may be the first one to witness a socialist revolution in a couple of decades? This, however, does not mean that we should just wait for the Event to surprise us—the art of revolutionary dreaming can play a crucial role in prerevolutionary times. Such dreaming is not limited only to radical forces: one can learn a lot also from the distorted way a conservative or liberal historical agent imagines the threatening shadow of an emancipatory Event. Even a virtual Event can leave traces, can serve as an ambiguous point of reference—therein resides the interest of a film like Christopher Nolan's *The Dark Knight Rises*, which can only be properly understood against the background of the Event it imagines.

Here is the film's (simplified) storyline. Eight years after the events of *The Dark Knight*, law and order prevail in Gotham City: under the extraordinary powers granted by the Dent Act, Commissioner Gordon (Gary Oldman) has nearly eradicated violent and organized crime. He nonetheless feels guilty about the cover-up of Harvey Dent's crimes (when Dent tried to kill Gordon's son before Batman saved him, Dent fell to his death, and Batman took the fall for the Dent myth, allowing himself to be demonized as Gotham's villain), and he plans to admit to the conspiracy at a public event celebrating

Dent but decides that the city is not ready to hear the truth. No longer active as Batman, Bruce Wayne (Christian Bale) lives isolated in his manor while his company is crumbling after he invested in a clean energy project designed to harness fusion power, but he shut it down after learning that the core could be modified to become a nuclear weapon. The beautiful Miranda Tate (Marion Cotillard), a member of the Wayne Enterprises executive board, encourages Wayne to rejoin society and continue his philanthropic works.

Here enters the (first) villain of the film: Bane (Tom Hardy), a terror-ist leader who was a member of the League of Shadows and who gets hold of the copy of Gordon's speech. After Bane's financial machinations bring Wayne's company close to bankruptcy, Wayne entrusts Miranda to control his enterprise and also engages in a brief love affair with her. (In this she competes with Selina Kyle (Anne Hathaway), a cat burglar who steals from the rich in order to redistribute wealth but finally rejoins Wayne and the forces of law and order.) Learning that Bane also got hold of his fusion core, Wayne returns as Batman and confronts Bane, who says that he took over the League of Shadows after Ra's al Ghul's death. Crippling Batman while in close combat, Bane detains him in a prison from which escape is virtually impossible: inmates tell Wayne the story of the only person to ever success-fully escape from the prison, a child driven by necessity and the sheer force of will. While the imprisoned Wayne recovers from his injuries and retrains himself to be Batman, Bane succeeds in turning Gotham City into an isolated city-state. He first lures most of Gotham's police force underground and traps them there; then he sets off explosions that destroy most of the bridges connecting Gotham City to the mainland, announcing that any attempt to leave the city will result in the detonation of the Wayne fusion core, which has been converted into a bomb.

Here we reach the crucial moment of the film: Bane's takeover is accompanied by a vast politico-ideological offensive. Bane publicly reveals the cover-up of Dent's death and releases the prisoners locked up under the Dent Act. Condemning the rich and powerful, he promises to restore the power of the people, calling on the common people to "take your city back," Bane reveals himself to be "the ultimate Wall Street Occupier, calling on the 99% to band together and overthrow societal elites."[1] What follows is the film's idea of people's power: summary show trials, executions of the rich, and streets littered with crime and villainy.

After a couple of months, Wayne successfully escapes prison, returns to Gotham as Batman, and enlists his friends to help liberate the city and stop the fusion bomb before it explodes. Batman confronts and subdues Bane, but Miranda intervenes and stabs Batman; the societal benefactor reveals herself to be Talia al Ghul, Ra's daughter: it was she who escaped the prison as a child, and Bane was the one person who aided her escape. After announcing her plan to complete her father's work in destroying Gotham, Talia escapes. In the ensuing mayhem, Gordon cuts off the bomb's ability to be remotely detonated while Selina kills Bane, allowing Batman to chase Talia. He tries to force her to take the bomb to the fusion chamber where it can be stabilized, but she floods the chamber. Talia dies when her truck crashes off the road, confident that the bomb cannot be stopped. Using a special helicopter, Batman hauls the bomb beyond the city limits, where it detonates over the ocean and presumably kills him.

Batman is now celebrated as a hero whose sacrifice saved Gotham City, while Wayne is believed to have died in the riots. As his estate is divided up, Alfred (Michael Caine) witnesses Bruce and Selina together alive in a cafe in Florence, while Blake, a young honest policeman who knew about Batman's identity, inherits the Bat cave. In short, "Batman saves the day, emerges unscathed and moves on with a normal life, with someone else to replace his role defending the system."[2] The first clue to the ideological underpinnings of this ending is provided by Alfred, Wayne's faithful butler, who, at Wayne's (would-be) burial, reads the last lines from Dickens's *A Tale of Two Cities*: "It is a far, far better thing that I do, than I have ever done; it is a far, far better rest that I go to than I have ever known." Some reviewers of the film took this quote as an indication that the film

> rises to the noblest level of Western art. The film appeals to the center of America's tradition—the ideal of noble sacrifice for the common people. Batman must humble himself to be exalted, and lay down his life to find a new one. . . . An ultimate Christ-figure, Batman sacrifices himself to save others . . . the film does not primarily champion one political philosophy over another, but presents the central premise of Western civilization.[3]

And, effectively, from this perspective, there is only one step back from Dickens to Christ at Calvary: "For whosoever will save his life shall lose it: and whosoever will lose his life for my sake shall find it. For what is a man profited, if he shall gain the whole world, and lose his own soul?" (Matthew 16:25–26). Batman's sacrifice as the repetition of Christ's death? Is this idea not compromised by the film's last scene (Wayne with Selena in a Florence café)? Is the religious counterpart of this ending not rather the well-known blasphemous idea that Christ really survived his crucifixion and lived a long peaceful life (in India or even Tibet, according to some sources)? The only way to redeem this final scene would have been to read it as a daydream (hallucination) of Alfred who sits alone in the Florence café. The further Dickensian feature of the film is a depoliticized complaint about the gap between the rich and the poor. Early in the film Selina whispers to Wayne while they are dancing at an exclusive upper-class gala: "A storm is coming, Mr. Wayne. You and your friends better batten down the hatches, because when it hits, you're all going to wonder how you thought you could live so large, and leave so little for the rest of us." Nolan, like every good liberal, is "worried" about this disparity, and he admits this worry penetrates the film:

> What I see in the film that relates to the real world is the idea of dishonesty. The film is all about that coming to a head. . . . The notion of economic fairness creeps into the film, and the reason is twofold. One, Bruce Wayne is a billionaire. It has to be addressed. . . . But two, there are a lot of things in life, and economics is one of them, where we have to take a lot of what we're told on trust, because most of us feel like we don't have the analytical tools to know what's going on. . . . I don't feel there's a left or right perspective in the film. What is there is just an honest assessment or honest exploration of the world we live in—things that worry us.[4]

Although viewers know Wayne is mega-rich, they tend to forget where his wealth comes from: arms manufacturing plus stock market speculations, which is why Bane's stock exchange games can destroy his empire—arms dealer and speculator, *this* is the true secret beneath the Batman mask. How does the film deal with it? By resuscitating the archetypal Dickensian topic of a good capitalist who engages in financing orphanage homes (Wayne) versus a bad greedy capitalist (Stryver, as in Dickens). In such Dickensian overmoralization, the economic disparity is translated into "dishonesty" that should be "honestly" analyzed, although we lack any reliable cognitive mapping, and such an "honest" approach leads to a further parallel with Dickens— as Christopher Nolan's brother Jonathan (who cowrote the scenario) put it bluntly: "*A Tale of Two Cities* to me was the most sort of harrowing portrait of a relatable recognizable civilization that had completely fallen to pieces. The terrors in Paris, in France in that period, it's not hard to imagine that things could go that bad and wrong."[5] The scenes of the vengeful populist uprising in the film (a mob that thirsts for the blood of the rich who have neglected and exploited them) evoke Dickens's description of the Reign of Terror, so that, although the film has nothing to do with politics, it follows

Dickens's novel in "honestly" portraying revolutionaries as possessed fanatics and thus provides

> the caricature of what in real life would be an ideologically com-
> mitted revolutionary fighting structural injustice. Hollywood tells
> what the establishments want you to know—revolutionaries are
> brutal creatures, with utter disregard for human life. Despite
> emancipatory rhetoric on liberation, they have sinister designs
> behind. Thus, whatever might be their reasons, they need to be
> eliminated.[6]

Tom Charity was right to note "the movie's defense of the establishment in the form of philanthropic billionaires and an incorruptible police"[7]—in its distrust of the people taking things into their own hands, the film "demonstrates both a desire for social justice and a fear of what that can actually look like in the hands of a mob."[8] Karthick raises here a perspicuous question with regard to the immense popularity of the Joker figure from the previous film: Why such a harsh disposition toward Bane when the Joker was dealt with so leniently in the earlier movie? The answer is simple and convincing:

> The Joker, calling for anarchy in its purest form, critically under-
> scores the hypocrisies of bourgeois civilization as it exists, but
> his views are unable to translate into mass action. Bane, on the
> other hand poses an existential threat to the system of oppres-
> sion. . . . His strength is not just his physique but also his ability
> to command people and mobilize them to achieve a political
> goal. He represents the vanguard, the organized representative
> of the oppressed that wages political struggle in their name to
> bring about structural changes. Such a force, with the greatest
> subversive potential, the system cannot accommodate. It needs
> to be eliminated.[9]

However, even if Bane lacks the fascination of Heath Ledger's Joker, there is a feature that distinguishes him from the latter: unconditional love, the very source of his hardness. In a short but touching scene, he tells Wayne how, in an act of love in the midst of terrible suffering, he saved the child Talia, not caring for consequences and paying a terrible price for it (Bane was beaten to within an inch of his life while defending her). Karthick is totally justified in locating this event in the long tradition, from Christ to Che Guevara, which extols violence as a "work of love," as in the famous lines from Che Guevara's diary: "Let me say, with the risk of appearing ridiculous, that the true revolutionary is guided by strong feelings of love. It is impossible to think of an authentic revolutionary without this quality."[10] What we encounter here is not so much the "Christification of Che" but rather a "Cheization" of Christ himself—the Christ whose "scandalous" words from Luke 14–26—"If anyone comes to me and does not hate his father and his mother, his wife and children, his brothers and sisters—yes even his own life—he cannot be my disciple"—point in exactly the same direction as Che's famous quote: "You may have to be tough, but do not lose your tenderness."[11] The statement that "the true revolutionary is guided by a great feeling of love" should be read together with Guevara's much more "problematic" statement on revolutionaries as "killing machines": "Hatred is an element of struggle; relentless hatred of the enemy that impels us over and beyond the natural limitations of man and transforms us into effective, violent, selective, and cold killing machines. Our soldiers must be thus; a people without hatred cannot vanquish a brutal enemy."[12] Or, to paraphrase Kant and Robespierre yet again: love without cruelty is powerless; cruelty without love is blind, a short-lived passion that loses its persistent edge. Guevara is here paraphrasing Christ's declarations on the unity of love and sword—in both cases, the underlying paradox is that what makes love angelic, what elevates it over mere unstable and pathetic sentimentality, is its cruelty itself, its link with violence—it is this link that raises love over and beyond the natural limitations of man and thus transforms it into an unconditional drive. So while Guevara certainly believed in the transformative power of love, he would never have been heard humming "all you need is love"—what you need is to *love with hatred*, or, as Kierkegaard put it long ago: the necessary consequence (the "truth") of the Christian demand to *love one's enemy* is "the demand to *hate the beloved* out of love and in love. . . . So high—humanly speaking to a kind of madness—can Christianity press the demand of love if love is to be the fulfilling of the law. Therefore it teaches that the Christian shall, if it is demanded, be capable of hating his father and mother and sister and beloved."[13] In contrast to erotic love, this notion of love should be given here all its Pauline weight: *the domain of pure violence*, the domain outside law (legal power), the domain of the violence which is neither law-founding nor law-sustaining, *is the domain of agape*.[14] Consequently, we are not dealing here with a simple brutal hatred demanded by a cruel and jealous God: the "hatred" enjoined by Christ is not a kind of pseudo-dialectical opposite to love but a direct expression of *agape*—it is love itself that enjoins us to "unplug" from our organic community into which we were born, or, as St. Paul put it, for a Christian, there are neither men nor women, neither Jews nor Greeks . . . So, again, if the acts of revolutionary violence are "works of love" in the strictest Kierkegaardian sense of the term, it is not because the revolutionary violence "really" aims at establishing a nonviolent harmony; on the contrary, the authentic revolutionary liberation is much more directly identified with violence—it is violence as such (the violent gesture of discarding, of establishing a difference, of drawing a line of separation) that liberates. Freedom is not a blissfully neutral state of harmony and balance but the very violent act that disturbs this balance. This is why, back to *The Dark Knight Rises*, the only authentic love in the film is Bane's, the "terrorist's," in clear contrast to Batman. Along the same lines, the figure of Ra's, Talia's father, deserves a closer look. Ra's is a mixture of Arab and Oriental features, an agent of virtuous terror fighting to counterbalance the corrupted Western civilization. He is played by Liam Neeson, an actor whose screen persona usually radiates dignified goodness and wisdom (he is Zeus in *The Clash of Titans*), and who also plays Qui-Gon Jinn in *The Phantom Menace*, the first episode of the *Star Wars* series. Qui-Gon is a Jedi knight, the mentor of Obi-Wan Kenobi as well as the one who discovers Anakin Skywalker, believing that Anakin is the Chosen One who will restore the balance of the universe, ignoring Yoda's warnings about Anakin's unstable nature; at the end of *The Phantom Menace*, Qui-Gon is killed by Darth Maul.[15]

In the *Batman* trilogy, Ra's is also the teacher of the young Wayne, and in *Batman Begins*, he finds the young Wayne in a Chinese prison. Introducing himself as "Henri Ducard," he offers the boy a "path." After Wayne is freed, he climbs to the home of the League of Shadows, where Ra's is waiting, although presenting himself as the servant of another man called Ra's al Ghul. At the end of a long and painful training, Ra's explains that Bruce must do what is necessary to fight evil, while revealing that they have trained Bruce with the intention of him leading the league to destroy Gotham City, which they believe has become hopelessly corrupt. Months later, Ra's unexpectedly reappears and reveals that he was not Henri Ducard, but Ra's al Ghul. In the ensuing confrontation, Ra's elaborates on the League of Shadows' exploits throughout history (sacking Rome, spreading the Black Death, and starting the Great Fire of London). He explains that the destruction of Gotham City is merely another mission by the league to correct humanity's recurring fits of decadence and presumably protect the environment. Ra's then has his henchmen burn down Wayne Manor with the intent of killing Bruce, stating, "Justice is balance, you burnt my home and left me for dead, consider us even." Wayne survives the fire and confronts Ra's as Batman; after overpowering him, he leaves Ra's for dead on a train that falls into a car garage and explodes. Ra's uses his last moment to meditate, and is presumed dead, though no body is found in the wreckage. Ra's is thus not a simple embodiment of Evil, rather, he stands for the combination of virtue and terror, for the egalitarian discipline fighting a corrupted empire, and thus belongs to the line that stretches (in recent fiction) from Paul Atreides in *Dune* to Leonidas in *300*. And it is crucial that Wayne is his disciple: Wayne was formed as Batman by him.

Two commonsense reproaches impose themselves here. First, there *were* monstrous mass killings and violence in actual revolutions, from Stalinism to the Khmer Rouge, so the film is clearly not just engaging in reactionary imagination. The second, opposite reproach: the actual Occupy Wall Street (hereafter, OWS) movement was not violent, its goal was definitely not a new reign of terror; insofar as Bane's revolt is supposed to extrapolate the immanent tendency of the OWS movement, the film thus ridiculously misrepresents its aims and strategies. The ongoing antiglobalist protests are the very opposite of Bane's brutal terror: Bane stands for the mirror-image of state terror, for a murderous fundamentalist sect taking over and ruling by terror, not for its overcoming through popular self-organization. What both reproaches share is the rejection of the figure of Bane, and the reply to these two reproaches is multiple. First, one should make clear the actual scope of violence—the best answer to the claim that the violent mob reaction to oppression is worse than the original oppression itself, was the one provided long ago by Mark Twain in his *A Connecticut Yankee in King Arthur's Court*:

> There were two "Reigns of Terror" if we would remember it and consider it; the one wrought in hot passion, the other in heartless cold blood . . . our shudders are all for the "horrors" of the minor Terror, the momentary Terror, so to speak, whereas, what is the horror of swift death by the axe compared with lifelong death from hunger, cold, insult, cruelty, and heartbreak? A city cemetery could contain the coffins filled by that brief Terror which we have all been so diligently taught to shiver at and mourn over; but all France could hardly contain the coffins filled by that older and real Terror, that unspeakably bitter and awful Terror, which none of us have been taught to see in its vastness or pity as it deserves.[16]

In order to grasp this parallax nature of violence, one should focus on the short circuits between different levels, say, between power and social violence: an economic crisis that causes devastation is experienced as uncontrollable quasi-natural power, but it *should* be experienced as *violence*. Then, it is not only Nolan's film that was not able to imagine authentic people's power—the "real" radical-emancipatory movements themselves also were not able to do it; they remained caught in the coordinates of the old society, which is why the actual "people's power" often was such a violent horror. Then, one should demystify the problem of violence, rejecting simplistic claims that the twentieth-century Communism used too much excessive murderous violence, and that we should be careful not to fall into this trap again. As a fact, this is, of course, terrifyingly true, but such a direct focus on violence obfuscates the underlying question: What was wrong in the twentieth-century Communist project as such; which immanent weakness of this project pushed Communists to resort to unrestrained violence? In other words, it is not enough to say that Communists "neglected the problem of violence": it was a deeper sociopolitical failure that pushed them to violence. (The same goes for the notion that Communists "neglected democracy": their overall project of social transformation enforced on them this "neglect.") And, last but not least, it is all too simple to claim that there is no violent potential in OWS and similar movements—there *is* a violence at work in every authentic emancipatory process: the problem with the film is that it wrongly translated this violence into murderous terror. Let me clarify this point with the detour through my critics who, when they are forced to admit that my statement "Hitler wasn't violent enough" is not meant as a call for even more terrifying massive killing, tend to turn around their reproach: I just use provocative language in order to make a commonsense non-interesting point, for example, that Gandhi was more violent than Hitler in terms of creating a massive social upheaval; that I go out of my way to present in a shocking manner, something we can all agree on, for example, that Gandhi did accomplish more through nonviolence than violence; that my claim that not only is the Jew inside the Nazi, but that the Nazi is also "in the Jew" belies a mutually reinforcing reciprocity without countering the anti-Semitisms of the Nazis.[17]

In both cases, the reproach is the same: I try to sell the common thesis that Gandhi aimed at changing the system, not destroying people, but since this is a commonplace, I formulate it more provocatively, weirdly expanding the meaning of the word "violence" to include institutional changes. The same goes for my statement about "the Jew is in the anti-Semite, but the anti-Semite is also in the Jew": it's just a garbled way to deliver the commonplace that, in the mind of every Nazi who hates Jews, there must also be a fictional Jew for that Nazi to hate . . . But is this the case? What if the key point gets lost in this translation of my "muddled word salad" into common sense? In the second case, my point is not just the (effectively obvious) claim that the "Jew" to whom the Nazi refers is his ideological fiction, but that his own ideological identity is also simultaneously grounded in this fiction (not simply depending on it): the Nazi is—in his self-perception—*a figure in his own dream about the "Jews,"* and this is far from an obvious commonplace. So why call Gandhi's attempts to undermine the British state in India "more violent" than Hitler's mass killings? To draw attention to the fundamental violence that sustains a "normal" functioning of the state (Benjamin called it "mythic violence"), and the no less fundamental violence that sustains every attempt to undermine the functioning of the state (Benjamin's "divine violence").[18] This is why the reaction of the state power to those who endanger it is so brutal, and why, in its very brutality, this reaction is precisely "reactive," protective. So, far from eccentricity, the extension of the notion of violence is based on a key theoretical insight, and it is the limitation of violence to its directly visible physical aspect that, far from being "normal," relies on an ideological distortion. This is also why the reproach that I am fascinated by some ultra-radical violence with comparison to which Hitler and the Khmer Rouge "didn't go far enough" misses the point, which is not to go further in *this* type of violence but to change the entire terrain. It is difficult to be really violent, to perform an act that violently disturbs the basic parameters of social life. When Bertolt Brecht saw a Japanese mask of an evil demon, he wrote how its swollen veins and hideous grimaces "all betake / what an exhausting effort it takes / To be evil." The same holds for violence that has any effect on the system. The Chinese Cultural Revolution serves as a lesson here: destroying old monuments proved not to be a true negation of the past. Rather it was an impotent *passage a l'acte*, an acting out that bore witness to the failure to get rid of the past. There is a kind of poetic justice in the fact that the final result of Mao's Cultural Revolution is the current unmatched explosion of capitalist dynamics in China: a profound structural homology exists between Maoist permanent self-revolutionizing, the permanent struggle against the ossification of state structures, and the inherent dynamics of capitalism. One is tempted to paraphrase Brecht again here: What is the robbing of a bank compared to the founding of a new bank; what were the violent and destructive outbursts of a Red Guardist caught in the Cultural Revolution compared to the true Cultural Revolution, the permanent dissolution of all life forms that capitalist reproduction dictates?

The same, of course, applies to Nazi Germany where the spectacle of the brutal annihilation of millions should not deceive us. The characterization of Hitler that would have him as a bad guy, responsible for the deaths of millions but nonetheless a man with balls who pursued his ends with an iron will, is not only ethically repulsive, it is also simply *wrong*: no, Hitler did not "have the balls" really to change things. All his actions were fundamentally reactions: he acted so that nothing would really change; he acted to prevent the Communist threat of a real change. His targeting of the Jews was ultimately an act of displacement in which he avoided the real enemy— the core of capitalist social relations themselves. Hitler staged a spectacle of revolution so that the capitalist order could survive. The irony was that his grand gestures of despising bourgeois self-complacency ultimately enabled this complacency to continue: far from disturbing the much despised "decadent" bourgeois order, far from awakening the Germans, Nazism was a dream that enabled them to postpone awakening. Germany only really woke up with the defeat of 1945. If one wants to name an act that was truly daring, for which one truly had to "have balls" to try the impossible but which was simultaneously an act of horrendous violence, an act which caused suffering beyond comprehension, it was Stalin's forced collectivization at the end of 1920s. Yet even this display of ruthless violence culminated in the Great Purges of 1936–1937, which were, again, an impotent *passage a l'acte*: "This was not a targeting of enemies, but blind rage and panic. It reflected not control of events but a recognition that the regime lacked regularized control mechanisms. It was not policy but the failure of policy. It was a sign of failure to rule with anything but force."[19]

Which, then, is the sublime violence with regard to which even the most brutal killing is an act of weakness? Let us make a detour through José Saramago's *Seeing*, which tells the story of the strange events in the unnamed capital city of an unidentified democratic country. When the election day morning is marred by torrential rains, voter turnout is disturbingly low, but the weather breaks by midafternoon and the population heads en masse to their voting stations. The government's relief is short-lived, however, when vote counting reveals that over 70 percent of the ballots cast in the capital have been left blank. Baffled by this apparent civic lapse, the government gives the citizenry a chance to make amends just one week later with another election day. The results are worse: now 83 percent of the ballots are blank. The two major political parties—the ruling party of the right (p.o.t.r.) and their chief adversary, the party of the middle (p.o.t.m.)—are in a panic, while the haplessly marginalized party of the left (p.o.t.l.) produces an analysis claiming that the blank ballots are essentially a vote for their progressive agenda. Unsure how to respond to a benign protest but certain that an antidemocratic conspiracy exists, the government quickly labels the movement "terrorism, pure and unadulterated" and declares a state of emergency, allowing it to suspend all constitutional guarantees and adopt a series of increasingly drastic steps: citizens are seized at random and disappear into secret interrogation sites, the police and seat of government are withdrawn from the capital, sealing the city against all entrances and exits and finally manufacturing their own terrorist ringleader. The city continues to function near-normally throughout, the people parrying each of the government's thrusts in inexplicable unison and with a truly Gandhian level of nonviolent resistance . . . *this*, the voters' abstention, is a case of truly radical "divine violence" that prompts brutal panic reactions of those in power.[20]

Back to Nolan's triad of *Batman* films: we can see now how it clearly follows an immanent logic.[21] In *Batman Begins*, the hero remains within the constraints of a liberal order: the system can be defended with morally acceptable methods. *The Dark Knight* is effectively a new version of the two John Ford western classics (*Fort Apache* and *The Man Who Shot Liberty Valance*) that deploy how, in order to civilize the Wild West, one has to "print the legend" and ignore the truth—in short, how our civilization has to be grounded on a Lie: one has to break the rules in order to defend the system.[22] Or, to put it in another way, in *Batman Begins*, the hero is simply a classic figure of the urban vigilante who punishes the criminals where police cannot do it; the problem is that police, the official law enforcement agency, relates ambiguously to Batman's help—while admitting its efficiency, it nonetheless perceives Batman as a threat to its monopoly on power and a testimony of its own inefficiency. However, Batman's transgression is here purely formal, it resides in acting on behalf of the law without being legitimized to do it: in his acts, he never violates the law. *The Dark Knight* changes these coordinates: Batman's true rival is not Joker, his opponent, but Harvey Dent, the "white knight," the aggressive new district attorney, a kind of official vigilante whose fanatical battle against crime leads him into killing innocent people and destroys him. It is as if Dent is the reply of the legal order to Batman's threat: against Batman's vigilante struggle, the system generates its own illegal excess, its own vigilante, much more violent than Batman, directly violating the law. There is thus a poetic justice in the fact that, when Bruce plans to publicly reveal his identity as Batman, Dent jumps in and instead names himself as Batman—he *is* "more Batman than Batman himself," actualizing the temptation Batman was still able to resist. So when, at the film's end, Batman takes upon himself the crimes committed by Dent to save the reputation of the popular hero who embodies hope for ordinary people, his self-effacing act contains a grain of truth: Batman in a way returns the favor to Dent. His act is a gesture of symbolic exchange: first Dent takes upon himself the identity of Batman, then Wayne—the real Batman—takes upon himself Dent's crimes. Finally, *The Dark Knight Rises* pushes things even further: is Bane not Dent brought to extreme, to its self-negation? Dent, who draws the conclusion that the system itself is unjust, so that in order to effectively fight injustice one has to turn directly against the system and destroy it? And, as part of the same move, Dent who loses last inhibitions and is ready to use all murderous brutality to achieve this goal? The rise of such a figure changes the entire constellation: for all participants, Batman included, morality is relativized, it becomes a matter of convenience, something determined by circumstances; it's open class warfare, everything is permitted to defend the system when we are dealing not just with mad gangsters but also with a popular uprising. Is, then, this all? Should the film just be flatly rejected by those who are engaged in radical emancipatory struggles? Things are more ambiguous, and one has to read the film in the way one has to interpret a Chinese political poem: absences and surprising presences count. Recall the old French story about a wife who complains that her husband's best friend is making illicit sexual advances toward her: it takes some time till the surprised friend gets the point—in this twisted way, she is inviting him to seduce her. It is like the Freudian unconscious that knows no negation: what matters is not a negative judgment on something but the mere fact that this something is mentioned—in *The Dark Knight Rises*, people's power *is here*, staged as an Event, in a key step forward from the usual Batman opponents (criminal mega-capitalists, gangsters, and terrorists). Here we get the first clue—the prospect of the OWS movement taking power and establishing a people's democracy in Manhattan is so patently absurd, so utterly nonrealist, that one cannot but raise the question: *Why does then a major Hollywood blockbuster dream about it, why does it evoke this specter?* Why even dream about OWS exploding into a violent takeover? The obvious answer (to smudge OWS with accusations that it harbors a terrorist-totalitarian potential) is not enough to account for the strange attraction exerted by the prospect of "people's power." No wonder the proper functioning of this power remains blank, absent: no details are given about how this people's power functions, what the mobilized people are doing (remember that Bane tells the people they can do what they want—he is not imposing on them his own order). One can even talk of necessary *censorship* here: any depiction of the self-organization of the people during Bane's reign would have ruined the effect of the film, laying bare its inconsistency.

This is why the film deserves a close reading[23]: the Event—the "people's republic of Gotham City," dictatorship of the proletariat in Manhattan—is *immanent* to the film, it is (to use the worn-out expression from the 1970s) its "absent center." This is why external critique of the film ("its depiction of the OWS reign is a ridiculous caricature") is not enough—the critique has to be immanent, it has to locate within the film itself a multitude of signs that point toward the authentic Event. (Recall, for example, that Bane is not just a brutal terrorist but a person of deep love and sacrifice.) In short, pure ideology is not possible, Bane's authenticity *has* to leave a trace in the film's texture. And one should also not shirk from imagining an alternate version of the film, something like what Ralph Fiennes did with *Coriolanus*: in his film, it is as if Coriolanus, obviously out of place in the delicate hierarchy of Rome, only becomes what he is, gains his freedom, when he joins the Volscians (with their leader Aufidius playing the role of Bane). He does not join them simply in order to take revenge on Rome; he joins them because he belongs there. In joining the Volscians, Coriolanus does not betray Rome out of a sense of petty revenge but regains his integrity—his only act of betrayal occurs at the end when, instead of leading the Volscian army on to Rome, he organizes a peace treaty between the Volscians and Rome, breaking down to the pressure of his mother, the true figure of superego Evil. This is why he returns to Volscians, fully aware what awaits him there: the well-deserved punishment for his betrayal.[24] So what about imagining a Batman who rejoins Bane's forces in Gotham City? After helping them to almost defeat the state power, he breaks down, mediates an armistice, and then goes back to the rebels, knowing he will be killed for his betrayal.

Focusing on the problem of taking power, *The Dark Knight Rises* is traumatic not only (and not even principally) for today's liberal right; it also touches the nerve of today's radical left whose motto is: "We have to be outside. This is a postmodern idea. The idea is that I must subtract myself from the game of power." This stance is typical of the contemporary French leftist political thought, which focuses on the state and its apparatuses: the radical emancipatory struggle is a struggle that should be led at a distance from the state, ultimately against the state. (It is here that one should also apply Hegel's lesson about *absoluter Gegenstoss*: it is this very resistance to the state that constitutes the state as its point of reference.) What one tends to forget here is the basic Marxist insight (which holds today more than ever) that the basic antagonism that defines today's society is not the resistance against the state but the "class struggle" *within society, at a distance from the state*. In short, the Marxist point is not directly anti-statist but, rather, how to change *society* so that it will no longer need a state.[25] So even if the emancipatory struggle begins as an opposition to state apparatuses, it has to change its target in its course. Alain Badiou opposes (what he considers) the classic dialectical logic of negativity that engenders out of its own movement a new positivity, a new "affirmative" dialectics: the starting point of an emancipatory process should not be negativity, resistance, will to destruction, but a new affirmative vision disclosed in an Event—we oppose the existing order out of our fidelity to this event, drawing out its consequences. Without this affirmative moment, the emancipatory process ends up necessarily imposing a new positive order that is an imitation of the old one, sometimes even radicalizing its worst features. One should oppose to this "affirmative" notion of dialectics the Hegelian notion of the dialectical *process* that begins with some affirmative idea toward which it strives, but in the course of which *this idea itself undergoes a profound transformation* (not just a tactical accommodation but an essential redefinition), because the idea itself is caught into the process, (over)determined by its actualization. Say, we have a revolt motivated by a request for justice: once people get really engaged in it, they become aware that much more is needed to bring true justice than just the limited requests with which they started (to repeal some laws, etc.).

The problem is, of course: what, precisely, is this "much more." Everyone knows Winston Churchill's quip about democracy usually quoted as: "Democracy is the worst possible system, except for all others." What Churchill effectively said (in the House of Commons on November 11, 1947) was slightly less paradoxical and scintillating:

> Many forms of Government have been tried, and will be tried
> in this world of sin and woe. No one pretends that democracy
> is perfect or all-wise. Indeed it had been said that democracy is
> the worst form of Government except for all those other forms
> that have been tried from time to time.[26]

The underlying logic is best rendered if one applies to Churchill's dictum Lacan's "formulae of sexuation" and rephrases it as follows: "Democracy is the worst of all systems; however, compared to it, any other system is worse." If one takes all possible systems as a whole and ranges them with regard to their worth, democracy is the worst and finishes at the bottom; if, however, one compares democracy one-to-one with all other systems, it is better than any of them.[27] Does something similar not hold (or seem to hold) for capitalism? If one analyzes it in an abstract way, trying to locate it in the hierarchy of all possible systems, it appears as the worst—chaotic, unjust, destructive, and so on; however, if one compares it in a concrete pragmatic way to every alternative, it is still better than any of them.

This "illogical" imbalance between the universal and the particular is a direct indication of the efficiency of ideology. An opinion poll in the United

States at the end of June 2012, just before the Supreme Court decision about Obama's healthcare reform, showed that "strong majorities favor most of what is in the law":

> Most Americans oppose President Barack Obama's healthcare reform even though they strongly support most of its provisions, a Reuters/Ipsos poll showed on Sunday, with the Supreme Court set to rule within days on whether the law should stand. The survey results suggest that Republicans are convincing voters to reject Obama's reform even when they like much of what is in it, such as allowing children to stay on their parents' insurance until age 26.[28]

Here we encounter ideology at its purest: the majority wants to have its (ideological) cake and to eat it (the real cake), that is, they want the real profits of the healthcare reform, while rejecting its ideological form (which they perceive as the threat to the "freedom of choice")—they reject water, but accept H_2O, or, rather, they reject (the concept of) fruit, but they want apples, plums, strawberries . . .

Notes

1. Tyler O'Neil, "*Dark Knight* and Occupy Wall Street: The Humble Rise," *Hillsdale Natural Law Review*, July 21, 2012, http://hillsdalenaturallawreview. com/2012/07/21/dark-knight-and-occupy-wall-street-the-humble-rise/ (date of access unknown).

2. R. M. Karthick, "*The Dark Knight Rises* a Fascist?," *Society and Culture*, July 21, 2012, https://wavesunceasing.wordpress.com/2012/07/21/the-dark-knight-rises-a-fascist/.

3. O'Neil, "*Dark Knight* and Occupy Wall Street."

4. Christopher Nolan, interview in *Entertainment Weekly* 1216 (July 2012): 34.

5. Karthick, "*The Dark Knight Rises* a Fascist?"

6. Karthick, "*The Dark Knight Rises* a Fascist?"

7. Tom Charity, "'Dark Knight Rises' Disappointingly Clunky, Bombastic," CNN Review, July 19, 2012, http://edition.cnn.com/2012/07/19/showbiz/movies/dark-knight-rises-review-charity/index.html?iref=obinsite (date of access unknown).

8. Forrest Wickman, "The Dickensian Aspects of *The Dark Knight Rises*," Browbeat: *Slate's* Cultural Blog, July 21, 2012, http://www.slate.com/blogs/brow-beat/2012/07/21/the_dark_knight_rises_inspired_by_a_tale_of_two_cities_the_parts_that_draw_from_dickens_.html (date of access unknown).

9. Karthick, "*The Dark Knight Rises* a Fascist?"

10. Quoted from John Lee Anderson, *Che Guevara: A Revolutionary Life* (New York: Grove Press, 1997), 636–637.

11. Anderson, *Che Guevara*, 27.

12. Anderson, *Che Guevara*, 27.

13. Søren Kierkegaard, *Works of Love* (New York: Harper & Row, 1962), 114.

14. A supreme literary example of such "killing out of love" is Toni Morrison's *Beloved*, where the heroine kills her daughter to prevent her falling into slavery.

15. One should note the irony of the fact that Neeson's son is a devoted Shia Muslim and that Neeson himself often talks about his forthcoming conversion to Islam.

16. Mark Twain, "The Two Reigns of Terror," from *A Connecticut Yankee in King Arthur's Court* (1889), Bartleby.com, http://www.bartleby.com/71/0530.html.

17. See Ari Kohen's blog, "According to Slavoj Žižek, No-one Understand Slavoj Žižek," http://kohenari.net/post/26498282819/zizek-responds (date of access unknown).

18. There is a homologous procedure in our language. In the domain of politics, one often uses (ironically) the passive form of an active verb—say, when a politician is forced to "voluntarily" step down, one comments that he was "stepped down." (In China, during the Cultural Revolution, one even used the neutral form—like "struggles"—in an artificial passive or active version: when a cadre accused of revisionism was submitted to a session of "ideological struggle," it was said that he was "struggled," or that the revolutionary group was "struggling" him (here, the intransitive verb was changed into a transitive one: we not only struggle, we struggle *someone*). Such distortions of "normal" grammar adequately expressed the underlying logic; consequently, instead of rejecting them as violent distortions of the normal use of language, we should praise them as disclosures of the violence that underlies this normal use.

19. J. Arch Getty and Oleg V. Naumov, *The Road to Terror: Stalin and the Self-Destruction of the Bolsheviks, 1932–39* (London: Verso, 2010), 481.

20. For a more detailed reading of Saramago's novel, see the conclusion of Slavoj Žižek, *Violence: Six Sideways Reflections* (New York: Picador, 2008).

21. I rely here on an idea developed by Srećko Horvat (Zagreb).

22. For a more detailed analysis of *The Dark Knight*, see chapter 1 of Slavoj Žižek, *Living in the End Times* (London: Verso, 2010).

23. I leave out of consideration the Aurora cinema killings, which in no way refer specifically to the film.

24. For a more detailed reading of Fiennes's *Coriolanus*, see chapter 9 of Slavoj Žižek, *The Year of Dreaming Dangerously* (London: Verso, 2012).

25. Stalinism was far from an unambiguous case of a strong state—Stalin had a point when, in a weird dialectical turn toward "organs without body," he once remarked that, in the process of constructing Socialism, the state is withering away through the very process of the strengthening of its organs (meaning, of course, principally the secret police apparatus).

26. Incidentally, it is not known to whom "it had been said" refers—is it a determinate individual or just a reference to common wisdom?

27. In logic and theory of judgment, we sometimes encounter a similar paradox of intransitivity: if A is better than B and B is better than C, it does not always follow that A is better than C—when one compares A and C directly, C can appear as better. It would be all too easy to explain away this paradox as relying on the change in criteria (when one ranges all systems, one applies the same set of criteria, but when one compares them one to one, criteria imperceptibly shift): in some way this, of course, has to be true, but the point is that the shift is immanent, not arbitrary. That is to say, the shift can occur because of the differentiality of features: let us say that we compare the beauty of three persons—A appears more beautiful than B and B more beautiful than C. However, when we compare A and C, it may happen that a strong contrast in some minor feature will ruin the beauty of A, so that A will appear inferior to C.

28. Patricia Zengerle, "Most Americans Oppose Health Law but Like Provisions," *Reuters*, June 24, 2012, http://www.reuters.com/article/2012/06/25/us-usa-campaign-healthcare-idUSBRE85N01M20120625 (date of access unknown).

15

The ["End"]

JAN JAGODZINSKI

The readily recognizable signifier "The End" that once served as the formal ending to film narratives provided a familiar and reassuring closure for spectators of classical Hollywood cinema. Its disappearance from the screen marked a transition from a closed organic narrative to an open one as stories, especially after World War II, became more existential. In the postwar era, film began exploring a world that was left devastated, one that required a future vision to restore stability as new forms of subjectivity began to be explored. Gilles Deleuze charts this transition within his two volumes: *Cinema 1: The Movement-Image* (1986) and *Cinema 2: The Time-Image* (1989), where he proposes that the cinema of the classical era prior to World War II revolved around the movement-image, which was challenged and supplemented by the time-image appearing in films after the war.

With the loss of the organic narrative, which coincided with the expansion of global capitalism and its ongoing depletion of the world's resources, we are now faced with the question: What if we now have to face "The End" literally? As in the end of our species as we know it, as well as the end of the planet as we know it. How can cinema "think" the impossible image of human extinction due to any number of cosmological or environmental cataclysms? Anxieties loom over whether a poweful plasma eruption will cause a solar storm that generates a flare able to reach the Earth. Even if the Earth manages to esape such a fate, there is the projected death of the sun in another five billion years. Alterntively, the image of total destruction might be envisioned as a lopsided start to a nuclear war, fulfilling the apocalyptic eschatological prophecies of the Bible, where we annihilate ourselves by unleashing hell on earth.

Films that address this problematic of the end of our species, especially Hollywood disaster films, *end* with a redepemption narrative of one sort or another, with humanity being saved and most often the family restored. We see this in the endings of such blockbuster hits as director Roland Emmerich's films *The Day After Tomorrow* (2004) and *2012* (2009), *World War Z* (Marc Forster, 2013), director Danny Boyles's *28 Days Later* (2002), and so on. Such endings offer the comfort that humanity will, through the cunning of reason, match Nature's sublimity and survive through various technological, scientific, or medical feats. Concurrently, the sustainability discourse, which is prevalent throughout green capitalism, promotes an impossible homeostasis, where the "world-without-us" is often presented as a fantasy scenario by a disembodied eye, an observing gaze by an Other whose nonexistence does not let go of a world "for us." It's like, as Slavoj Žižek puts it, "the fantasy of witnessing the act of one's own conception, parental copulation, or the witnessing of one's own burial."[1] The spectacle of our own destruction is somehow naturalized and internalized. Primary examples include such films as *The Age of Stupid* (Franny Armstrong, 2009), a drama-documentary taking place in 2055 wherein a lone archivist presides over the entire digitalized archive of humankind. He pieces together snippets and stories of actual news and documentary footage charting the story of human demise, ending in a desperate attempt to beam the information into outer space so that the same "mistake" is not repeated by another cosmic civilization. The final screen shot is of a cliché of the Earth surrounded by orbiting satellites like the rings of Saturn with a question mark punctuating the signifier: "The End?"

WALL-E (Andrew Stanton, 2008) is yet another example of this domesticating genre where the planet Earth has turned into a garbage dump and an eponymous robot digs through the ruins, looking for "treasures" that have become discarded "shit." Acting as a kind of proxy for humanity, *WALL-E* places viewers in a position posterior to their own extinction. The message is that we will ultimately survive but as obese humans needing to be transported by space cars. Yet, finally, humanity comes to "see the light" as spaceships return to Earth to begin a new era, thanks to the bot, which provides the ethical lesson of the cost of human excess. Throughout the narrative of *WALL-E*, a technological old-timer symbiotically falls in love with an ultra-modernized she-bot, showing that it is possible to wed old and new technologies together. The Earth's resilience is restored as plants begin to emerge everywhere in the final scenes, even springing up from the garbage.

The end is again presented as a cliché: the Earth (what looks like North America to be precise) is shown shimmering, as it is about to be restored.

Of course there are other postapocalyptic narratives that attempt to provide a much bleaker ending. Lars von Trier's *Melancholia* (2011) explores the psychological reaction to the planet's end via the dichotomous dispositions of two sisters: Justine (Kirsten Dunst) and Claire (Charlotte Gainsbourg). *Melancholia*'s ending leaves no doubt as to what happens as the asteroid named "Melancholia" destroys the Earth. We see a white screen immediately follow as the bare-boned teepee tent "protecting" Justine, her sister Claire, and Claire's nine-year-old boy Leo (Cameron Spurr) are swept away into oblivion by the force of the approaching planet.

The Road (John Hillcoat, 2009), another powerful postapocalyptic film narrative based on Cormac McCarthy's book, relates "the end" through a focus on a father (Viggo Mortensen) and his son (Kodi Smit-McPhee) attempting to survive on a desolated dying planet. *The Road* explores the question of death, nihilism, and the future uncertainty of the boy as his father dies upon reaching an ocean beach that was supposed to be a place of comfort and hope. The boy, left alone, is then befriended by a family who continues their relentless existence of survival. Both *Melancholia* and *The Road* have received a great deal of attention and commentary concerning human ethics and the question of human mortality. Both films end with what Deleuze and Guattari would identify as "becoming-child"; that is, the question of how the future that is being extinguished will be able to exist for an upcoming generation that is without hope. In *Melancholia* the make-believe protection of the teepee simply serves as a way for Leo to bear the impending annihilation, to make it pass, like having an injection that stings only for a short time. In *The Road*, the boy has nothing to live for except to hold "the fire" that his father passed on to him, namely, the fantasy that survival is the only value to cherish.

While these endings move past the usual Hollywood catastrophe porn, up until "the end" the "world-for-us" remains intact. What do I mean by this? Eugene Thacker makes a very useful distinction between three onto-logical positions that are helpful in the approach to the problematic of what I am calling "The End." A "world-without-us" is contrasted to a "world-in-itself" and a "world-for-us."[2] Through "the labor of the negative," according to Hegel, we transform the "world-in-itself" to a "world-for-us," whereas a "world-without-us" brings us to the realization that we are not necessary to the planet. It will simply transform and survive, barring of course any natural catastrophe that would extinguish it, like the explosion of the sun. The science, for example, in Lars von Trier's *Melancholia* is purely science fiction. It can never happen the way it is envisioned in the storyline. Our future is what *was*, should the archaeological remains ever be excavated by another life form. This "world-without-us" can only act as the threshold of an Imaginary scenario for us to bump up against. Up until now, the endings of these postapocalyptic films do not or are unable to address an *end* that grips the imaginary threshold of a "world-without-us."

Here a slight diversion will be offered as this metaphysically presents a problem that necessarily has to do away with subjectivity as generated by various philosophies that address the "world-in-itself" and a "world-for-us," which include all forms of humanist thought, particularly phenomenology, hermeneutics, critical theory, and psychoanalysis. While "speculative realism" is too broad a term, since there is no cohesive agreement as to what it consists of, it is this philosophical direction that best addresses a "world-without-us." A radical materialist metaphysics seeks to consider a reality devoid of subjectivity. It is human thinking that accepts the ontological power of rationality back into the world itself. The realism sought is a reality where it is possible to consider what the world was like—or will be like—without human beings. All forms of humanist philosophies posit a "correlationism" according to Quentin Meillassoux.[3] That is to say, an object/subject dichotomy wherein we are always dealing with a correlate or relationship between the two; being (as object) or the in-itself, like the Lacanian Real becomes inaccessible in this approach to materialism and reality. A so-called purely "objective" view is inconceivable or not possible because of some condition that taints the co-relation with reality. But this means that we are caught in a perpetual self-referential loop as our human finitude continually bumps up against an absolute "outside" world. We are constantly interpreting the world, rationalizing it to give it meaning and to stave off nihilism. For Deleuze this "outside" is the unthought, as it is independent of thought consisting of the multiplicity of natures or worlds. This is not the same position we find in post-Kantian postmodern philosophies that claim a reality that is seen in constructivist terms where all forms of thought are epistemologically filtered. The difficulties of getting around correlationism and not falling into forms of scientific rationalist materialism are certainly obvious, which makes the term "speculative realism" problematic in that it does not address the problem of value. Should the value of human experience be completely dropped, or if included in the materialist metaphysics, how might it be situated within the nonhuman other? In both cases, what is being raised is an inhuman position, which is very disturbing for many. The question still remains: How do we then bump up against an ending that presents a "world-without-us"?

My tact will to be to turn to Deleuze and Guattari as they address the "world-without-us" in machinic terms. Thought in their view is not absolutized as being human. Rather the eye is "torn" from the body and becomes a machine, but it is not a computer that functions through algorithms; rather, it is like a synthesizer. Thought *is* a synthesizer. With Deleuze and Guattari philosophical discourse disentangles itself from the dialectics of form and matter and opts for the synthesis of the molecular and the cosmic and forces such as densities, intensities, and duration—all aspects of the "world-without-us," or what they term a "Mechanosphere," which contains the mute and unthinkable forces of the Cosmos.[4] When forces become necessarily cosmic, the material world becomes necessarily molecular, with forces operating in an infinitesimal space and speed. In this state of affairs the problem is no longer that of a beginning; the search is not for some foundational ground. Synthetic thought is not caught by Kantian a priori synthetic judgments as epistemological forms that process the world; rather the question becomes a form of pragmatism: How does one consolidate heterogeneous material and make it consistent, so that it can harness the unthinkable, invisible, and nonsonorous forces of the "outside," which participate in the infinity of the Cosmos? The proviso they make is that such a synthesis is not always necessarily successful. "Sometimes one overdoes it, puts too much in, works with a jumble of lines and sounds"; then instead of producing a cosmic machine capable of "rendering sonorous," one lapses back to a machine of reproduction that "ends up reproducing nothing but a scribble effacing all lines, a scramble effacing all sounds."[5]

Philosophy, and by extension film, becomes a synthetic thought *experiment* to bump up against the threshold of a "world-without-us." Schizophrenia is given a privileged position, as thought that appears inhuman is more likely to tap into the cosmic outside and avoid being caught by correlationist propositions, since the world is, neurobiologically speaking, processed entirely differently and irrationally. The schizophrenic synthetically brings heterogeneous elements together that nevertheless have a strange plane of consistency about them, forming rhizomatic links that are truly creative. They appear likely, yet we cannot be sure, as a virtual dimension is tapped that is out of joint with normative perception. While still "human," their thought patterns may be inhuman in terms of the myriad of becomings they may take: animal, mineral, bacterial, machinic, and so on. Such a position, it should be stated, is entirely contra to other speculative realist positions proposed, for example, by Quentin Meillassoux in *After Finitude* (2008) and Ray Brassier in *Nihil Unbound* (2007), who posit a "transcendental nihilism." The powers of reason through the ontological methods of mathematics eliminate the human. There is no need to consider any forms of axiology. Within the context of this essay, accepting a strong sense of nihilism, following Brassier would mean that humanity would have to face up to a "Truth," with a capital letter: Truth as exposed through the power of reason. If there is a mind-independent reality, which is indifferent to human existence, then this means accepting a fundamental nihilism that would require a realist ontology that does away with all forms of transcendentalism so as to accept the cold hard facts: that is, the end of the planet when the sun has had its cycle. Period. End of metaphysics. The end *is* "The End."

Deleuze and Guattari are not so skeptical or pessimistic. They seek another solution as influenced by the Stoics in their attempt to believe in the world, but they do so by confronting the Outside creatively via the escape attempt of creative synthesis as hinted to earlier. Neurobiology plays a significant role as it is the brain that generates multifaceted worlds to bridge the Outside. Deleuze and Guattari present a way to still speculate on the absolute via a metaphysics that continues to decenter the human, but they do so through anomalous figures who stalk the edges of being human. I turn to a full-length discussion of a film that is able to think the "world-without-us" in what I take as a uniquely Deleuzian-Guattarian way, which positions us between the dichotomous choice of nihilism *or* some form of axiology within a flat ontology where all life forms search for parity, human beings not having any special privileges in this matter. It is a thought experiment in the best meaning of the term.

The film I have in mind is *Save the Green Planet* directed by Joon-Hwan Jang, released in 2003, a darkly gothic futuristic film mainly using the mise-en-scène of the protagonist's dimly lit dungeon-like laboratory. The film rewrites Stanley Kubrick's *A Clockwork Orange* and *2001: A Space Odyssey* for the twenty-first century, and it is a fine example of "intellectual cinema." As Deleuze writes, "Kubrick is renewing the theme of the initiatory journey because every Journey in the world is an explanation of the brain."[6] In *Save the Green Planet*, director Jang is involved in a similar quest. He explores the futility, or shall we say the impossible deadlock, we find ourselves in today in relation to the values that circulate in globalized capitalism that generate the worst of living conditions for the majority of the population while holding the belief that this capitalist system provides the best benefits for all.

The film is a mixture of science fiction, dark comedy, detective story, and horror story all rolled into one, where the audience is subjected to a series of revelations that play with the virtual and actual dimensions of time and space. It is truly a synthesizing machine in this sense. The narrative carries on until the "end" is truly reached with the destruction of planet Earth, followed by an extradiegetic epilogue, to which I will return because it offers a novel variation on the notion of "The End" in film. The anomalous figure is Lee Byeung-gu (Ha-kyun Shin), a young man who is clearly, or so it seems, delusional and schizophrenic. He is a serial killer whose paranoia has been shaped by a series of events that have unhinged his life. Once an employee of Yuje Chemical, his girlfriend was beaten up and killed during an out-break of a worker's strike. His mother, who also worked for Yuje Chemical, lies in a deep coma from chemical poisoning, which doctors are unable to explain or treat. Lee keeps her on a life support system at the high cost of hospital maintenance. We further learn that as a child Lee was often bullied and beaten and lost his father to suicide after witnessing the latter's loss of an arm in a coal mining accident. Lee's entire history, it seems, is a series of ill-fated tragedies, and he sets out to avenge his adversaries who, he is convinced, are aliens that have invaded the planet. As such, Lee vibrates in a world of delirium. His hallucinations describe the presence of the unreal within a world of the real, an intrusion of the not-there into what-is-there; a feeling that manifests itself as paranoia, a nostalgia for his past, and his belief that aliens are haunting the planet. His delirium is a complete colonization of the Real by fantasy. Addicted to amphetamines to soothe his pain, Lee generates psychotic hallucinations that have been shaped by his readings of sci-fi and UFO stories about alien invasions. His plan is to save the human race by meeting the prince of the aliens who is coming by spaceship during the upcoming lunar eclipse.

The song "Somewhere over the Rainbow" plays prominently twice throughout the film in two different variations, to assure us, the audience, that Lee is truly mad regardless of the space he occupies, which is not of this world. Lee's delirium does not refer to things in the world that are *not* there; he does not cover the world with a different world. Rather, his is an otherworldly cosmic perception of the world that exists concurrently, like a palimpsest, within the singular space that we all occupy. Lee's hallucinations occupy and invade a space between, in Thacker's terminology, the Earth and the Planet, between a "world-in-itself" and a "world-without-us." There is no "world-for-us" in Lee's consciousness. To save the Green Planet Earth, the "world-in-itself," Lee must identify the aliens on Earth. In his psychotic state he is able to see past the "world-for-us," much as in John Carpenter's science fiction B movie *They Live* (1988). In this film the protagonist who puts on special sunglasses is able to "see" another world of seductive signs and walking aliens disguised as humans.

Lee's primary target is the CEO of Yuje Chemical, Kang Man-Shik (Yun-shik Baek), whom he believes is from the planet Andromeda. Kang is a stereotype of the powerful male elite in Korea, a brusque and boorish man who displays an arrogance characteristic of the male executive. Lee captures Kang and takes him to an underground cellar, strapping him into a makeshift barber's chair. This "throne" chair becomes his permanent residence and is an allusion to Kubrick's *A Clockwork Orange* where Alex (Malcolm MacDowell) is subjected to the Ludovico treatment to cure his violence. But here a reversal takes place. Kang is subjected to the "Lee Byeung-gu treatment," not to rid him of his brain of violence (as in Alex's case) but rather to subject him to bodily torture so that he will admit to his crimes of being an alien, an alien who does not realize himself *as* an alien. The brain is meant to surrender to the body. Rather than deploying psychology to treat Alex's mind as alien, an "inside" job so to speak, so that he becomes an automaton by losing his violent streak, thereby becoming a good citizen, Kang is tortured to reveal his involvement in the "outside" as part of the social order, so to speak, to confess to his violent streak as an alien. While Alex becomes "civilized," Kang is not so easily domesticated. Even after Kang is electrically shocked, branded by hot irons, nearly blinded by methanol, and even impaled and crucified by his palms on a wooden beam, so that he appears like a Christ figure, he does not break.

With this torture scene director Jang has staged for us Artaud's Theatre of Cruelty. We are made to feel the unexpressed emotions of Lee's unconscious aimed directly at Kang and our nervous system. Kang seems to be a phantasm that bleeds, like the Marquis de Sade's tortured victims, but Lee is unable to reach the "alien" through such torture. With the narrative so established, the viewer has no difficulty accepting that Lee is psychotic, out for revenge, and that his attempt to save the planet from aliens is some sort of delusional heroic dream that he has concocted to give meaning to his life, while Kang's redoubtable resolve gives the impression that he is indeed superhuman in his ruthless, strong-willed, and absolutely self-assured will to survive.

In one pivotal scene Kang presents a fabulated tale of the Andromeda aliens' mission on Earth. Unlike Alex's torture in *A Clockwork Orange*, the images presented are a straightforward projection of Kang's narrative, not ideologically meant to manipulate as in the former case; rather they are transcendent, cosmic, and come from a nonhuman standpoint. The atrocities of history and the apologia for a neoliberal order are presented in a matter-of-fact way without any need of justification. The aliens' utopian ideologies, whether from the left or right, are carried out in the name of progressive humanity; those opposing the vision are to be destroyed through whatever means are necessary. An ironic twist now presents itself: the Andromedans are *not* there to destroy humanity but to save it from its most dangerous impulses—namely, its proneness to violence. In a hilarious montage composed of cartoonlike images from popular UFO legends, Biblical illustrations, historical footages of wars and massacres, and a number of scenes of early *Homo sapiens* (directly paying homage to Stanley Kubrick's *2001: A Space Odyssey* where the black obelisk plays such an iconic role for the mystery of origins), Kang's story unfolds.

In a film that is largely structured as a movement-image, the shift in this sequence is to that of a time-image. Kang explains how the Andromedans had discovered Earth, but inadvertently wiped out the dinosaurs. Out of remorse and guilt they created a life form that resembled them to repopulate the planet. Hilariously, they create Adam and Eve, who are still joined by an umbilical cord to Kubrick's famous black obelisk, thus confirming that humans are descendants of a superior alien life. Kang tells Lee that a society in harmony with nature was born (Atlantis flashes on the bottom of the screen), but things went terribly wrong. Humans decided that they wanted to be more powerful than their Andromedan creators and started a reckless project of genetic engineering, ending up implanting their offspring with a destructive gene that results in a long history of carnage and atrocity. The consequence of this aggression led to a planetary atomic war that opened up a hole in the ozone, resulting in the melting of the polar ice caps. Yet one man, Noah, was able to save his family and along with genetic samples of animal life in a kind of submarine, was able to float for centuries until he came upon dry land. However, the cumulative effects of this genetic manipulation reversed the course of evolution, and human beings regressed or devolved rapidly into apes (the *Planet of the Apes* series being the obvious allusion here).

Such a devolution becomes worrisome for the Andromedans, as the primate holds an in-between space in human evolution: the indeterminacy of a qualitative advancement of intelligence or a continuation of evolution on yet another plane. Rather than an ape that speaks (a human), we might have an ape that becomes telepathic (transhuman) or something else entirely. Who knows how punctuated evolution works? When this happened the Andromedans decided to intervene once more by reversing the effects of this degradation and evolution is repeated once again. A Nietzschean return of difference occurs, as now an ape sits in front of the 2001 alien obelisk, just as in Kubrick's sequence, holding a large bone, which then becomes a weapon. It is thrown up in the air, but the camera does not cut to a spaceship—primitive man to technological man as in Kubrick's film—but rather to grim documentary footage of various historical horrors. The montage presents images of the national socialism of Hitler, mounds of concentration camp victims' bodies being bulldozed into a pile, bombings during the Vietnam War, children badly burned by napalm, and scenes of slaughter, strife, and grief in Africa, Latin America, and the Middle East. In these crystal-images the movement has no real progress; it follows from primitive man to primitive man where the past and present are the same. Modernity held the promise of technology in Kubrick's time, but in postmodernism it holds no such promise because the original sin, the flaw of human aggression, remains. Kang ends his story by maintaining that the Andromedans launched a series of experiments on several thousand people to find a way to isolate and destroy this malignant gene that causes violence. Both Lee and his mother were one of those experiments, which were unsuccessful as the idea was that, as Kang admits, "physical and mental suffering stresses organisms, forcing them to adapt and develop more quickly." It seems that hypothesis was itself flawed.

While Kang's tale is as absurd and every bit as mad as Lee's own psychotic vision, the viewer is uncertain whether this narrative was told in this way so as to appease Lee. Earlier in the narrative Kang was able to go through the mounds of material that Lee had written outlining his cosmic plan to save the planet. It could well be that Kang pieced the tale together from reading the many allusions to history and sci-fi popular culture that Lee had lying around. The tale, it seems, is too mad to be taken seriously, yet Lee is fascinated by it, convinced more than ever that he has finally found the alien he was looking for. Lee's suspicion that Kang has made this up is quickly dismissed when Kang correctly calculates via the principle of relativity how many Earth years make up a single Andromedan year, as if he were a genius equivalent to Einstein. The redemptive narrative of globalizing modernity is linked with a cosmic and nonhuman standpoint of Ufology; it is radically de-anthropomorphized. The reduction of salvation to a technological biological fix is no more strange than the ufologists who see environmental destruction, the accelerated pace of technology, and the emergence of the political world order all as signs that the end time is near.

It is perhaps here that the point of the film reveals itself. Lee is both a victim and perpetrator as he struggles against the globalization that Kang represents. Kang's unbelievable narrative is every bit as fantastic as the belief of progressive capitalization, which promises, through new technologies, to continue to save the Earth. Kang challenges Lee's insatiable and improbable plan to stamp out the aliens: "Saving the planet—for whom, for what? The people who bullied you; the ones that made you crazy? If you kill them all, does that mean you are saving the planet?" Lee's psychosis simply repeats the desire to purify the race, thus confirming the "flaw" Kang was exposing. His experiments on unwilling victims, his torturing and dismembering them so as to reveal the cosmological dimension of the conspiracy, are revealed as a salvation project that is just as harmful as Kang's and equally as paranoid in trying to control the human order.

Kang and Lee are locked in mortal combat—one the savior of human-kind from the point of view of utopian globalism and technological advance-ment and the other an angel of vengeance fighting for all those victims of "alien" abuse. If Lee is without cause, he falls into nihilism. All he might do is blow up the earth in a showdown with the Andromedan Prince, reduced to being a terrorist without cause. Kang is caught by the following contradiction: Andromedans want to get rid of human enmity but not at the expense of losing their own superiority. Yet, it is precisely enmity that is humanity's mur-derous disorder, which is, in turn, the flaw that prevents the Andromedans from helping humanity achieve peace through superior technological means. But coming to the aid of humanity and retaining sovereign authority doesn't work. So, oddly, the Andromedans' killing humanity "softly" through experi-mentation is matched by their victims' killing them "hard" through torture: the vengeful slave wanting to get back at his master or at least identify who the master is so that he might—what? Save the earth, or blow it up inad-vertently? Kang is further riven by sincere sorrow and the sympathy he feels after reading Lee's diaries, for in them he recognizes the atrocities the latter has suffered. Yet, at the same time he flips emotions, wanting to wipe out all human life, as Lee persists in wanting to kill him by strapping on a bomb. The wild oscillation occurs between the impossible attempts to find consistency and the absurd inconsistency of actions and explanations. The edge of chaos is reached as, ultimately, Lee is shot and Kang is beamed up to his spaceship as a solar eclipse occurs. *It turns out that Kang is the Prince of the Andromedans after all!* He declares the human experiment a failure and blows up the planet. Mankind is terminated, both physically and symbolically.

A number of subtle contingencies are revealed throughout the story. The finger of a fallen mannequin points to a secret door where Lee's labo-ratory is concealed; the flip of a coin determines whether a random detail holds a vital clue or not; the chief of police arrests a disgruntled worker who had bullied Lee as the culprit behind a CEO's kidnapping; Su-ni (Jeaon-min Hwang), his girlfriend, tries to save Lee based on her own premonitions. The story is shaped by the divine transcendental hallucination of Lee and Kang's grand design for humans, as well as the demonic revelation of contingency and horror that accompanies such transcendentalism. We cannot exactly tell who the alien is and who is madder.

The horror genre, like Le Théâtre du Grand-Guignol (The Theater of the Big Puppet), which specialized in naturalistic horror shows at the turn of the twentieth century in Paris, had to have a comedy played on alternative weeks to release the heightened effects that were generated in that abandoned church-turned-theater. Similarly *Save the Green Planet* has its comedic flourishes to sustain the horror, to distance it from becoming too close to the Real. Schopenhauer seems appropriate to quote here: "The life of every individual, viewed as a whole and in general, and when only its most significant features are emphasized, is really a tragedy; but gone through in detail it has the character of a comedy."[7] The characters do come across as cartoonlike figures: Su-ni is just a bit too plump to be believable as a trapeze artist; Kang is just too indestructible given the ultraviolence he is subjected to; Lee's attire is just too strange with his helmets, rubber boots, and what look like rain coats; the barber-torture chair too bizarre; the cartoon sketches that map out the alien weak spots and defenses are all too over-the-top to be taken seriously. These are all elements of the carnivalesque. Beethoven's Ninth Symphony, as heard by Alex in *A Clockwork Orange* as he undergoes media torture to rid him of his violent streak, is replaced by "Somewhere over the Rainbow," made famous by Judy Garland in *The Wizard of Oz*, an obvious fantasy narrative with its tornado serving as an allusion to Lee's delirium. The director also plays on religious symbolism to show that a theological discourse is also of no use here but rather to be made fun of.

After accidently killing his mother by giving her Benzene, Lee sees her spirit descending from the ceiling, surrounded by angelic light, in the traditional costume of a Korean shaman with long strips of cloth that have been cut from her patient's nightdress. The extraterrestrials also sport oversized earlobes, similar to what one finds on Buddha statues, and even the deity of Shiva and the principle of destruction and creation is suggested as there are eight long spiderlike arms holding various implements emerging from the barber's chair ready for torture. It seems all the deities that are toyed with are placed as question marks, incapable of offering a way out of the dilemma and affirming once again that this is no morality play but a mapping of routes that lead to nihilism as the planet is destroyed. Jang's mode of address, like that of Kubrick, is ethical. His clichés in reference to other horror films are meant as a good laugh to continue the dark humor. In this tragicomedy, Jang stages the question of human existence as the psychotic Lee faces the horror of his own symbolic death.

And yet . . . in the epilogue to the film we return once more to *2001: A Space Odyssey*, with an allusion to the star-child that forms the last sequence in that film. After the astronaut Bowman's (Keir Dullea) death, a star-child is born whose eyes turn back toward the earth, offering a space for a new potential. As Deleuze writes, "At the end of *Space Odyssey*, it is in consequence of a fourth dimension that the sphere of the foetus and the sphere of the earth have a chance of entering into a new, incommensurable, unknown relation, which would convert death into a new life."[8] Jang pays homage to this in yet another way. After the planet has been blown up, amid the debris floating through space is a television with a cracked screen that comes to rest at the lower corner of the frame. The same background noise is heard as in *2001*; it is otherworldly and cosmic.

We could say that this television set also alludes to a monolith, an obelisk just as in Kubrick's film—the active and reactive forces of pure potentiality shown by the electric photons vibrating across the television screen as if the activity in a vacuum tube has been made visible. The TV switches on and the sequence that follows, nondiegetic in character, serves as a counterpoint to the montage that Kang's confession offers. It shows Lee's life prior to becoming mad. It is an anamnesis that offers us another entirely different line of flight, wherein we see Lee's loving childhood memories with his parents, his dad showing him star charts, being hugged by his family, holding an ET figure, loving a puppy, enjoying the days with his first girlfriend when he played the harmonica for her, and his watching Su-ni perform in the circus—all tender and sad moments of his life.

This is another reference to "becoming child" but quite unlike the last scene of Lars von Trier's *Melancholia* and John Hillcoat's *The Road*. If it is meant to be a rebirth or a redemption of sorts, it is a strange one, as there is no future. Maybe it is an awakening to childhood that is being denied. It seems to say that the subject is confronted today with having to choose another virtuality, another potential of not becoming alien, with all the violence that this entails. The endgame is the realization that one cannot save the planet this way. Alluding to the floating fetus at the end of *2001*, the suggestion is made of the unconditional fidelity to the intimate moments that bring us love and joy. While this is no solution, it is posited as a life of affirmation, which as we know Deleuze struggled with until his own end: to "believe in this world" despite the carnage we see around us. The dark obelisk keeps on standing for a return of difference—not as apes or humans but as a species that must decide who we are to become—the future anterior of our future as we face extinction. This is the ["The End"].

Notes

1. Slavoj Žižek, *Living in the End Times* (London: Verso, 2010), 80.

2. Eugene Thacker, *In the Dust of This Planet: Horror of Philosophy*, vol. 1 (Winchester: Zero Books, 2010).

3. Quentin Meillassoux, *After Finitude*, trans. Ray Brassier (London: Continuum, 2008).

4. Gilles Deleuze and Félix Guattari, *A Thousand Plateaus: Capitalism and Schizophrenia*, trans. Brian Massumi (Minneapolis and London: University of Minnesota Press, 1987), 69.

5. Deleuze and Guattari, *A Thousand Plateaus*, 343–344.

6. Gilles Deleuze, *Cinema 2: The Time-Image*, trans. Hugh Tomlinson and Robert Galeta (Minneapolis: University of Minnesota Press, 1989), 206.

7. Arthur Schopenhauer, *The World as Will and Representation*, vol. 1, trans. E. F. J. Payne (New York: Dover, 1958), 322.

8. Deleuze, *Cinema 2*, 206.

Contributors

Rex Butler is a reader in the School of English, Media Studies, and Art History at the University of Queensland. In addition to authoring books on Baudrillard, Borges, and Deleuze and Guattari, he has written *Slavoj Žižek: Live Theory*, edited *The Žižek Dictionary*, and coedited *Interrogating the Real* and *The Universal Exception*.

David Denny teaches critical theory, film, and literature in the Culture and Media Department at Marylhurst University in Portland, Oregon. He has published essays on film, psychoanalysis, and politics. He is currently working on an edited volume entitled *Lars von Trier's Women*.

Ryan Engley is a doctoral candidate at the University of Rhode Island. He is currently working on a book-length project for Bloomsbury Press on Howard Hawks, *Bringing Up Baby*, and Auteur theory. He also loves Indian food and non sequitur.

Jennifer Friedlander is Edgar E. and Elizabeth S. Pankey Professor and chair of media studies at Pomona College. She is the author of *Moving Pictures: Where the Police, the Press, and the Art Image Meet* (1998) and *Feminine Look: Sexuation, Spectatorship, and Subversion* (2008), as well as various articles in journals such as *Discourse: Journal for Theoretical Studies in Media and Culture*, *(Re)-turn: A Journal of Lacanian Studies*, *Journal for the Psychoanalysis of Culture and Society*, and *International Journal of Žižek Studies*.

jan jagodzinski is a professor of visual art and media education in the Department of Secondary Education at the University of Alberta, Canada. His most recent books include: *Youth Fantasies: The Perverse Landscape of the Media* (2004), *Musical Fantasies: A Lacanian Approach* (2005), *Television and Youth: Televised Paranoia* (2008), *Art and Education in an Era of Designer*

Capitalism: Deconstructing the Oral Eye (2010), *Misreading Postmodern Antigone: Marco Bellochio's "Devil in the Flesh" (Diavolo in Corpo)* (2011), and the edited collection *Psychoanalyzing Cinema* (2012).

A. Kiarina Kordela is a professor of German and director of the critical theory program at Macalester College and honorary adjunct professor at the University of Western Sydney. She is the author of *$urplus: Spinoza, Lacan* (2007), *Being, Time, Bios: Capitalism and Ontology* (2013), and coeditor, with Dimitris Vardoulakis, of *Freedom and Confinement in Modernity: Kafka's Cages* (2011) and *Spinoza's Authority* (2015). Beyond her essay "The Gaze of Biocinema" (in *European Film Theory*, 2008), her articles on various topics appear in journals, such as *Angelaki, Cultural Critique, Political Theory, Rethinking Marxism, Differences,* and *Umbr(a)*.

Henry Krips is chair of cultural studies and Andrew W. Mellon All Claremont Professor of Humanities at Claremont Graduate University. His publications include *Fetish: An Erotics of Culture* (1999) and *The Metaphysics of Quantum Theory* (1989). He has coedited several collections, including *Event and Decision: Ontology and Politics in Badiou, Deleuze and Whitehead* (2010), *Der Andere Schauplatz: Psychoanalyse, Kultur, Medien* (2001), and *Science, Reason and Rhetoric* (1995).

Sheila Kunkle is an associate professor of Individualized Studies at Metropolitan State University. She has published articles on psychoanalysis, film, and culture in journals such as *Paradoxa: Studies in World Literary Genres, American Imago, Journal of Lacanian Studies, International Journal of Žižek Studies,* and *Journal for the Psychoanalysis of Culture and Society,* and contributed chapters to *Skin, Culture, and Psychoanalysis* (2012) and *Psychoanalyzing Cinema* (2012), as well as coedited a collection, along with Todd McGowan, entitled *Lacan and Contemporary Film* (2004).

Juan Pablo Lucchelli was born in Buenos Aires in 1966. He is a psychoanalyst living in Paris, a member of the World Association of Psychoanalysis, and author of many essays and books about psychoanalysis, including *La Perversion* (2005), *Le transfert, de Freud à Lacan* (2009), *Le Malentendu des sexes* (2011), *Clartés de tout* (with Jean-Claude Milner, 2011), *Métaphores de l'amour* (2012), and *Lacan avec et sans Lévi-Strauss* (2014).

Hugh S. Manon is an associate professor and director of the Screen Studies Program at Clark University where he specializes in Lacanian theory, film noir, and glitch aesthetics. He has published in *Cinema Journal, Film Criticism, Framework, International Journal of Žižek Studies*, and numerous anthologies, including articles on Tod Browning, Edgar G. Ulmer, George Romero, Billy Wilder's *Double Indemnity*, Michael Haneke's *Caché*, and Stanley Kubrick's films noir. His current work investigates Gothic film and literature as a means of theorizing the current fascination with audiovisual glitching, wherein the perfectibility of modern digital technology is haunted by forgotten analog impulses.

Todd McGowan teaches theory and film at the University of Vermont. He is the author of *Enjoying What We Don't Have: The Political Project of Psychoanalysis* (2013), *Rupture: On the Emergence of the Political* (2012, with Paul Eisenstein), monographs on the films of Christopher Nolan and David Lynch, among other works. His articles on various topics appear in several collections and journals, including *The International Journal of Žižek Studies, Umbr(a)*, and *Cinema Journal*.

Hilary Neroni is an associate professor of film and television studies at the University of Vermont. She is the author of *The Violent Woman: Femininity, Narrative, and Violence in Contemporary American Cinema* (2005) and *The Subject of Torture: Psychoanalysis, Biopolitics, and Media Representations* (2015). She has also published essays on women directors such as Jane Campion and Claire Denis.

Fabio Vighi is a professor of critical theory and Italian at Cardiff University (UK), where he codirects the Žižek Centre for Ideology Critique. Among his recent books are *Sexual Difference in European Cinema: The Curse of Enjoyment* (2009), *On Žižek's Dialectics: Surplus, Subtraction, Sublimation* (2010), *Critical Theory and Film: Rethinking Ideology through Film Noir* (2012), *Critical Theory and the Crisis of Contemporary Capitalism* (with Heiko Feldner, 2015).

Brian Wall is an associate professor and chair of the Cinema Department, Binghamton University. He has published articles on Beckett, Bataille, *The Big Lebowski* and *Buffy*, and most recently a book, *Theodor Adorno and Film Theory: The Fingerprint of Spirit* (2013). He is currently working on a monograph on blindness in cinema.

Slavoj Žižek is a senior researcher at the Institute for Sociology and Philosophy at the University of Ljubljana (Slovenia). His publications in

English include *Everything You Always Wanted to Know about Lacan but Were Afraid to Ask Hitchcock* (1992), *The Parallax View* (2006), and *Less than Nothing: Hegel and the Shadow of Dialectical Materialism* (2012), among many other titles. He has published widely on themes concerning politics, theology, philosophy, psychoanalysis, cultural studies, and film.

Index